Personality-Guided
Relational Psychotherapy

Personality-Guided Relational Psychotherapy

Jeffrey J. Magnavita

Series Editor Theodore Millon

AMERICAN PSYCHOLOGICAL ASSOCIATION
WASHINGTON, DC

Published by
American Psychological Association
750 First Street, NE
Washington, DC 20002
www.apa.org

To order
APA Order Department
P.O. Box 92984
Washington, DC 20090-2984
Tel: (800) 374-2721
Direct: (202) 336-5510
Fax: (202) 336-5502
TDD/TTY: (202) 336-6123
Online: www.apa.org/books/
E-mail: order@apa.org

In the U.K., Europe, Africa, and the Middle East, copies may be ordered from American Psychological Association
3 Henrietta Street
Covent Garden, London
WC2E 8LU England

Typeset in Goudy by World Composition Services, Inc., Sterling, VA

Printer: Edwards Brothers, Inc., Ann Arbor, MI
Cover Designer: Berg Design, Albany, NY
Technical/Production Editor: Gail B. Munroe

The opinions and statements published are the responsibility of the authors, and such opinions and statements do not necessarily represent the policies of the American Psychological Association.

Library of Congress Cataloging-in-Publication Data

Magnavita, Jeffrey J.
    Personality-guided relational psychotherapy: A unified approach / Jeffrey J. Magnavita.—1st ed.
        p. cm. — (Personality-guided psychology)
    Includes bibliographical references and index.
    ISBN 1-59147-213-X
    1. Interpersonal psychotherapy. 2. Personality assessment. 3. Personality disorders. I. Title. II. Series.

    RC489.I55M34   2005
    616.89'14—dc22   2004017103

British Library Cataloguing-in-Publication Data
A CIP record is available from the British Library.

Printed in the United States of America
First Edition

CONTENTS

SERIES FOREWORD

The turn of the 20th century saw the emergence of psychological interest in the concept of individual differences, the recognition that the many realms of scientific study then in vogue displayed considerable variability among "laboratory subjects." Sir Francis Galton in Great Britain and many of his disciples, notably Charles Spearman in England, Alfred Binet in France, and James McKeen Cattell in the United States, laid the groundwork for recognizing that intelligence was a major element of import in what came to be called *differential psychology*. Largely through the influence of psychoanalytic thought, and then only indirectly, did this new field expand the topic of individual differences in the direction of character and personality.

And so here we are at the dawn of the 21st century, ready to focus our attentions ever more seriously on the subject of personality trait differences and their impact on a wide variety of psychological subjects—how they impinge on behavioral medicine outcomes, alter gerontological and adolescent treatment, regulate residential care programs, affect the management of depressive and PTSD patients, transform the style of cognitive–behavioral and interpersonal therapies, guide sophisticated forensic and correctional assessments—a whole bevy of important themes that typify where psychologists center their scientific and applied efforts today.

It is toward the end of alerting psychologists who work in diverse areas of study and practice that the present series, entitled *Personality-Guided Psychology*, has been developed for publication by the American Psychological Association. The originating concept underlying the series may be traced to Henry Murray's seminal proposal in his 1938 volume, *Explorations in Personality*, in which he advanced a new field of study termed *personology*.

It took its contemporary form in a work of mine, published in 1999 under the title *Personality-Guided Therapy*.

The utility and relevance of personality as a variable is spreading in all directions, and the series sets out to illustrate where things stand today. As will be evident as the series' publication progresses, the most prominent work at present is found with creative thinkers whose efforts are directed toward enhancing a more efficacious treatment of patients. We hope to demonstrate, further, some of the newer realms of application and research that lie just at the edge of scientific advances in our field. Thus, we trust that the volumes included in this series will help us look beyond the threshold of the present and toward the vast horizon that represents all of psychology. Fortunately, there is a growing awareness that personality variables can be a guiding factor in all spheres of study. We trust the series will provide a map of an open country that encourages innovative ventures and provides a foundation for investigators who wish to locate directions in which they themselves can assume leading roles.

Theodore Millon, PhD, DSc
Series Editor

PREFACE

This volume is the current expression of my evolution as a psychotherapist, clinical investigator, psychodiagnostician, and theoretician. It is my belief that all clinical mental health practitioners are also theoreticians, although many have not spent the time, as I have done in this and other volumes, trying to formally articulate their unique model that intuitively guides their work. The unified model presented in this volume has emerged from the rich matrix of clinical and theoretical systems that have been advanced during the first century of modern psychotherapy and clinical sciences. Many whose works are cited, and others whose are not, developed the constructs, theoretical models, and technical advances that are the foundation of a unified system. It is impossible to reference adequately all the contributors to this system, but I hope that the primary ones are apparent to the reader. To those whom I have overlooked, I offer my sincere apologies. We are a young science that has only begun to unravel the mystery of consciousness, the nature of humanity, and methods by which to ameliorate human suffering. This rich heritage of knowledge from the 20th century, gleaned mostly by innovators and their experiences with the suffering individuals we call patients, has prepared us to enter a new phase of development with increasing access to mind–brain and mind–body connections offered by the neurosciences. Never before has there been so much excitement evident across disciplines and among various schools. It is now becoming commonplace to attend a psychoanalytic lecture and hear the speaker discuss the latest neurobiological findings and how they help us understand how the mind functions as well as provide a useful tool to explore theoretical constructs that previously were untested. This is an exciting time as we follow one of the major advances in natural sciences, the completion of the human genome. We are now approaching a time when we may be able to prevent and treat some of the major medical diseases of our era. Wilber (2000a) calls for a "Human Consciousness Project" to similarly map the dimensions of the personality system. It is clear, however, that other medical and emotional disturbances are caused by problems in the sociocultural–familial matrix. These include major health problems such as obesity, which accounts for related illnesses such as diabetes, cardiovascular disease, and cancer. On the emotional front, we are witnessing an increase in severe forms of personality dysfunction in adolescents and adults, characterized by more commonly known syndromes such as eating disorders, addictions, and a variety of other Axis I disorders or clinical syndromes such as anxiety, depression, and others.

Fundamental to my thinking is the assumption that was advanced by the early psychoanalytic workers and reformulated more contemporaneously by Millon, Grossman, Meagher, Millon, and Everly (1999) that personality is the organizing system from which to understand the organic, fluid process, as well as the fixed aspects of our patterns of behavior. These networks or complex systems define who we are and the sociocultural systems in which we operate and on which we operate. As readers of this volume will discern as they navigate the terrain of concepts and paradigms, the construct of "personality" is used in a nontraditional manner to signify what Bronfenbrenner (1979) described as the nested systems in which human functioning is embedded and he terms the "ecology of human development." This concept of nested structures to describe development and structure is expanded in this volume to encompass the total ecology of the personality system, which includes four basic matrices based on triangular configurations representing increasingly macroscopic perspectives. We know that personality is shaped in the relational matrix and is the result of evolutionary processes that occur at various levels of the ecological system. Each matrix represents a different level of functioning within the context of relational forces. At the primary level, we are concerned with the intrapsychic–biological triangle, which depicts how internal forces are given expression. Even this system is relational in that it is shaped and structured by attachments and the schematic representations that create our intrapsychic structures and endow us with identity, character, and so forth. All this brings us to the major point of this volume that Millon urged: Personality should guide therapeutic intervention, not the syndromes or symptomatic expression of dysfunction or maladaptation, which are expressed when the personality system falters as the result of stress or trauma. The levels of the personality system then become the central ones of our science and of our theoretical formulations.

The goal of this volume is to present the reader with the scaffold of this unified system. It would have required multiple volumes to flesh out the specific techniques and methods required. Readers who want more specific information about the major methods of working with the personality system may refer to my previous works that detail more precisely modes of action in the four triangles. My first volume, *Restructuring Personality Disorders: A Short-Term Dynamic Approach* (1997a), primarily describes processes in the intrapsychic–biological triangle, and my next volume, *Relational Therapy for Personality Disorders* (2000a), expands my thinking to the dyadic and triadic systems. Finally, a range of approaches is presented in the *Comprehensive Handbook of Psychotherapy: Psychodynamic/Object Relations*, edited by Florence Kaslow (2002). Each of these volumes, the first of which is devoted to psychodynamic/object relations (Magnavita, 2002a), presents a sample of many of the cutting-edge approaches to psychotherapy in various modalities and populations. Readers who are interested in gaining a better appreciation of the foundation of the theoretical model presented in this volume as well as Millon's can refer to my text *Theories of Personality: Contemporary Approaches to the Science of Personality* (2002a). Finally, those who are interested in treating personality systems can refer to the *Handbook of Personality Disorders: Theory and Practice* (2004d).

Readers may encounter various names such as *short-term restructuring psychotherapy* (STRP), the model in my first volume based on my work in short-term dynamic therapy; *integrative relational therapy* (IRP), the evolution and expansion from the intrapsychic–dyadic domain to the triadic and familial; and finally, *relational psychodynamics*, based on my work published in the *Comprehensive Handbook of Psychotherapy* (2002e). Finally, my thinking evolved to a unified *component system model* (CSM) presented in the *Handbook of Personality Disorders: Theory and Practice* (2004d) and elaborated in the present volume. The various models were not an attempt to obfuscate the subject but represent my own evolutionary stages as a theoretician and clinical investigator–practitioner. I am hopeful that a unified approach better encompasses the range of methods and constructs that most clinicians draw from and use to guide their clinical work.

ACKNOWLEDGMENTS

There are many people who have influenced my clinical work and theoretical modeling. First and foremost, I would like to express my appreciation to Theodore Millon, who is one of the most prolific theoreticians of the later half of the 20th century and continues to advance cutting-edge ideas that will spawn the work of many for years to come. Ted has been most influential and supportive of my theoretical work, even though it diverges in some critical ways from his own conceptual model. Many of the concepts in this volume owe their genesis to his rich trove of conceptual work that is multilayered and will continue to be mined for many decades to come. His construction of personality-guided therapy resonates deeply with my own thinking and my quarter century of clinical and theoretical work. The personality system is a vital conceptual advance that can be a unifying one for the field. It is an honor to be invited to join this personality-guided series. A caveat is in order. Even though many of my conceptualizations either directly emerge from Millon's work or parallel his, the unified model presented in this book is a departure, and thus I alone assume responsibility for any inconsistencies or flaws that successive theorists, clinicians, and researchers may discover.

That said, I also owe a great debt to those who have influenced my clinical conceptualization of the intrapsychic and dyadic system by offering elegant theoretical constructs in the form of triangular configurations. It was the genius of David Malan to bring these two constructs together as a way of understanding the action of psychodynamics. Malan has influenced the work of many current-day clinical theorists, clinicians, and researchers. His continued support and encouragement to those he has influenced continue to be a beacon to all, encouraging the use of audiovisual recording as a way to advance clinical science, sometimes against the tide. Another master clinician to whom I owe much is Habib Davanloo, who has made technical advances that have furthered the methods of treatment in powerful ways. He also has been one of the voices urging the field to adopt audio-visual recording as a main investigative tool. My opportunity to train with Davanloo altered my beliefs about what could occur in the personality system often in brief but intensive treatment formats.

There are a number of individuals who have provided me with a rich intellectual treasure trove of constructs, methods, and ways to understand complex systems. Some of these pioneers I have had the opportunity to observe in workshops and seminars, others I have come to know through their written work. I owe much of my early interest in systemic thinking to the pioneering work of Salvador Minuchin, who early in my career, while I trained as a family therapist, offered a way to understand the structure of family systems that was cogent and useful in my clinical practice on an inpatient adolescent unit. I have also been influenced by the work of Gregory Bateson, whose cross-disciplinary approach to learning remains a model for me in my own development. Theoretically, I owe a debt to the pioneering work of Murray Bowen, whose theoretical system appeals to me because of its clinical utility and comprehensiveness in understanding human function-ing and dysfunctioning. As a psychologist, it was not until later in my career that I found the enormous value in the work of Urie Bronfenbrenner, whose volume *The Ecology of Human Development* is one of the great psychological works of the 20th century. Last, and most important, is the theoretical work of Ludwig von Bertalanffy, who also had tremendous influence on the social, biological, and natural sciences with his work developing general system theory. As has been said by many, "I stand on the shoulders of these individuals" and only hope that I do them and their work justice.

There are many contemporary figures whom I would also like to thank for their keen intellectual and clinical interest in the field and their influence on me. My understanding of the dyadic configuration has been propelled by the groundbreaking work of Lorna Smith Benjamin, who is an intellectual force to contend with. My discussions and collaboration with her have always been stimulating and fruitful. I also thank Diana Fosha, who is a most generous and prolific force in the field and who continues to remind us that affective processes are central aspects of the human personality and of change mechanisms. Her broad-ranging mind and personal presence have been a gift to the sometimes-stuffy field of psychotherapy and to me personally. I am also thankful to Michael Mahoney for his unifying work and his grasp of the complexity of the field. Stanley Messer deserves thanks for his support of my work even while, I believe, not agreeing with some important aspects of unification. I appreciate his open-minded critiques and his affirmation. Other influential members of the Society for the Exploration of Psychotherapy Integration who have been important influences are Paul

Wachtel, whose integrative work was a decisive advance for the field, and Marvin Goldfried, who has also been supportive in offering a behavioral perspective to my theorizing. John Clarkin has been a valuable influence on me as he combines the best of theorizing and clinical work, grounded on a research foundation.

Special thanks are due to Jack C. Anchin, who painstakingly reviewed this volume while in manuscript form and who produced one of the most extensive reviews that the American Psychological Association has ever received. I am grateful to him for his unflagging support and his belief in this effort toward unification. His efforts have made this volume a much better one, and any mistakes are mine alone. Many passages are in Jack's own words and are written with great clarity. Jack's range of knowledge, simply put, is "awesome!"

I also would like to thank the anonymous reviewer for the helpful comments that shaped the volume. I know being an anonymous reviewer can be a thankless task, but in this case, "many thanks."

I also would like to thank a core group of individuals who help keep me grounded and who share the joys as well as the trials and tribulations of clinical practice. Our central group has been a forum for all of us to deal with our struggles to master the work. These colleagues include Frank Knoblauch, Vincent Stephens, William Alder, and Thomas Carlson.

I also thank my students from the doctoral program in clinical psychology at the University of Hartford, whose hunger for theoretical guidance that offers clinical utility always urges me on, I hope, to clearer conceptualization.

A great debt of gratitude is owed to those who have sought me out for psychotherapy. The gift of working with you all has been a greatly cherished privilege from which I have learned more than you can imagine. The impetus for this volume has emerged from this endeavor and has made me a more effective clinician.

Most important, I express my deepest gratitude to the unifying force in my life, Anne Gardner Magnavita. She not only is the best editor I know but also delivers critique in a generous way and always strives to propel me to greater conceptual clarity and parsimony of thought. Her respect and support of my work is unwavering and a beacon. Last, our three daughters, Elizabeth, Emily, and Caroline, provide us with loving inspiration as they joyfully express their unique emerging personalities.

I

THEORETICAL MODEL

This part of the volume, divided into three chapters, introduces the historical precursors and theoretical advances of a unified model. The evolutionary phases of the brief history of psychotherapy, moving from single-school approaches to integrative, are reviewed. This has set the stage for what appears to be a paradigmatic shift toward a unified approach to the components and methods that are introduced. Four triangular configurations representing the total ecosystem of human functioning are presented as a guide toward conceptualization of the interrelationships necessary for personality-guided relational therapy.

1

UNIFIED RELATIONAL PSYCHOTHERAPY: BEYOND INTEGRATION

A human being is part of the whole called by us the universe, a part
limited in time and space. He experiences himself, his thoughts and
feelings as something separated from the rest, a kind of optical delusion
of his consciousness. This delusion is a kind of prison for us, restricting
us to our personal desires and to affection for a few persons nearest to
us. Our task must be to free ourselves from this prison by widening our
circle of compassion to embrace all living creatures and the whole of
nature in its beauty.

—Albert Einstein

All therapeutic action and process occurs within relationships, actual
or representational, through schema, structures, and matrices. The primacy
of the relational matrix is the unequivocal crucible of development and
change (Kaslow, 1996; Magnavita, 2000a; Mitchell, 1988). Mobilizing and
channeling forces within the relational matrix is analogous to releasing the
forces within the atom—the release of energy can be massively destructive
or profoundly transforming. Experienced clinicians have repeatedly seen
some individuals and relational systems self-destruct and others transform
themselves. What accounts for this phenomenon? The forces within the
relational matrix can be understood and channeled using a unified model.
This volume presents a new, unified system of personality-guided psychotherapy that harnesses the power of these forces and offers a system to
intervene in complex systems at four levels representing the entire matrix
of human functioning: (a) *intrapsychic–biological*, (b) *interpersonal–dyadic*,
(c) *relational–triadic*, and (d) *sociocultural–familial*. None of these domains
can be ignored without a loss of theoretical clarity and clinical potency.
This volume attempts to articulate these interconnected domains more fully
and to move the field toward unification.

The 20th century was ushered in with the development of psychoanalysis, the first wave of the modern psychotherapy movement. Since then, we

3

have accrued the major components of a comprehensive system of personality, psychopathology, and psychotherapy. Mahoney (1991) describes this period, one marked by great advances in the field of psychology:

> There are many indications that we are now in the midst of sweeping conceptual shifts that mark a clear turning point in the history of human understanding. It is an exciting and challenging time for the sciences, and a period of dramatic conceptual development in psychology. (p. 48)

The model that is considered to be the foundation of contemporary psychotherapy, the *component system model,* is the result of this remarkable century of clinical, scientific, and theoretical developments, and it is presented in this volume. Recent years have seen an explosion of advances in the science and art of psychotherapy, as well as in many other disciplines.

This chapter presents some of the main historical advances that have relevance to personality-guided relational psychotherapy and the component system model and serves as a framework in which to place other contemporary theories and treatment models. The chapter also presents the reader with an introduction to the constructs and an overview of the model.

Of course, unification is not a new idea and has been suggested by others. William James (1890), when he wrote *The Principles of Psychology* more than a century ago, felt that the unification of psychology was premature because the component systems were not yet sufficiently developed. Gregory Bateson (1979), another innovative thinker, wrote in his volume *Mind and Nature* that "a mind is an aggregate of interacting parts or components" (p. 102). He elaborates, "In a word, I do not believe that single subatomic particles are 'minds' in my sense because I do believe that mental process is always a sequence of interaction *between* parts. The *explanation* of mental phenomenon must always reside in the organization and interaction of multiple parts" (p. 103). Angyal (1941, 1982) articulated many of the aspects required for what he termed a "holistic" or unified model. In *Neurosis and Treatment: A Holistic Approach,* he wrote the following:

> The holistic approach postulates that man is to be understood not in terms of specific functions or traits, but in terms of the broad system principles which organize these traits into a hierarchy of systems and subsystems. (1982, p. 203)

And further:

> The basic tenet of the holistic approach is that personality is an organized whole and not a mere aggregate of discrete parts. Its functioning does not derive from the functioning of its parts; rather the parts must be viewed in light of the organizational principles governing the whole. (p. xvi)

In what appears to be advanced conceptualizing, Angyal described in 1941 the basic framework for a unification paradigm:

> Of the total process of life a *unified system of factors* can be separated by abstraction. However, not every moment of the life process is organized into that system. The life process in its concrete form also contains factors alien to the system, or "random" from the point of the system. The biological total process results from the interaction of system-determined (self-governed, autonomous) factors and factors which are alien to the system (governed from outside the system, heteronomous). (pp. 93–94)

One can see unarticulated elements of chaos theory (Gleick, 1987) in his conceptualization, as well as a strong systemic (von Bertalanffy, 1968) bent. Whether he was aware of von Bertalanffy's system theory is unclear because it is not cited in either of Angyal's volumes. What is also so impressive about Angyal's (1941) work is that he places a strong emphasis on the cultural subsystem, which he describes thus: "Culture can be defined as an organized body of behavior patterns which is transmitted by social inheritance, that is, by tradition, and which is characteristic of a given culture" (p. 187).

Others, such as Harry Stack Sullivan, wanted to expand the field to include the cultural matrix, as is evident in his collaboration with the anthropologist Edward Sapir (1963), who had great influence on Sullivan. Sapir wrote, "But we do maintain that such differences of analysis are merely imposed by the nature of the interest of the observer and are not inherent in the phenomenon themselves" (p. 546).

Arthur Staats (1983, 1987, 1991) is also a strong proponent of unification. He explored the ramifications and need for a "grand unified theory" for the field of psychology, an ambitious task revisited more recently by Sternberg and Grigorenko (2001) in an article in the *American Psychologist*. Staats (1983) wrote in his volume *Psychology's Crisis of Disunity: Philosophy and Method for a Unified Science*:

> The optimistic message in the present work, nevertheless, is that what psychology has achieved in its 100 or so years of self-conscious striving does provide the raw materials for making the leap to the status of a unified science. I believe psychology is ready for the revolution to the unified state that must inevitably occur, for there is now a deep tension in psychology produced by disorganization. (p. vi)

Royce (1987) and Yancher and Slife (1997), contemporaries of Staats, also sought unification. The search for psychology's grand unifying theory, important as it may be for the field, is not as urgent as unification in the clinical sciences, which although less ambitious is vital for ameliorating unnecessary human suffering. More currently in the area of clinical science, Millon and colleagues (Millon, Grossman, Meagher, Millon, & Everly, 1999) emphasized the task of finding "the person," a concept that is lost in reliance on diagnostics and manualized treatment and that represents a unified approach. They wrote of

> the primacy of the overarching gestalt of the whole person. The gestalt gives coherence, provides an interactive framework, and creates an organic order among otherwise discrete clinical techniques. Each personality is a synthesized and substantive system; the whole is greater than the sum of its parts. The problems that our patients bring to us form an inextricable interwoven structure of behavior, cognitions, and intrapsychic processes, all bound together by feedback loops and serially unfolding concatenations that emerge at different times and in dynamic and changing configurations. (p. xi)

Millon and Davis (1996) view the personality as a complex system and write, "Such complex and dynamic interdependence is cause for both optimism and pessimism" (p. 184). Optimistically, at any fulcrum point, if the system is affected, it can change; this change can reverberate throughout. Pessimistically, systems strive for homeostasis and maintaining equilibrium, a force often called *resistance*.

MILLON'S PERSONALITY-GUIDED THERAPY

Millon's major advance, termed *personality-guided therapy*, sets the stage for the next evolutionary phase of psychotherapy. Millon et al. (1999) offered a model to unify the field of psychotherapy that makes sense to most clinicians who seek to practice holistically. Yet to achieve the goal of unified practice may take years of clinical experience and training. Until recently, we did not have enough components to easily incorporate a holistic perspective. Rangell (2002), too, has promoted a "total composite psychoanalytic theory" with features of unification, but focusing solely on components derived from psychoanalysis.

PARADIGMATIC SHIFTS IN THE FIELD OF PSYCHOTHERAPY

It is often necessary in the development of scientific disciplines to make paradigmatic shifts in the way we understand, view, and conceptualize certain problems. In the field of psychotherapy, there have been models that represented quantum shifts in the way we think about our subject.

There is no doubt that many of these that may appear quaint to us now were remarkable in their time. It also seems necessary and timely, as we begin a new millennium, to examine where we have come from and whether there is a better way in which to understand the clinical phenomenon and challenges that clinicians face in their day-to-day practice, regardless of the setting in which they work and the populations they treat. A look at the current state of psychotherapy reveals a fragmented field, scattered with numerous schools and models of psychotherapy, models that in some ways hold very different assumptions and emphases, yet share many commonalties. How did this fragmentation come about?

There have been a number of phases in the evolution of psychotherapy, some of which represent paradigmatic shifts over the course of the 20th century, many of which spawned new models of psychopathology and treatment and theories of personality. Some, which seemed groundbreaking at the time, have faded into the history books; others continue to exert influence on the field (Jackson, 1999). Clinical sciences are not static but are continually evolving as new models for understanding phenomena are offered and as scientific discoveries add to our empirical knowledge. Because this text is not primarily concerned with a history of psychology or psychiatry but the narrower discipline of psychotherapy, only five major evolutionary phases that occurred during the 20th century are presented—those that are essential to unified component system model. Readers may refer to these excellent references for further information: *Healing the Mind: A History of Psychiatry From Antiquity to the Present* (Stone, 1997), *History of Psychotherapy: A Century of Change* (Freedheim, 1992), *The Story of Psychology* (Hunt, 1993), and *Masters of the Mind* (Millon, 2004).

The First Five Evolutionary Phases of Psychotherapy

During the first half of the 20th century, we witnessed the remarkable birth of modern psychotherapy and the development of various schools of the discipline. The development of psychoanalysis gave birth to the first century of modern scientific psychotherapy (Magnavita, 2002b). Various schools of therapy emerged to challenge the ascendancy of psychoanalysis, which itself was a major theoretical leap. In its genius, Freud's work is often compared with Albert Einstein's theory of relativity and Charles Darwin's theory of evolution (Bischof, 1970). The five major paradigmatic shifts were psychoanalysis–psychodynamic therapy, radical behaviorism–behavior therapy, the cognitive revolution–cognitive therapy, general systems theory–family therapy, and the existential–humanistic movement. Much overlap existed among these evolving and shifting paradigms, and some represent "true" paradigmatic shifts more than others.

Psychoanalysis—Psychodynamic Therapy

Although fraught with controversy, there is little doubt among most scholars that Freud's metapsychology represented a major development in the 20th century in its conceptualization of a dynamic model of the mind, which was based in part on a metaphor of fluid hydraulics. Freud offered a mechanical but flexible model that did not artificially reduce its subject, and since his pioneering work, there has been a proliferation of psychodynamic approaches that, as Havens (2002) eloquently wrote, were "stimulated by the limitations of traditional psychoanalysis and by infusion of existential thought, with emphasis on selfhood and being with the other, as in Kohut's self psychology, and interpersonal or social concepts, centering on relationship patterns and their reoccurrence in therapy, as in object relations and intersubjective analysis" (p. xi). Within the contemporary psychodynamic model are five primary branches: ego psychology, object relations, self psychology, interpersonal psychology, and relational psychoanalysis.

1. *Ego psychology* emphasized adaptation and aspects of healthy functioning (Hartmann, 1958, 1964). This offered the clinician a new lens through which to view psychic functioning and provided considerable utility for understanding and developing useful assessments. Although ego psychology is not considered a fertile development in that it has not evolved or led to many other innovations, it represents in itself an important dimension of psychic functioning.

2. *Object relations* offered a new theoretical development that emphasized attachment instead of placing the emphasis on the biological substrate or drive. This perspective maintained that the primacy of attachment is a drive of the human infant, and it emphasized the bond between infant and mother. This view shifted the emphasis from the intrapsychic matrix of Freud's structural-drive theory to a dyadic matrix. Object relations created new concepts and terms such as the concept of the "good-enough mother" (Winnicott, Shepherd, & Davis, 1989, p. 44).

3. *Self psychology* is another way of understanding certain clinical phenomena. Kohut's (1971, 1977, 1984) expansion of the conceptualization of narcissism is considered to be a remarkable development in psychodynamics. Emphasizing attachment experiences, he formulated the construct of narcissism, which was seen not as a conflict but as a deficit in self-structure.

4. *Interpersonal psychiatry* was pioneered by Harry Stack Sullivan (1953) and constituted a radical departure because he declared that what was important was not what was going on *inside* of

people but *between* them. He eschewed the theory of repressed emotions and intrapsychic forces. Sullivan's work was a major departure that has inspired many later and contemporary theorists such as Anchin and Kiesler (1982), Benjamin (1996), Carson (1982, 1983), Kiesler (1996), Leary (1957), Levenson (1995), and Strupp and Binder (1984).

5. *Relational psychoanalysis* is a hybrid that incorporates various aspects of the other branches but also includes many versions of existentialism. This model emphasizes the intersubjectivity of therapeutic process and seems to be ascendant to the psychoanalysis reflected in the works of Aron (1996), Frank (1999, 2002), Greenberg and Mitchell (1983), Mitchell (1988, 1993), and Skolnick and Warshaw (1992).

Radical Behaviorism—Behavior Therapy

The second paradigmatic shift was the development of behaviorism. The first credible attack on psychoanalysis was launched by the behaviorists, who rightly challenged the "ungrounded" theoretical system of this model. James Watson, a major figure in academic psychology, initiated one of the early attacks, ridiculing many psychoanalytic notions that he believed were not supported empirically. Hans Eysenck (1952) launched the most notorious attack on psychotherapy—and psychoanalysis in particular—because he was dissatisfied with its lack of empiricism. Behaviorism offered a new empirical basis for understanding behavior, devoid of overly reified psychological theory. Behavior technology was clearly proven effective in shaping the behavior of animals and humans. New treatment models emerged from this research, including Stampfl's (1966) implosive therapy, Skinner's (1953) conditioning model, Wolpe's (1958) systematic desensitization, and Seligman's (1975) learned helplessness. Dollard and Miller (1950) offered their comprehensive learning-based theory of personality, effectively bridging a gap between psychoanalytic and behavior theory.

The Cognitive Revolution—Cognitive Therapy

Many followers of the behavior movement became disillusioned with the shortcomings of behaviorism. The computer drew the attention of behaviorists and the possibilities it offered, for it seemed to provide a useful model for how the mind works. The roots of cognitive therapy are in the information-processing models developed at the time that demonstrated how schema organized and stored information for later access. The leaders of this movement, Beck (1976) and Ellis (Ellis & Harper, 1961), began to apply these concepts to emotional disorders.

Existential–Humanistic Movement

The movement to phenomenology of an individuals' subjective experience represents another major shift in paradigms. Pioneered by Carl Rogers (1951), Abraham Maslow (1962), and Rollo May (1953), among others, the existential–humanistic movement has been referred to as the "third force." This shift represented a marked departure from radical behaviorism's external approach by revitalizing the importance of the inner phenomenon of self and experience.

General System Theory—Family Therapy

The development of general system theory (von Bertalanffy, 1968) fueled the new field of family therapy. Family therapy represented a major departure from conceptualizing and treating intrapsychic psychopathology and extended the parameters of treatment to the family and relational systems. Instead of viewing psychopathology as occurring within (intrapsychic) or between individuals (dyadic), general system theory offered a radically different perspective of how dysfunctional patterns are perpetuated, controlled, and reinforced through reciprocal feedback loops. Thus, the concept of the relational triangle was introduced as a central "molecule" of human relations (Bowen, 1976). The ability of an individual to regulate the polarity of intimacy–closeness versus distance–disconnection became crucial in understanding self–other differentiation, emotional differentiation, and how triangular configurations result when differentiation is low.

THE SIXTH PHASE—A PARADIGMATIC SHIFT

The necessary components were now in place for another form of psychotherapy to begin to take hold, which necessitated leaving behind the parochialism of previous eras. This sixth phase represents a shift in paradigms from single models and their evolutionary branches to new ways of seeing commonalities and synergistic combinations of various approaches.

The Movement From Individual Schools to Integrative Psychotherapy

In the second half of the 20th century, a new paradigmatic shift was beginning to take hold. As the various schools of psychotherapy evolved and developed, a novel and heretical way of thinking began to emerge in the 1980s, which became known as the *psychotherapy integration movement*. In 1989, Beitman, Goldfried, and Norcross wrote, "Psychotherapy systems appear and vanish with bewildering rapidity on the diffuse, heterodox scene in the United States" (1988, p. 138). Karasu (1986) reported that there were more than 400 schools of psychotherapy. In their classic article, Beitman et al. discussed the psychotherapy integration movement, a movement that led to a new stage of rapprochement among the various schools of psychotherapy. The movement is characterized by four somewhat distinct perspectives: assimilative integration, technical eclecticism, theoretical integration, and common factors (Norcross & Goldfried, 1992), each of which has a growing and sizable literature.

BEYOND INTEGRATION TOWARD UNIFIED THEORY

A new paradigm is necessary for convergence in the field. The "old school" model of psychotherapy, although an essential evolutionary process in the field of psychotherapy, creates unnecessary fractionation of the field. If one examines the major systems of psychotherapy as clinicians practice them, the overwhelming reaction is that the therapeutic process is remarkably similar. Beitman et al. (1989) described this phenomenon as *convergence*, rather than *rapprochement* or *eclecticism*. Furthermore, they wrote, "There appears to be an emerging preference for theoretical synthesis (integration) as opposed to technical synthesis (eclecticism)" (p. 140). This is not to say that various proponents of these models do not emphasis one domain (e.g., cognition, affect, defense, interpersonal process, attachment) over another, but that generally they nonetheless pay attention to the components they do not emphasize. A unified theory is an effort to advance the field and further the theory and science of psychotherapy. It is hoped that science and compassion can guide our understanding of the ethical and social issues involved in all forms of human suffering.

A NECESSARY REQUIREMENT FOR A UNIFIED THEORY

Unified psychotherapy requires a fluid relationship among basic domains of clinical science. There are three essential ones that need to cohere. These are reviewed in this section.

The Three Sister Disciplines

Three "sister disciplines" are required for a thorough understanding of contemporary clinical science: *personality theory, psychopathology*, and *a theory of psychotherapy* (Magnavita, 2002d). Numerous authors have identified explicitly or implicitly the intimate relationship among these domains. Rychlak (1973), a major thinker and writer in the area of personality theory, wrote the classic *Introduction to Personality and Psychotherapy*, in which he explores the relationship between personality, psychotherapy, and psychopathology. He wrote as follows:

> If the question "What is personality?" is difficult to answer then "What is psychotherapy?" is doubly so. The two questions are not unrelated, however, since it is historical fact that many of our major personality theorists have come from the medical profession, or they have taken considerable interest in man's level of psychological health even as they were explicating his temperament, character, or "personality." (p. 17)

Rychlak (1973) also explored the relationship among personality theory, psychotherapy, and psychopathology. He raised three important questions that must be considered as the first step toward formulating a unified theory:

> (1) How does a personality "get sick" or "become maladjusted" or "begin behaving in an unrewarding fashion"? (2) How does the therapist go about curing, resolving, or controlling (changing) this condition? And (3) does he have any unique procedures in his approach distinguishing him from other psychotherapists? (p. 21)

In his book, *Personality Development and Psychopathology*, Cameron (1963) explored the relationship between personality and psychopathology. He discussed societal problems: "Everyone has potentialities for developing psychopathology—personality disorder, psychosomatic disorder or psychosis, as well as neurosis—just as we all have potentialities for other kinds of illness" (p. 2). He discussed what we have come to know about personality and stress, which has been a driving theme of Millon's work: Personality is like the immune system, and when we are stressed, we all have a preferred symptomatic expression. In another important work, *Personality and Psychotherapy: An Analysis in Terms of Learning*, Dollard and Miller (1950) explored the relationship among personality theory, psychopathology, and psychotherapy in their translation of psychoanalytic theory into behavior theory.

Millon, a more contemporary influence, has also emphasized the relationship among psychopathology (Millon, 1969/1985), theories of personality (Millon, 1981, 1990; Millon, Davis, Millon, Escovar, & Meagher, 2000), and models of psychotherapy (Millon et al., 1999). His writing suggests these are important elements of contemporary clinical science. A great deal of overlap exists between theories of personality and models of psychopathology. Many personality theorists were also clinical practitioners who used their patients' experiences and personal suffering to understand what occurs when development goes awry.

Personality Theory

Personality theory (Magnavita, 2002a) is the guide or model used to understand how individuals function, or, if we expand this notion, how the personality system operates more broadly (as we consider in this volume). All clinicians use personality theory, applied either formally or informally, to guide their treatment approach. Each theoretical model makes certain assumptions about the nature of humans, their capacity for change, and the influential factors that shape developmental progression. Thus, one's understanding of personality theory will determine how one predicts dysfunction and how psychopathology will be expressed, and offers insight about the mechanisms of change. Theories of personality disorders also offer models of how dysfunctional personality are conceptualized (Clarkin & Lenzenweger, 1996).

Psychopathology

Cameron (1963) wrote, "The task of differentiating between what is normal and what is abnormal has always been a vexatious one. Different people define normality and abnormality in different ways, from different points of view, and for different purposes" (p. 8). This opinion is still widely held in the therapeutic community. Researchers might find value in one system, clinicians in others, and theoreticians in yet another. Within the field of psychopathology, some diagnosticians are shifting from the concept of disorder to harmful dysfunction (Wakefield, 1999). A harmful dysfunction represents an evolutionary deviation in adaptation. This warrants a greater emphasis on systemic modeling as opposed to other systems such as categorical or factorial. The current categorical conceptualization of personality disorder as presented in the *Diagnostic and Statistical Manual of Mental Disorders* (4th ed.; *DSM–IV*; American Psychiatric Association, 1994) is fraught with problems (Magnavita, 2004a). There is a high degree of overlap among the various personality disorders as well as lack of refinement about the variation so prevalent in the human personality system. According to Adams, Luscher, and Bernat (2001):

> The goal of any system designed to classify behavior is that the assignment of an individual or response pattern to allocation on a dimension or certain category permits useful statements about the behavior based on membership in that category" (p. 4). Problems exist with all classification systems. Each system offers a view of the phenomenon but is limited by its lens or perspective (e.g., intrapsychic, factorial, prototypal, categorical, relational). Adams et al. stated, "Attempts to define abnormal, deviant, disordered, or psychopathological behavior in psychology have been disastrous, although the process is necessary to develop a classification system. (p. 7)

Theory of Psychotherapy

Approaches to psychotherapy inherently emerge from personality theory and psychopathological models. There exists congruence among these three domains. It has been said that a poor theory is better than no theory at all. Even a poor theory capitalizes on the placebo and expectancies that can be made more potent by a practitioner's belief in his or her model. A map is a way for us to organize and navigate a complex terrain. Theories of psychotherapy offer clinicians constructs with which to conceptualize treatment such as transference and countertransference, repression and resistance, schema and so on, as well as codified methods, techniques, and processes with which to orient and guide treatment interventions. Without a theory of psychotherapy that offers the necessary paradigms, constructs, and methods, psychotherapy would be a mostly haphazard process.

COMBINING TWO KEY PARADIGMS

Various paradigms have been formulated over the past century that have demonstrated utility for understanding personality development and the way in which dysfunction can occur. Combining two of these paradigms offers increased explanatory power and assists in understanding and organizing the complexity of personality variables, the multifactorial nature of human personality systems, and both dysfunctional and functional processes. The two models to be combined are the biopsychosocial (Engle, 1980) and the diathesis-stress (Monroe & Simons, 1991).

The Biopsychosocial Model

A remarkable breakthrough conceptualization offered by Engle (1980) is the biopsychosocial model, which highlights the multiple substrates from the cellular level of abstraction to the sociocultural level. The biopsychosocial model views the individual holistically and does not ignore the potential contributing effects of various domains from the molecular to the ecological. Engle reminded us not to ignore any of these levels of abstraction to ensure that individuals are viewed holistically and to counter the reductionistic thinking of medicine in particular but also of psychology.

The Diathesis–Stress Model

One way of understanding why people develop certain physical and emotional problems when under stress is to conceptualize this relationship by applying a diathesis–stress model (Monroe & Simons, 1991). The diathesis is the area in the personality–physical system of increased vulnerability determined by genetic predispositions and psychological susceptibility, based on multiple developmental factors. The diathesis–stress model is an important development in understanding the relationships among genetic vulnerability, psychological vulnerability, and the point at which stress can result in symptomatic outbreak or personality dysfunction. According to Paris (1999), "The diathesis–stress model provides a general theory of the etiology of most mental disorders" (p. 696). He also believes that temperamental vulnerabilities are exacerbated or amplified by trauma and environmental challenges, and that the organism breaks down where the weakness exists. For example, the diathesis for some might be a vulnerability to depression, anxiety, schizophrenia, alcoholism, and so forth. Future genetic research might elaborate these vulnerabilities more clearly. Diathesis may also exist in the intrapsychic, dyadic, triadic, and sociocultural–familial system. One person may be more vulnerable to symptoms as a result of borderline organization, a couple might be prone to express a weakness in the marital dyad by triangulating a child or a lover, and a culture might have a diathesis to increased fundamentalism when under duress.

When the biopsychosocial model and the diathesis–stress paradigm are combined, it is possible to depict how the personality system might react under stress (see Figure 1.1). Consider a case in which stress impinges on the personality system (in this case, we are referring to the biological and intrapsychic domain of the individual personality system, which represents one level of the biopsychosocial sphere), and a symptom complex of anxiety and depression emerges (in this case, the diathesis is the vulnerability to anxiety and depression). However, the ensuing anxiety and depression may then begin to impinge on the marital dyad and the family as the effects cascade and amplify themselves bidirectionally. Later I discuss how this combined biopsychosocial and diathesis–stress amalgam may operate in various other subsystems of human functioning.

Problems With the Current System of Classification

There has been endless controversy about the preferred system of classifying mental disorders, especially personality disorders. The essence of this controversy is whether mental disorders should be classified in separate categories or placed along a continuum with statistically derived cut-off points that differentiate between "normal" and "abnormal." All the systems of diagnosis and classification offer a valid perspective, but it seems that none has established itself as completely satisfactory. What may be a more practical system is a multiperspective approach that combines the various

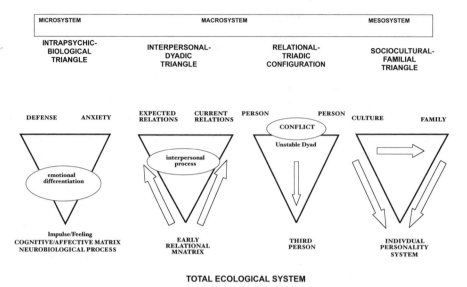

Figure 1.1. From the microlevel to the macrolevel of a unified model of personality systems.

systems. "Probably the most useful way to approach diagnosis is to use a multiperspective that eschews a narrow band formulation and classification based on limited data" (Magnavita & MacFarlane, 2004).

Simple Versus Complex Clinical Syndromes

The concept of comorbid disorders has recently become an area of acute interest and relevance for clinicians and researchers (Tyrer, Gunderson, Lyons, & Tohen, 1997). It refers to the co-occurrence of two or more clinical syndromes or personality disorders (Magnavita, 1998a). This term, which is useful in alerting clinicians and researchers to the likelihood that many patients have multiple symptom clusters or disorders, does not convey information regarding the interrelationship among the symptom constellations and personality traits from which many patients suffer. Often, these comorbid disorders are not unrelated but emerge from the personality system matrix (Magnavita, 1998a). Such cases are important because of the challenge they present to clinicians, who often refer to such patients as "treatment refractory," "difficult to treat," or "complex." Comorbid disorders may include any combination of the following, all of which emanate from various personality configurations: anxiety disorders, depressive spectrum disorders, interpersonal problems, marital problems, and substance use disorders. Millon et al. (1999) make a vital distinction between simple versus complex clinical syndromes: "Simple clinical reactions, complex clinical syndromes, and personality styles/disorders lie on a continuum such that the first is essentially a straightforward singular symptom, unaffected by other clinical domains of which the persona as a whole is composed" (p. 111). At the other end of the spectrum are the extreme personality disorders and, in the middle, complex clinical syndromes "akin to simple syndromes but interwoven and mediated by pervasive personality traits and embedded vulnerabilities" (p. 111).

The treatment of complex clinical syndromes is among the most challenging issues clinicians face (Magnavita, 1997c). It requires a model that is comprehensive and capable of intervening at multiple domain systems.

THE VIABILITY OF "SYSTEM THEORY"

Personality is the system that links various aspects of functioning at the intrapsychic, dyadic, triadic, and mesosystem level of process. Millon et al. (1999) offered a major breakthrough in the development and explication of personality-guided therapy, which emphasizes interrelated systems that function synergistically. Personality-guided therapy takes into consideration the domains of the total ecological system in treating mental disorders. Millon et al. (1999) also eschewed a static view of the individual and endorsed the position that personalities are probably best conceptualized not as disorders, but as systems: "The systems model argues for periods of rapid growth during which the psychic system reconfigures itself into a new gestalt, alternating with periods of relative constancy" (p. 153). Millon's perspective parallels that of many earlier systemic theorists and has served as the foundation for many ideas in this volume. He wrote in detail about many of the fundamental conceptualizations presented later in the text:

> The individual person represents but one structural level of life's systems; other levels of organization might also be considered and analyzed. Thus, individuals may be viewed as systems units that exist within larger ecological milieu, such as dyads, families, communities, and, ultimately cultures. Like the personality system, these higher-level systems contain homeostatic processes that tend to sustain and reinforce their own unique patterning of internal variables. (Millon et al., 1999, p. 155)

This excerpt from Millon et al.'s (1999) groundbreaking volume encapsulates the primary emphasis of this entire volume. The individual, structural, and trait systems, which have been the bulwark of contemporary personality theory, psychopathology, and psychotherapy, will largely be jettisoned;

instead, a systemic model will be emphasized. Historical and accepted constructs will not be entirely abandoned but incorporated as important aspects of the larger component systems.

Many clinicians find that the static maps offered by categorical and dimensional classifications of personality have limited applicability to actual clinical practice and case formulation. It is necessary to know more, to know how the multiple domains of human personality functioning interrelate to express themselves. As Millon and Davis (1996) remind us, systems theory assumes the whole is greater than the sum of its parts. Denton elaborates: "General systems theory (and the biopsychosocial model) maintains that dysfunction in one system level will impact the other system levels" (1996, p. 40). Diagnosing someone with a dependent personality and a concomitant anxiety disorder, for example, provides minimal useful information about the manner in which these disorders interrelate, are contextualized in social systems (marriage, family community, nation), and can be treated. It is possible to draw some inferences about this person; for example, the person will probably be overregulated in his or her affective life and likely to use cognition in his or her interpersonal experience and coping style. A clinician might suspect that this patient uses a certain array of defenses, such as intellectualization, rationalization, and isolation of affect. It would not be clear how this person's defenses might shift under stress, however, and whether the patient might be susceptible to clinical depression or to explosive behavioral outbursts. There is no hint of the influence of the family dynamics and multigenerational transmission processes that are often a sign of a dysfunctional personologic system (Magnavita, 2000c). There is no mention of the importance of sociocultural factors that may influence a certain symptomatic expression or personality adaptation.

Experienced clinicians are apt to draw information from subtle clinical criteria that they have observed over years of clinical practice and combine this with knowledge of the total ecological system of their patient(s). Clinicians often have an intuitive sense about how symptom manifestation is an expression of a complex system, with the parts being greater than the whole. Millon et al. (1999) described the way personality systems operate: "Clinical signs in *personality disorders* (PD) reflect the operation of a pattern of deeply embedded and pervasive characteristics of functioning, that is, a system of traits that systematically 'support' one another, and color and manifest themselves automatically in all facets of the individual's everyday life" (p. 112). Experienced clinicians will observe the way in which patients tell their story and how they understand themselves—what we call "psychological mindedness." Such clinicians will observe physiological signs of anxiety and depression and subtle affective shifts as patients discuss aspects of their lives. For example, in some circumstances, an individual who initially seems obsessive may later show signs of a more primitive organization.

Categorical and dimensional classification artificially places an individual in a category or on a continuum, such as highly to mildly obsessive. Individuals cannot truly be captured by these static, inorganic systems, or even by a prototype that combines both categorical and dimensional. Structural–dynamic diagnosis places too much emphasis on one domain; intrapsychic and interpersonal diagnoses often miss the triadic and the intrapsychic systems.

All diagnostic approaches have some clinical utility, but their limitations make many clinicians hunger for a more fluid model that better captures the complexity of the human experience. Millon and Davis (1996) described this conundrum as follows: "As a construct, personality seeks to capture the entire matrix of the person, to distill from the swirl of the behavioral stream some set of underlying, logical, organizing principles that precisely capture individual functioning" (p. 8). But how can this be achieved with current models? The categorical and prototypical systems, although an important starting point in classification, have probably outlived their usefulness for the psychodiagnostician and psychotherapist.

Millon and Davis (1996) wrote of the importance of what seems like the next major evolution in personality, psychotherapy, and psychopathology:

> the authors believe that the concept of a *system* offers an optimal level of scope and precision for purposes of bridging nomothetic and idiographic perspectives. By definition, a system is an integrative construct consisting of both structural and functional elements. Part and whole are bound together by self-regulating processes. (p. 8)

Systemic principles are necessary for understanding the complex interrelations that occur at various levels of the biopsychosocial model and can be viewed as ever-enlarging relational matrixes from the intrapsychic to dyads, triads, and larger systems. The relational matrix is the central aspect of human functioning and the focus of study. Relational science is emerging as a new discipline (Berscheid, 1999); the branches of relational theory include "(a) the intersubjectivity of the dyadic relationship, (b) the development of triadic theory, (c) the centrality of relationships in women's development, (d) the therapeutic alliance, and (e) a new model of relational diagnosis and treatment" (Magnavita, 2000b, p. 999).

THE CENTRALITY OF THE RELATIONAL MATRIX

The foundation of the relational model emerged at the beginning of modern psychotherapy, at the start of the last century, in the work of Sandor Ferenczi. Ferenczi eschewed the distant, neutral stance endorsed by the psychoanalytic approach and instead identified *relational psychodynamics* in the family "as a central issue in the development of psychopathology" (Rachman, 1997, p. 236). He emphasized the *real* as opposed to the transference relationship with the patient, believing that the neutral stance was retraumatizing to the patient. Relationships are the matrix in which personality is formed, first by early attachments and then in the relational experiences of family and community. All psychotherapy occurs in relationships, which are a fundamental requirement for healing. In an earlier volume, I first presented the centrality of a relational perspective as follows:

- Personality is formed by the relationships present from the earliest interpersonal experience and attachments.
- Personality is organized and shaped by the relationships in the interpersonal matrix that is unique to each family system.
- People with personality disorders consistently demonstrate disturbances in the relational matrix.
- People with personality disorders have major defenses against intimacy and closeness (or disturbances in attachment) that interfere with the healing possibilities of human connectedness.
- The restorative or healing aspect of the therapeutic relationship is the quality of the therapeutic alliance.
- The benefits of enhanced relational capacities and family support are evident in almost every line of research.
- Personality disturbances are reinforced and often exaggerated by cultural and family systems. (Magnavita, 2000a, pp. 10–11)

The following section presents an overview of the model of personality-guided relational psychotherapy.

ESSENTIAL COMPONENTS OF PERSONALITY-GUIDED RELATIONAL PSYCHOTHERAPY

The essential constructs of the unified model of personality-guided relational psychotherapy are shown in Exhibit 1.1. The exhibit summarizes the important paradigms that serve as the scaffold for the unified model.

The component system model of personality-guided relational therapy presented in this volume uses a spectrum of triangular configurations to organize the components that account for personality systems as they exist from the microscopic level to the macroscopic level (see Figure 1.1). As we move from left to right on the spectrum, we move from the microcosm of the internal workings of an individual's personality system to the macrocosm of broader sociocultural forces in relation to the individual. As we move from left to right the power of magnification increases, moving from the internal workings of the personality system of an individual to the

EXHIBIT 1.1
Essential Paradigms of Model

The centrality of the relational matrix as the framework with which to contextualize personality functioning

The blending of the biopsychosocial and diathesis–stress models to form a stronger amalgam

The use of system theory to provide the interconnections among related domains of personality

The emphasis on the personality system as it is expressed in the intrapsychic, dyadic, triadic, and sociocultural–familial (mesosystem) matrices

---

broader sociocultural forces at play. Starting at the left of the spectrum is the *intrapsychic–biological triangle*, which comprises the interrelationship of cognitive–affective elements, anxiety functions, and defensive functions. Next along the spectrum is the *interpersonal–dyadic triangle*, which includes interpersonal processes emanating from the early relational matrix and expressed in current relationships and expected or transference relationships. The third triangle along the spectrum depicts the *relational–triadic configuration*, which represents the tendency for unstable dyads to form triads in an attempt at stabilization. Such triads often result in symptomatic expression in the third party. Finally, the *sociocultural–familial triangle* comprises cultural, familial, and individual personality system processes.

Restructuring the Triangular Matrices

Each of the four triangular configurations can be used to guide the clinician when selecting from various methods of restructuring the personality system that have been developed over the last century. Using these triangles as guides, modifying or restructuring can be attempted by using four major methods. Working at the *intrapsychic–neurobiological triangle*, various methods of *intrapsychic restructuring* (IR) have been developed, including *defensive restructuring* (DeR), *cognitive restructuring* (CR), *affective restructuring* (AR), *cognitive–behavioral restructuring* (C-BR), and *neurobiological restructuring* (NR).

At the *interpersonal–dyadic level*, methods of *dyad restructuring* (DR) are used. When the restructuring focus is between the therapist and patient, this is best described as *self–other restructuring* (McCullough Vaillant, 1997); when the focus is the dyad, such as parent–child or couple, it is termed *relational–dyadic restructuring*.

When the focus of therapeutic intervention is the relational–triadic configuration, we term the method *triadic restructuring* (TR). TR restructuring refers to processes and techniques that work with any larger (dyad + *n*) system and occurs as the process unfolds. *Symbolic–relational restructuring* occurs in subsystems with one or two individuals and uses the triangular relational formations to assist individuals or couples in symbolic working through of triangular relationships with other members. These are the inner triangular schemata that are reenacted emotionally and interpersonally. For example, in one case, a mother of a patient told him he would not amount to anything, but this communication was a deflection and triangulation of her anger toward her husband that she displaced on their son. The patient then sabotaged everything that was a step toward his success.

When the process of restructuring occurs at the sociocultural–familial triangle, we call this *mesosystem restructuring* (MR).

In the following chapter, I discuss the origins and advantages of the systemic model and explain how this can be used to create a holograph of the personality system.

SUMMARY AND CONCLUSIONS

An evolution of psychotherapy from a single-school to an integrative phase has occurred. The next paradigmatic shift will be toward a phase of unification. This volume presents one such model of a unified theory based on a component system model of personality-guided relational therapy. This model has a number of essential paradigms that have been developed over the last century that allow us to more clearly understand the complex interrelated domains that comprise the personality system as it exists at the intrapsychic, dyadic, triadic, and sociocultural-familiar (mesosystem) levels of organization. The remaining chapters introduce the reader to this model and continue the evolutionary process in the development of a scientific psychotherapy that does not ignore the complexity of the interrelated domains of personality. The manner in which I adapt and develop dysfunctional personality systems and the complex clinical syndromes that psychologists routinely see in clinical practice can best be understood as complex and irreducible phenomena that must be understood as part–whole relationships.

2

THEORETICAL FOUNDATION

We live in an extraordinary time: All of the world's cultures, past and present, are to some degree available to us, either in historical records or as living entities. In the history of the planet Earth, this has never happened before.

(Wilber, 2000a, p. I)

This chapter presents the theoretical underpinnings of a unified model that is the foundation for personality-guided relational therapy. This theoretical scaffold encompasses the three related fields of personality, psychopathology, and psychotherapy. At this stage in the development of contemporary psychotherapy, we have the benefit of the accrued work of the previous highly productive century in science and psychology. As Urie Bronfenbrenner (1979) wrote over 20 years ago, any scientist is aware of being among "a community of scholars": "We stand on the shoulders of giants, and mistake the broad vision for our own" (p. xi). He mentioned individuals such as Kurt Lewin, Sigmund Freud, Kurt Goldstein, Otto Rank, and Jean Piaget, to name a few. I would add Murray Bowen, Ludwig von Bertalanffy, Sandor Ferenczi, David Malan, Theodore Millon, Gordon Allport, and many others whose work is presented in this volume. The most important, however, may be those not mentioned, those whose work we take for granted, such as William James, Charles Darwin, Albert Einstein; many of the great scientists of the brain, such as Roger Sperry, Charles Sherrington, and Santiago Ramon y Cajal (Finger, 2000); and many other notables. At no other time has so much knowledge in so many fields been accrued in such a short period. The emergence of the scientific revolution during the 15th and 16th centuries marked the beginning of this remarkable period and the prelude to advances in numerous disciplines during the 20th century. The new scientific disciplines of psychiatry and psychology, which share seminal roots in the musings of ancient philosophers, healers, early physicians, and theologians, did not become a scientific discipline until the 19th century with the work of those who began to systematize illness and incorporate the tools of empiricism in understanding the mind and brain (Millon, 2004; Stone, 1997). Although much knowledge has been accumulated and advanced, fragmentation of science in this era of specialization remains an issue. Psychiatry, a once-prestigious medical specialty, is in an identity crisis (Hobson & Leonard, 2001) and split between the "brain scientists" and the "psychodynamic therapists" (Luhrmann, 2000). Interdisciplinary rivalry remains an obstacle to further advances, although this is beginning to change as some call for a renewed interdisciplinary emphasis in science and the social sciences.

TOWARD A UNIFIED MODEL FOR THE 21ST CENTURY

Gordon Allport (1968) was one of the great proponents of what he termed *systematic eclecticism* (which we might better describe from our vantage point as theoretical synthesis or *convergence*): "Eclecticism is often a word of ill-repute. An artist or composer, or even a psychologist who is 'eclectic' seems to lack a mind and style of his own" (p. 3). What Allport proposed was not a hodgepodge but rather a synthesis. He described his vision for eclecticism as "a system that seeks the solution of fundamental problems by selecting and uniting what it regards as true in the specialized approaches to psychological sciences" (pp. 5–6). He described the problem at the time as follows:

> The situation at present is that each theorist typically occupies himself with one parameter of human nature, and builds himself a limited model to fit his special data and personal style. Those who concern themselves with either the brain or phenomenology may be said to focus on one important parameter (body–mind); depth psychologists on the conscious–unconscious parameter; trait theorists on the stability–variability parameter; others on self and non-self. Trouble arises when an investigator maintains that his preferred parameter, or his chosen model, overspreads the whole of human personality. (1968, p. 10)

Following the efforts of Staats (1983, 1987, 1991) and others, Sternberg and Grigorenko (2001) recently proposed a "unified psychology" by which they mean "multiparadigmatic, multidisciplinary, and integrated study of psychological phenomena through converging operations" (p. 1069). They contended that this attempt to unify psychology requires giving up three bad habits:

> The bad habits are (a) exclusive or almost exclusive reliance on a single methodology (e.g., response-time measurements or fMRI measurements)

rather than multiple converging methodologies for studying psychological phenomena; (b) identification of scholars in psychology in terms of psychological subdisciplines (e.g., social psychology or clinical psychology) rather than in terms of the psychological phenomena they study; and (c) adherence to single underlying paradigms for the investigation of psychological phenomena (e.g., behaviorism, cognitivism, psychoanalysis). (p. 1069)

The search for a unified system is not a new one in psychology. Sternberg and Grigorenko (2001) reviewed other attempts in their groundbreaking article, which were similar to the unified component systems–based model proposed in this volume. They summarized the previous work as follows:

Lerner (1998) has also taken a systems approach, arguing that the multiple levels of organization that constitute human life—from the biological to the individual to the social and beyond—all need to be understood within a common framework. Cairns (1998) has made a similar suggestion. Bronfenbrenner (1979; Bronfenbrenner & Morris, 1998) has actually proposed such a framework, with interlocking systems of development, such as the microsystem, which encompasses the individual; the mesosystem, which encompasses the family, the school, the peers, religious institutions and so forth; the exosystem, which includes the extended family, neighbors, mass media, social welfare and legal services, and so forth; the macrosystem, which includes the attitudes and ideologies of the culture. (p. 1070)

Grand Unification Theories

Psychology is not alone in its attempts to develop a unified theory. The noted psychobiologist Edward O. Wilson (1998) suggested that consilience in human knowledge is attainable. What he suggested by the term *consilience* is that various disciplines can be united in a coherent way to explain the world. Consilience, which means "jumping together," was "coined by William Whewell in 1984" (Gould, 2002, p. 104). Gould (2002) used consilience as a "principle tactic of bringing so many different points of evidence to bear on a single subject, history wins assent as an explanation of overwhelming confirmation and unique coordination" (p. 104). Wilson was concerned with the value of scientific theorizing and emphasizes the systemic nature of this endeavor: "The greatest challenge today, not just in cell biology and ecology but in all of science, is the accurate and complete description of complex systems" (1998, p. 85).

Among the most ambitious—and indeed compelling—attempts to create a grand unifying theory is the work of Ken Wilber. In his grandly titled book, *A Theory of Everything* (2000a), he presented an integral vision of the interconnected nature of knowledge. Wilber termed the current research in synthesizing knowledge of psychological dimensions "the human consciousness project," which he suggested to be crucial to a "theory of everything." He explained:

> In a sense, this research is the psychological correlate of the Human Genome Project, which involves the scientific mapping of all of the genes in human DNA. Just so, this overall psychological research— this Human Consciousness Project—is a cross-cultural mapping of all the states, structures, memes, types, levels, stages, and waves of human consciousness. This overall map, as we will see, then becomes the psychological component of a possible Theory of Everything, where it will be supplemented with findings from the physical, biological, cultural, and spiritual dimensions. (p. 7)

Wilber proposed a *holonic* model (p. 52). He defined the *holon* as

> a whole that is a part of other wholes. A whole atom is a part of a whole molecule; a whole molecule is part of a whole cell; a whole cell is part of a whole organism. Reality is composed of neither wholes nor parts, but whole/parts, or holons.

He suggested that an integral map of human consciousness should include the following:

1. multiple levels or *waves* of existence, a grand holarchy spanning the entire spectrum of consciousness, matter to body to mind to soul to spirit
2. numerous different *streams*, modules, or lines of development, including cognitive, moral, spiritual, aesthetic, somatic, imaginative, interpersonal, and so on. Moreover, at virtually any stage of development, one is open to
3. multiple *states* of consciousness, including waking, dreaming, sleeping, altered, nonordinary, and meditative (many of these altered states can occur at any level; thus, for example, one can have a variety of religious experiences at virtually any stage of development).
4. numerous different *types* of consciousness, including gender types, personality types. These types can occur in levels, lines, and states.
5. multiple organic factors and brain states (this . . . quadrant today receives most of the attention from psychiatry, cognitive science, and neurobiology; but as significant as it is, it is still only "one-fourth" of the story).
6. the extraordinary important impact of numerous *cultural* factors, including the rich textures of diverse cultural realities, background contexts, pluralistic perceptions, linguistic seman-

tics, and so on, none of which should be unwarrantedly marginalized, all of which should be included and integrated in a
broad web of integral-perspectival tapestries. (And, just as
important, a truly "integral transformative practice" would
give considerable weight to the importance of relationships,
community, culture, and intersubjective factors in general, not
merely as a realm of application of spiritual insight, but as a
means of spiritual transformation.)

7. the massively influential forces of the *social* system, at all levels
(from nature to human structures, including especially the
techno-economic base, as well as the profoundly important
relationship with nonhuman social systems, from Gaia to
ecosystems).

8. although I have not mentioned it in this simple overview, the
importance of the self as the navigator of the great River of
Life should not be overlooked. It appears that the self is not
a monolithic entity but rather a society of selves with a *center
of gravity*, which acts to bind the multiple waves, states,
streams, and realms into something of a unified organization;
the disruption of this organization, at any of its general stages,
can result in pathology. (pp. 53–54)

Wilber's comparison between the Human Genome Project and a unified psychology is an apt one, an important component of which is multiple
perspectives and multiple methodologies.

SINGLE VERSUS MULTIPLE METHODOLOGIES

Bronfenbrenner (1979) described the tension between empiricism and
clinical utility as follows: "To corrupt a modern metaphor, we risk being
caught between a rock and a soft place. The rock is rigor, and the *soft* place
relevance. The emphasis on rigor has led to experiments that are elegantly
designed but often limited in scope" (p. 18). Sternberg and Grigorenko
(2001) emphasized that no single methodology is likely to be a panacea for
any problem that science addresses: "At one time, exploratory factor analysis
was seen in this way by some psychometric investigators, until its limitations
became increasingly apparent (e.g., the existence of an infinite number of
rotations of axes, all representing equally legitimate solutions statistically)"
(p. 1072). They encouraged the use of multiple methodologies in the development of a unified psychology and favored "multiple converging operations," which they described thus:

Ultimately, the converging operations and perspectives that are brought
to bear on a problem can and generally should go even beyond those

of psychology. Investigations of many psychological phenomenon can be enriched by the ideas of other disciplines, such as biology, anthropology, neuroscience and so forth (Woodward & Devonis, 1993). For example, psychologists can enrich their perspectives of child rearing by understanding how people in other cultures rear children, or they can broaden their perspectives on aggressive behavior by taking into account what is considered to be aggressive in the first place in one culture versus another. (p. 1073)

In my own work in the area of personality theory, elaborated in *Theories of Personality: Contemporary Approaches to the Science of Personality* (2002a), I have arrived at the same conclusion as Sternberg and Grigorenko (2001), although I suggest the somewhat less ambitious project of unifying clinical science. We clinical theorists are now prepared to begin to put the building blocks together to create a flexible system that allows for evolution as new ideas and paradigms are developed.

THE INTERDISCIPLINARY SCIENCE OF A UNIFIED MODEL— THE COMPONENT SYSTEMS

Contemporary models of psychotherapy have been strengthened by an interdisciplinary collaboration and synthesis among a number of related disciplines and the domains they represent (Magnavita, 2002d). These are interrelated domains that happen to be the favored focus of a particular discipline. Important new scientific disciplines that have emerged in the last half of the 20th century are offering exciting points of convergence and multiple methodologies. Some of the more prominent developments include the following.

- *Cognitive science.* According to Mahoney (1991), "The cognitive sciences represent one of the most powerful developments of the twentieth century" (p. 67). A scientific revolution was created when cognitive science emerged from behaviorism, using computer models to understand cognitive processes (Gardner, 1985). Wilson and Keil (1999) underscored that the foundation of cognitive science spans multiple domains, including (a) philosophy, (b) psychology, (c) neurosciences, (d) computational intelligence, (e) linguistics and language, and (f) culture, cognition, and evolution.

    What the cognitive sciences have taught us, and what cognitive psychotherapies are attempting to practice, are lessons in understanding and influencing the fundamental processes by which individual humans attend to, learn, forget, transfer, adapt, relearn, and otherwise engage with the challenges of life in development. (Mahoney, 1991, p. 67)

- *Neuroscience*. One of the most exciting new disciplines emerging from a combination of related disciplines such as physiological psychology, genetics, cognitive science, and medicine, neuroscience is primarily concerned with understanding consciousness (Dennett, 1991). Neuroscience has been influenced by connectionism, which disputes the computer modeling of how the mind works in a linear fashion. Mahoney (1991) summarized the basic features as follows:

  1. A reliance on models and theories in neuroscience (rather than computer science) in model building
  2. A rejection of traditional (serial linear) models of information processing in preference to multiplex "massively distributed parallel processing" models
  3. In some versions, the acknowledgment of "subsymbolic" processes that cannot be expressed in explicit symbolic form. (p. 82)

These three features underscore the connectionism inherent in a systemic model.

- *Affective science*. The findings from affective science are promising in understanding the personality system and dysfunctional processes (Rottenberg & Gross, 2003). Emerging from Darwin's (1872/1982) seminal work (the first scientific examination of emotion) and furthered in the 1960s by Silvan Tomkins (1962), the topic of emotion was downplayed by academic psychology and was later rediscovered and energized by the work of Plutchik (1980, 2000) and Ekman and Davidson (1994), pioneers of the field of affective science. It should be underscored that separating affect from cognition is artificial. Mahoney (1991) wrote: "The impossibility of segregating emotional process from those in thinking and action as been recently highlighted by attempts to do just that—for example, in debates about the relative primacy of cognition versus affect in human experience" (p. 188). The affect system represents a portion of the cognitive–affective matrix.
- *Developmental science*. Hetherington (1998) defined the term *developmental science,* which is the study of development over the life span. Mahoney (1991) described the roots: "Concepts of development, growth, and education were significantly influenced both by their heritage in evolutionary studies and by the pressing need for practical information about the care and

teaching of infants and children" (p. 145). Mahoney wrote that one of the major changes in the field "has been the conceptual shift from stages and structures to systems and process" (p. 147).

- *Relational science.* Berscheid (1999) wrote of the birth of relational science: "Today, if you squint your eyes and cock your head just so, you can see the greening of a new science of interpersonal relations" (p. 79). Relational scientists emphasize the study of what transpires between and among individuals, in dyadic and triadic configurations. As with the study of affect, theory and research about interpersonal relationships has a rich history that has produced an extensive array of relational dimensions, variables, and processes.

- *Sociobiological and evolutionary science.* Evolution has been a powerful model that has been applied to various disciplines. Evolutionary psychology and sociobiology have applied the principles of natural selection and survival of the fittest to understand behavioral patterns and social structures (Buss, 1984; Wilson, 1975). Darwin's (1859) evolutionary theory changed the structure of science and our understanding of how complex systems change, adapt, and struggle for survival (Gould, 2002).

- *Clinical science.* Efforts to classify, understand, and treat psychological disturbance bring together a number of related disciplines, the focus of which are primarily clinical rather than academic. Contemporary clinical sciences have offered remarkable advances in knowledge of psychopathology, epidemiology, psychopharmacology, and statistical methods and research design, as well as a rich heritage of clinical observation for over 100 years (Magnavita, 2002d, p. 598).

These related domains and their relationship to personality theory, psychopathology, and psychotherapy are depicted in Figure 2.1. There are also a number of highly influential and related disciplines from which the unified model also draws evidence and theoretical constructs, including biological anthropology, sociology, ethnology, biological science, and philosophy.

BRONFENBRENNER'S ECOLOGICAL MODEL—A FORERUNNER OF THE COMPONENT SYSTEMS MODEL

Bronfenbrenner (1979) developed a "theoretical perspective for research in human development" (p. 3) that has some essential similarities with

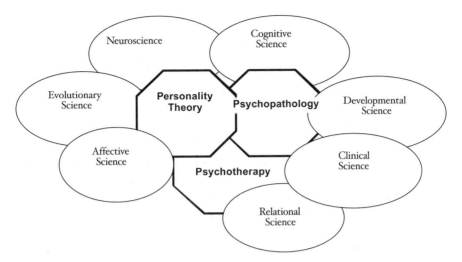

Figure 2.1. The relationship among new scientific disciplines, personality theory, psychopathology, and psychotherapy.

the component system model. His stated goal was to "attempt theoretical integration" (p. 11). Another prominent theorist, Kurt Lewin (1935, p. 73), was a great influence on Bronfenbrenner, offering what the latter described as the "classic equation: $B = f(PE)$" (p. 16), which refers to behavior (B) being the function of the interplay between the person and the environment (PE). It represents the functional relationship between nature and nurture. A metaphor for his model is a set of nested Russian dolls, each representing an aspect of the structure of the ecological environment.

Bronfenbrenner's model seems advanced for the time, with its emphasis on interrelationships between the individual and his or her total ecological system. He (1979) described "The ecology of human development involves the scientific study of the progressive, mutual accommodation between an active, growing human being and the changing properties of the immediate settings in which the developing person lives, as this process is affected by relations between these settings, and by the larger contexts in which the settings are embedded" (p. 21). Although he alluded to the importance of systems, his work does not seem to draw directly from general system theory, nor did he cite von Bertalanffy's influential work. He described the basis for his model and emphasized the centrality of both dyadic and triadic relational fields as follows:

> Different kinds of settings are also analyzed in terms of their structure. Here the approach departs in yet another respect from that of conventional research models' environments are not distinguished by reference to linear variables but are analyzed in systems terms. Beginning at the innermost level of the ecological schema, one of the basic units of

analysis is the *dyad,* or two-person system. . . . For instance, from dyadic data it appears that if one member of the pair undergoes a process of development, the other does also. Recognition of this relationship provides a key to understanding developmental changes not only in children but also in adults who serve as primary caregivers—mothers, fathers, grandparents, teachers, and so on. The same consideration applies to dyads involving husband and wife, brother and sister, boss and employee, friends, or fellow workers. (p. 5)

For Bronfenbrenner, unlike most developmentalists of his era, the triadic relationship is essential. The triad has been underused in academic psychology until relatively recently with the emergence of relational science (Berscheid, 1999), although it has been incorporated by clinicians and clinical theorists in the family therapy movement. Brofenbrenner underscored the importance in his model of extending beyond the dyad as follows:

> In addition, a systems model of the immediate situation extends beyond the dyad and accords equal developmental importance to what are called *N + 2 systems*—triads, tetrads, and larger interpersonal structures. Several findings indicate that the capacity of a dyad to serve as an effective context for human development is crucially dependent on the presence and participation of third parties, such as spouses, relatives, friends, and neighbors. If such third parties are absent, or if they play a disruptive rather than a supportive role, the developmental process, considered as a system, breaks down; like a three-legged stool, it is more easily upset if one leg is broken, or shorter than the others. (p. 5)

Bronfenbrenner described the various component systems in his theoretical model. He used the term *microsystem* to refer to the interrelationships within the immediate setting (p. 7), the term *mesosystem* to incorporate linkages among settings "in which the developing person actually participates," and *exosystem* for "those that he may never enter but in which events occur that affect what happens in the person's immediate environment" (pp. 7–8). Finally, he used the term *macrosystem* to describe "the complex of nested interconnected systems" that are "a manifestation of overarching patterns of ideology and organization of the social institutions common to a particular culture or subculture" (p. 8). He stated further that "within a given society or social group, the structure and substance of micro-, meso-, and exosystems tend to be similar, as if they were constructed from the same master model, and the systems function in similar ways" (p. 8).

According to Brofenbrenner, "Most of the building blocks in the environmental aspect of the theory are familiar concepts in the behavioral and social sciences: molar activity, dyad, role, setting, social network, institution, subculture, culture" (p. 8). He defined "development" as "the person's evolving conception of the ecological environment, and his relation to it, as well as the person's growing capacity to discover, sustain, or alter its properties" (p. 9).

Bronfenbrenner's terminology is apt for our subject, although it seems more useful when combined with the biopsychosocial model. Its explanatory power can be multiplied and a conceptual system expanded. Here I redefine the terms to make them applicable to a contemporary model. One of the limitations of his model is the lack of inclusion of the role that is ascribed to the intrapsychic system, which needs to be positioned in the microsystem.

COMPONENT DOMAIN SYSTEMS

Various unified models have been presented in the literature, the most notable of which are Lazarus's (1973, 1981) multimodal model, which endorses systematic eclecticism offering a type of component systems approach to psychotherapy that is atheoretical (Millon et al., 1999). The component systems model attempts to use theories, research, and clinical findings of the last century and organize them into various subsystems that place them within a coherent overall model. These component systems are not static but are part of holonic relationships organized by simple and complex systemic regulatory processes. These include but are not limited to the following domains.

- *Neurobiological domain.* The neurobiological system includes an individual's genetic endowment, neurobiological function, and temperamental variation. We are beginning to understand the neurobiology of many of the domains of human functioning and have a deeper appreciation for the complexity of consciousness (Rennie, 2004). The developments of positron emission tomography and magnetic resonance imaging have added to our quest to determine the seat of consciousness (Metzinger, 2000; Roth & Wullimann, 2000), as well to determine the structural and functional impact of psychotherapeutic intervention (Kandel, 1998). Nobel Prize-winning psychiatric researcher Eric Kandel (1998) noted that "as a result of advances in neural science in the last several years, both psychiatry and neural science are in a new and better position for a rapprochement, a rapprochement that would allow the insights of the psychoanalytic perspective to inform the search for a deeper understanding of the biological basis of behavior" (pp. 459–460). He further described the importance of this line of research and understanding: "when a therapist speaks to a patient and the patient listens, the therapist is not only making eye contact and voice contact, but the action of neuronal machinery in the therapist's brain is having an indirect and, one hopes, long-lasting effect on the neuronal machinery in the patient's brain; and quite likely, vice versa" (p. 465).

- *Attachment domain.* The attachment system emerges from the neurobiological and interpersonal domains and is crucial to shaping the personality system (Bowlby, 1973, 1977, 1980). The attachment system sets the parameters for many important functions and processes such as self–other differentiation, interpersonal patterns, and styles of parenting, all of which can be transmitted by the multigenerational transmission process (Cassidy & Shaver, 1999). Thus attachment may be conceived of as the first stage in the epigenesis of family mutuality (Wynne, 1984).

- *Affective domain.* The affective system includes the emotional, affective, experience, and activation-deactivation patterns. *Activation* refers to the attenuation and intensification of emotions and deactivation of the processes by which emotion is contained or reduced in intensity. Key terms include, *emotional regulation-dysregulation* (Linehan, 1993), *core affective experience* (Fosha, 2002), and *affective processing* or *metabolization* of emotions (Magnavita, 1997a).

- *Cognitive domain.* The cognitive system includes schema, thoughts, and beliefs and includes the internalized voices that influence an individual's emotional, behavioral, and interpersonal response pattern (Firestone, 1997).

- *Defensive domain.* The defensive system includes both intrapsychic and interpersonal operations and mechanisms that function as part of the regulatory system vis-à-vis painful or unacceptable feelings and impulses, self-esteem, and ego adaptation.

- *Behavioral domain.* The behavioral system encompasses the complex sequences of overt behavior that operate by well-established rules of learning such as operant and classical conditioning paradigms, as well as those operating in observational learning. On a microanalytic level, the overt behavioral system is composed of multiple nonverbal components (e.g., body movements, facial expressions, posture, gestures, etc.) that form an interpersonal perspective. These nonverbal behaviors are also viewed as channels of communication that convey expressive meanings and messages.

- *Interpersonal domain.* The interpersonal domain is the dyad or two-person attachment systems that are the foundation of developmental processes. These include primary attachment systems such as the maternal–infant system. This domain is concerned with the centrality of communication processes, which are a crucial component of the interpersonal domain and an integral determinant of the relative level of closeness within a given relational system, be it a dyad, a triad, or a larger family system. It is the very nature of the content and processes that characterize reciprocal communication.

- *Relational domain*. The relational system is defined as the triadic relationship configurations whereby three individuals are in an interrelated process. The triangle is an essential construct used in this domain. L'Abate (1986) wrote, "No single dimension (i.e., a dyad) is sufficiently strong to survive by itself. Furthermore, it could be maintained that, in nature, dyads per se do not exist and that even dyads (such as marriage) have a relationship that furnishes the third element" (p. 90). Relational triangles are ubiquitous and can be observed multigenerationally (Guerin, Fogarty, Fay, & Kautto, 1996; Magnavita, 2000a).

- *Sociocultural domain*. This system encompasses the social, economic, and cultural factors that organize and shape groups, institutions, society, and cultural expression. "It is . . . clear that the active human psyche cannot be reduced to its common biological substrate, abstracted from the conditions of its development and the particular environment within which it is functioning at any given time" (Shore, 1996).

The interrelationships of these domain subsystems comprise the relational system. The processes, structures, and mechanisms of interaction are the realm of unified clinical science.

PROCESSES AND STRUCTURE OF A UNIFIED MODEL

In the following section, the processes and structure of a unified model are presented. The four embedded subsystems are further elaborated.

von Bertalanffy's General System Model

Before we embark on a discussion of the principles and methods of psychotherapy using a component systems model, it is imperative to present one of the major developments of 20th-century scientific thinking, one that represents a major paradigmatic shift. A number of disciplines were advanced when von Bertalanffy (1968) developed his *general system theory* (often referred to as general systems theory). Systems theory was an attempt to understand the universal rules and principles by which systems in general operate. "This perspective emphasized the need to look at the world as a complex mixture of interrelated variables affecting one another in a way that made the system greater than the sum of its parts" (Magnavita, 2002a, p. 334). von Bertalanffy (1968) described all living systems as "open systems," which he defines "as a system in exchange of matter with its environment, presenting import and export, building-up and breaking-down of its material components" (p. 141). This process of assimilation and accommodation is termed *metabolization* (Magnavita, 1997a). von Bertalanffy contrasts this to a machine model, which he described as the basic model for psychoanalysis and behaviorism. As I discuss in the final chapter, using current metaphors from other scientific disciplines advances science. A basic assumption of the system model is that it is essential to understand how the interplay of factors adds much more to our understanding than an overly reductionistic perspective that artificially isolates factors without understanding the holonic–part–whole interrelationships. Any static perspective necessarily misses the drama of the movement or synergy of the system. This is not to suggest that static information is not useful but rather that it is insufficient. For example, the results of a neuropsychological evaluation of a patient who experienced a massive cerebral stroke that left him unable to talk and read could not predict the courage and stamina of this man in mastering the most rudimentary tasks and finally returning to his position as CEO of his company. The support of his family system, the adaptability of his organization, and the acceptance of his limitations only partially explain his remarkable adaptation. Although still experiencing major neuropsychological deficits, his ability to guide his organization remains intact and, as he has noticed, even improved.

According to Mahoney (1991),

> evolutionary studies have challenged some cherished beliefs about our unique and changeless character. . . . These studies have also revealed that, beneath the surface order of our lives, there teems ceaseless and complex activity. Variation is pervasive, and yet order emerges. (p. 140)

He summarized and paraphrased the characteristics and complexity of personality system, citing the work of Janstch and Waddington (1976):

1. A state of dynamic nonequilibrium (both within the system and between it and its environment).
2. The complementarity (mutual determination) of the system's structures and functions.
3. The complementarity operation of deterministic and indeterminate (random or chance) processes.

4. The capacity to undergo qualitative changes between dynamic and stable states or "regions."
5. Autocatalysis (self-precipitation) "drives" the system through an ordered succession of such changes.
6. The system's resilience is inversely related to its stability.
7. In the long run, flexibility is favored over (is more viable than) rigidity.
8. Exploratory, experimental, and variational processes are apparent at many levels.
9. Adaptations between the system and its environment are reciprocal; in humans, social and symbolic influences outweigh genetic ones.
10. Heterogeneity (variation) becomes symbiotic (mutually advantageous) to coordinating systems.
11. A "healthy" (viable) system both seeks and resists qualitative change; resilience implies the capacity for flexible transformation.
12. The openness inherent in evolving systems requires their imperfection, perennial uncertainty, and a strength of "courage" that helps them transcend these existential contingencies. (Mahoney, 1991, pp. 140–141)

THE MICROSYSTEM, MACROSYSTEM, MESOSYSTEM, AND TOTAL ECOLOGICAL SYSTEM OF THE BIOPSYCHOSOCIAL MODEL

A holonic system must take into account the part–whole relationships that exist among the various component systems and subcomponents. The best way to do so is by expanding the biopsychosocial model (Engle, 1980) to include the relational systems (Magnavita, 2000a). The biopsychosocial model is equivalent in scope to the total ecological system, with the added benefit of viewing the systems as they cohere and interact.[1]

Part–whole relationships exist at literally every level of analysis and among every level of the biopsychosocial matrix. For example, the attachment system emerges from the neurobiological system and the influence of

---

[1] Although many endorse a biopsychosocial model, Gabbard and Kay, psychiatric leaders, suggested that this model for psychiatry "has been relegated to political lip service in our managed care environment" (2001, p. 1956). Their article focuses mostly, however, on the separation of the biological and psychological aspects of treatment narrowly defined by the often separation of medication and psychotherapy.

early dyadic relationships, leading to the structuralization of the intrapsychic system in complex circular feedback systems. In an effort to simplify the terminology, the levels of the system can be arranged according to Bronfenbrenner's concepts of microsystem, macrosystem, and mesosystem as they exist in and comprise elements of the total ecological system.

Systems of Analysis

Any level of analysis or attempt to carve nature at its joints artificially maps the terrain we are exploring. We nonetheless must attempt to define the system and subsystems. In so doing, I rearrange Bronfenbrenner's terms to make them more consistent with a unified model.

Microsystem

The microsystem is the individual system, which entails the phenomenon in the intrapsychic–biological triangle. At the level of the microsystem, we may examine neurotransmitter interaction, or *nanosystems,* or how anxiety and defenses are used. We may elaborate the cognitive schema and affective system within the individual. The microsystem is formulated and shaped by genetics, attachment, bonding, interpersonal experience, and socioeconomic factors but is viewed at the intrapsychic–biological level.

For example, at the microscopic level of analysis, we can hypothesize that deficiencies of certain neurotransmitters such as serotonin may be related to depression. We may concern ourselves with the neurotransmitter action and what is needed to resolve the deficiency. The lack of this vital neurotransmitter may leave an individual unmotivated and, over the course of a lifetime, might result in limited attainment and further depression in a chronic downward spiral. We might enhance the neurotransmitter system with an antidepressant medication that may enhance mood, but the individual will then be faced with enhanced mood but the lack of attainment from a lifetime of low energy and impaired motivational system remains. Enhancing neurobiological function alone will affect the total system to a degree. This may not necessarily lead to greatly enhanced functioning because the individual may not know how to focus this new energy, and this could potentially result in anxiety. Further intervention may be required—specifically, understanding the relationship between the biological system and the personality system.

Macrosystem

Here I redefine the macrosystem as the complex interpersonal or relational fields that occur in dyadic and triadic relationships. The macrosystem entails the interpersonal matrices of an individual, whether dyadic or triadic—*N* + 2, as Brofenbrenner (1979) defined them. Brofenbrenner described the importance of these constructs as follows:

> The dyad is important for development in two respects. First, it constitutes a critical context for development in its own right. Second, it serves as the basic building block of the microsystem, making possible the formation of larger interpersonal structures—triads, tetrads, and so on. (p. 56)

Although Brofenbrenner made a distinction among three functional forms of dyads, current theory (Muran & Safran, 2002) and research (Schuldberg & Gottlieb, 2002; Stern, 1985) suggests that all dyads are intersubjective and reciprocal.

Mesosystem

"A mesosystem is thus a system of microsystems" (Bronfenbrenner, 1979, p. 25). The mesosystem entails the elements of culture and society. The macrosystems include the social and cultural institutions, both formal and informal, of which we are all members. These can include school, church, and other organizations that are essentially extrafamilial. They also include systems such as subcultures (e.g., followers of a rock group, such as The Grateful Dead).

Ecosystem

The ecosystem entails the entire system and would then necessarily entail cosmos and spiritual dimensions of which we may not be aware. Personality can only be fully understood when the entire ecology of the individual is considered. One cannot characterize personality in absence of the socioeconomic and political systems to which we are directly or indirectly related.

A GUIDEBOOK FOR USING THE UNIFIED COMPONENT SYSTEM MODEL

Although no one would discount the importance of the biopsychosocial model in the understanding and treatment of mental disorders, few systematically use the model for maximum benefit. There are some rules to follow that to many may seem intuitive but are worth underscoring before we proceed.

1. Do not remain fixated on any one level of abstraction. Multiple perspectives are required to understand complex phenomena.
2. Strive to account for as many aspects of the biopsychosocial matrix (e.g., biological vulnerability to major psychiatric

disorder, quality of early relationships, family function, cultural forces) as possible when formulating plans and making interventions.

3. Maintain flexibility to understand and use metaphoric language at various levels of abstraction, from the biological to the sociocultural.

4. Begin treatment at the level where the most obvious need exists. For example, a homeless depressed person needs a place to sleep and eat, and thus the sociocultural system must be addressed and mobilized before attending to other levels.

5. Be aware of and incorporate metaphors based on the lexicon of abstraction of a particular domain. For example, some patients may initially be relieved to know that they have a "chemical imbalance" and that medication is needed to shock and recalibrate their neuronal system. Others may recoil from this metaphor, preferring to hear that they are emotionally blocked and need to metabolize their affect.

Triangular Configurations

Triangular configurations are ubiquitous in the psychological literature and may represent a foundational structuring of human nature. Social psychologists and clinical theorists often depict various aspects of psychological dynamics, including intrapsychic, interpersonal, relational, and sociocultural configurations, using the triangular construct. Psychological growth and development may, in fact, involve a dialectic process in which two ends of a continuum oscillate until a new state of equilibrium is attained. Developmentally, for example, adolescence is a struggle between dependency strivings and independence, and, if navigated well, results in a new autonomous position capable of "healthy" dependency. L'Abate (1986) conceptualized life roles visually with triangular configurations. He described six roles that can be depicted by triangles: "(1) Family formation: father–mother–child, (2) Ego states: parent–adult–child, (3) Language: I–we–you, (4) Drama triangle: victim–persecutor–rescuer, (5) Family development: self–mate–parent, and (6) Societal structures: home–work–leisure" (pp. 88–89). Heider (1958), a social psychologist, described human relationships as triangular. Bowen (1976, p. 76) may have identified a universal phenomenon of the social sciences when he called the triangle "the molecule or basic building block of any emotional system." Triangles may in fact be more broadly applied to the human personality system. A triangular lens provides a perspective with which to observe processes. "Triangles, of course, are basic in navigation and in any process involving localization in space" (L'Abate, 1986, p. 91). They have been used in the psychological literature to depict the synergistic movement among three interrelated sets of variables and thus are ideal constructs for a component systems model. According to L'Abate (1986), "All dyads are triangles to the extent that the relationship of the two members of the dyad is the third element of a triad" (p. 90).

Freud developed one of the most notable triangular relationships, which he termed the "oedipal complex." This triangle depicts the tension and dynamic processes that occur in development when there are two parents and a child who is attempting to navigate the dual attachments and competitive strivings and emotional sexual longings that emerge in development. Freud believed that successful navigation of this period would allow for healthy adult relationships. Others have also used the triangle to depict psychological processes and dynamics. Ezriel (1952) coined the term *triangle of conflict* to depict the intrapsychic interplay among underlying emotions, anxiety, and the defensive processes developed to contain and regulate these. Yet another triangle proposed by Menninger (1958) was termed the *triangle of insight*, essentially an interpersonal construct that depicts the schematic re-creations that occur in all relational patterns and thus captures the goal of many forms of therapy. The triangle of insight enables the therapist to sample and observe the repetition of the early relationships with primary attachment figures and intervene therapeutically.

Cognitive therapy has been depicted in a triangular matrix with the following three corners: (a) affect and feeling, (b) conscious cognition, and (c) behavior, "which also shows the interrelationship among limbic system, neocortex, and motor strip" (Groves, 1992, p. 44). Bowen (1976) believed that the triangle was the basic building block of any emotional system, terming it the *molecule* (p. 76). This was a remarkable new paradigm, offered when two-person psychology was also in vogue. When tension in a dyad is too great, a relational triangle is formed, involving a third often-vulnerable party. L'Abate (1986) described this process as follows: "The less the self is present in any member of a dyad, the more likely that an issue (i.e., a symptom) will be substituted for a third member of the triangle" (p. 90). Destabilizing a triangular configuration can release a great deal of force (e.g., anxiety, emotion, will, hope, despair, transformation). The model is not dissimilar to atomic physics, in which some elements are more stable than others and certain ones, such as uranium, can express enormous force when destabilized.

Hoffman (1981) describes the cybernetics of this type of change:

> The natural history of a leap or transformation is usually this: First, the patterns that have kept the system in a steady state relative to its environment begin to work badly. New conditions arise for which these patterns were not designated. Ad hoc solutions are tried and sometimes work, but usually are abandoned. Irritation grows over small but persisting difficulties. The accumulation of dissonance eventually forces the

entire system over an edge, into a state of crisis, as the stabilizing tendency brings on ever-intensifying corrective sweeps that get out of control. The end point of what cybernetic engineers call a runaway is that the system breaks down, or creates a new way to monitor the same homeostasis, or spontaneously leap to an integration that will deal better with the changed field. (pp. 159–160)

The Model in Motion—The Four Primary Triangles of the Unified Model

In the previous chapter, the reader was introduced to four triangles that depict the processes of the personality system at the intrapsychic, dyadic, triadic, and sociocultural–familial levels of organization. The following sections take a more in-depth look at these components.

Intrapsychic–Biological Triangle (The Person)

The intrapsychic–biological triangle is what is traditionally viewed as the personality system and encompasses what occurs at the biological and psychological level of organization. This type of separation is only for heuristic purposes because the intrapsychic system is organized and develops "structure" on the basis of the developmental processes that shape this matrix through relational experiences and attachments. The neurobiological and intrapsychic structure emerges and has a degree of plasticity. Trauma can alter the neurobiology as well as the structure of the intrapsychic system, although the capacity to change neurocircuitry in adulthood has been suggested (Davidson, 2000).

Interpersonal–Dyadic Triangle (Two People)

The dyad is the basic unit of an interpersonal system (Sluzki & Beavin, 1977). In many theories of psychotherapy and psychopathology, the dyad may be internalized so that the original dyadic configuration is addressed by examining beliefs, cognitive and relational schema, object relations, attachment systems, and so forth, depending on the predilection of the orientation. The dyad then is really the original unit in the formation of the self. Long-lasting dyadic configurations seek to maintain equilibrium. This equilibrium is maintained by homeostatic regulation. The equilibrium of a dyad can be regulated by two processes: symmetry and complementarity (Bateson, 1958). Bateson provided an example from his anthropological studies. If an individual is assertive and another responds submissively, a complementary pattern can gradually increase the assertiveness of one and the submissiveness of the other in a *complementary* feedback loop. Haley (1963) called this the *one up, one down* relationship. Bateston (1958) offered another example in which one individual enjoys boasting and another responds by boasting so that there is a competitive escalation of boasting in a *symmetrical* fashion. Hoffman (1981) wrote, "One could, and probably should, make an argument for not treating couples as a separate universe. It is entirely possible that no purely dyadic cycle exists independent of third parties" (p. 184).

Relational–Triadic Triangle (Two + N People)

Sluzki and Beavin (1977) noted that "triads, tetrads, and so forth, are far more complicated systems which we would attempt to deal with only after thorough analysis of dyadic interaction" (p. 74). Byng-Hall (1999) summarized the work of Emde (1991) regarding the complexity resulting from the permutations possible in dyadic and triadic configurations as follows:

> For instance, a triad has only three dyadic relationships influencing one another, whereas in a family of four there are 15, and in a family of eight are 378. This suggests that studying the triad is a good way to build on dyadic research. Emde (1991) discussed why triads are considered particularly meaningful in therapy, and suggests that this may be because so many feelings are evoked by a person's being either left out of or included in dyads. For example, children have fears and wishes about exclusion from or inclusion in the parents' relationship, as well as parent–sibling relationships. (p. 626)

Haley (1977) discussed what he terms *the perverse triangle*, or ones that generate pathological systems, ones in which there is continual conflict, or ones that create "symptomatic distress in one or more family members" (p. 37). He described some of the characteristics of these triadic relationships that are worth remembering as follows:

1. The people responding to each other in the triangle are not peers, but one of them is of a different generation from the other two. *Generation* is used to mean a different order in the power hierarchy, as in a human generation of parent and child or in an administrative hierarchy such as manager or employee.
2. In the process of their interaction together, the person of one generation forms a coalition with the person of the other generation against his peer. *Coalition* means a process of joint action taken *against* the third person (in contrast to an alliance in which two people might get together as the result of a common interest independent of the third).
3. The coalition between the two persons is denied. That is, certain behavior indicates a coalition exists but, when the two persons are confronted, they will deny the existence of a coalition. More formally, behavior at one level indicating a

coalition exists is qualified by meta-communicative behavior indicating there is not a coalition.

Haley (1977) reminded his reader that the oedipal triangle in psychoanalysis is an example of a perverse triangle, which is a central tenant:

> Sigmund Freud at one time proposed that hysteria was the result of a sexual assault on the patient by an older relative. In this sense he proposed that here was a breaching of generations which should not have occurred and, insofar as it was a secret act, could be considered a covert coalition across generations. However, he then discovered that in certain cases the sexual indecent could not actually have happened, and shifted from the idea of a familial cause of this malady to an intrapsychic cause—a fantasied wish for the sexual act. This was the birth of the Oedipal conflict, the wish of the boy to have sexual relations with his mother and the consequent fear that his father would not take this coalition kindly and would castrate him. The Oedipal conflict became a universal explanation for neurosis. (pp. 38–39)

Freud has been severely criticized by disciples (Ferenczi & Rank, 1925) and by contemporary workers for his abandonment of his discovery of the trauma theory. The importance and ubiquity of less "perverse" triangles besides those that occur in incestuous relationships was not developed until later in the 20th century with the work of system theorists.

These relational triangles (Guerin et al., 1996) have enormous clinical and theoretical utility. Triangles are in some way an attempt to change (Haley, 1977). Haley described the potential for triangular relations in a marital dyad as follows:

> For example, it is possible that the wife joins child against husband not merely because of internal dissatisfaction but as an adaptive response to her relationship with her parents. To maintain stability in relation to her parents, she may find it necessary to join child against husband because an amiable relationship with her husband would have repercussions in the way she is dealing with her parents and the way they are dealing with each other. In this sense, "cause" is a statement about regularities in larger networks. (pp. 44–45)

L'Abate (1986, p. 90) viewed triangles as "solutions to polarities," by which he means, "no single dimension (i.e., a dyad) is sufficiently strong to survive by itself."

Sociocultural–Family Triangle (Mesosystems)

The field of sociogenesis reminds us that we are embedded in and co-construct our social system (De Graaf & Maier, 1994). Firestone (2002) wrote of one aspect of this bi-directionality between the individual and social system: "Society represents a pooling of the individual psychological defenses that later reflect back on individual personality development" (p. 225). "It is a fundamental fact of human life that [wo]man is a social animal" (Bradburn, 1963). The sociocultural influences on personality, both normal and dysfunctional, cannot be overemphasized. Bradburn wrote of the importance of this system as follows:

> For most people the greater part of their adult life is spent with other people who have grown up under basically similar socialization pressures, who share the same language, who have many of the same basic ideas about the ways in which the world should be organized and who desire the same goals in life. Although each individual is unique, he also shares many attributes with others who live in his culture. It is important for the student of personality to consider the cultural context within which human personality develops and functions, lest he confuse factors specific to a particular culture with those that are more general in their influence on personality development and functioning. (p. 333)

von Bertalanffy (1968) emphasized the value of a system model for the social sciences because "the difficulties are not only in the complexity of phenomena but in the definition of entities under consideration" (p. 197). He described this challenge as follows:

> At least part of the difficulty is expressed by the fact that the social sciences are concerned with "socio-cultural" systems. Human groups, from the smallest of personal friendships and family to the largest of nations and civilizations, are not only an outcome of social "forces" found, at least in primitive form, in subhuman organisms; they are part of a man-created universe called culture.
>
> Natural science has to do with physical entities in time and space, particles, atoms and molecules, living systems at various levels, as the case might be. Social science has to do with human beings in their self-created universe of culture. The cultural universe is essentially a symbolic universe. Animals are surrounded by a *physical* universe with which they have to cope: physical environment, prey to catch, predators to avoid, and so forth. Man, in contrast, is surrounded by a universe of *symbols*. Starting from language which is the prerequisite of culture, to symbolic relationships with his fellows, social status, laws, science, art, morals, religion and innumerable other things, human behavior, except for the basic aspects of the biological needs of hunger and sex, is governed by symbolic entities. (p. 197)

The sociocultural–family triangle represents the interrelationship among the individual at the lower corner, the family at the right, and social and cultural influences and structures at the left.

Basic Systemic Principles and Processes

In the next section we will review some of the critical principles and processes necessary for a unified model. The complexity of human functioning requires that bidirectionality among component subsystems and structures be depicted. "Thus, in relational terms, what we have here is a unity in which its phases and aspects are not related to each other as separable, existentially identifiable component parts, but related only as sensibly distinct and distinguishable" (Shotter, 1994, p. 87).

Systemic–Cybernetic Theory

One of the most important insights of system theory is the process by which component domains of nonlinear systems interrelate and alter each other by a process of continual feedback and correction or circular causality. The term *cybernetics*, coined by Wiener (1961), refers to the flow of information between components of the total ecological system and the control or feedback mechanisms that shape them (Ashby, 1964). It is the study or mapping of networks or pathways of information. Anchin (2003) described the difference between system theory (von Bertalanffy, 1968) and cybernetics thus: "System theory focuses primarily on the structure of systems, whereas cybernetics focuses more on how this structure functions—that is, characteristic processes that govern how systems operate" (p. 336). One component affects and alters the other, which feedbacks in a circular loop corrections for maintaining the system. The infant–mother dyad is an example of a circular feedback loop in which deviations are corrected by subtle and overt feedback, such as crying, cooing, stroking, holding, and feeding. This system is directed toward survival of the infant. Thomas and Chess (1977) described this dyad when it is in a positive feedback loop as having "goodness of fit" referring to the mutually attuned feedback between the infant's temperament and the mother's personality.

Feedback Loops

In the personality system, there is a constant flow of information from all component domains, both internal and external. The personality system responds to positive and negative feedback loops, which effect input channels. The four triangular configurations are a way in which to organize and map these process centers.

Ajaya (1983) described this central feedback system in the personality system as follows:

> Positive or deviance-amplifying feedback increases change from the original standard or norm in a system. If there were only negative

feedback in systems, they would always remain static; there would be no change. There is a preponderance of negative feedback in systems that do not evolve, whereas in those that are modifying themselves, positive feedback plays a more significant role. If negative feedback in a system is slight, deviance-amplifying feedback may lead to a significant alteration in the system. The shift may be a "quantum jump" through which the system suddenly reorganizes itself in a new and more comprehensive way. (p. 108)

This may be a similar phenomenon reported by Gould (2002) in evolutionary theory called *punctuated equilibrium*. Evolution is not only gradual but can also reflect radical or quantum shifts.

Complex systems have multiple feedback loops and are often characterized by chaos. This allows for abrupt changes to occur with oscillating phases between order and chaos called *bifurcations* (Feigenbaum, 1980). Affective experience and responding is a major evolutionarily endowed regulatory process of the human personality system and greater sociocultural context (King, 2002). Anchin (2003) described how affective processes can cause dysfunctional perturbations in personality systems: "Processes transpiring within and among different subsystem domains are impeding the system's capacity to effectively navigate toward its goals, with feedback loops connecting the different subsystem components keeping the system locked into— and thus perpetuating—the dysfunctional systemic state" (pp. 339–340).

The Importance of Novelty and High Impact in Learning and Change

Learning and change are often fueled by novelty. Emotional experiences that have high impact seem to make for more durable learning (Omer, Winch, & Dar, 1998): "Impact refers to the characteristics of a therapeutic intervention that make it memorable for the client and easily retrievable in times of need. To be effective, even a good therapeutic message must overcome the client's many ways of disregarding, neglecting, and forgetting it" (Omer et al., p. 1313). Anchin (2003) wrote of the importance of the affective system: "In the human cybernetic system, a primary source of comparative feedback is the individual's affective state" (p. 339). In research applying this principle to therapeutic change, there is some evidence to suggest, as reported by Omer et al. (1998), that high impact either by extension of the length of the session (making it a more memorable encounter) or increased emotional arousal seems to help in smoking cessation (Dornelas & Magnavita, 2001). Mahoney (1991), in his volume *Human Change Processes*, noted:

> The essential challenge in change—the existential heart of learning, if you will—is the experience of novelty. As the pioneering educator John Dewey noted early in this century, learning requires novelty

(McDermott, 1981). Without novelty—that is, without a difference that makes a difference—the individual projects past and familiar personal life theories onto each arriving moment and, not surprisingly, life flows as usual. Novelty entails challenge, but not all novelties or challenges are necessarily good for the developing individual. Rates, ranges, and rhythms of learning are highly individualized. The facilitation and pacing of individually appropriate developmental challenges are therefore fundamental to all educational and therapeutic experiences. (p. 104)

Chaos Theory

Chaos theory offers a useful perspective consistent with general systems theory about the manner in which complex systems function. Chaos theory is being applied to clinical science and offers a new explanatory foundation (Butz, 1997; Chamberlain & Butz, 1998). According to Mahoney (1991), "The study of 'dynamic systems' became increasingly popular in the 1970's, and a veritable revolution in both method and theory resulted in more and more conferences, books, and journals devoted to the study of physical change processes and what some have termed 'the science of becoming' (as contrasted with the earlier preoccupation with fixed states of being). Some proponents of this new perspective claim that twentieth-century science will be remembered for three things; relativity, quantum mechanics, and chaos" (p. 412). Gleick (1987) described the explanatory power of this theory as follows:

> In science as in life, it is well known that a chain of events can have a point of crisis that would magnify small changes. But chaos meant that such points are everywhere. They were pervasive. In systems like the weather, sensitive dependence on initial conditions was an inescapable consequence of the way small scales intertwined with large. (p. 23)

Chaos theory seeks to understand the complexity of systems. For example, in understanding weather, "Errors and uncertainties multiply, cascading upward through a chain of turbulent features, from dust devils and squalls up to continent-size eddies that only satellites can see" (Gleick, 1987, p. 20).

> This 'sensitive dependence on initial conditions' is termed "the Butterfly Effect" in meteorology, on the basis of the half-facetious notion that the air turbulence created by a butterfly's wings somewhere over the Mediterranean today may influence the development of a hurricane off the coast of North America next month. As far-fetched as that metaphor may seem, it captures the essence of the principle. (Mahoney, 1991, p. 412)

Chaos theory attempts to explain multiplicative events that can result in major transformations. "Small perturbations in one's daily trajectory can have large consequences" (p. 67). "For example, a personality disorder is a disorder of a complex system that can be set in motion by the introduction of small events that reverberate throughout the biopsychosocial system" (Magnavita, 2002a, p. 399). One often reads, for example, about horrendous antisocial acts committed by these types of cascading events. A mere slight might reactivate a hair trigger temper of a sociopathic individual, resulting in murder or other forms of violence. Mahoney (1991) summarized: "The point is that models embracing complex nonlinear dynamics have begun to demonstrate their superiority over traditional and simplistic accounts of our experience. 'Disorder' is not an aberration but a necessary aspect of the essential tension that characterizes self-organizing systems" (p. 414).

Evolutionary Theory

It is hard to conceive of any comprehensive theory of human functioning that does not include evolutionary principles. Individuals, groups, and societies are shaped and transformed by evolutionary principles. Societies that do not adapt to the changing environmental demands do not survive. Individuals and their systems of adaptation evolve over a lifetime as well as over successive generations. Millon (1990) described these evolutionary requirements as follows:

> During its life history an organism develops an assemblage of traits that contribute to its individual survival and reproductive success, the two essential components of "fitness" formulated by Darwin. Such assemblages, termed "complex adaptations" and "strategies" in the literature of evolutionary ecology, are close biological equivalents to what psychologists have conceptualized as personality styles and structures. (p. 21)

SUMMARY AND CONCLUSIONS

This chapter presents the theoretical foundation of a unified model on which personality-guided relational psychotherapy is based. Researchers and theorists from various disciplines, including biological and social sciences, have proposed a move toward a unifying science. The fields of psychotherapy, personality theory, and psychopathology should not be deemed separate disciplines but overlapping areas with a common theme. The unification of psychotherapy draws from many of the conceptualizations that others seeking convergence have offered. The major conceptual framework for the unified theory presented in this volume encompasses the work of Bronfenbrenner, whose ecological model of the mind has strong implications for the field of psychotherapy. The ecological model attempts to encompass all the major aspects of personality systems from the individual to the sociocultural level of process and structure.

It is vital in a unified theory that we account for the total ecological system of those we treat. To best serve this purpose, we can conceptualize human functioning as a nested set of embedded subsystems and depict the processes at the micro-, macro-, and mesosystem levels. Using the four triangles, we can operationalize structure, function, and processes at these various levels from the microscopic to the macroscopic. This provides us with multiples lenses with which to understand functioning and dysfunctioning personality systems.

3

COMPONENTS OF A UNIFIED TREATMENT APPROACH: PSYCHOPATHOLOGY, PERSONALITY THEORY, AND PSYCHOTHERAPY

This chapter presents the three interrelated or "sister disciplines"—psychopathology, personality theory, and psychotherapy—that are necessary for a unified model of personality-guided relational therapy. Personality-guided therapy (Millon et al., 1999) is based on the premise that understanding and navigating the personality system is essential to effective treatment, especially with more complex clinical syndromes and treatment refractory cases. Psychopathology or dysfunctional adaptations emerge from poorly functioning or overly stressed personality systems. Psychotherapeutic strategies and interventions are derived from an understanding of how this system works and become more focused and potent when applied at critical subsystems, at the very nexus. It is vital that any comprehensive system of psychotherapy has a theoretical and empirical connection to personality theory and psychopathology to construct a holonic map of human functioning and dysfunction. This enables us to know how, when, and where in the personality systems to intervene and which methods of psychotherapy to select. Techniques and methods of treatment not anchored to a theoretical system are not the realm of a unified model. Unified psychotherapy requires much more. One must have a deep appreciation for the complexity of the personality system and the cybernetic mechanisms through which feedback flows. This chapter explores some of the relevant issues and related constructs among these disciplines. I begin our discussion with psychopathology.

"PSYCHOPATHOLOGY" AND DYSFUNCTIONAL PERSONALITY SYSTEMS

Many current schools of psychopathology often endorse implicitly a systemic model without naming it as such; others schools do not rely on a systemic model. Psychopathology is often not grounded in the dynamic personality system. By and large, the field of psychopathology is so highly disembodied that specialists often spend a career researching one disorder such as anxiety or depression. Thus, we have chapters in the major texts on psychopathology devoted to the various disorders that generally correspond to the *Diagnostic and Statistical Manual of Mental Disorders* (3rd ed.; *DSM–III*; American Psychiatric Association, 1980) categorical classification system (Adams & Sutker, 2001; Millon, Blaney, & Davis, 1999; Turner & Hersen, 1997). Essentially, then, the study of contemporary psychopathology is primarily disorder driven. One cannot separate the pathological expression of the complex system without losing something. In his chapter on biological variables in psychopathology, Fowles (2001) wrote as follows:

> It should be clear from these examples that dichotomies between psychological and biological influences are inappropriate. Experience and behavior affect gene expression and brain structure, and reciprocally genes and brain structure affect behavior and experience. There should be no conflict between these perspectives but rather an effort to sort out the processes involved and complex interactions. (p. 87)

The texts by and large are still organized around various pathological classifications.

A noteworthy exception is Cummings, Davies, and Campbell's (2000) volume, *Developmental Psychopathology and Family Process: Theory, Research, and Clinical Implications*, which offers a more systemically oriented model. Their work is firmly rooted in Bronfenbrenner's (1979) ecological model. In the foreword to their book, Dante Cicchetti wrote the following:

> In particular, there has been an emphasis on increasingly specific process-level models of normal and abnormal development, an acknowledgment that multiple pathways exist to the same outcome and that the effects of one component's value may vary in different systems, and an intensification of interest in biological and genetic factors related to the development of maladaptation and psychopathology. (p. ix)

Cummings et al. (2000), in their developmental psychopathology model, were "concerned with the search for the dynamic mediating processes that account for patterns of adaptation and maladaptation over time. . . . a developmental psychopathological perspective emphasizes dynamic processes on interaction between multiple intra- and extraorganismic factors" (p. 124). It is interesting that the authors do not cite von Bertalanffy's (1968) work in the reference section, but it is clear that the general system theory tenants have been assimilated and are foundational. Their model of psychopathology is consistent with the holistic view presented in this volume, and I highly recommend this volume. The authors described a central principle of holism:

> The principle of holism posits that interdependency among parts exists in systems. Thus, development cannot be understood by dissecting the system into a series of parts because each component gains critical meaning and purpose from the other parts. Synthesis is the rule in holism; that is, parts must be examined in the fabric of the whole. (p. 28)

There have been other noteworthy exceptions to such reductionism, such as the clinical theorist Angyal (1982), who endorsed a "holistic" model of personality, psychopathology, and psychotherapy. He emphasized the central position of the personality system in his model, described as follows:

> Personality may be viewed as a highly organized whole, a *hierarchy of systems*. . . . The significant positions in its overall organization are occupied by parts which themselves are systems; the constituents of these secondary systems may also be systems and so on. Since in systems the dimensional domain in which the parts are distributed participates in their patterning, the dimensions enumerated also provide the general bases for the formation of these hierarchies of systems. (p. 50)

Werner (1957) offered another important developmental principle, the *orthogenetic principle*, which states that "development proceeds from a state of relative globility and lack of differentiation to a state of increasing differentiation, articulation, and hierarchic integration" (p. 126). This phenomenon is also an important principle of the unified components system model presented. Within each of the triangular configurations, higher levels of functioning are evident when there is increasing differentiation and then reintegration of the component domains and their systems into a new organization. Thus, as an example, in the intrapsychic–biological triangle, increased differentiation and integrations of the three corners (i.e., anxiety, affect, defense) and cognitive awareness of this system results in increased emotional differentiation—a necessary aspect of intimacy and closeness in the interpersonal–dyadic configuration.

von Bertalanffy (1968) stated that "Mental disease is essentially a disturbance of system functions of the psychophysical organism. For this reason, isolated symptoms or syndromes do not define the disease entity" (p. 218). For example, anxiety is a signal of a variety of systemic operations. If anxiety is too high, the system can be flooded and become paralyzed; if too low, there is a lack of motivational signaling to survive and adapt. Where does normal behavior end and abnormal behavior begin? This question has preoccupied psychopathologists for more than a century. A systemic model gives some guidance to this conclusion and allows us not to "lose the person in psychopathology," a pitfall of the medical disease model and its assumption of biological etiology. Most clinicians intuitively conceptualize the array of symptoms and disturbances in a systemic fashion whereby they try to understand the interrelationships of domains of the total personality system. Minuchin (1974) described the complex interplay and reciprocity among various component domains of the total ecological system and their mutual influence as follows:

> The individual influences his context and is influenced by it in constantly recurring sequences of interaction. The individual who lives within a family is a member of a social system to which he must adapt. His actions are governed by the characteristics of the system, and the characteristics include the effects of his own past actions. The individual responds to stresses in other parts of the system, to which he adapts; and he may contribute significantly to stressing other members of the system. The individual can be approached as a subsystem, or part, of the system, but the whole must be taken into account. (p. 9)

Human beings are much too complex to ever be reduced to a purely biological model and this view necessarily limits our perspective of psychopathology. "Psychiatric disturbances can be neatly defined in terms of system functions" (von Bertalanffy, 1968, p. 218). von Bertalanffy foreshadowed the component system model: "our normal world is shaped also by emotional, motivational, social, cultural, linguistic, and the like factors, amalgamated with perception proper" (p. 218). Systemic models have evolved and new versions have been advanced that add to our understanding of human personality systems.

Jackson (1977) also proposed a view of psychopathology based on the systemic discoveries. This model represented a paradigmatic shift away from the linear model of cause-and-effect relationships to a cybernetic one of informational feedback systems. The feedback model takes into account how information about an event impinges on another event, and how, in a circular fashion, events influence one another. The essence of this model is on communication. Watzlawick and Beavin (1977, p. 57) described this process as "pragmatics" and emphasized the reciprocal process and avoiding reductionism. "We would not even say 'sender–receiver' relation, if this could be avoided in our language, in order to be able to focus on a reciprocal process in which both (or all) persons act and react, 'received' and 'send,' in such detail and complexity that these terms lose their meaning as verbs on individual action." He wrote:

> symptoms, character structure and personality can be seen as terms describing the individual's typical interactions which occur in response to a particular interpersonal context. Since the family is the most influential learning context, surely a more detailed study of family process would yield valuable clues to the etiology of such typical modes of interaction. (Jackson, 1977, p. 2)

One of the important features that Jackson emphasized in the interactional model was *homeostatic mechanisms*, which are the way in which a system's norms are enforced and behavior regulated. "Homeostatic mechanisms are . . . an extension, in an ongoing relationship, of the give and take of relationship definitions by which the original rules are worked out" (p. 13).

Again, another noteworthy exception to the overly reductionistic and linear perspective is seen in the prescient work of Angyal (1982), who placed dysfunction in the sphere of the personality system, which he described as a lack of system integration:

> The discussion of the disturbances of integration has led us into the field of pathological behavior. However, since we are discussing not only severe but also mild and transitory conditions, we shall substitute the term *bionegative* for the term *pathological*. Bionegativity can best be defined in terms of integration. In an ideally healthy organism the various part processes are integrated in such a way that they subserve and promote the total function of the organism—its twofold dynamic pattern. *Abnormality, or bionegativity, may be defined as a personality constellation in which one or more part processes disturb the total function of the organism.* (p. 58)

The term *bionegativity* and its opposite, *biopositivity*, appear to be useful and suggest a more solid grounding in systemic processes than the standard psychopathology designation for dysfunctional systems.

Minuchin (1974) offered the view that "When the mind is viewed as extracerebral as well as intracerebral, to locate pathology within the mind of the individual does not indicate whether it is inside or outside the person" (p. 9). Further, he wrote, "The individual influences his context and is influenced by it in constantly recurring sequences of interaction" (p. 9). To understand bionegativity, it is critical to understand the disruptive effect that trauma exerts on the personality system.

TRAUMA THEORY AND THE ROOTS OF "PSYCHOPATHOLOGY," BIONEGATIVITY, AND DYSFUNCTIONAL PERSONALITY SYSTEMS

An understanding of the nature and impact of trauma on the personality system is vital to understanding how humans develop and maintain maladaptive behavior. Trauma creates perturbations in the systems affected and can result in a cascading series of reactions and feedback loops that exacerbate symptoms and often lead to developmental psychopathology, especially if the trauma occurs early or is chronic, such as neglect and ongoing abuse. The majority of trauma occurs within the relational matrix, which is also the main source of resilience and healing. In the following section we will explore some of these issues.

Historical Background

Early in the development of modern psychotherapy, Sigmund Freud originally conceived of sexual trauma as being the causative agent of hysteria. As we know, he later renounced this theory (Magnavita, 2002a). Trauma theory did not disappear but remained a central tenant of Sandor Ferenczi, who was originally a "favorite son" of Freud but was renounced by the psychoanalytic community because of his theoretical and technical departures, which were much more relational in practice, from classical theory. Much of Ferenczi's work was suppressed until relatively recently. In one of his seminal chapters (Ferenczi, 1933), *Confusion of the Tongues Between Adults and the Child,* he discussed the impact of child sexual abuse. Although this work has been called "one of the most significant contributions in the history of psychoanalysis" (Rachman, 1997, p. 414, citing Fromm, 1959), Ferenczi was severely criticized for his "wild analysis" and failure to follow "psychoanalytic technique" with more relationally oriented therapy.[1]

The Roots of Bionegativity and Dysfunction

There is clear evidence from over a century of both clinical work and research that the roots of most bionegativity and dysfunction are traumatic experience (Magnavita, 2004a). Trauma creates systemic disruption that can be amplified in negative feedback loops until it becomes an attractor state. Angyal (1982) wrote the following:

---

[1] It is interesting to note that psychoanalysis as actually practiced by Freud was much different from the form he espoused in his technical papers. In a review of 43 of Freud's cases from 1907 to 1939, Lynn and Vaillant (1998) discovered that Freud had deviated from his own recommendations: "Indeed, his actual method could be seen as a quite different process, characterized by expressiveness and a tendency to be forcefully directive" (p. 169).

Trauma is a biospheric event, an instance of interaction between the world and the organism, and it can be defined only in terms of its outcome; important is not what it is but what it does, and this is not so easily predictable. ... *a trauma is a persistent interference with the person's basic pattern of life which cannot be managed by him in accord with this pattern.* It leads to a distortion of the healthy pattern and eventually, through a generalization of the experience, to the emergence of a competing pattern governed by different attitudes toward himself and the world. (pp. 117–118)

Mahoney (1991) summarized the matrix of factors and insights about trauma on the personality system as follows:

Rescued from scientific rhetoric, one [sic] fact now stands clear, naked, and ugly to the entire world:

1. The physical, emotional, and psychosocial neglect, abuse, and rejection of human beings is potentially hazardous to their health and well-being.
2. The risks of such hazards are substantially amplified when experiences of neglect, abuse, or rejection occur *(a)* very early, *(b)* repeatedly, *(c)* with emotional intensity, and *(d)* with experienced reference to the capacities or appraisal of the self.

... The earliest clinical and scientific evidence for these assertions came from observations and studies of the ill effects of institutional care on children's—and especially infants'—development. Pioneering figures here included Lauretta Bender, John Bowlby, Dorothy Burlingham, Anna Freud, William Goldfarb, David Levy, and Rene Spitz. The "failure to thrive" of these children was attributed to "anaclitic depression" by psychoanalytic specialists, but Bowlby and his colleague Mary Ainsworth were among a group who would blaze new paths in the study of infant–mother relations and later psychological development. (p. 157)

Clearly, converging lines of evidence showed that it was the lack of a loving, secure attachment that led to severe problems. There is a vicious cycle of trauma, personality dysfunction, and dysfunctional parental subsystems evident in multigenerational process. Harlowe's primate studies have also been supported by nonprimate animal models of trauma and the pervasive effects of relational disconnection (Blum, 2002).

Trauma as an Attractor State

Traumatic experiences can become attractor states that in turn become a central station for external and internal inputs. Chaos theory (Gleick, 1987) posits that complex systems are prone to states of chaos that self-organize around attractor states—called "strange attractors"—which are forces within complex systems in which elements converge in a bionegative or biopositive direction (Magnavita, in press-a). Trauma can be viewed within this perspective as causing systemic disruption and then leading to a bionegative reorganization of the system. This phenomenon can be seen, for example, in the sexually traumatized child who develops a dissociative disorder that results in changes at all levels of the personality system, feeding back the original input about the world and relationships being untrustworthy. From here patterns are often reenacted and continue to reinforce bionegativity. Mahoney (1991) described this process as follows:

> The new dynamic equilibrium that emerges is not a return to some prior (homeostatic) set point, however. Rather, it is an irreversible leap in the structural identity of the system. If and when such restructuring occurs, the more complex system that emerges is capable of assimilating perturbations like the ones that initiated the transformation (as well as others not yet encountered). The emergence of a more viable organization is not, however, an inevitable outcome of runaway fluctuations: some systems will settle into a less viable structure and suffer the consequences. In other words, the dynamics of the disorder create opportunities for reorganization, but do not create or guide a system in its structural metamorphosis. Some systems will lack the capacities, resources, or good fortune to sustain a successful transformation, in which case they will struggle (chronically) and/or degenerate in the process. (p. 419)

The impact of trauma at all levels of the total ecological system can no longer be minimized.

Impact on Family Systems

With regard to the impact on family systems, child abuse, neglect, and rejection have a major impact. Mahoney (1991) wrote of these:

> the evidence is now considerable that these dysfunctional patterns of parent–child interaction are (1) frequently related to patterns of emotional distress, self-abuse, and psychopathology in the family, and (2) often perpetuated across generations and through spouse selection ("assortative mating"). (p. 157)

Further, he wrote as follows:

> Although it may sound oversimplifying, Virginia Satir (1972) captured much of the essence of such dysfunctional families in summarizing their three most common and absolute injunctions (to the child and to one another): DON'T TRUST, DON'T FEEL, and DON'T TALK ABOUT IT. (p. 157)

Impact of Trauma on the Personality System of the Individual

Focal and chronic trauma can result in a severe perturbation of the individual, dyadic, triadic, and familial system. Trauma to the larger ecological system can also produce severe disturbance in the sociocultural-domain subsystems. The impact of trauma and mistreatment on the personality system of the individual and the resulting psychopathology and dysfunction can be profound or subtle. Traumatic experiences can disrupt the neurobiological mechanisms and, if prolonged, lead to actual structural changes in the hippocampus (Shore, 2003a)—or as William James (1890) suggested more than 100 years ago, they can "scar" the cerebral cortex. Although James recognized a relationship between trauma and brain structure, it took almost another century and tools of neuroscience to locate the structure as the hippocampus and not the cerebral cortex. Relational trauma disrupts attachments, and prolonged trauma results in disorganized and disoriented attachment systems (see chap. 5) that are often apparent in those experiencing severe personality dysfunction and complex clinical syndromes such as complex posttraumatic stress disorder. Evoy (1981) identified many of the effects of trauma:

- "deeply damaged self-esteem," with feelings of self-rejection and even self-hate;
- "convictions of personal worthlessness" which are very resistant to challenge or change;
- feelings that their worthlessness is "transparent' to other people;
- a desperate longing to be loved co-existent with the simultaneous conviction that they are unlovable;
- feelings of aloneness and not belonging;
- fears of mental illness;
- chronic anxiety and vigilance about being rejected again;
- chronic problems with intimacy, usually related to the rejected person's inability to genuinely "give" or "receive" love;
- chronic (though often stifled) feelings of anger, resentment, guilt, hostility, and depression; and
- in some, a feeling that "something inside them had died." (p. 70)

The effects of trauma must be metabolized by actively restructuring the critical subsystems that have been affected (Magnavita, 2001b).

Classifying Trauma—"Big-T" and "Small-t" Trauma

All psychopathology and dysfunction has its roots in trauma: the trauma of faulty attachments or of overwhelming experiences that have not been metabolized from responsive attachments and subsequently leave a damaging effect on the personality system, making one more vulnerable to psycho-pathological adaptations and symptom complexes.[2] Previously, I summarized the findings of a century of clinical evidence about the roots of psychopathol-ogy (Magnavita, 1997a): "(1) insufficient attachment and responsivity of early caretakers, (2) incidents of sexual and or physical abuse, (3) patterns of neglect, (4) loss of object, (5) injuries to the self (narcissistic exploitation), and (6) unresolved oedipal issues" (p. 73). Neborsky and Solomon (2001) arranged trauma on a continuum that progresses from "*Small-t*" to "*Big-T*":

> One way almost trivializes the concept of trauma, but in common usage it means an event that causes emotional disruption (today we refer to this as Small-t trauma); the second way is what we call Big-T trauma—an overwhelmed state wherein the individual is powerless to exert control over the environment. (p. 162)

They arrange trauma as it progresses from Small-t to Big-T, as follows:

1. RELATING: (a) Faulty attunement by either or both caregivers, (b) Faulty empathy by either or both caregivers
2. PARENTING: (a) Faulty application of boundaries by caregivers, (b) Favoritism; sibling rivalry, (c) Defective affect regulation
3. EXPLOITATIVE: (a) Sexual abuse, (b) Physical abuse, (c) Power: children as pawns or scapegoats, (d) Triangulation
4. ENVIRONMENTAL: (a) Death of parent or sibling, (b) Injury of person or body part, (c) Divorce, (d) Poverty, (e) Natural disasters, (f) Social discrimination: sex, race, culture. (Neborsky & Solomon, 2001, p. 163)

The Nature of Trauma

The earlier, more severe, and more chronic the trauma, the more likely it will be detrimental (in the absence of secure attachment that is able to mitigate and reduce the overwhelming impact on the neurobiological systems and personality). Traumatic experience that occurs earlier in development generally has a more profound effect and is retained in the personality system in affective arousal and body memories that are not attached to symbolically encoded memory. Thus, there is a profound difference in the experience of trauma prior to and after the development of language. Trauma experienced

---

[2] As previously stated (Magnavita, 2000a, p. 78): "Ferenczi believed that character neurosis, or personologic disturbance as we currently refer to it, in the form of 'parental psychopathology—narcissism, rage, empathic failure, sadism, perversion—are considered the locus for trauma (not the child's internal process of oedipal fantasy)'" (Rachman, 1997, p. 318).

at the prelanguage level of development has long-term impact on many component domains of the personality system. This type of trauma is much more difficult for the clinician to access and remediate and thus takes longer to restructure the personality system because the fragmentary experiences must be put into a cohesive narrative. Abundant research has demonstrated the morbidity of severe trauma in those who lack sufficient attachments, termed "failure to thrive," which can result in death. This phenomenon has also been documented in primate studies and shows the traumatic effect of severe attachment disruptions (Harlow & Harlow, 1962). Judith Herman (1992) described the impact of trauma as follows:

> Traumatic reactions occur when action is of no avail. When neither resistance nor escape is possible, the human system of self-defense becomes overwhelmed and disorganized. Each component of the ordinary response to danger, having lost its utility, tends to persist in an altered and exaggerated state long after the actual danger is over. Traumatic events produce profound and lasting changes in physiological arousal, emotion, cognition, and memory. Moreover, traumatic events may sever these normally integrated functions from one another. The traumatized person may experience intense emotion but without clear memory of the event, or may remember everything in detail without emotion. (p. 45)

The type of effect Herman described in this excerpt is a depiction of the result of Big-T trauma and generally of the recurrent type found in the "physically/sexually traumatizing personologic system" described later in chapter 6 (Magnavita, 2000a). Small-t trauma often seems to have a less obvious impact, but on closer inspection one can see the manifestation of this type of relational trauma in the covertly narcissistic dysfunctional personologic system as well as other systems described later in this volume (chap. 6).

TRAUMA—A COMMON PATHWAY OF PSYCHOPATHOLOGY IN THE DIATHESIS–STRESS OF MENTAL DYSFUNCTION

It is evident to most in clinical science that trauma is one of the most robust etiological factors in the development of various forms of psychopathology. There is ample evidence to support the position that both Big-T and Small-t trauma cause stress that triggers the vulnerability in the diathesis–stress matrix. Accruing neurobiological evidence from neuroscience is documenting the effects that child abuse has on the developing brain, which may be very difficult to heal (Teicher, 2000, 2002).

The types of trauma that have been described are fairly circumscribed, but the variety and combinations are infinite. No person's experience and biological makeup can be the same as another's; even in the cloning of animals, certain differences, although subtle, are apparent to researchers. How, then, does one who is traumatized in a certain manner develop one personality system and clinical syndrome(s) while another develops an entirely different matrix? The diathesis–stress model offers a way to bridge the psychological, biological, familial, and sociocultural domains to account for the expression of psychopathology seen in contemporary society. A major conceptual breakthrough occurred with the development of Monroe and Simons's (1991) diathesis–stress model of psychopathology. When a personality system is under stress, it is likely that, on the basis of genetic vulnerabilities, temperamental variation, and attachment experience, a specific symptomatic response may occur. Millon and Davis (1999) described this model as follows: "personality disorders create an enduring diathesis that lowers the threshold at which an Axis I disorder might develop" (p. 35). The stressor, broadly speaking, is trauma in all its varieties and expression.

Millon (1981) conceived of personality as a psychological immune system. This fits nicely with the diathesis–stress model:

> Here, however, it is not the immunological defenses or enzymatic capacities but the patient's personality pattern—that is, coping skills and adaptive flexibilities—that will determine whether or not the person will master or succumb to his/her psychosocial environment. Just as physical ill health is likely to be less a matter of some alien virus than it is a dysfunction in the body's capacity to deal with infectious agents, so too is psychological ill health likely to be less a product of some intrusive psychic strain than it is a dysfunction in the personality's capacity to cope with life's difficulties. Viewed this way, the structure and characteristics of personality become the foundation for the individual's capacity to function in a mentally healthy or ill way. (Millon, 1981, pp. 5–6)

Stone (1993) likened personality to a radial tire: "I find it useful, for didactic purposes, to picture the self, in relation to psychological stresses, as a 'radial tire'—kept inflated (i.e., preserving self-esteem) under all but the most adverse circumstances and able to absorb shocks without its inner layers being breached" (p. 8).

If we conceive of personality as a system that has multiple subsystems ranging from the microsystem to the total ecological system, we can then begin to understand personality in a much broader way. We can take into consideration the fluctuation in personality based on the evolving cultural, societal, political, and economic systems at the broader level and also increase magnification to look more closely at the microlevel, even to the level of genetic makeup and neurotransmitter potentials.

AN ECOLOGICAL SYSTEM FOR UNDERSTANDING PSYCHOPATHOLOGY AND DYSFUNCTION

Millon and Davis (1999) used the term *ecology* to refer to "the sum total of contextual influences in the living environment in which an organism exists" (p. 36). The systemic and ecological foundations of the Millonian model of psychopathology are apparent in the following excerpt:

> Intensive study of phenomena at a particular level of organization may lead some scientists into a "reductionism to the whole." Here, the reciprocal and multilevel influences that transact across all levels of organization and social structure are reduced to one level alone. . . . The lesson is that most psychopathologies are likely to be underdetermined at every level of analysis. Only by considering all sources of influence in conjunction can some picture of the development of personality and psychopathology be constructed. And if ecological structures change, developmental scenarios are free to change as well. (p. 37)

A trauma model alone will never be sufficient in and of itself to explain dysfunction of the personality system, but using the diathesis–stress model allows us to explore various areas and networks of impact.

"Outbreak" or Symptom Dysfunction

The main premise of a personality-guided system of psychotherapy is that the personality system is the most useful framework for understanding how psychopathology is developed and maintained and where and how to intervene systematically. The artificial dichotomies depicted in current conceptual systems of psychopathology offer little that is useful to the clinician. Take anxiety, for example, a popular outbreak of Axis I disorder. Anxiety disorders, although currently well documented and researched, are presented in the literature (and now in the media) as existing almost as an entity separate from the individual and from society (Barlow, 1988). We diagnose anxiety disorders and administer empirically validated treatment, which tends to be a cognitive–behavioral, anxiolytic medication, or combined therapy approach. We are continuously being urged to treat the disorder. Where is the person in this contemporary schema? As any experienced clinician knows, most anxiety disorders are multifaceted and best understood in context of the personality system, with its resiliency and maladaptive defensive operations.

Axis I "disorders" are really a unique expression of a personality system. As catalogued in Millon et al.'s (1999) *Personality-Guided Therapy*, there are logical combinations and expressions. They may be better conceived of as a meta-communication about the seat of enduring pain an individual is carrying instead of a reified disorder. Change the context, and you change the individual. This may be an exaggeration in some cases, but not in others. Put anyone into a maximum-security prison and see whether his or her personality system changes radically to adapt.

Psychopathology—Bionegativity and Health

It is difficult to be healthy in a dysfunctional system or society, but it is possible. This is known as *resilience*. It seems, however, that we have left the period of cultural relativity behind. Some societies have more pathology than others. Individuals, couples, families, and institutions within these dysfunctional societies have a difficult time functioning in a healthy way. An example is the mutual cascading pathology of violence in the Middle East between Israel and Palestine. Children growing up in these societies are affected profoundly by these dysfunctional mesosystems. The effect is bidirectional. The dysfunctional society creates cultural, familial, and individual disruption, which then feeds back to the society in a difficult to alter positive feedback loop.

Wakefield's Harmful Dysfunction

A major debate rages in the field of psychopathology concerning the nature of disorder or abnormal variants of normal behavior. Wakefield (1999) wrote, "There is no more fundamental conceptual challenge for the field of abnormal psychology—and none that has generated more heated controversy—than the analysis of the concept of disorder that underlies the field" (p. 374). Wakefield proposed that

> *disorder means harmful dysfunction*, where dysfunctions are failures of internal mechanisms to perform naturally selected functions. The harmful dysfunction (HD) analysis rejects both the view that disorder is just a value concept referring to undesirable or harmful conditions and the view that disorder is a purely scientific concept. Rather, the HD analysis proposes that a disorder attribution requires both a scientific judgment that there exists a failure of designed function and a value judgment that the design failure harms the individual. (p. 374)

Spitzer (1999) regarded "Wakefield's HD formulation as a major conceptual advance over previous attempts (including mine) to define medical and mental disorders" (p. 431). I necessarily must limit the scope of our discussion in a volume of this nature and therefore focus on the controversy over the conceptualization of personality "disorder."

CLASSIFICATION AND DIAGNOSIS OF THE PERSONALITY SYSTEM

The manner in which psychopathology is described and categorized necessarily influences how we conceptualize dysfunction and influences the treatments offered. It is therefore crucial to briefly explore some of the central tenets of contemporary systems of classification and how they relate to the personality system.

Current Systems of Classification of Psychopathology

The classification of mental disorders has been one of the scientific milestones of 19th- and 20th-century clinical science. The development of a system of classification for mental disorders was the beginning of the science of psychology and psychiatry and an essential step in the evolution of a scientific discipline. Classification enables investigators to begin the process of "carving nature at its joints." The organization and systematization of knowledge is then able to accrue and unfold as the new science takes root. Some of the major advances in classification were achieved in the 19th century with the groundbreaking work of Emil Kraepelin (1857–1939) and Eugene Blueuler (1857–1939; Stone, 1997). Kraepelin is considered by many to be the "great classifier," and his work marks the beginning of psychiatric taxonomy (classification) and nosology (naming) of disease and groups of symptom constellations. Bleuler was considered to be the major contributor to interpretative psychiatry with his emphasis on the hidden meanings of symptoms. Major advances in classification did not occur until later in the 20th century with the development of the modern system of classification introduced in 1980.

The Modern Era of DSM

The development of the current diagnostic system (American Psychiatric Association, 1980) was a genuine advance in the cataloguing of mental disorders. Tucker (1998) described this advance as follows:

> The criteria were polythetic in that not all the criteria need to be present to make the diagnosis. It provided a diagnostic system that contained other pertinent information (e.g., it was multiaxial) in which IQ, medical illnesses, stressors, and social functioning could be taken

into account. It also necessitated that we look at the patient longitudinally rather than at a moment in time. The explicit and understandable criteria of *DSM–III* and its successors have been very useful in educating patients. *DSM–III* spurred a great deal of research, particularly in anxiety and affective disorders, as well as laying the foundation for treatment outcome studies, such as the important Epidemiologic Catchment Area Program (Narrow, Regier, Rae, Manderscheid, & Locke, 1993). In fact, the new *DSM* diagnostic process has dominated the research, teaching, and contemporary practice of psychiatry (Kendell, 1988). The *DSM* diagnosis has almost become a thing itself—a certainty of "concrete" dimensions. The *DSM* diagnosis has become the main goal of clinical practice. (p. 159)

DSM has achieved an ascendant position in modern clinical sciences. Yet for all the good that has resulted, there are limitations of this model, and in particular for those clinicians who are faced with the array of human suffering seen in clinical practice. Although clearly the ensuing research that this codification offered is unparalleled, where DSM is most lacking is in its application to the real-life treatment of mental disorders. This is especially evident to most clinicians in the Axis II personality disorder dimension. As Shedler and Westen (2004) write: "A clinically useful and empirically sound classification of personality disorders has been an elusive ideal. A clinically useful diagnostic system should encompass the spectrum of personality pathology seen in clinical practice and have meaningful implications for treatment" (p. 1350). Although for many of the Axis I disorders, DSM is a useful guide, it falls far short of its mark for the personality disorders. Even for the Axis I clinical disorders, there is a danger of seeing the patient as a disorder instead of a human being who is suffering in a unique way, as each of us do.

Other problems for the clinician exist as well:

One, we have lost the patient and his or her story with this process; two, the diagnosis, not the patient, often gets treated; three, surprisingly, the study of psychopathology is almost nonexistent; and four, the strict focus on diagnosis has made psychiatry boring (this never seemed to be a problem in our field before). (Tucker, 1998, pp. 159–160)

Dimensional Classification Systems

Stone (1993) likened the categorical system of DSM "to the *digital* computer (where quantities are counted one by one)" (p. 25). The other main type is the dimensional system, which "corresponds to an *analog* computer (where the *degree* to which a certain tendency is present is estimated by the relative position of a dial, by the height of a column as in the thermometer, or by some other device)" (p. 25). Many current theorists believe that personality can be captured with the use of five dimensions, termed the "five-factor theory" (Costa & McCrae, 1990; Costa & Widiger, 1993). These models are based on statistically derived factors based on lexical descriptions of personality pioneered by Cattell (1957). Others have postulated three factors based in part on the early Greek study of temperament (Eysenck, 1982).

Prototypical Classification Systems

Millon and Davis (1996) proposed a system using prototypes based on three polarities (1) active–passive, (2) self–object, and (3) pleasure–pain. Prototypical systems combine elements of categorical and dimensional systems to better account for the variations in personality and gradation from normal to abnormal manifestations. Shedler and Westen (2004) have also been developing a "clinical prototype" classification that shows promise in capturing "the richness and complexity of clinical personality descriptions while providing reliable and quantifiable data" (p. 1350).

Circumplex Classification Systems

Another innovative system was developed by Leary (1957) and expanded on by Benjamin (1993) and Wiggins and Trobst (1999). These models arrange personality on various axes in a circle and were a conceptual leap over the more static factorial models. They are all based on the work of Sullivan (1953), who emphasized the interpersonal aspects of personality.

Structural–Characterological Classification

Over the past century, psychoanalytic workers, particularly during the first half of the century, observed and wrote about various characterological presentations seen in clinical practice. Many of these offered rich formulations and descriptions of various typologies of character. Modern-day psychodynamic models continue to rely on this type of classification. In this system character types are arranged on a continuum—psychotic → borderline → neurotic → normal—based on the intrapsychic integrity of a patient's mental apparatus according to an assessment of ego-adaptive capacity (McWilliams, 1994).

Relational Classification Systems

A much less recognized system is a relational system that is much more fluid and focuses on dysfunction in dyads, triads, and family systems. This work was originally pioneered by Ackerman (1957). Some four decades later, a movement was undertaken to develop a relational diagnostic system that would offer an alternative to the individualistic categorical system of *DSM* (Kaslow, 1996). On the basis of this work and the work of Bowen

(1976), an initial relational system describing 10 dysfunctional personologic systems has been elaborated (Magnavita, 2000a).

The Danger of Focusing Too Much on Diagnosis and Psychiatric Reductionism

It should be underscored that the present trend toward "diagnostic" psychotherapy poses an eminent danger: *overemphasis on the diagnosis with loss of the person as the focus of treatment*. Although diagnosis has its place and current diagnostics is required knowledge for the psychotherapist, it does not eliminate the need to view and understand the whole person or personality system of an individual, which exists in the rich context of relationships and is influenced by cultural, social, and political forces. The current diagnostic system has been developed in part to allow for evaluators to do rapid and "accurate" diagnoses with substantially less training than is required to understand whole-person systems. Diagnostic formulation is an important *ongoing* psychotherapeutic activity, but, when understood and practiced simplistically, it does not do justice to the enormity of the task of formulation and intervening when people have complex clinical syndromes. Almost anyone with an average level of intelligence can understand and use *DSM* with some accuracy.

The Value of Various Perspectives

Each system of diagnostic classification has its usefulness and its drawbacks. The academic research psychologist might find greater resonance with the statistically derived factorial models. Clinical researchers and epidemiologists are likely to be more attracted to the relative simplicity of the categorical system with "clear-cut" criteria for various disorders. Clinicians, on the other side of the coin, are often looking for something that has greater resonance with what they see in clinical practice. They tend to gravitate toward structural, interpersonal, and relational systems. Psychopharmacologists might also like the relative clarity of the categorical system or of pharmacological diagnosis—that is, diagnosis by the response to psychotropic medication. They can diagnose, prescribe, and follow for maintenance.

A Holonic Approach

None of the current systems for diagnosing and classifying personality can capture the phenomenon of personality and the sociocultural–political matrix in which it is expressed. The systems covered to date do not take into account the ecological factors that have a major impact on personality functioning. A holonic approach is needed, one that allows us to understand

and conceptualize the person and his or her interrelationship to the ecosystem in which we all operate. Nosology (classification and diagnosis) and psychopathology are related disciplines. One must have some idea of normal versus pathological, what represents function versus dysfunction, or what is bionegative as opposed to biopositive, to describe a holonic map.

A SYSTEMIC FRAMEWORK FOR PERSONALITY THEORY

The component systems that determine personality have been fairly well articulated after a century of modern psychological science. Much is still unknown, but the point is not to accumulate knowledge that trivializes the subject. We are not at the point where we can develop an algorithm; the data points would be considerable and the instrumentation is not yet developed, but the component systems have been identified. These are stipulated in the biopsychosocial model. We know they are not separate substrates and that personality development will be shaped and directed by the cascading energy of all the forces. There are some obvious hypotheses. For example, if an individual grows up in what we would consider a functional family with no traumatic experiences but who nevertheless fails to develop a sufficiently adaptive personality system, we can assume that the neurobiological or societal systems were malfunctioning.

Personality Systems Versus Personality Disorders

The construct of personality disorders was a major advance in clinical science and nosology in the 20th century but may have reached a stage at which it no longer has tremendous clinical relevance and usefulness. Although it still has some value to guide research and epidemiology, its value for clinical work is questionable. Personality is not the static system depicted by the *DSM*. The *DSM*'s attempt to classify personality into various categories based on behavioral criteria artificially reduces the complexity of personality to a static system that does not take into consideration the organic processes at work. A far more useful way in which to conceptualize personality is within a systemic context, like that pioneered by von Bertalanffy with his general system theory.

The first use that could be found of the term *personality system* was in Smelser and Smelser's (1963) volume, *Personality and Social Systems*. In this volume the authors and contributors presented a synthesis of the extant individual personality and social systems models expanding the range of the current levels of analysis in the field at that time. In many ways this volume was quite advanced in bridging theoretical and disciplinary chasms between personologists and social theorists.

A number of early theorists incorporated von Bertalanffy's system theory into their models. Allport (1961a, 1961b), who had a major interest in personality theory, gave this model much emphasis when he conceptualized "personality as system." Menninger (Menninger, Mayman, & Pruyser, 1963) also used general system theory, which he blended with organismic biology as the basis of his system of psychiatry. The great personality theorist Gardner Murphy (1947) emphasized "personality as a biological system, an organic matrix, from which, through outer and inner pressures, evolves the socially known individual" (p. 18). Although there was a surge of interest in personality as a system model in the late 1950s and early 1960s, this initial enthusiasm waned. As von Bertalanffy (1968) wrote, "The question arises why such a trend has appeared" (p. 205). The more interesting question from our perspective is "Why has this trend disappeared?"

Systemic Theory for Conceptualizing Personality

Although it is beyond the scope of this volume to adequately explore this interesting topic, it does seem that the answer to the question is that a systems theory of personality and personality disorder has not disappeared. Rather, systems theory has been incorporated in a limited way into most theoretical models that recognize the importance of a biopsychosocial framework. What is lost is a more rigorous use of the systemic–cybernetic model, especially its application to personality "disorders." A number of prominent 20th-century workers placed systemic theory in a central role in personality theory.

von Bertalanffy (1968) wrote, "In a variety of modern currents, there is one common principle: to take man not as reactive automaton or robot but as *an active personality system*" (p. 207). Instead of relying on the current static model of personality, it is more clinically and theoretically relevant to view personality as a system with various organizing principles and operating systems that affect the way in which personality is expressed. "In contrast to physical forces like gravity or electricity, the phenomena of life are found only in individual entities called organisms. Any organism is a system, that is, a dynamic order of parts and processes standing in mutual interaction" (von Bertalanffy, 1968, p. 208). Personality is not a rigid, static system, but one that represents a complex array of multiple components that interrelate and are governed by multiple feedback loops, both positive and negative. Murphy (1947) emphasized that the study of personality necessitates that we "stress the maintenance of a stable complex individual system" (p. 36). These systems "are forever in flux" (p. 37). Fromm (1970) also used the construct of a system:

> Man is a system—like an ecological or political system, the system of
> the body or of the cell, or a system of society or an organization. In

analyzing the system "man," we understand that we are dealing with a system of forces, and not with a mechanical structure of individual particles. (p. 63)

The concept of *personality as a system* has a long and controversial heritage in personality theory. Murray (1959) questioned both a narrow approach and what he believed was seductively holistic, hurling "a challenge at exponents of its extreme that is fully as biting as that leveled at the opposite extremists" (Maddi, 1963, p. 168).

> The terms "personality-as-a-whole" and "personality system" have been very popular in recent years; but no writer, so far as I know, has explicitly defined the components of a "whole" personality or of a "system of personality." When definitions of the units of a system are lacking, the term stands for not more than an article of faith, and is misleading to boot, in so far as it suggests a condition of affairs that may not actually exist. (Murray, 1959, p. 19)

According to Murphy (1947), there are at least three levels of complexity that must be considered when conceptualizing personality. He suggested at the first level that personality be conceived of "as an object or an event in a larger context—a dot on a chart, a billiard ball on a table. It is identifiable, strictly localized in time–space, and homogeneous" (p. 3). Next, at the second level of complexity, he likens personality to a chrysalis: "It is again identifiable and strictly bounded, but it has internal structure. It is no longer homogeneous; it is organized" (p. 3). At the third level, he suggests that there is no sharp boundary between "self and an non-self." He called this the "organism–environment field" (p. 5). There are many other ways to organize the domains of the field of study. One is to move from the individual system, to the family system, and finally to the cosmos or the entire system. Finally, we should not only include the sociocultural system but must necessarily include the entire ecological system of the individual, family, and society.

Personality systems are organized at three primary levels: individual, family, and societal. These various systems are inextricably interrelated and are separated for heuristic purposes. As we know, none of these systems are static but are constantly in motion of organization–reorganization, evolution–extinction, homeostasis–disequilibrium, stability–instability, growth–regression, chaos–reordering. We may take a static measurement such as we would if we diagnosis, classify, label, and so forth, but these are inadequate conceptualizations of the phenomena.

The Individual Personality System

The individual personality system includes all of the elements from the intrapsychic–biological triangle. Individual personality systems are organized in various ways as described earlier in this chapter. A psychotically organized system is the most disturbed, with the highest level of dysfunction. As we move from the left of the continuum to the right, the system becomes more functional. These are not static structures or states of personality system organization. As most clinicians have witnessed, individuals can often rapidly shift from borderline to psychotic levels and normal to neurotic under stressful circumstances.

The Interpersonal Personality System

The dyad, depicted in the interpersonal dyadic triangle, is the basic unit of the interpersonal system and the building blocks of all relational systems. The most fundamental dyadic unit is the mother-infant relationship, from which the individual personality system emerges in the rich matrix of mutual communication and repeated attunements and disruptions of connection. The dyad is also the critical dyad in Western culture for marital relationships and is fundamental to family functioning. Tracking the dyadic system helps us identify patterns of communication in the interpersonal process and identify problematic reoccurring patterns and how these are mutually reinforced. In the therapeutic relationship, the dyadic processes are evident to the therapist, who is the participant-observer in the process. One of the main functions of the dyad is modulating intimacy–closeness between the twosome.

The Relational Personality System

The relational system, depicted by the relational triadic matrix, is primarily composed of triadic configurations. These triadic configurations often exist in multigenerational, overlapping configurations. The relational system includes roles, hierarchies, communication channels, and patterns that define the structure of these triads. When dyads are unable to effectively manage anxiety, the tendency is to seek a third person to absorb the anxiety whereby stabilizing the unstable dyad. These triads are ubiquitous in human relationships.

The Family Personality System

The family personality system includes the dyadic and triadic relationships depicted by the intrapsychic biological triangle and the relational triadic configurations. The family system includes nuclear and extended family networks and muligenerational hierarchies. When family systems are functioning, the individuals within the system are able to make developmental transitions effectively. The family system needs to be fluid enough to withstand the developmental pressures that require it to change and have sufficient structure to provide security to its members.

The Societal–Cultural Personality System

The societal–cultural domain takes into account elements that include the relationships developed outside of the family in broader society, including those with social and political institutions that are structures of society.

Key Systemic Constructs—Ludwig von Bertalanffy

von Bertalanffy introduced several systemic constructs that have influenced the unified model of component systems.

- *Centralization.* Some components may dominate the nature of a system. A small change in a component system may lead to amplification of changes in the total system.
- *Regression.* "Regression is essentially disintegration of personality; that is, *dedifferentiation* and *decentralization*" (von Bertalanffy, 1968, p. 214).
- *Boundaries.* "Any system as an entity which can be investigated in its own right must have boundaries, either spatial or dynamic. Strictly speaking, spatial boundaries exist only in naive observation, and all boundaries are ultimately dynamic" (p. 215). von Bertalanffy used the concept of ego to illustrate that

   the boundary of the ego is both fundamental and precarious. . . . it is slowly established in evolution and development and is never completely fixed. It originates in proprioceptive experience and in the body image, but self-identify is not completely established before the "I," "Thou," and "it" are named. Psychopathology shows the paradox that the ego boundary is at once too fluid and too rigid. (p. 215)

- *The symbolic basis of human behavior.* With the exception of satisfaction of basic human needs, "man lives in a world not of things but of symbols" (p. 215). Further, "In consequence, mental disturbances in man, as a rule, involve disturbances in symbolic functions. . . . This is the ultimate reason why human behavior and psychology cannot be reduced to biologistic notions like restoration of homeostasis, conflict of biological drives, unsatisfactory mother–infant relationships, and the like" (p. 217). Language, cognition, symbolization and mentation then are essential elements of the human personality system, and are embedded codes in various of the subsystems.

Thus, wherever possible, psychologists try to understand the dynamic rather than the static system. We are interested in boundaries but only as interfaces with other component systems, such as the boundary between individual and other, self and family, family and culture, and so forth.

Creating Maps of the Holonic System Rather Than Diagnosing

When clinicians diagnosis, we necessarily reduce the complex phenomena into a simplistic, label-category. Much is lost when we do so exclusively. As Angyal (1982) noted, "The position within the personality system of any factor, subjective or environmental, is characterized by its function; determined by whether the given factor promotes or handicaps the realization of the basic dynamic pattern and by the specific ways in which it does so" (p. 49). Tucker (1998) commented as follows:

> We now tend to study how a patient fits a diagnosis, or how groups of patients fit a diagnostic category, not psychopathology. Not only has this led to a boring, voluminous new literature, but tends to force fit all patients into the diagnostic categories we have, rather than study the varieties of psychopathology. With our current polythetic system and our lack of attention to observational skills, it is possible that we are often comparing two different groups of patients in the same diagnostic category or similar groups in different diagnostic categories. (p. 160)

Adopting Multiple Perspectives to Characterize a Holonic View

Understanding and treating mental dysfunction requires shifting perspectives. Good clinicians oscillate among various perspectives in a seamless fashion. Multiple perspectives are required to produce a holonic view of the vital personality systems in operation, which create dysfunction and psychopathological adaptation. The following are necessary, and no single perspective is sufficient:

1. *Patient narrative and phenomenology.* "A narrative story must emerge on how each individual copes and adjusts to his or her life, and from this, a hypothesis of understanding of the patient's problems should develop [other than that the patient has some 'biochemical defect']" (Tucker, 1998, p. 161). The narrative is the story of ourselves as it is retained in our symbolic system of language.
2. *Conventional diagnostic classification.* The point is not that we jettison the current *DSM* diagnostic system but that we de-emphasize its position as the primary mode to understand psychopathology and dysfunctional relationships. The *DSM* gives us a static picture that provides some of the topography of the patient system, basic personality characteristics, and symptom complexes.

3. *Relational classification.* The model presented in this volume emphasizes what occurs in dyads, triads, and larger systems, examining and identifying the communication process, organization, and structure of relational systems. Various models of family progress and topology have been offered (Hoffman, 1981; Kaslow, 1996; Magnavita, 2000a).

4. *Intersubjective experience of patient–therapist dyad.* Another important relational perspective is the phenomenology of the therapist–patient dyad that can be a rich source of information about expected transactive and reciprocal interactions.

5. *Experience of family system process.* The experience of the therapist as he or she sits with the family offers rich diagnostic information about the tone and process that occur within the system.

6. *Standard psychodiagnostic findings.* Standard psychological tests and assessment instruments can add to or corroborate impressions and formulations.

7. *Sociocultural assessment.* An understanding of the cultural, ethnic, religious, and political factors that influence the personality system are vital.

8. *Ecological assessment.* The total ecological system of the patient and his or her social matrix are vital to understanding how the system functions and how to organize interventions.

Unified Psychotherapy

Emerging from psychopathology and personality theory is the third interrelated discipline of psychotherapy. Unified psychotherapy is naturally embedded in the processes of the domains of the personality system and is concerned with dysfunctioning that leads to "psychopathology," or bionegativity at various levels in the total ecological system (Magnavita, 2004c). Psychotherapy uses the various matrices of relational systems to mobilize movement toward more adaptive and functional repertoires. These various methods of psychotherapy have been identified within the major forms of psychotherapy and can be conceptualized as restructuring or reorganizing the networks or systems with which they are concerned. I discuss these processes and methods in greater detail in the following chapters.

SUMMARY AND CONCLUSIONS

This chapter presents a brief overview of interrelated constructs and domain areas that are necessary in creating a holonic perspective for organizing

a treatment package to alter functioning of systems that are operating ineffi-
ciently or maladaptively. The holonic perspective encourages us to understand how complex systems such as personality are interconnected networks
of related domains that cannot be fully understood without an idea of how
they are organized and structured and of the processes that represent their
underlying architecture. Assessment of the personality system requires samples from multiple domain areas, using multiple perspectives. Personality-
guided relational psychotherapy requires a systematic application of methods
for reorganizing these networks so that the structure can be modified.

II

COMPONENT SYSTEMS
AND ASSESSMENT

In the following three chapters of this part of the volume, the component domains of the personality system are identified and guidelines with which to assess them offered. The component domains of the personality system encompass important spheres of structure and process, which practitioners from various therapeutic schools emphasize to one degree or another. It is important in adopting a unified perspective to underscore the embedded nature of these various domains and their spheres of mutual influence, keeping in mind their reciprocal channels of influence. For example, the affect subsystem is vital to regulating emotional responses in each of the four levels of triangular processes, and this subsystem will affect individual, dyadic, triadic, familial, and societal function and process.

4

COMPONENT SYSTEMS OF
THE RELATIONAL MATRIX

This chapter presents a more detailed presentation of the component systems of the relational matrix, the central elements of a unified model of personality-guided relational psychotherapy. Understanding the components of the relational matrix and their interrelationships is essential for assessment and treatment. Angyal (1982) described the challenge as follows:

> For holistic study of personality we need logical tools adequate for dealing with structure of wholes. We need, in fact, a new type of logic of holistic systems, which would be the counterpart of the conventional logic of relations. This is a large order and a task for the future. (p. 45)

I begin by focusing on the microsystem and then proceed to the macrosystem and mesosystem.

THE VIEW FROM THE MICROSYSTEM TO THE MESOSYSTEM

Assessing an individual's personality system requires knowledge of the way in which the personality system works. Tracking the ecology of a patient's personality system is an essential and ongoing part of treatment. The component systems elaborated in this chapter will assist clinicians in orienting themselves to the vital aspects of personality system dysfunction and bionegativity and provide the foundation for assessment. At the onset of the treatment process, the clinician's task is to establish a therapeutic alliance, gather initial information, and take a reading of how the component systems that comprise the total ecology of the patient(s) operate. Assessment is not a one-time event that occurs at the beginning of treatment; it is instead a process that requires continual attention as a holonic view of the patient is developed and refined.

CREATING A HOLONIC MAP

Formulating a holonic map requires that the personality system be viewed as interconnected "part–whole" processes. A *holograph* is a three-dimensional or holonic map of phenomena. Triangular configurations are useful in formulating a holograph because they allow for three-dimensional representations. One may ignore or focus exclusively on a single domain of the personality system, but there is an inevitable loss in this type of single-domain orientation. The best way to achieve an understanding of a patient is to use the holonic approach, that is, ongoing multiple sampling from various perspectives, as opposed to focusing exclusively on the *DSM* diagnosis. Personality can be reduced to traits, but these are limited for understanding the individual and his or her system. The meaning of a particular symptom constellation and trait is often difficult to understand when it is not viewed in the multiple component systems of personality. This allows for inevitable change, both positive and negative, in the personality system. A holonic view attempts to understand the patient's total ecology as it continues to unfold in his or her life process. Again we are emphasizing relationships in two essential ways: (a) the relationships among any components of the system, and (b) the domain of human relationships as they exist in the sociocultural and family spheres. We are interested in the functional relationships, mechanisms, processes, and attractor states.

> The position within the personality system of any factor, subjective or environmental, is characterized by its function; it is determined by whether the given factor promotes or handicaps the realization of the basic dynamic pattern and by the specific ways in which it does so. (Angyal, 1982, p. 49)

Assessment cannot be static, but must convey a rich relational matrix in constant process. Within this matrix each person has a unique individual personality system, a shared social system, and an ecological system in which he or she functions. A holonic perspective avoids unnecessary reductionism of the patient's complexity to isolated component aspects of the biopsychosocial model. Reductionism has its place, but only when each element is considered in light of its part–whole dynamical state. Instead, a holonic assessment is based on an oscillating or dialectic process among the various microscopic and macroscopic levels of understanding. A true diagnostic appreciation of a patient requires a tremendous amount of flexibility and tolerance for uncertainty in the clinician.

THE FOUR TRIANGLES AND THEIR COMPONENT SYSTEMS

The four triangles of the personality system offer a useful matrix with which to organize the various interconnected component domains and processes. As we move from the *intrapsychic–biological triangle* to the *sociocultural–familial triangle*, we are increasingly shifting our orientation from a microscopic to a macroscopic level, so the level of magnification decreases and the perspective widens. Even though we may focus our attention on elements from any one or another of these triangles, we must keep in mind that powerful forces from the other domains of the remaining triangles continue to shape and influence the system on which we have focused our attention. In the next part of the chapter, I review the component domains as they operated in the four triangles. Again, I begin at the microscopic and proceed to lesser degrees of magnification and a wider perspective.

ESSENTIAL COMPONENTS AND PROCESSES OF THE INTRAPSYCHIC–BIOLOGICAL TRIANGLE

At the intrapsychic level, we attempt to understand how the internal biopsychological components of an individual are organized and how various dynamic processes relate to one another. At this level, we are interested in the dynamic processes that occur at the neurobiological level and cognitive–affective matrix. The cognitive schema and affective processes are part of the system that shapes self-esteem and self-concept. If the internalized schematic representations are negative, the belief system will be filled with negative injunctions about the self. Firestone (1997) called this the internalized "voice": "I have found that not only are people driven by unconscious forces, but they internalize an alien aspect of personality in the form of destructive voices that are basically suicidal in intent and diametrically opposed to happiness and well-being" (Firestone, 2002, p. 229). Negative or maladaptive schematic representations require restructuring (see chap. 7, Intrapsychic Restructuring) but must first be identified and brought to the patient's awareness because they are often out of consciousness. When functioning optimally, the affective system keeps anxiety at manageable limits; when functioning ineffectively, the result is emotional dysregulation or severe disconnection or repression of affective responding. In intrapsychic systems that are not functioning adequately, anxiety can be overwhelming or, conversely, absent, as in the case of those experiencing some expressions of antisocial personality. The affective–cognitive system is inherently endowed by biogenetic factors and vulnerabilities and shaped by attachment experience and influences from the total ecological system. In addition, anxiety is managed internally by the unique system of defenses that an individual develops through his or her experience in relationships and the complex feedback loops that structuralize the internal system.

The Attachment System

The attachment system includes a number of domains and processes that exert a primary influence on the development, structure, and process of adult attachments. Our relationships throughout our lives are influenced by the attractor states that result from our attachment system. In the relational model, the attachment system begins to develop before birth in the parental dyads expressed in fantasy, expectations, and wishes. The substrate of the attachment system is the neurobiology and genetic endowment of the neonate.

Neurobiological Components and Processes

> The functioning of the brain as a complex system of neuronal circuits requires it to have some way of determining which firings are useful, neutral, or harmful. Without such an appraisal mechanism, stimuli from the outside world and internally generated states and representations would all be equally welcome. (Siegel, 1999, pp. 136–137)

Determining an individual's biological vulnerabilities is crucial to our understanding. Thus, having an understanding of the basic principles of neuroscience can help to explain why certain conditions are difficult to remedy. A predisposition to depression (Nemeroff, 1998), schizophrenia, bipolar disorder, and anxiety disorders are often seen in successive generations. "Geneticists have provided some of the oldest proof of a biological component to depression in many people" (Nemeroff, 1998, p. 44). There is some evidence that even suicide may have a biological basis (Ezzell, 2003). Taking a careful history can alert the clinician to a biological vulnerability that may have or may emerge as a diathesis–stress mechanism. It is thus imperative to understand the *total ecological system* of those treated. This can alert the clinician to the need for preventative intervention with the patient as well as other members of the family. As a result of generations of untreated depression, some families may develop signs of a DepDPS (depressiogenic dysfunctional personologic system; see chap. 6 for description of various types of DPS; Magnavita, 2000a).

The brain has the most *plasticity* in early development. Early in life, the brain's neuronal networks are pruned through experience. Stimulation of neuronal networks increases organization and structure of certain areas and understimulation or a lack of stimulation prunes other areas. This may be one reason why, for example, it is difficult, but not impossible, to learn a foreign language as an adult learner. Evidence is accruing that neurobiology is altered by stress and trauma (Teicher, 2002). As Teicher (2002) reported, "Subsequent work by other investigators using magnetic resonance imaging (MRI) technology has confirmed an association between early maltreatment and reductions in the size of the adult hippocampus. The amygdala may be smaller as well" (p. 71). Neuroscientists suspect that the limbic system plays "a pivotal role in the regulation of emotion and memory" (p. 70). More specifically, Teicher noted that "The hippocampus is thought to be important in the formation and retrieval of both verbal and emotional memories, whereas the amygdala is concerned with creating the emotional content of memory—for example, feelings related to fear conditioning and aggressive responses" (p. 70). These neuroscientific findings that support a unified model are reviewed in greater detail in the final chapter of this volume.

Temperamental Components and Processes

It is imperative to understand the contribution of temperamental variation on the personality system and its development and to make an assessment of an individual's temperamental predisposition. Temperament is subject to neurobiological and genetic parameters but can be modified to a degree. This type of developmental insight can be achieved following any number of systems, such as that developed by Greenspan (1997a, 2002). Greenspan (1997a) offered a developmentally based approach. "The overarching principle of a developmentally based approach to psychotherapy is mobilization of the developmental processes associated with an adaptive progression of the personality throughout childhood and adulthood" (Greenspan, 2002, p. 19). He suggested that "certain processing patterns are coupled with certain environmental patterns" (p. 20). In this way, Greenspan offered an explanation for the interrelationship among temperamental variables, diathesis–stress, trauma, and the development of defenses that are a major aspect of the personality system. After extensive observation, Greenspan learned how to read the system and offers us the following guidelines:

- Individuals who are overreactive to touch or sound have stronger auditory processing abilities and relatively weaker visual–spatial ones and tend toward the hysterical, depressive, and anxiety disorders. Those who have difficulty with movement in space tend toward phobic disorders.

- Individuals who are underreactive to sensations and have low motor tone tend toward more withdrawn behavior. They tend to escape into fantasy and, in the extreme, evidence more schizoid and autistic patterns.
- Individuals with hyporeactivity to sensations along with stimulus-craving patterns, coupled with high activity levels and organized gross motor patterns, tend toward risk taking and, if there is emotional deprivation, antisocial patterns.
- Individuals with relatively stronger visual–spatial processing and overreactivity to certain sensations tend toward patterns characterized by negativism, stubbornness, and compulsiveness.
- Individuals with marked motor planning and sequencing challenges tend toward attentional problems. (pp. 20–21)

Knowledge of temperamental variation and perceptual and processing preferences not only assists us in understanding an individual's developmental trajectory but also offers suggestions for developing optimal treatment strategies. Greenspan suggests that developmental vulnerabilities be strengthened and competencies supported.

Attachment Style and "Goodness of Fit"

Individuals' temperament and their relationships with early caregivers affect their attachment style.

> Attachment theory and research can help provide a much needed developmental perspective on personality pathology. In addition, attachment theory highlights the interpersonal dimensions of personality difficulties, both as an important aspect of personal adaptation and as a social context in which pathology may be developed. (Bartholomew, Kwong, & Hart, 2001, p. 196)

Attachments are the framework for the developmental process. There are clear converging lines of evidence that severe attachment disruptions lead to psychopathological or maladaptive personality systems (Blum, 2002). This evidence has accrued from almost three quarters of a century of research with animal models, clinical observation, and developmental psychology. "The quality of early attachment relationships is seen as rooted largely in the history of interactions between infants and their primary caregivers (or attachment figures)" (Bartholomew et al., 2001, p. 197). Bartholomew et al. (2001) reviewed four types of attachments: secure, preoccupied, fearful, and dismissing.

There is evidence to support the view that attachment styles are fairly stable over time (Bartholomew et al., 2001). Although not conclusive, "a growing body of research focuses on intergenerational continuity by assessing the concordance of attachment patterns across generations" (Bartholomew et al., 2001, p. 208). Thus, there is some support for the contention that attachment styles developed in childhood will emerge in the clinical process but may also be witnessed through the intergenerational transmission process (see chap. 5).

Mary Main is one of the leading figures in attachment theory. Siegel (1999) summarized Main's work (Main & Morgan, 1996), which includes the following principles:

- The earliest attachments are usually formed by the age of 7 months.
- Nearly all infants become attached.
- Attachments are formed to only a few persons.
- These "selective attachments" appear to be derived from social interactions with the attachment figures.
- They lead to specific organizational changes in an infant's behavior and brain function. (p. 68)

The attachment style at childhood can confer a degree of resiliency if secure or make the individual more susceptible to mental disorders. Insecure attachments do seem to create "a risk of psychological and social dysfunction" (Siegel, 1999, p. 84). Early attachment experiences are directly converted to neurobiological structure. Siegel (1999, p. 86) described this interaction as follows: "early life histories of absence of any attachment experience (as in severe neglect) or the experience of overwhelming trauma (as in physical, sexual, or emotional abuse) may markedly alter the neurobiological structure of the brain in ways that are difficult if not impossible to repair."

Basically one can divide people into two groups regarding attachment: those who have difficulty forming *trusting attachment* and those who have difficulty tolerating *intimacy and closeness*. The former group represents those who have major disturbance in their attachment system, usually the result of trauma, insufficient attachment, or disturbed attachment or of some neurobiological dysfunction. For example, a patient with autism has a severe dysfunction in his or her ability to form attachments, but evidence suggests that this is a genetic predisposition or prenatal insult. On the other side of the coin, someone who early in his or her life experiences extreme or chronic trauma may also develop a severe disruption of the attachment system, leading to severe difficulty forming attachments (see Table 4.1).

The second group comprises those who are capable of forming attachments but have conflict and anxiety over intimacy and closeness. Maintaining intimacy and closeness are one of the central functions of the relational system. Individuals in this group generally have formed attachments with significant early-life figures to build relational schemas that are positive but

TABLE 4.1
Severe Versus Milder Developmental Disruption

Severe Trauma or Neurobiological Insult	Minor Trauma or Relational Injuries
Issues with establishing basic trust Likely neurobiological change	Issues with intimacy and closeness No likelihood of neurobiological change or mild changes

may have endured a nonmetabolized injury or loss that is reactivated when intimacy becomes too intense.

The Vital Importance of Secure Attachment

The importance of secure attachment in the development of the personality system cannot be underestimated. Secure attachment in the absence of trauma, loss, or developmental derailment leads to an adaptive and resilient personality system. The research to support this contention is unequivocal. Mahoney (1991) wrote:

> Over all, the combination of laboratory findings, longitudinal, self-report studies suggest that, relative to their insecurely attached peers, children, adolescents, and adults who feel secure in their intimate relationships:
>
> 1. Exhibit earlier greater flexibility and resilience in their engagements with their worlds
> 2. Exhibit and experience themselves as more competent in a variety of realms
> 3. Are more likely to engage in exploratory behavior and to remain behaviorally organized in the face of novelty and stress
> 4. Are more sought out and popular among their peers
> 5. Report higher self-esteem
> 6. Are more capable of establishing and maintaining secure and satisfying relationships with others
> 7. Are less at risk of developing major psychological disorders
> 8. Are more likely to express their feelings directly, to seek comfort when they are distressed, and to offer comfort to their distressed companions. (p. 171)

Positive attachment is the basis of the development and structuralization of the intrapsychic personality system (Magnavita, 1997a) and the basis for the dyadic and triadic configurations covered in this chapter. Essential to the attachment system and what activates attachment in primates is the affect system. Evolutionary processes generate affective responses between infant–caregiver so that the human neonate can survive the extended period of development necessary for survival. I continue, then, with the affective component of the intrapsychic–biological triangle.

Affective System Components and Processes

The affect system emerges from neurobiological factors and temperamental variation and is fueled by the attachment system, shaping the earliest experience of the infant. Antonio Damasio (1999), a leading neuroscientist, has been interested in unraveling the complexities of consciousness. "Without exception," he wrote,

> men and women of all ages, of all cultures, of all levels of education, and of all walks of economic life have emotions, are mindful of the emotions of others, cultivate pastimes that manipulate their emotions, and govern their lives in no small part by the pursuit of one emotion, happiness, and the avoidance of unpleasant emotions. (Damasio, 1999, p. 35)

Although for heuristic purposes I discuss the components of the affective–cognition–defense matrix in separate sections, they are part and parcel of the same system (Mischel & Shoda, 1995). Affective responding is inextricably linked to both the defense system and the cognitive system. Lazarus (1991) commented on the value of a systems perspective:

> Some aspects of system theory are particularly well suited to the task of bringing the complex set of person-centered variables that affect emotion and adaptation together with the complex set of variables that comprise the environments in which persons must function, and it is especially useful for examining the cognitive processes of decision making on which human adaptive and maladaptive action is predicated. (p. 11)

The affective system entails the individual's capacity to tolerate, identify, process, and express emotion and is a part of one's emotional intelligence (Goleman, 1994). Key components include emotional regulation and dysregulation, which are vital processes that must be assessed and modified where necessary (see discussions on defensive and affective restructuring in chap. 7). Patients who have personality systems that tend to overregulate or overcontrol their emotional responses will exhibit one set of symptomatic reactions; and those whose systems are underregulated, will have a different type of response, as in borderline systems and those who exhibit traumatic disorders and are prone to dissociation.

The affective system in humans has been shaped over the course of evolution to the present state. Emotional responding is a necessary precursor for adaptation at a symbolic level necessary for the development of civilization and complex social processes. Emotional responses alert the organism to what is important to attend to in the environment. Without emotion to guide the neuropsychological apparatus, humans would be overwhelmed and unable to make meaning out of the plethora of incoming events that compete for attention. On the most basic level, the emotional system at the limbic-system level of organization informs us about potential danger in our environment; before the cerebral cortex is fully informed, it is capable of guiding the organism to a flight-or-fight response (Johnson, 2003). In particular, "The amygdala has been studied more than any other appraisal center and has been found to play a crucial part in the fight-or-flight response" (Siegel, 1999, p. 132).

> Because the fear response can play a direct role in life-and-death struggles, it is not surprising to find that the brain contains elaborate machinery dedicated to its routines. The fact that the amygdala's basic architecture reappears in so many species is testimony to its evolutionary importance: Natural selection generally doesn't tinker with components that have proved essential to basic survival. (Johnson, 2003, p. 39)

As Lazarus (1991) noted, "Emotions are normally interpersonal, whether in reference to a real person or imagined one" (p. 224).

When the human affective system is functioning well, it is a remarkable evolutionary advance over that of early primates. It allows for us to imbue life with the meaning and motivation to be creative, nurture others, develop society, advance science, express ourselves in the arts, and so on. When the system is malfunctioning, however, severe suffering often ensues, and dysfunction is likely. In affective systems that are overregulated, an individual often functions like the character Mr. Spock from *Star Trek*, or what is described in the clinical literature as the alexithymic: a person who seems unable to experience or label affect (Krystal, 1988). Krystal described the epigenesis of affect: "Every significant event, whether developmental, maturational, or incidental, creates an affective state, thereby simultaneously posing both a challenge to oneself and an opportunity for one emotion to be highlighted and raised to a new level of verbalization, desomatization, and differentiation" (p. 45).

Affect and the Case of Alexithymia

The study of alexithymic individuals presents us with an opportunity to understand the consequences of severe impairment in the emotional system and therefore is worth examining at greater depth. Krystal (1988) described the result of the affective disturbance:

> Alexithymic patients' impaired ability to utilize emotions as signals to themselves is based in the *form* that their emotional responses take. Their reactions are basically somatic, consisting of the "expressive," or physiological, aspects of affects, with minimal verbalization. In addition,

their emotions are often undifferentiated; they are vague and unspecific, as if they represented an undifferentiated form of common affect precursors, so that separate responses of such feelings as depression and anxiety do not seem to appear. Because of the concomitant diminution in the verbalization of affects, these patients experience somatic, often distressing reactions rather than complete emotions. Only when one experiences the cognitive aspect of an emotion—the meaning of the affect and some indication of the "story behind it"—and simultaneously has the expressive reaction and an adequate capacity for reflective self-awareness, can one observe that one is experiencing a "feeling" and identify it. Alexithymics often cannot tell whether they are sad, tired, hungry or ill. They are not accustomed to recognizing their feeling states and discovering their reaction to events in their lives. Sometimes they complain of the physiological aspects of affects, but they neither recognize nor can name a specific emotion or even such states as pain, thirst, or hunger. (p. 243)

Core Emotions and the Affect System

Fosha (2000b) emphasized the centrality of the affective system in personality development and change: "While personality is shaped by experiences with attachment figures over time, it is also shaped by intense emotional experiences of short duration (p. 19). Affective science has been a rapidly developing discipline crucial to understanding the personality system. According to Mayne and Ramsey (2001), "Emotion manifests across physiological, cognitive, behavioral, social and cultural systems; thus it is no surprise that specialists in each domain have constructed definitions, measures, and theories of function as they relate to that specific domain." They continued, "Perhaps one of the hottest current debates in the emotion field is whether there are discrete, basic, universal emotions, or whether emotions are best characterized as points within two-dimensional space" (p. 2). These authors suggested that emotions are best conceived of as operating in a nonlinear dynamic system and state: "emotions may be seen, literally, as the coupling of various organismic subsystems" (p. 18). Fosha (2000b) wrote as follows:

> Core affect, or more precisely, core affective experience, refers to our emotional responses when we do not try to mask, block, distort, or severely mute them. Defining aspects of the experience of core affect include: a subjective, personally elaborated experience; some change in bodily state; and the release of an adaptive tendency toward some expressive action. (p. 15)

Emotional differentiation emerges from the early attachment experiences. Fosha (2000b) noted that "feelings of relatedness and intimacy are relationally constructed phenomena with roots in the sharing of affects between infants and parents" (pp. 148–149).

Intrapsychic Anxiety and Channels

In the intrapsychic domain, anxiety triggers defensive reactions, and defensive reactions inhibit core emotional experience (Fosha, 2000b; Wachtel, 1993). Anxiety may be stimulated by intrapsychic conflict or interpersonal or ecological factors such as war or natural disaster. Anxiety has various ways in which it can be intrapsychically channeled, and each of us has a primary and secondary pathway. Some channel anxiety into the soma, and it becomes expressed in various somatic ways such as muscle tension or disturbances of the gastrointestinal tract (e.g., irritable bowel syndrome). Tension and migraine headaches are another common channel of anxiety. Others channel anxiety into psychological symptom complexes such as panic or depression. Yet another channel of anxiety is directly to the defensive zone, which manifests in rigid character patterns. Others may tend to channel anxiety to the cognitive–perceptual field and have disruption of thoughts or perceptual distortion.

Emotional Development, Empathy, and Intelligence

"The assumption that other people's emotional responses are like our own is the basis of empathy and as such is basic to all human intercourse" (Krystal, 1988, p. 242). Empathy is a key aspect of human discourse and, from an evolutionary psychological perspective, one that has probably developed to allow for the survival of our species. Without being able to put us in the proverbial "shoes of the other," the human experience would be much different. We can attest to this when we are confronted with the dysfunctional antisocial personality system either in individual or group composition. The foundation for empathy is in the unfolding of "emotional intelligence" (Goleman, 1994) based on sound attachments with primary caregivers. Aggression may also be considered a relational disconnection. According to Weinfield et al. (1999),

> Empathy is in many ways the complement or counterpoint to aggression. Whereas aggression often reflects alienation from others, empathy reflects an amplified connectedness, and whereas aggression reflects a breakdown or warping of dyadic regulation, empathy reflects heightened affective coordination. (p. 78)

Empathy unfolds over the course of time and secures self–other relationships, in which one experiences attunement with an attachment figure.

Izard (1994, p. 356) said that "Emotional development consists of the processes whereby the emotions system achieves an ever increasing complex matrix of functional links with other sub-systems of the individual—the physiological–drive, perceptual, cognitive, and action systems." The emotionally driven attachment system that develops may in fact provide the vital architecture of the mind (Greenspan, 1997b). As Greenspan noted,

> Our developmental observations suggest, however, that perhaps the most critical role for emotions is to create, organize, and orchestrate many of the mind's most important functions. In fact, intellect, academic abilities, sense of self, consciousness, and morality have common origins in our earliest and ongoing emotional experiences . . . the emotions are in fact the architects of a vast array of cognitive operations throughout the life span. Indeed, they make possible all creative thought. (p. 7)

Habitual emotional activation activates cognitive development, and thus the cognitive–affective matrix develops simultaneously. The unfolding emotional system gives rise to the defensive organization and structure. Greenspan (1997b) proposed that the activation of intellectual growth is inextricably linked to the affective stimulation in the maternal–infant dyad. In the next section, I explore the components and processes of the defensive system.

DEFENSIVE SYSTEM COMPONENTS AND PROCESSES

The pioneering work in the identification and cataloging of defenses was part of the Freudian heritage, with the use of the term *defence* first appearing in 1894 in a paper titled *The Neuro-Psychoses of Defence*, which was expanded by Anna Freud (1966), Wilhelm Reich (1933), and others. In a cogent article about the demise of depth therapy, Firestone (2002) wrote of the drawbacks to understanding core defensive operations: "Another major factor limiting the effectiveness of psychotherapy is the fact that its practitioners often have a misunderstanding of core defensive processes" (p. 228). The ability to understand core defensive process is essential in effective treatment. Firestone (2002) explained, "Essentially, by their responses, therapists are either supporting their clients' defenses and cutoff emotional states, or they are challenging their clients' defenses by helping them expose their self-attacks and express the accompanying feelings of anger, sadness, and grief" (p. 228). A catalogue of the patient's defensive system is another important element to attend to when formulating a holonic representation. "The clinician must be adept at systematically identifying and categorizing the array of defenses that the patient brings to therapy. This skill is vital to successful strategic psychotherapeutic planning and treatment" (Magnavita, 1997a, p. 107). Defensive operations occur at the intrapsychic, interpersonal, triadic, and sociocultural levels. At the intrapsychic level, defenses are generally used in the way Freud and his followers conceived them, modulating overwhelming or painful affects. They can also be used to maintain self-cohesion. Firestone (2002) described what I have often observed in supervising therapists in clinical practice and observing the clinical video-tapes of a wide array of therapies:

> Conventional therapies that attempt to restore clients to their premor-bid anxiety-free state by strengthening their defenses inadvertently do these clients a disservice. In trying to relieve their clients' pain and help them reestablish psychological equilibrium, proponents of these therapies are condemning their clients to a limited life experience. In this case, clients' defenses will continue to restrict them and interfere with their lives even though they may feel more comfortable. (p. 228)

All therapists, I believe, need to be trained in core defensive processes. This requires one to be familiar with defenses and be able to identify them. The best way to do this is to watch videotapes of any type of therapy and conduct careful *microprocessing* by stopping the tape and identifying defense processes. This is best done in a small supervisory or training group in which discussion of the process is encouraged. I have found this approach in introductory and advanced courses on psychotherapy, training seminars for experienced professionals, and intensive supervisory groups.

The Process of Mapping the Core Defenses

To obtain a catalogue of defenses, the clinician can both listen to descriptions of interpersonal interactions and note which are the preferred defenses of a patient. As the patient is describing a conflictual situation, the therapist essentially examines the interpersonal–behavioral sequence—*What did you say? How did you or he react? What happened then?*—and so forth until a crisp rendition of the incident has been portrayed. This line of direct questioning of the sequence of behavior and reactions has two functions: The first is to create a window in which to view the defensive functioning; the second is to intensify feelings by bringing the situation alive in the here and now. To track these processes, we can refer to the *interpersonal–dyadic triangle* (see Figure 1.1) and examine the current rela-tional patterns or future expected relations. For example, a patient is discuss-ing a conflict with his wife and reports feeling upset and storming out of the house after an explosive verbal tirade. We can identify that the patient has a tendency to use explosive *discharge of affect* (the verbal tirade) and *avoidance* (leaving the house to avoid further affective arousal and defensive responding). When he returns, he is sullen and verbally cutting. He is now demonstrating *withdrawal* and *sarcasm*. Conversely, one can also attain a fairly accurate description of the defensive constellation of significant attach-ment figures. By encouraging a patient to describe conflictual interpersonal interactions, one can begin to develop an accurate picture of this component of an individual's personality system. It is of utmost importance to encourage "incident specificity," which requires the patient to recall as many details of a particular conflictual event as possible (Magnavita, 1997a).

Another way in which to elaborate the patient's defensive constellation is to observe defensive responding in the therapeutic matrix. Specifically, this regards the interpersonal process with the therapist, which is the most useful and accurate way in which to catalogue defenses. This can be an accurate way to develop a picture of the defensive constellation because one is witnessing and participating in the here-and-now process with the patient.

Anxiety and affective regulation also play a major part in the dynamic processes that occur in this venue. Often sufficient anxiety needs to be mobilized within the therapeutic matrix to observe the defensive system in operation. A patient may behave in one manner during the therapy session and in quite another at home. In the natural ecological setting, defensive responding is usually triggered by interpersonal conflict, attachment disruptions, challenges to intimacy–closeness capacity, and other ecosystem stressors. The transactional pattern may include a feedback system by which defenses are stimulated by the other, in a dyadic process, and lead to rapid escalation and shifting to a more primitive constellation of defenses. It is critical to have a sound understanding of defenses. The following schema is one that includes defenses from a number of theoretical systems. Defenses can be classified hierarchically as psychotic, immature, neurotic, or mature (Meissner, 1981; Perry & Cooper, 1989; Vaillant, 1971, 1992). A list of the following defenses can be used as a basic template for conducting a comprehensive catalogue of the defense constellation.

Catalogue of Defensive Operations

Psychotic Defenses

> *Delusional projection.* The individual grossly distorts external reality and feels persecuted.
> *Denial (psychotic).* The individual denies external reality to a significant degree.
> *Distortion.* The individual reshapes reality to better match internal needs.

Immature (Primitive) Defenses

> *Projection.* A person's perceives his or her undesirable impulses and feelings as belonging to another. Although projection is ubiquitous, it is only pathological and overused when it is an unacknowledged perception.

Schizoid fantasy. This is an overindulgence in fantasy wherein the person retreats from conflict and seeks primary satisfaction and gratification in his or her fantasy preoccupation. The fantasy life is more gratifying than real life. Individuals with computer addictions often exhibit this defense.

Hypochondriasis. The individual is plagued by physical symptoms that result from unmet emotional needs and unacceptable impulses or feelings. The person is often highly distressed and seeks relief from various medical specialists, to no avail. Anxiety changes to physical experience and the individual often becomes hypervigilant in monitoring and misinterpreting these sensations.

Passive–aggressive behavior. The individual expresses unacceptable feelings of anger indirectly and through passive means. Anger is often expressed by forgetting, not cooperating, and moving slowly.

Acting out. The individual acts on unconscious feelings and conflict without their becoming conscious, so that they are never experienced. The person's capacity for mentation (putting experience into language) is often compromised.

Dissociation. The individual is dramatically disconnected from one's experience, which serves to mitigate emotional distress. In extreme cases the personality becomes compartmentalized with different ego states that are unaware of the others. The personality structure is like a honeycomb, with separate cells.

Blocking. The individual temporarily inhibits emotions, thoughts, or impulses.

Introjection. An individual internalizes the characteristic(s) of another in an attempt to establish closeness. Introjections can be negative, as with self-abuse, or they can be positive. The patient often responds with a phrase or statement that does not appear to be his or her own.

Regression. The individual returns to early, more primitive periods of development and behavior. Regression entails a loosening of more mature defenses and a slide into less mature ones. For example, some patients at the neurotic level of organization appear on occasion to throw temper tantrums similar to those of very young children.

Externalization. The individual exhibits a tendency to see the source of difficulty as residing in the external world and fails to see his or her influence in a behavior.

Splitting. The individual separates positive and negative qualities of the self. Things are viewed as all good or all bad; integration in not attained. There is usually oscillation between poles.

Projective identification. The individual projects unacceptable impulses onto another. The projection is often so intense that the person who is the target of the projection responds in a manner that befits the projection.

Devaluation. Negative qualities toward another person or oneself are exaggerated.

Idealization. The opposite of devaluation, the individual unrealistically exaggerates positive attributes of oneself or another.

Omnipotence. The individual acts as if he or she or others possess special powers or abilities that are not based on reality.

Withdrawal. The individual moves away or disengages from others and the external world as a means to avoid painful affects.

Explosiveness of affect. The individual releases pent-up anxiety and affect through explosive discharge. These are typically intense emotional catharses after which the person often feels relieved.

Weepiness. The individual becomes tearful, but there is no experience of the affect, as would occur if the individual were experiencing grief or sadness. Tears just flow as if the person is leaking and not crying as in true experience and expression of grief.

Depression. Many individuals use depression as a defense against feeling. Often, aggressive impulses are channeled into depression, but many other feelings are also defended in this way, particularly unmetabolized grief.

Sleep deprivation. Another defense that numbs many people is avoiding sleep.

Neurotic Defenses

Repression. The individual loses ideas and feelings from awareness in a seemingly unexplainable loss of memory. This defense also encompasses unacceptable thoughts and feelings that never reach conscious awareness.

Displacement. Feelings are shifted from one object to another, usually to one that holds less importance for the individual.

It is the tendency to take out our feelings on an inno-
cent party.

Reaction formation. The individual changes emotions and impulses
from unacceptable to acceptable by reversal. Someone who
is titillated by pornography might become a vocal crusader
against it.

Intellectualization. Intellectualization is an individual's separation
of ideas from his or her feelings by an abstract discussion
that keeps the feeling repressed. It is often seen in those who
overuse logic and rational thinking to explain away feelings.

Somatization. The individual converts psychic energy into bodily
symptoms and derivatives. Various vulnerable parts of the
body absorb the unacknowledged conflict or feeling.

Controlling. The individual excessively manages events or people
in the environment as a way to ward off anxiety.

Inhibition. The individual dampens or limits potential sources
of ego gratification, often for fear he or she will spin out
of control

Isolation. The individual splits affect from cognition and represses
or displaces either element. There often appears to be a
mechanical or wooden quality to the individual who uses
this defense excessively.

Rationalization. The individual justifies feelings, behaviors, or
thoughts that may be deemed unacceptable to the conscious ego.

Sexualization. The individual attributes sexual significance that
does not exist to people or objects or exaggerates this
significance.

Undoing. The individual negates thoughts, feelings, or actions of
oneself or another. The undoing often occurs as soon as the
uncomfortable thought or feeling comes to awareness.

Detachment. Detachment is comparable to dissociation but is
a less intense variation. The individual seems not to be
emotionally present. Such patients appear preoccupied and
emotionally distant or chronically distracted.

Avoidance. The individual circumvents or turns away from situations or feelings that are conflictual or anxiety provoking.

Compartmentalization. The individual is able to separate various
elements of his or her life without experiencing the conflict
that would inevitably result in their acknowledgment.

Complaining. Complaining is a rather insidious defense that serves
to siphon off anxiety and impede true action.

Mature Defenses

Altruism. This represents an unselfish interest in service to others. It provides substantial gratification to the individual with no compromise to the integrity of self, as would exist in codependent patterns.

Humor. The individual explores the capacity to express feelings without untoward effect on others through wit or sense of the ludicrous. Humor can also be a neurotic defense if it is used to protect oneself from genuine emotional expression.

Suppression. This reflects the individual's capacity to maintain an awareness of conflict without repressing the emotion, reacting to it, or becoming unduly anxious. It indicates a high tolerance for experiencing one's emotions without becoming symptomatic or using neurotic defenses.

Anticipation. The individual is able to plan for the future in a realistic fashion. He or she experiences emotional reactions in a limited fashion and exercises the ability to plan and problem solve.

Sublimation. The individual expresses instincts indirectly without a loss of pleasure and without negative consequences. (Magnavita, 1997a, pp. 110–114) The individual is able to use his or her potential fully in work and intimate relationships.

Reich's Character Defenses and Davanloo's Tactical Defenses

In addition to the categories of defenses just presented, Reich identified others that were subsequently expanded on and termed *tactical defenses* by Davanloo (1980). Reich and Davanloo seemed to refer to similar phenomena. Anna Freud (1966) noted how

> bodily attitudes such as stiffness and rigidity, personal peculiarities such as a fixed smile, contemptuous, ironical, and arrogant behavior—all these are residues of very vigorous defensive processes in the past, which have become dissociated from their original situations (conflicts with instincts or affects) that have developed into permanent character traits, "the armor-plating of character." (p. 33)

These are usually ancillary defenses but can, as Anna Freud reminded us, become ego-syntonic. They can be further divided into the following three categories, but this list is in not comprehensive (Magnavita, 1997a):

Interpersonal defenses. These include smiling, sarcasm, argumentativeness, negativity, compliance, submission, blaming, poor eye contact, criticizing, defiance, stubbornness, seductiveness, complaining, provocation, teasing, and distancing. Such defenses serve to put distance between the patient and therapist or significant other, as well as between the patient and his or her feelings. Some of these can become chronic character defenses with certain patients, for example, as with a histrionic patient who relies on seductiveness as a method of influencing others' responses.

Cognitive defenses. These include rumination, tentativeness, vagueness, retraction, generalization, ambivalence, and equivocation. These defenses can also be major character defenses, such as with patients who experience major ambivalence that results in difficulty making and following through on decisions in all aspects of life.

Anxiety-siphoning defenses. These include chewing gum, cursing, fidgetiness, pacing, smoking, eating and drinking, and rocking. These defenses seem to directly reduce anxiety by acting as a siphon (Magnavita, 1997a, pp. 114–115).

Ego-syntonic versus ego-dystonic. Another useful construct has to do with whether defenses are ego-syntonic versus ego-dystonic. *Ego-syntonic* personality systems are ones in which the defensive responding of the individual is virtually outside the awareness of that individual. These are the patients that Reich (1933) focused on in his classic book *Character Analysis*. He discovered that the verbalizations of these individuals made little contribution to the communication. Instead, he found that more was communicated through the body and nonverbal channels of communication. Reich's work still stands as an enormous contribution in understanding and treating these patients. *Ego-dystonic* personality systems, on the other hand, experience anxiety and have some notion about how the psychological system is related to the symptom constellation. In a subsequent discussion on methods of restructuring (chap. 7), I discuss how defensive restructuring is often an optimal approach for those with ego-syntonic personality systems and other forms more applicable to ego-dystonic personality systems.

Characteristics of Defensive Systems

We must recognize some of the properties of the defensive system to work effectively with them. The manner in which defenses are expressed intrapsychically and interpersonally provide significant information that should not be overlooked. Gabbard (2001) reminded us that even though defenses are considered intrapsychic, they are expressed and observed interpersonally: "Particularly in the realm of personality disorders, defenses are most usefully conceptualized as embedded in relatedness" (p. 368). Summarizing the findings, we can make some useful generalizations about the way they operate:

1. Defensive systems are not static but are constantly changing and shifting, even though there are limitations based on the unique capacities of a patient. On a moment-to-moment basis, we continually call forth one defense or another, but generally an array of them that is unique to us.
2. The fewer the defenses that an individual system uses, the more rigid and brittle that system tends to be.
3. The more an individual is identified with his or her defenses (believes that they are part of the self), the more unaware that person usually is of the impact on his or her functioning and on relationships with others.
4. The higher the degree of individuation, the more mature the defensive system and conversely the lower level of individuation the more primitive the defenses.
5. Defensive systems shift under stress, sometimes to higher level defenses, but generally, and especially under prolonged stress, to lower levels of defensive operation. This is termed *regression*, and can be a destabilization of the intrapsychotic, dyadic, and triadic matrices.
6. Each individual's defensive system is unique, although it might share some basic array of defenses with others who have similar personality systems.
7. Most personality systems can be destabilized either by outside events or therapeutic experiences. A system may oscillate between rigidity and chaos, and, if managed effectively, a higher level of organization may result.
8. Personality systems that use primarily primitive defenses are extremely sensitive to destabilization and usually do not reorganize at higher levels of functioning.
9. Some primitive defenses, such as dissociation, are so powerful that even systems that appear relatively stable can create a reverberation of defenses, leading to a rapid downward spiral of the individual. As the defenses are activated, increased anxiety-feeling creates multiple feedback loops, whereby the system increasingly relies on primitive defenses and reactions. As the anxiety increases, panic over the dissolution of the self

and disengagement from the other increases in a cascading downward trend.

10. Empirical support suggests that the commonly held clinical observation that defensive operations develop along developmental lines is likely valid (Cramer, 1987). What is appropriate for a child is often maladaptive for an adolescent or young adult and signifies a developmental pathway has not been successfully navigated.

11. Defense systems cannot be explained away, although awareness is the key in modifying a poorly adapted system. They are only enhanced by successive exercise of the emotional and attachment system.

12. Interpersonal feedback loops often reinforce defenses that are no longer adaptive.

Gabbard (2001) described the way in which defenses operate to contain affect in the person with obsessive–compulsive personality disorder:

> Powerful affective states are highly threatening to the individual with obsessive–compulsive personality disorder, so these defenses tone down affects and emphasize cognition instead. Hence the defensive repertoire unfolds in the psychoanalytic situation as careful avoidance of any strong feeling in the patient accompanied by behaviors designed to control the analyst's affective state. Patients with obsessive–compulsive personality disorder may talk about a wide variety of subjects with considerable insight and psychological awareness while also displaying a flattened affect and monotonous vocal intonation. (p. 368)

For example, the defense constellation of a prototypical obsessive–compulsive individual usually includes repression, displacement, intellectualization, controlling, isolation (of affect), detachment, inhibition, and when stressed, explosiveness of affect.

COGNITIVE SYSTEM COMPONENTS AND PROCESSES

The cognitive system is another major, interactive domain of the intrapsychic system. "The relationship between emotion and memory suggests that emotionally arousing experiences are more readily recalled later on" (Siegel, 1999, p. 48). The way in which we process and store information, based on our neurophysiology, and interpersonal experience shape our core beliefs and schematic representation of both self and other. Learning is enhanced and laid down in the neuronal networks with the help of emotion. "In other words, emotion involves a modulatory process that enhances the creation of new synaptic connections via increases in neuronal plasticity" (Siegel, 1999, p. 48).

Schema

The construct of schema was based on the work of Bartlett (1932). Hunt (1993) commented on this important discovery:

> Bartlett's idea has been revived and elaborated in recent years. Schemas—also known as "frames" and "scripts"—are now thought of as packages of integrated information on various topics, retained in memory, on which we rely to interpret the allusive and fragmentary information that ordinary conversation—and even most narrative writing—consists of. (pp. 530–531)

Different types of schemas serve various functions and are not limited to cognition. These include:

> *Cognitive schemas* "are concerned with abstraction, interpretation, and recall."
> *Affective schemas* "are responsible for the generation of feelings."
> *Motivational schemas* "deal with wishes and desires."
> *Instrumental schema* "prepare for action."
> *Control schemas* "are involved in self-monitoring and inhibiting or directing action." (Beck & Freeman, 1990, p. 33)

Schema are templates in which information about past experience is stored and used to guide future responses. Beliefs about oneself often are not noticed until another points them out. Thus, one of the essential systems for maintaining dysfunctional patterns of behavior associated with affective modulation problems is the interrelation among cognition, affect, and self-representation. Experience is interpreted on the basis of one's schematic representation, and these interpretations can trigger positive or negative affective responses that reinforce the schema. An individual who, for example, was told that she was "stupid" much of her life dropped out of high school and never applied herself. When tested during a psychiatric hospitalization, she attained an 80 on her standardized IQ test and admitted that she answered so that she would prove what the internalized voice believed. Later when she returned to school and attained her GED and then started to excel in college, she would become triggered (her internal voice would say, "You are too stupid to succeed") when she did well, which often occurred. The internalized beliefs about her lack of intellectual ability were not confirmed, creating an intrapsychic crisis. She was caught in a maelstrom of conflicting emotions and beliefs concerning her core identity. Extensive cognitive restructuring of her belief system needed to be achieved to allow her to build a new, healthier, and more accurate schema based on a realistic self-appraisal.

ESSENTIAL COMPONENTS AND PROCESSES OF THE INTERPERSONAL–DYADIC SYSTEM

The dyadic system may be one of the key organizers of the structure and developmental process of the brain. Siegel (1999) also supported one of the basic assumptions of this volume: "Understanding the behavior of complex systems can provide insights into the sometimes automatic ways in which relationships with others seem to evolve" (p. 223). As I have noted, the early relational configuration, the hallmark of which is attachment experiences, is essential to the development of the personality system and sets the parameters for later relationships.

The Dyad as the Primary Attachment System and the Matrix for the Emergent Self

Who we are and how we become who we are emerge from the attachment experiences that have been presented in the previous section. The process of development presented in the following chapter begins with the primary caregiver–infant dyad. When optimal, this dyadic configuration creates the necessary field for the development of trust (Erikson, 1950) and begins to shape the schematic representations. These schemas are carried as internal guides or maps to be applied to future relationships. These relationships are represented in the upper right hand corner of the *interpersonal–dyadic triangle* as current relationships (see Figure 1.1).

Current Relationships

These interpersonal processes are observed when we have the opportunity to witness two individuals in a relationship who are communicating as one might in couples therapy. We can also sample the interpersonal system when an individual describes a relational interaction.

Expected Relations

Most therapists also traditionally observe and participate in the "expected (or transference) relationships" corner of the interpersonal–dyadic triangle (see Figure 1.1) when we experience and perceive how a patient relates to us. This includes the interpersonal forces that impinge on the therapist, creating reactions and counterreactions in the interpersonal field.

The expected relation, traditionally termed *transference*, is basically the activation of schematic representations in the interpersonal process between patient and therapist.

Past Relations

We can conceptualize the past-relationships corner of the *interpersonal–dyadic triangle* (see Figure 1.1) as the primary origin of dysfunctional schematic representations. These relational schemas may not be directly accessible and may only be brought to awareness by examining the patterns in the current and expected corners of the triangle.

Interpersonal Components and Processes

Interpersonal processes occur in the dyad and triad and are internalized in the intrapsychic system as schematic representations or object relations. These internal or intrapsychic structures, which include the component attachment systems, attachment, relational and cognitive schema, and defensive functions, presented earlier in this chapter, are expressed in various forms in current and future relationships. Glickauf-Hughes and Wells (2002) summarized key features and relations between the intrapsychic and dyadic triangles:

1. Personality and psychopathology are influenced by relationships with significant others during critical stages of social and emotional development.
2. Hypothetical psychic structures (e.g., the self, the ego, the superego) that perform critical mental functions (e.g., reality testing, the ability to self-observe, the capacity to have concern for the well-being of others) normally develop in relationships with others during these periods.
3. One's early formative relationships are affected by one's innate temperament as well as character style and current life status (e.g., health, marital satisfaction) of one's childhood caretakers.
4. One's early interpersonal experiences are internalized and become organized into a mental template of relationships (i.e., an image of oneself interacting with an image of an object–other) that determines one's perceptions of and behavior with others.
5. Psychopathology is a function of inaccurate and maladaptive mental templates.

6. One's mental template can be changed in psychotherapy through interpretations leading to insight about oneself and one's relationships, along with a corresponding corrective interpersonal experience. (p. 287)

From Primary Attachment to Intimacy and Closeness— The Driving Force in the Dyadic System

The ability to form relationships lies in the earliest experiences with attachment. As the capacity for positive attachment is sparked by secure and responsive caregivers, the capacity for developing intimate and close relationships as an adult becomes possible. One of the assumptions of this model is that humans are social beings and that healthy functioning requires interpersonal connections. To recapitulate: Attachment theory posits that humans have an innate tendency to seek and maintain relationships. Attachments lead to the formation and expression of intense human emotions, which strengthen and renew these bonds. Furthermore, these attachments serve as a major source of human survival and security in relations with caretakers when young (Magnavita, 2002a). Positive experience with intimacy and closeness facilitate emotional responding, the presence of which provides some degree of inoculation against stress and mental dysfunction (Magnavita, 2002a).

Dyadic Anxiety as Expressed in the Interpersonal–Dyadic Triangle

Dyadic anxiety emerges from interpersonal conflict and is greater at lower levels of differentiation. Movement toward intimacy and closeness can stimulate dyadic anxiety. When a couple first meet, intimacy and closeness are very high as they enjoy the natural merger that occurs in the initial stage of a relationship. Later, however, as the couple becomes more attached to one another, there may be a movement away from this level of intimacy, which may begin to become too anxiety provoking because it begins to stimulate unresolved attachment and intimacy–closeness issues that have not been adequately resolved.

Social Roles and the Personality System

Dyadic relationships are influenced by the roles that individuals adopt or are ascribed, such as mother, father, child, sibling, student, or teacher. Roles within the family, workplace, community, and friendships are the major point of focus (Klerman et al., 1984). "These relationships between the individual and others, the self and others, have a structure, and this structure is provided by the position of the individual within the social system—most precisely by the specific roles the individual plays" (p. 48).

Interpersonal–Dyadic Themes and Processes

Murray (1938) was an pioneer in the examination of dyadic processes. He suggested that dyadic configurations require a transmitter who needs to inform and a receptor who needs the information, out of curiosity or interest. Other interpersonal theorists have elaborated many subsequent conceptions about the key components, elements, and themes of dyadic processes (Hinde, 1979; Kelley, Berscheid, Christensen, Harvey, & Huston, 1983; Kiesler, 1996; Swensen, 1973; Wilmot, 1987). Other types of dyadic themes include reciprocity, cooperation, competition, and opposition. Leary (1957) developed the interpersonal circle, or circumplex, to account for interpersonal interaction. Benjamin (2003) identified three primary interpersonal processes that she termed *copy process*: (a) identification—be like him or her; (b) recapitulation—act as if he or she is still there and in control; (c) introjection—treat yourself as he or she treated you. She (Benjamin, 1993) used five predictive principles to determine what may have happened before or after an interpersonal event:

1. *Complementarity*. In a dyadic unit, each participant in the interaction is matched in terms of interdependence and affiliation. For example, on the affiliation dimension, if the *Other attacks and Self recoils*; or, another possibility, *Other shows love and Self shows reactive love*. Along the interdependence dimension, if the *Other emancipates and Self separates* or *Other controls and Self submits* (Benjamin, 1996).
2. *Introjection:* Individuals treat themselves as they have been previously treated by significant figures.
3. *Similarity*. A person acts like or copies another through a desire to identify with that person.
4. *Opposition:* A person desires the opposite interpersonal pattern that another is exhibiting, for example, seeking affirmation from someone who is blaming.
5. *Antithesis:* The individual feels pulled to engage in interpersonal behavior that is opposite to how one's dyadic partner is, or was, treated by other(s), for example, wanting to protect someone who is neglected.

Working in the interpersonal–dyadic triangle, the goal is to bring interpersonal patterns to awareness and assist in the reshaping of these patterns to more functional ones.

ESSENTIAL COMPONENTS AND PROCESSES OF
THE RELATIONAL–TRIADIC SYSTEM

Triadic processes are depicted in the *triadic–relational configuration* (see Figure 1.1, p. 16) and occur when the dyad is overwhelmed with anxiety that cannot be managed. Anxiety will then be absorbed by a third party and used to stabilize the dyad. Triadic processes can occur in any situation where there are $N + 2$ groups.

Triadic Components and Processes

Triadic processes are constantly in operation in all relationships but are more likely to occur in unstable social systems. We can witness triangular processes in childhood relationships, a twosome forms, a third party becomes friendly with one or another, and the triangle shifts. Managing triangular relationships are a normal part of development. However, when triangular configurations become fixed, they may become an impediment to development. Rigid or fixed triangular relationships require energy that keeps the corners locked in and unable to shift adaptively to other configurations. Processes of growth, individuation, and integration are thwarted. In extreme cases, there may be a denial of normal developmental processes and an attempt to hang on to modes of interaction from earlier stages of development by all members of a relational triangle. Family systems may become emotionally stuck and be unable to navigate important successfully transitions, such as childhood to adolescence and adolescence to early adulthood.

Triadic Anxiety

Triadic anxiety has its roots in a system that is threatened externally or internally. The flow of anxiety can occur along vertical or horizontal directions (Bowen, 1978). *Vertical anxiety* involves generations of unresolved feelings that accumulate, and great energy is required to maintain these at a submerged level. This repression primarily occurs through emotional triangulating (Hoffman, 1981; McGoldrick & Gerson, 1985). These dynamics often create chronic anxiety and tension that is defended against by characteristic defenses in a perpetual feedback loop. *Horizontal anxiety* results from current external stressors such as coping with forces from the sociocultural–familial triangle that are impacting the family.

Attachment, Differentiation, and Autonomy

Triadic processes are highly contingent on the level of development that has been achieved by members of dyads. If both members of a dyad are relatively undifferentiated, the likelihood of forming triangles is more likely. As I discuss in later chapters, the lower the level of differentiation, the greater the tendency toward "fusion" with another (Bowen, 1976). This may be a normal experience when falling in love, during the initial stages of which most people experience this type of merger with the loved one. The attachment system provides the basic foundation for later interpersonal processes. If attachment figures are undifferentiated, it makes the process of differentiation more complex, which is discussed in greater detail in the following chapter on developmental progression of the personality system.

The emotional currents within triangles are continually in motion, even in periods of calm. When there is relative calm, the favored position is the dyad, where "togetherness" is preserved. In periods of stress, however, the favored position is outside the dyad. If tensions are very high within a family, the system may seek to involve an individual from outside the family (Magnavita, 2000a).

Family Processes and Mechanisms

There are important family processes and mechanisms that operate within the relational system and shape the nuclear family system and transmit information across generations. The process includes channels of communication, both conscious and those out of awareness, that exert pressure on the roles and behavior of its members. Also included are role expectations, family projections, and styles and modes of communication.

Nuclear Family Emotional System

This refers to the way in which a nuclear family functions on an emotional level within one generation. Basic relationship patterns may replicate the past and be transmitted from one generation to another. The functioning of the emotional system within the nuclear family is the basis on which intimacy and closeness is regulated and enjoyed. Low levels of emotional differentiation in family members may result in higher levels of enmeshment or disengagement. Higher levels of differentiation enhance capacity for intimacy and closeness and effective communication.

Family Projection Process

"The process through which parental undifferentiation impairs one or more children operates within the father–mother–child triangle" (Bowen, 1976, p. 81). By this mechanism undifferentiation is projected to other family members. Some of this is absorbed into the marriage or as a sickness in the spouse, which will reduce the amount projected onto the child. Bowen (1976) described the multiple processes:

> The children selected for the family projection process are those conceived and born during stress in the mother's life; the first child, the oldest son or oldest daughter, and only child of either sex, one who is emotionally special to the mother, or one the mother believes to be special to the father. Among common special children are only children, and oldest child, a single child of one sex among several of the opposite sex, or a child with some defect. Also important are the special children who were fretful, colicky, rigid, and nonresponsive to the mother from the beginning. A good percentage of mothers have a basic preference for boys or girls, depending upon their orientation in the family of origin. It is impossible for mothers to have equal emotional investment in any two children, no matter how much they try to protest equality for all. (pp. 82–83)

Emotional Cutoff

Some unresolved emotional attachments with parents are handled by cutting off the parents. In these cases, the normal process of healthy separation is foreshortened by emotionally or physically distancing, or staying in physical proximity but being "allergic" to intimacy and closeness (Bowen, 1976, p. 84). Emotional cutoffs are equivalent to the level of emotional differentiation; in other words, an individual who cuts off his or her family in an attempt to start over is carrying the unresolved process to the next generation through the family projection process.

Multigenerational Transmission Process

The family projection process occurs throughout successive generations, often with increasingly fewer levels of emotional differentiation from one generation to the next. In healthy families, the level of differentiation is reasonably consistent throughout generations. Those children who are in triangulated positions generally do less well than siblings who tend to function at the same level of differentiation as their parents.

The Family System—Dyadic and Triadic Processes

The family is the primary system for the development of humans. Within the family system are essential processes and features that determine the way in which relationships are established and maintained. These processes include nonverbal and verbal communication patterns, quality of attachment subsystems, and stability—these represent the functionality of a family structure and multigenerational processes whereby relational templates are transferred from one to another.

ESSENTIAL COMPONENTS AND PROCESSES OF THE SOCIOCULTURAL–FAMILIAL TRIANGLE

The sociocultural–familial triangle includes the *individual personality system* (intrapsychic–biological triangle processes and components), interpersonal–dyadic and relational–triadic processes and components as they are organized in the *family* and *community* and shaped by the *social* and *cultural systems* and *institutions*. An individual's personality is shaped and expressed through a process of mutual influence, each domain influencing the other, in multidirectional feedback loops. Angyal (1941) stated that

> The integration of the individual into the social group, the assimilation of its culture, of its written and unwritten codes, are just as essential for the personality development and personality organization as any of the physiological functions. Thus it appears that personality is a larger unit than a mere individual organism, because it also includes those factors through which it functions as a participant in the superindividual units of society and culture. (p. 170)

The interrelationships among these systems are crucial and expressed in this configuration. Glass and Mackey (1988) described the importance of the interrelations of these component systems: "Human systems do not exist in isolation. Rather, they have multiple interactions among themselves as well as with the external and internal environment" (p. 10). The degree of complexity is such that no simple explanation of these phenomena will ever suffice. It seems more efficacious to view this triangle using nonlinear models, such as that offered by chaos theory. These complex systems are self-organizing. The essential elements and processes interact to organize the system in a certain form, which is continually reorganized and reshaped as it evolves. The expression of dysfunction may vary with changing historical circumstances. We have seen, for example, hysteria in Freud's time, fugue states in France in the 1900s, and computer addiction in the 20th century. Chaos theory suggests that at each level of triangular representation, the elements of the intrapsychic–biological triangle will be reproduced in similar fractal patterns.

Component Systems and Processes

In the following section, we discuss the component systems and processes of the sociocultural family triangle. As we do so, we continue to widen our perspective and examine the larger system-structure in which the previous levels are embedded.

Cultural and Social Factors

Personality systems are embedded in cultural contexts that shape and are themselves shaped in a continual complex feedback loop. Dominant cultural forces and subcultural forces shape individual and family processes as well. Shotter (1994), a proponent of sociogenesis, described this interrelated system:

> Thus, in relational terms, what we have here is a unity in which its phases and aspects are not related to each other as separable, existentially identifiable component parts, but are related only as sensibly distinct and distinguishable aspects of the same flowing totality. Each loci is a region of structurizing activity (an agency?), within which a diffuse, dynamic unity is continually, creatively sustained by the (disorderly) exchanges at its boundaries, exchanges between it and the other activities surrounding it, which depend in their turn upon dynamic exchanges at greater and lesser levels, and so on. (Shotter, 1994, p. 87)

Cultural ideals about beauty, success, and values are transmitted through mass media and societal forces. Family systems are continually responding to and assimilating or rejecting these cultural images and expectations. The pervasiveness of eating disorders is an example of the complex interaction among cultural influences that idealize thinness and the affluence of our society to create an epidemic of eating disorders. Multifactorial in nature, family influences and the roles and expectations of children and parents are also in operation. Technological advances can further compound the problem. Access to the Internet now allows those with eating disorders to join others to reinforce their eating disorders.

Cultural influences are also central to shaping of dysfunctional systems that are evident throughout the world and often manifest in mistreatment and subjugation of minorities, women, and children. A frightening example of this is in the emergence of a new epidemic of slavery throughout the world. Bales (2002) described the complexity of slavery: "The psychology of the slave is mirrored by that of the slaveholder. Slavery is not a simple matter of one person holding another by force; it is an insidious mutual dependence that is remarkably difficult for the slaveholder as well as slave to break out of" (p. 97). Thus, we are witnessing is a dysfunctional dyadic system cultivated by powerful cultural influences.

Economic and Political Systems

The influence of economic and political systems on individuals and families is enormous. Poverty, economic downturns, and other factors can have a substantial impact on family stability and functioning. This has been demonstrated by various economic and political events of the previous century and currently in the unfolding new world order that arrived with the end of the Cold War. The increasing disparity between the affluent and the poor in the United States is a major social dysfunction; 35 million Americans live in a state of poverty (Shipler, 2004). The relationship among economic forces and personality systems was well illustrated by the Great Depression and, more recently, by the impact of corruption and unethical business practices among corporate executives in U.S. businesses.

Sociocultural–Familial Triangle Anxiety

The sociocultural–familial triangle component systems can be the source of substantial levels of anxiety. This is obvious to anyone who has struggled during financial downturns to maintain their family system and intrapsychic equilibrium. We all know the stories of the stockbrokers and shareholders who jumped out of windows when they learned of their financial ruin. There is no escape from the anxiety of existence.

THE TOTAL ECOLOGICAL SYSTEM

The total ecological system incorporates the four triangles presented here that examine the phenomena of the human personality system at all levels of analysis. Jones and Lindblad-Goldberg (2002) noted that "an ecological approach involves giving attention to the total field of a problem, including extended family, friends, other professionals, community agencies and institutions" (p. 3). A unified model requires that all the processes within the total ecological system are understood in their dynamical processes and interconnections. As Shore (2003b) acknowledged,

> A central tenet of dynamic systems theory holds that at particular moments, a flow of energy allows components of a self-organizing system to become interconnected, and in this manner organismic form is constructed in developmental processes. As the patterns of relations among the components of a self-organizing system become increasingly interconnected and well ordered, it is more capable of maintaining a coherence of organization in relation to variation in the environment. (p. 266)

Thus, we must move flexibly from microsystem to the mesosystem. "When we try to connect a social system to a psychological one, such as the emotion process in individual persons, we have the problem of translating a macro level analysis (that is, the social system) to a micro level (the mind of the individual person)" (Lazarus, 1991, p. 353). The following chapter reviews the developmental progression of a unified model.

SUMMARY AND CONCLUSIONS

This chapter presents an overview of the component domains and systems of personality and their interrelationships at various levels of abstraction. These component systems and processes must be understood to achieve a holonic map and to enable clinicians to develop an accurate assessment that will allow us to select the most efficacious treatment strategy at the various levels of organization.

5

THE DEVELOPMENTAL PROGRESSION: FROM INFANCY TO ADULTHOOD

The personality system is fluid and in continual evolution from the time of conception. Human existence entails growth, evolution, and change. There is no component of the total ecological system that does not evolve and reconfigure over time. Some would even suggest that the powerful forces that shape us and our social systems are in operation before conception when the family system begins the process of projection, imagining the child, exploring names, and beginning the emotional attachment based on one's wishes and hopes. This chapter is concerned with the perpetual unfolding of the developmental progression and reorganization of the personality system as various life-cycle transitions are navigated, as we move from conception to maturity to decline. To assess and intervene effectively when systems require "intentional" or therapeutic reorganization or restructuring, one needs to understand the developmental progression from infancy to adulthood. A unified model is well suited for understanding dysfunction and maladaptation because it emphasizes the interrelationships among developmental process, pathological organismic expression or bionegativity, and "personality systemics" based on understanding of complex human biopsychosocial systems. Here I introduce two new theoretical terms, *personality systemics* and *developmental personology* (Magnavita, 2004a).

PERSONALITY SYSTEMICS

Personality systems are central organizing matrices along with their mechanisms and processes, which account for important aspects of development and human functioning and adaptation. *Personality systemics* emphasizes the study of personality systems in their various forms and associated processes (Magnavita, 2004a). These include the interrelated domains that are reviewed in previous chapters. Human beings are enormously complex and cannot be reduced to single domain systems or units of observation, without a concomitant loss of understanding. Personality systemics eschews overly reductionistic views, preferring to understand basic processes and organizing principles and accepting the irreducibility of human existence. Personality systemics encourages social scientists to place personality at the center of clinical and psychological science or *unified clinical science* (Magnavita, 2004c). Personality systemics relies on complexity theory as a guiding principle for trying to capture personality organization, developmental progression, and function–dysfunction and bionegativity. Erikson (1968) described central aspects of this view: (a) each item of the vital personality to be discussed is systematically related to all others, and they all depend on the proper development in the proper sequence of each item; and (b) each item exists in some form before its decisive and critical time normally arrives (pp. 94–95).

DEVELOPMENTAL PERSONOLOGY

The field of psychopathology traditionally attempts to isolate and study "discrete" mental disorders by investigating the relevance and validity of various diagnostic and psychopathological conditions. This way of approaching dysfunction runs the risk of being overly fragmenting and reductionistic and often has little clinical relevance for practitioners. When this model of "discrete" disorder is followed, treatment becomes a case of diagnosis, labeling, and application of a packaged treatment. Labeling has inherent problems, as if a particular label such as "alcoholic," "borderline," "narcissist," or any other term can define the individual (Dass, 1991). Cummings et al., (2000) described the fundamental assumption of a similar approach to developmental psychopathology:

> Another fundamental principle of the developmental psychopathology approach is holism. The principle of holism posits that interdependency among parts exists in any system. Thus, development cannot be understood by dissecting the system into a series of parts because each component gains critical meaning and purpose from the other pars. *Synthesis*

is the rule in holism; that is, parts must be examined in the fragment of the whole. (p. 28)

Oftentimes, both pharmacological and psychological treatment interventions are delivered in a symptom-based approach, which ignores the holistic interrelationships among domains. The disorder becomes the guiding force in conceptualizing and organizing treatment, not the person and their systems. A new view is to look at psychopathological adaptations or bionegativity and dysfunctional systems through a developmental framework using personality systemics as the theoretical guide. The fundamental engine of human personality development is interpersonal or *relational experience* (Siegel, 1999; Shore, 2003a, 2003b). This is not to discount other (e.g., instinctual) forces, but even these arise in the relational matrix. The force of the human attachment system is one that seeks connections with others, and when this is not satisfied, the results may be catastrophic, as in failure-to-thrive syndrome in infants, in which they ostensibly die as a result of emotional starvation.

THE DEVELOPMENTAL PROGRESSION

The family develops through a progression of stages, and at each transition point there is opportunity for reorganization and restructuring that allows adaptation to the next stage of development. Individual and family development unfolds in a close oscillating dance of assimilation and accommodation. In the next section of this chapter, various aspects of this progression are identified and discussed.

The Familial Container and Organizer of the Personality System

The family system is the container for various aspects of the personality system, so it makes sense to approach the developmental process through this relational lens with a focus on the family. Cummings et al. (2000) described the importance for the researcher, but also for the clinician, of maintaining a view of the whole system:

Components of any whole that is studied are themselves wholes. For example, while parent–child attachment is a component of the "whole" of the family system, it is also a whole that warrants study in itself. This hierarchical, nested structure of part–whole relations can be further extended in both directions toward the more specific (e.g., components of attachment such as appraisals of parents and emotional reactivity) and more general (e.g., family system as part nested in the larger whole of the community or neighborhood). Since an element itself is a whole, floating holism asserts that the elements and the whole may both be appropriate areas of inquiry depending on the goals of the researcher. (p. 30)

The importance of the family system is a cross-cultural phenomenon. Personality organization and structure, psychopathology, and psychotherapy cannot be fully understood without a sound theoretical foundation in this family matrix. The individual personality system evolves as one proceeds through the developmental progression from birth and infancy to old age and death. As the individual personality system unfolds and is shaped within the powerful force field or attractor states within the family, the importance of the family takes on less of a basic survival role, both psychologically and physically, and moves toward more of a symbolic one. This is not meant to suggest that the valence the family exerts is less powerful but that it often shifts to an internal symbolic level, the influence of which may continue in both functional and dysfunctional ways. The development of language and symbolic encoding allows the experiences to be maintained in the cognitive perceptual system of the individual, dyad, family, and society. Intrapsychically, these codes are maintained through schematic representations or *engrams* (endurable mark or trace) that shape and guide behavioral response patterns and relational expectancies. These codes are also expressed in repetitive maladaptive behaviors, reenacted dyadically and triadically, and expressed in larger institutional and social processes, in outbreaks of social pathologies such as racism, slavery, child abuse, poverty, and subjugation of women. These are cross-cultural phenomena, and these larger symptomatic outbreaks are frequent occurrences in contemporary society. The family system, with its complex relations and life cycles, becomes codified in relational and cognitive–affective templates or schemata (as presented in chap. 4 and further explored in this and later chapters). The engrams, then, are embedded in and can be expressed at various process levels of the dynamic triangular configurations that we have explored. We may even portray these as fractals or attractor states, which hold the fundamental codes that must be decoded and converted to narrative. The developmental pathway moves in a series of coordinated steps from attachment–relational experience toward internalization through assimilation, and codification in intrapsychic and relational structure and process. Lyons-Ruth and Zeanah (1993) espoused a similar model to the unified model presented in this volume, one that embraces complexity:

> It cannot be emphasized enough that focusing on dyadic interaction alone provides only one dimension of the family context of infant development and infant mental health. As Emde (1991) has pointed out, there are increasing levels of interdependent influences within families that are far more complex than our theories or our empirical efforts to date are able to accommodate. Although many advocate

moving to a systemic level to consider family context, even this bypasses a myriad of individual, dyadic, and triadic influences on development within a family. Given that our knowledge base about any of these levels is limited, continued exploration of each of them is warranted. (p. 14)

The Infant–Caretaker Personality System

"The biological birth of the human infant and the psychological birth of the individual are not coincident in time. The former is a dramatic, observable, and well-circumscribed event; the later a slowly unfolding intra-psychic process" (Mahler, Pine, & Bergman, 1975, p. 3). As we have re-viewed, most clinical theorists agree that the personality system is anchored in the maternal (primary caretaker)–infant dyad from which psychological organization begins to emerge and take form. This process was initiated by previous generations, in their attachment experiences and parenting styles, and continues in an unfolding of generational processes that exert a powerful influence on human development. Positive dyadic configurations tend to spawn a healthy personality system, and those that are insufficient engender bionegativity and maladaptation. Pine (1985, p. 192) called the dynamic interaction between infant and maternal figure *core-relatedness*, which en-compasses the affective attunement between the two. This emotional matrix is critical to understand. According to Fonagy and Target (2002), Anna Freud (1965) was a major contributor to theory that linked emotional development to psychopathology "and made the powerful suggestion that equilibrium between developmental processes was a key aspect of normal development" (p. 106). Margaret Mahler and her associates (Mahler, 1968; Mahler et al., 1975) studied the development of children during the first 3 years of life.

Key Developmental Processes—Separation and Individuation

Two key developmental processes are the increasing differentiation from the maternal dyad and establishment of a separate identity. Mahler et al., 1975) described this dual developmental process of separation and individuation as follows:

One is the track of individuation, the evolution of intrapsychic auton-omy, perception, memory, cognition, reality testing; the other is the intrapsychic development track of separation that runs along differentia-tion, distancing, boundary formation, and disengagement from mother. All of these structuralization processes will eventually culminate in internalized self-representations, as distinct from internal object repre-sentations. (p. 63)

Mahler depicted the progression as a three-stage unfolding. Benedict and Hastings (2002) modified this schema by changing the first stage from autism. They suggested the following:

- *Presymbiosis* (autism). Occurs over the first month of life.
- *Normal symbiosis*. Dual unity between infant–caregiver dyad (2–4 months)
- *Separation–individuation*. Mahler identifies four subphases: (1) *Differentiation* (4–11 months) during which the infant shifts from inner to outer-directedness; (2) *Practicing* (11–17 months), when the infant moves out of the symbiotic dyad but returns for "refueling"; (3) *rapprochement* (18–24 months), when the infant struggles between need for the protection of closeness and experiences states of vulnerability; and (4) *object constancy*, during which the infant tolerates increasing separateness, maintaining both good and bad aspects of the attachment figure.

As the infant, with his or her unique neurobiological, temperamental, and attachment system interacts, the personality system becomes increasingly more differentiated and organized. Mahler et al. (1975) described the systemic shift in the developing personality system as follows:

> Metapsychologically, the focus of the *dynamic* point of view—the conflict between impulse and defense—is far less important in the earliest months of life than it will come to be later on, when structuralization of the personality will render intra- and intersystemic conflicts of paramount importance. Tension, traumatic anxiety, biological hunger, ego apparatus, and homeostasis are near-biological concepts that are relevant in the earliest months and are the precursors, *respectively*, of anxiety with psychic content, signal anxiety, oral or other drives, ego functions, and internal regulatory mechanisms (defense and character traits). The *adaptive* point of view is most relevant in early infancy—the infant being born into the very crest of the adaptational demands upon him. (p. 5)

Major disruptions or trauma, especially early in the child's experience, can have dire consequences, in extreme cases fragmenting or destabilizing the fledgling system. At some point, the child's personality becomes organized in a maladaptive manner that may be refractory to change and moreover continue a positive feedback cycle whereby the child gravitates toward and becomes increasingly reinforced in his or her style of adaptation and personality organization. We are all familiar with examples of these systems, such as batterer–abuse victim or master–slave, that are difficult to reshape.

Sameroff's System Codes

The primary and extended family system carry and transmit multiple codes. Society carries and transmits memes, and these converge in multiple operations that will be discussed as we proceed. As Sameroff (1993) noted, "The experience of the developing child is partially determined by the beliefs, values, and personality of the parents; partially by the family's interaction patterns and transgenerational history; and partially by the socialization beliefs, controls, and supports of the culture" (p. 10). He proposed that "developmental regulations at each of these levels are carried within codes that direct cognitive and social–emotional development, so that the child will ultimately be able to fill a role defined by society" (p. 10). He suggested the following codes—cultural, family, and individual:

- *Cultural code.* This is the societal established child-rearing system, which includes socialization and educational practices. The cultural code is the interaction of processes in the sociocultural–familial triangle, which regulates "the fit between individuals and social system" (p. 10).
- *Family code.* This includes the dynamic family processes that socialize the individual within the family constellation. This is achieved through rituals, role attributions, shared myths, and stories.
- *Individual code.* Individuals also have influence on the family system in which they function. Sameroff (1993) stated, "there is also no doubt that each individual brings his or her own contribution to family interactions" (p. 11). The individual code is embedded in the intrapsychic–biological triangle in the schematic representations based on that person's unique developmental process and family experience.

These codes capture some of the ways in which the individual, familial, and cultural systems interact, each element shaping, regulating, and altering each other. As should be clear by now, the dynamical processes among the four triangles are not bidirectional but multidirectional.

Individual Differences in Infants

Individual differences are observable in infants. Anyone who has more than one child has observed this and is often astounded by the variations. Brody and Siegel (1992) described the early aspects of these differences as follows:

Fine individual differences may be seen among normal infants in the first weeks and months of life. They appear most readily in the tempo and force of an infant's physical movements and in the degree of satisfaction he has in feeding and sleeping. They appear in the degree of his freedom to show spontaneous and responsive facial expressions that reflect his passing affective states. Usually the most significant individual differences among infants have to do with the breadth and intensity of their beginning cathexes of people and of things in their near environment, and the pleasure sought in passive and active behaviors. (p. 453)

Individual differences are often evident before birth, when the mother can feel differences in the activity level and rhythms that the developing fetus expresses. Even during this phase, the maternal–infant and paternal–infant attachment is stimulated.

Dysfunctional Infant–Parent Personality Systems

We understand the importance of the primary dyadic relationship in the formation of the personality system. "Parental psychopathology has long been recognized as a contributor to the poor developmental status of children" (Sameroff, 1993, p. 11). Winnicott's oft-quoted statement "there is no such thing as a baby" but only a maternal–infant dyad is an apt one (Rayner, 1991, p. 60). Because the infant–parent or caretaker dyad is so influential, disturbances in this subsystem can have dire consequences to the emergent personality system of the infant. Infants who are born to and left in the care of severely dysfunctional attachment figures are likely to experience disastrous effects without mitigating attachments or intervention. We are all aware of these systems in clinical practice or from viewing the evening news. Sameroff and Chandler (1975) used a "transactional model" in which "the development of the child is seen as a product of a continuous dynamic interaction between the child and the experience provided by his or her family and social context" (Sameroff, 1993, p. 6).

THE CHILD PERSONALITY SYSTEM

The question of whether childhood personality disorders exist is controversial, with proponents on both sides. Many theorists believe that diagnosing personality disorder in a child is premature and does a disservice. Others believe there is compelling evidence that these disorders do exist and that not to diagnosis a personality disorder does a disservice because appropriate intervention is then not available (Kernberg, Weiner, & Bardenstein, 2000).

At what point is the child's personality system no longer tied to the family system? There is no clear empirical evidence to answer this question. Clinical and developmental observations indicate that as development proceeds, the family system becomes less of an influence because the personality organization and adaptation of the child takes hold. As most clinical scientists understand, however, these experiences are codified and carried in some form, often being recreated. The family system, although greatly overlooked in 20th-century psychopathology, is central to understanding how development proceeds and dysfunction occurs. What is fairly clear is that there are multiple pathways to the same personality organization and symptom formation. For example, a conduct disorder may be heavily biologically influenced when a child has a high level of aggressiveness, but this may be ameliorated in a family that provides adequate structure and socially approved outlets, such as athletics. In a family where the goodness of fit is not as beneficial, the aggressiveness may take hold and be amplified. A recent example is of the father who killed another player's father in an escalating, highly aggressive disagreement, witnessed by both men's sons. (Of course, the sociocultural matrix here is significant as well and will be discussed later in this chapter.)

The question of personality disorder versus no disorder is interesting, but one that can be better handled if we use the conceptualization of a personality system. This might be unacceptable for researchers, which is understandable because they need to quantify what they measure; for clinical practice and theoretical development, however, the vital question is how we understand, conceptualize, and shape the ecosystem of children to maximize the health of the "individual" personality system.

In one of the few volumes on personality disorders in children, Kernberg et al. (2000; see also Bleiberg, 2001) described the following components of the child's personality system:

- *Temperament*—a biologically based disposition that influences the child's interaction with his world by affecting both the nature and style of the child's approach and the reactivity of others.
- *Identity*—an internal mental construction that involves the child's developing sense of self-sameness across time and situation.
- *Gender*—a fundamental dimension, itself a component of a developing identity, that defines individuals across cultures and embodies certain behavioral expectations; a dimension in which the type and frequency of psychopathology varies.
- *Neuropsychological development disorders*—deficits in cognitive and ego functioning that include neuropsychological processes

and affect how the child may process, organize, and recall information.

- *Affect*—the child's emotional reactions and internal, mental "glue" that links self- and other-representations.
- *Defense mechanisms*—the child's characteristic mode of coping with and adapting to internal and external stress and, as such, an important element in the diagnosis and treatment of personality disorders. (pp. 15–16)[1]

The Centrality of the Family System

As has been stated, a major assumption of a unified approach to psychotherapy is that the family is central to personality, psychopathology, and psychotherapy. This view is increasingly supported from other related areas such as relational science and developmental psychopathology. In their excellent volume on developmental psychopathology, Cummings et al. (2000) offered their view on the importance of family influences:

> The complexity of interrelationships among family subsystems, genetic inheritance, and broader social contexts and ecologies makes the study of causal relations in children's normal development and in the development of psychopathology as a function of family factors particularly challenging. This field is especially likely to benefit from the developmental psychopathology approach, which provides a sophisticated framework for unraveling causal processes in development. Although family systems approaches are prevalent, they rarely consider relations between family processes and child development in the context of developmental time. Furthermore, systematic accounts of family functioning in the developmental psychopathology literature are typically limited to relatively narrow substantive areas (e.g., divorce, child maltreatment). These considerations also reflect the need at this time for a more integrative approach to understanding children's development in families. (p. 8)

Developmental psychopathology offers an exciting new approach to the often-stagnant model of psychopathology that most clinicians rely on for diagnosis and classification. "Developmental psychopathology is not a narrow specialty area, but, rather, is a broadly conceptualized approach to

---

[1] It should be noted that Kernberg et al. (2000) also referred to the personality using the term "organization" as opposed to "structure" in "several incarnations" that take the form of "neurotic, borderline, and psychotic personality organizations" (p. 49). Their approach, which is strongly anchored in object relations theory, also emphasizes, as this volume does, the cataloging of defenses in children to make a comprehensive assessment.

understanding the complexities of human development" (Cummings et al., 2000, p. 17). This new discipline offers a utilitarian framework with which to understand the developmental trajectories of those we treat, to offer more insight and awareness about how to mend the inevitable disruptions that occur in life, disruptions that are more prominent in those experiencing emotional disorder. As discussed previously, the classic medical model that views emotional disorder as a "static" disease that requires diagnosis is often too simplistic for the clinician. Instead, the developmental approach to psychopathology "emphasizes multifactorial causation and the importance of identifying the dynamic processes that underlie disturbance" (Cummings et al., 2000, p. 18).

Theoretically, a child with a high degree of biological vulnerability to hyperactivity, showing signs, for example, of temperamental difficulties, will become more or less susceptible to further developmental disturbance, depending on the quality of dyadic attachment in the early phase of development. On the basis of his studies of infants, Stern (1985) suggested there are few cases that provide evidence of pathology in infants: "When there are deviations, it is the relationship with the caregivers and not the infant that appears deviant" (p. 186).

If the attachment is poor, then vulnerability is increased; if the attachment is strong, resiliency is enhanced. This matrix gives rise to the personality system, which is further shaped by the type of family system and ecological system in which the individual functions (see Figure 5.1). As one can see, the number of permutations are enormous, which accounts for the infinite variability in personality while allowing for similarities of the component systems. If the developmental pathway is toward the right side of the figure (i.e., positive sociocultural matrix, low biological vulnerability, good attachment, healthy psychological organization and functional family system), then we can predict overall resiliency and stability of the personality system. Conversely, as component domains congregate toward the left, the likelihood for psychopathology and maladaptation increase. Resiliency can result from any part of the domain system on the right side of the figure. One can have a biological–temperamental hardiness, a mitigating relationship that is positive with, for example, a coach, teacher, clergy person, member of the extended family, or one can have the good fortune to be raised in a positive sociocultural setting that offers escape and support.

The Organization and Structure of the Family System

It is clear that the organization and structure of the family system exerts a powerful influence on the personality development of children. We can examine some of the basic features of the family.

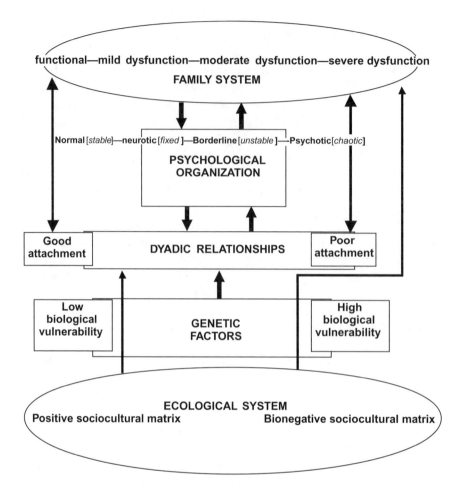

Figure 5.1. The interrelationship among various component systems that shape personality. Personality system dysfunction increases as you move from the left to the right side.

Stable–Unstable

Family systems can be characterized along a continuum from stable to unstable. Stable families tend to have functional and adaptive processes over time. Unstable ones are characterized by punctuated disequilibria, which continually engender anxiety among its members.

Organized–Disorganized

We can also place families on a continuum from organized to disorganized. Organized families have well-established processes that allow for maximal adaptation. Family communication is effective, and hierarchy is apparent. Disorganized systems are more prone to chaotic reactions and covert and changing processes that create a sense of insecurity.

Constricted–Flexible

We may also arrange families on a continuum from flexible to constricted. Flexible families have strong, functioning defense and coping systems that enable the system to readjust as developmental demands require. Constricted families, at the other end of the spectrum, have less adequate coping and defensive systems and are emotionally more constrained.

The family's organization and structure will clearly be reflected in the child's unfolding personality system. Attachment systems, family functioning, and temperamental variation interact and influence the way in which the personality system is expressed and how it will become consolidated as the child enters into one of the most challenging and ultimately defining periods of development: adolescence.

THE ADOLESCENT PERSONALITY SYSTEM

The adolescent personality system undergoes a remarkable and often stormy reconfiguration as the individual navigates the period from prepubescence to adolescence. Sometimes the level of dysfunction of the adolescent personality requires active intervention (Bleiberg, 2001; Kernberg et al., 2000). Although there may be a number of character traits observable in the child, Blos (1985) proposed that "character as an integrated system of behavior shares with the ego ideal the time of its structuralization, which is adolescence" (p. 160). There are a number of critical systemic shifts and structural changes that occur in both the individual personality system of the adolescent and in the nuclear and extended family system in which they belong.

Identity Consolidation

During the course of adolescent development, remarkable physical, psychological, and social changes occur. To cope with the physical and sexual–hormonal changes that the early adolescent undergoes, early attachments that are secure and have sufficiently met the child's unfolding needs are vital. During this period, earlier developmental complexes are aroused as the individual searches for his or her identity configuration. Issues related to trust, intimacy–closeness, separateness and autonomy, and emotional regulation are intensified as the individual attempts to form identification patterns. Identity consolidation requires the individual to develop a cohesive and ideal self. Important aspects of this process include establishing sexual orientation and future goals and beginning to define the type of career path one will take.

The Pull Away From the Family and Toward the Peer Group

The adolescent process of separation and individuation is fueled in part by the development of a sexual–hormonal/psychological process that encourages a shift from the parental–familial subsystem to the peer group. This phase of renewed separation–individuation can tax family systems, especially because of the adolescent's oscillation between earlier childhood modes of attachment and emergent attachment patterns. The adolescent often moves rapidly between needs for dependency on parental subsystems and needs for autonomy; this can be quite confusing and disorganize or threaten stability in some families. There are clinical examples in which this process is stunted, described as a *developmentally delayed dysfunctional personologic system* (see chap. 6). In these systems, individuals often struggle with the adolescent issues of separation–individuation into their 20s, 30s, or even later in life. There are cases of children who never leave home, marry, or establish independent lives but remain home until their aging parents die.

Patterns of Chronic Substance Abuse

Substance use is an all-too-common problem in adolescent development that can have a profound effect on the personality system. Often psychoactive substances such as alcohol, marijuana, amphetamines, or cocaine are adopted as a way of offsetting the emotional *sturm und drang* of adolescence. Emotional development usually becomes fixated when a pattern of chronic substance abuse takes hold. The emotional challenges of identity consolidation become muted when substances are relied on as an escape. Often adolescents who become addicted enter into a phase of severe self-destructiveness in which their developmental process is severely derailed. Bright and gifted students may drop out of school or take menial jobs, frustrating their families. Chronic substance abuse causes a disruption in drive and motivation and creates a pattern of low tolerance for frustration and the expectation of immediate gratification. Systemically, substances become an attractor state for all levels of the system. In cases of addiction, which have become epidemic in the United States, almost every level of the personality system converges to the pull of the substance, which reconfigures the total ecological system. If allowed to continue, adolescents find themselves lost and despairing in early adulthood as they realize the developmental lag they experience in comparison to more successful peers.

Inappropriate Sexual Stimulation and Precocious Sexuality

Another unfortunate problem is the easy access to inappropriate and overly stimulating sexual material available to children and adolescents. When exposed to these materials, the affect system of the child or adolescent is unprepared and may become easily addicted, developing perverse expectations about sexuality that become consolidated with repeated exposure. Levant (1997) suggested that these and other social factors have created a generation of young men for whom "nonrelational sexuality is normative" (p. 23).

Inappropriate Exposure to Aggression and Violence

Yet another unfortunate social pathology is the exposure of children to images of violence and aggression commonly displayed on television and now in violent computer games to which children and adolescents have free access. This can be another factor that has a major impact on social development and personality system formation.

The Exacerbation of Family Dysfunction, Divorce, Remarriage, and Coming Out

Family dysfunction is often exacerbated during the adolescent phase of development. There are multiple causes of this phenomenon. The stress of adolescent development can take a toll, and a marginally functioning system can potentially destabilize. Issues that have lain dormant in the adolescent's parents can surface in powerful forms. It is not uncommon in clinical practice to witness an increased divorce rate among empty-nesters who are unable to redefine their relationship without children. Parents who have suppressed or ignored difficulties are often experiencing their own midlife or existential crises at about the time their children enter adolescence. It is also more common to see blended families in contemporary clinical practice that have very complex triangular configurations and dynamics. Also, another increasingly common phenomenon is that of a parent "coming out" by announcing that his or her sexual orientation is not heterosexual.

The Family Life Cycle

Along with the level of function versus dysfunction in a family are the inevitable life-cycle stages that must be navigated. Although often positive, they are periods of increased destabilization for most systems as family members try to accommodate, adjust, and assimilate new levels of organization and structure. The progression of the family through successive stages is elucidated by Carter and McGoldrick (1980), who described six stages:

1. The launching of the single young adult.
2. The joining of families through marriage.
3. Families with young children.
4. Families with adolescents.
5. Launching children and moving on.
6. Families in later life. (p. 17)

Regardless of a family's configuration, these stages are aspects of most families, from traditional to unconventional. Crises often occur and systems may become destabilized when navigating these and other transitions (Gerson, 1995, p. 99).

Separation and Divorce

Because separation and divorce is such a common occurrence in Western society, this transition must also be added to those of Carter and McGoldrick (1980). Separation and divorce can create powerful aftereffects for adolescents who are beginning to explore relationships and identity and to examine their notions about marriage and commitment.

Parenting Style and Approaches

Another factor that has shown to be of significant importance in the developmental model is the parenting capacity and style of primary caregivers. The style of parenting is often related to the experiences a parent had with his or her own parents. Parental control strategies can alter the relational matrix in a positive or negative direction. It is obvious that abuse and neglect have a negative impact, but there is also a cascade of systemic reverberations that occur with negative parenting styles. According to Cummings et al. (2000),

> Direct commands, threats, and physical force used by power-assertive parents engender frustration, hostility, and tension, and work against empathy as a precursor of prosocial behavior and interpersonal compassion. Motivated by fear for their well-being, children may temporarily and overtly comply with threats. However, they may have difficulty accepting and internalizing the moral message and accepting it as their own values. The arousal and fear for their own well-being may disrupt their cognitive attempts to understand the consequences of the transgression. (p. 167)

In summarizing the literature, Cummings et al. (2000) presented the work of Baumrind (1967, 1971), who developed a classification of various styles of parenting, and the fourth was added by Maccoby and Martin (1983): (a) authoritative, (b) authoritarian, (c) permissive, and (d) indifferent–uninvolved. Parenting styles are, to a certain degree, preordained by cultural influences, but they are also shaped by a parent's experience and the modeling of his or her own parents. Parenting practices and styles are not generally fixed throughout development and should change with the increasing autonomy and shifting emotional–psychological needs as the child proceeds through various developmental stages (Cummings et al., 2000).

Differentiation and the Orthogenetic Principle

Werner's (1948) orthogenetic principle is important in understanding personologic development. Development "proceeds from a state of relative globality and lack of differentiation to a state of increasing differentiation, articulation, and hierarchic integration" (Werner, 1957, p. 126). Development becomes increasingly complex, with each successive stage being based on the process and structure of the previous ones. The concept of differentiation is one that has been used by many theorists in psychology. Bowen (1976) believed that the concept of differentiation was essential to understanding personality systems at all levels. He developed a model that includes two primary types of differentiation crucial to development: emotional differentiation and self-differentiation.

Emotional Differentiation

Emotional differentiation refers to the increasingly complex differentiation of emotional responses that form the affective matrix of the individual personality system. Emotional differentiation includes the capacity to experience emotions in their subtle forms and being able to withstand the force to act on these or project them onto others. It also entails the capacity to label and express emotion in a modulated fashion to establish intimacy and closeness with significant attachments.

Self-Differentiation

Self-differentiation refers to the capacity to remain separate in relationships with others, without losing one's sense of self, as in fusion–enmeshment, or unnecessarily distancing oneself from another because intimacy is too threatening. This requires a consolidated and mature personality system that does not rely on projection in relations with others. Emotional and self-differentiation are integral processes that are artifacts of the separation-individuation process. If basic processes that impel the individual toward autonomous functioning are blocked, the individual will not proceed to more mature modes of development. This has dire consequences because individuals with lower levels of differentiation have greater difficulty building the more complex self-structures that are essential for intimate and mature adult relationships.

The Ecological System

One of the basic assumptions of this volume is that the power and influence of the ecological setting in which the individual and family is embedded is critical to include in any formulation or conceptualization. Ram Dass (1991) spoke of "dysfunctional cosmology" evident in the political and social pathologies evident of our time, such as the increasing disparity between the "haves and the have-nots" and the historical marginalization of African Americans. Cummings et al. (2000) described the contextual approach endorsed in this volume as follows:

> contexualism regards development as embedded in series of nested, interconnected wholes or networks of activity at multiple levels of analysis, including the intraindividual subsystem (e.g., interlay between specific dimensions within a domain such as affect or cognition), the interpersonal (e.g., family or peer relationship quality), and ecological or sociocultural system (e.g., community, subculture, culture). Thus, development regulates and is regulated by multiple factors, events, and processes at several levels that unfold over time. (p. 24)

Further, Pawl and St. John (2002) wrote as follows:

> Children's likelihood of survival and every aspect of their experience are shaped by the quality of the social structures in which they live. These include the nature of their family, their immediate culture and community, and their society's health, and educational, legal, and political systems. Children's well-being, importance, and value rest on the attitudes expressed through these very complex systems. (p. 81)

One of the assumptions of this book is that labeling of such "entities'" as personality disorders, anxiety disorders, and so forth is often irrelevant and lacks a deeper appreciation for the system. Cummings et al. (2000) supported this view:

> Labeling or categorizing abnormal behavior is not the same as explaining how or why maladaptation occurs; that is, maladaptation, when it occurs, evolves over time and prior adaptation interacts with current situations in predicting current functioning. Moreover, "disorder" does not necessarily lie within an individual but may in some instances be due to

social contexts, at least in part (e.g., families, communities, or society as a whole may be "dysfunctional"); that is, what is viewed as "disorder" may be due to the interaction between the individual and the environment (Jensen & Hoagwood, 1997), and may in some respects actually reflect the successful adaptation of individuals to difficult circumstances (Wakefield, 1997). (p. 20)

Sociocultural and Ethnic Influences on Families and Parenting

Sociocultural and ethnic influences exert an important influence on family functioning and parenting. Lyons-Ruth and Zeanah (1993) described this influence as follows: "despite intense family efforts, family structures and values are often eroded in impoverished communities by unemployment, high infant and adult mortality rates, health hazards associated with job conditions and poverty, and alternative adolescent value systems born of hopelessness" (p. 15). When conditions are more conducive to development, a resiliency process can mitigate other negative conditions:

> Conversely, in affluent communities, children may experience a variety of conditions that buffer the impact of family problems, including other adult role models available through friends and their families, schools that maintain access to productive jobs, after-school programs with good adult supervision, safe neighborhoods in which lack of effective family supervision is less hazardous, and peer cultures that promote hopefulness and motivation. (p. 15)

A good example of the influence of the ecological matrix and the multiple systemic outcomes is evident in the study of the style of parenting and the psychosocial adjustment of children.

THE ADULT PERSONALITY SYSTEM

The adult personality system is not static but proceeds through developmental and life changes until death. An enormous amount of literature has accrued over the last quarter of century elaborating the findings about adult developmental processes (Colarusso & Nemiroff, 1981; Levinson, Darrow, Klein, Levinson, & McKee, 1978; Nemiroff & Colarusso, 1990; Vaillant, 1977). The success with which the individual has navigated early stages will determine to a large extent the adaptive capacity of the adult personality system. The genetic psychorelational codes continue to exert an influence in all aspects of the life cycle and within the various triangular configurations. The adult personality system is embedded in the relational matrices in which it operates. Therefore, aspects of the system and the way in which it operates can be observed in the various relational and interpersonal matrices in which it is expressed.

Capacity for Intimacy and Closeness

A vital aspect of the adult personality system is the individual's capacity for intimacy and closeness that, in optimal developmental progression, allows for the establishment and maintenance of close relationships. If conditions have not been optimal, issues with intimacy and closeness will be expressed in most dimensions of the relational field. If severe attachment disruptions or incompatibility in the early primary relationships are evident, there will be evidence of severe disorders of the self-system and difficulties establishing basic trust in others.

Integrity of the Defensive System

Another feature of the adult personality system that can be viewed in relational expression is the integrity of the defensive system. Individuals who have navigated their developmental transitions with relative success and have not experienced nonmetabolized traumatic insults will have developed increasingly mature and adaptive defenses. For example, O'Leary (1999) found that dyadic aggression is associated with abusers who characteristically experience personality dysfunction. Summarizing the literature, he wrote, "Hamberger and Hastings (1986) found that batterers had three major types of profiles: narcissistic–antisocial, schizoidal–borderline, and dependent–compulsive. Only about 12% of the men had no discernable psychopathology" (p. 410). Poorly developed individual defensive functioning in the individual places great strain on the dyadic relationship and impairs positive intimacy and attachment.

THE COUPLE PERSONALITY SYSTEM

Because most individuals establish significant, long-term relationships, the couple dyadic configuration becomes an important aspect of the adult personality system (Johnson, 1999; Johnson & Greenberg, 1995; Wallerstein, 1994, 1996). Ackerman (1958) emphasized the importance of relational dynamics and catalogued the following relational diagnoses: (a) disturbances of marital pairs, (b) disturbances of parental pairs, (c) disturbances of childhood, (d) disturbances of adolescence, and (e) psychosomatic illness and family disturbance. He offered an early conceptualization emphasizing the importance of relational aspects of couple and family dynamics. "The special problems of marital and parental pairs can best be understood in terms of the mutuality and interdependence of the respective family role adaptations, the complementarity of sexual behavior, the reciprocity of emotional and social companionship, the sharing of authority and the division of labor" (p. 148).

The emotional system has tremendous influence in the functioning of the dyad. Johnson and Whiffen (1999) noted that

> Emotion is primary in organizing attachment behaviors and how self and other are experienced in an intimate relationship. Emotion guides and gives meaning to perception, motivates and cues behavior, and when expressed, communicates to others. It is a powerful link between intrapsychic and social realities. (p. 367)

The couple personality system has its own unique configuration and must be taken into consideration whenever assessing the function of an individual personality system. Synder (1999) endorsed a similar "pluralistic" approach to understanding and working with couples:

> Of particular importance are previous relationship injuries resulting in sustained interpersonal vulnerabilities and related defensive strategies interfering with emotional intimacy, many of which operate beyond the partners' conscious awareness. Consequently, interpretation of maladaptive relationship patterns evolving from developmental processes comprises an essential component of an informed pluralistic approach to couple therapy. (p. 352)

Flexible couple systems are often generative and capable of advancing the development of each member of the couple. When couple systems are maladaptive, a more nefarious process may operate that can create a process of multiple projections and have a tendency to bring out the worst in each other.

THE FAMILY PERSONALITY SYSTEM

The joining of family systems through marriage and committed relationships, as well as the beginning of a new family, add another dimension to the personality system. One cannot be understood outside of his or her family dynamics and process. We exist within these systems and both influence and are shaped by the processes. The choices that are made in the course of family life have great impact on developmental processes (e.g., to marry or not marry; to have or not have children; to engage one's "in-law" family; to have or not have contact with one's extended family) and on both the individual and dyadic personality system. These choices also influence the unfolding of one's personality system by creating complex relationships that can mature or cause regression.

THE UNFOLDING CORE GENETIC CODE

The core genetic code is the nodule of experiences that form and consolidate aspects of the cognitive–affective matrix and are expressed in relational patterns and symptomatic expression. It is important to underscore that the core genetic code does not refer to the biological substrate as it does in biology, although a portion of it is expressed in the genes. The genetic code in a sense is the convergence of domains or the "attractor states." It is evident or coded in language, reenactments, patterns, fractals, hot spots, core affect repetitive maladaptive patterns, cultural pathologies, and so forth. Within each of the four triangular matrices exists the core genetic code for personality. When examining and conceptualizing complex systems, chaos or complexity theory suggests that within each substrate there exists a basic structure and organization that is elemental. The core genetic code unfolds as the process of assessment and psychotherapy proceeds. This core genetic code is expressed in various forms in the patient narrative of his or her unique developmental experience and history. Psychotherapists learn to read the genetic code book of patient systems and establish the central aspect of their system. Stern (1985) suggested that the process of establishing the code is best when it is most open and flexible:

> No longer prescribed by theory, it poses a mystery and a challenge, and the therapist is freer to roam with the patient across the ages and through the domains of senses of the self, to discover where the reconstructive action will be most intense, unimpeded by too limiting theoretical prescriptions. . . .The fact is that most experienced clinicians keep their developmental theories well in the background during active practice. They search with the patient through his or her remembered history to find the potent life-experience that provides the key therapeutic metaphor for understanding and changing the patient's life. This experience can be called the narrative point of origin of pathology, regardless of when it occurred in actual developmental time. Once the metaphor has been found, the therapy proceeds forward and backward in time from that point of origin (p. 257).

The genetic code is the narrative that unfolds in the therapeutic process with special emphasis on nodal points in development and experience. These nodal points are often experiences that have in some way been traumatic, resulting in sufficient affective arousal to cause a defensive reorganization or developmental derailment. I return to this essential aspect of psychotherapy in the following chapter but underscore here that the core genetic code is established in the pattern recognition that occurs in the therapeutic matrix.

SUMMARY AND CONCLUSIONS

This chapter reviews the developmental progression that occurs as the personality system becomes more differentiated and complex, as transitions are navigated, and as challenges are met. The personality system is embedded in matrices of interrelated domain systems that begin with one's earliest attachment experiences. To develop a holonic representation of the personality system, the essential component systems must be identified and how they unfold in increasingly complex form over time must be assessed. The basic building block of the personality system is the early attachment configuration of maternal–child dyad. This dyad exists or is nested in triadic, family, and societal structures and processes that influence myriad aspects, such as parenting styles, family models of functioning, and roles and early genetic codes.

6

PERSONALITY SYSTEMICS ASSESSMENT: CLASSIFICATION, TYPOLOGIES, AND PROCESS

Personality systemics emphasizes an approach to assessment that attempts to depict accurately the interactions of the component domains and systems and to capture the chaos of complex nonlinear systems as they reconfigure, move through chaos, and self-organize. The intent of this chapter is not to review specific assessment measures, which would be far beyond the scope of this volume. Rather, the goal is to describe a conceptual framework with which to organize one's clinical assessment.

Assessment should never be construed as a "shotgun" approach in which every instrument and technique possible is used in the hope of capturing the phenomenon. A theoretical model that allows one to use instruments and clinical assessment procedures *selectively* to refine one's holonic understanding should drive assessment.

The assessment of the personality system is an essential phase in the early stage of the treatment process but continues to be an ongoing focus of clinical attention. We can never perfectly map the complex systems in which humans are embedded and that shape us. Each attempt can only get incrementally closer to holonic mapping, and, frustrating as it is, this is all we can hope for. Nonetheless, informed assessment using a unified model is more efficacious in this endeavor.

ASSESSING THE PERSONALITY SYSTEM

In the following sections of this chapter, we examine the important assumptions of assessing the personality system using a unified personality-guided relational approach. A brief review of the nature of anxiety and how it is expressed through various pathways using the four triangular matrices is presented.

Microsystem, Macrosystem, Mesosystem, and Total Ecological System Processes

Using the components from the biopsychosocial model as our guide and orienting our formulations using the four triangles described in previous chapters, we can effectively achieve an assessment of the component domains of the personality system, from the microscopic to the ecological. We can then draw from various assessment methodologies, selecting the most useful to broaden or deepen out understanding as they are indicated. Assessing the personality system is an attempt to conceptualize the dynamic processes of the various component systems of personality in a way that enhances our understanding of the individual or larger system with which we are working. There are certain assumptions and philosophical differences between this unified model and a more static model of diagnosing and labeling that has become predominant in clinical psychology and psychiatry. This model emphasizes a relational diagnostic approach first emerging in the early 1950s and posing a challenge to the predominant psychoanalytic model. This is not to suggest that the intrapsychic or other levels of process are not crucial but underscores the central organizing system of personality in the relational matrix. Necessarily, this complicates treatment by expanding the range of options. Some therapists refuse to combine multiple relational configurations for fear of boundary violations and the increased complexity of managing multiple relationships. Early on, Ackerman (1958) began to question the taboo of treating and evaluating family members together. He wrote as follows:

> The task of therapy cannot be simplified by the magic device of avoiding contact with other family members. Life is not simple, nor are the problems of family relationships simple. When a therapist refuses to see other family members, he has not thereby reduced the complexity of his position. He is a silent presence in the patient's family life anyway. Even though the therapist rejects face-to-face contact with other family members, he is a live image to them. He is a psychic force in the day-to-day emotional interchange among family members. In this sense, the therapist can no more avoid relatedness to the family group than can the patient cut off relations with his family while undergoing therapy.

The real question is not the artificial control of the simplicity or complexity of the therapeutic situation, but rather the need to explore the dynamic implications of different methods. Does one deal with these family members *in absentia*, through a medium, or does one deal with them directly? The position of the therapist cannot be an easy or simple one with any approach. It is conceivable that a therapist who deals with one patient faces one set of complications, whereas a therapist who deals with multiple family members faces another. (p. x)

This movement toward the development of a relational diagnostic system has regained momentum with the leadership of Kaslow (1996), who has sought to develop a diagnostic system based on current knowledge and research from family systems. Although still in its infancy, this enormous undertaking manifested the discontent with the individualistic system of *DSM–III* (American Psychiatric Association, 1980), which predominates the field. In previous work (Magnavita, 2000a), I listed some of the assumptions of a relational approach toward personality:

- Personality is formed by the relationships present from the earliest interpersonal experience and attachments.
- Personality is organized and shaped by the relationships in the interpersonal matrix that is unique to each family system.
- Personality "disordered" [quotation marks added] individuals consistently demonstrate disturbances in the relational matrix.
- Personality "disordered" [quotation marks added] individuals have major defenses against intimacy and closeness that interfere with the healing possibilities of human connectedness.
- The restorative or healing aspect of the therapeutic relationship is the quality of the therapeutic alliance.
- The benefits of enhanced relational capacities and family support are evident in almost every line of research.
- Personality disturbances are reinforced and often exaggerated by cultural and family systems.

In addition to these assumptions, the following are assumptions based on expanding the view of the personality as a system, intertwined with the sociocultural system (Angyal, 1941). When we consider personality as a system that exists at various levels of interaction and process, we expand our ability to understand how these complex entities function and can then more easily assess them.

Further Assumptions of a Unified Model

There are a number of assumptions that we can use to guide our formulations and assessment strategies:

1. Personality systems are not static but in continual motion; they cannot be captured by reductionistic labeling.
2. Personality systems cannot be reduced to their parts without considering the function of the entire system.
3. A static assessment should never be considered an accurate rendition of a personality system.
4. The system is more than a sum of its parts. An assessment might emphasize one aspect of the biopsychosocial matrix, but comprehensive assessment considers the impact of the other aspects and the interrelations of all the components of a system.
5. Assessment is never complete but is an ongoing process of refining one's understanding.
6. An understanding of systems theory is a prerequisite for determining the operation of any complex system such as personality.
7. Multiple data points increase the accuracy of our conceptualization.
8. Personality systems can be arranged on a continuum from functional to dysfunctional. A personality system can appear functional in one sociocultural context and dysfunctional in another.
9. Personality systems are to be considered in light of the environment in which they must adapt and evolve.

Understanding the manner in which anxiety is channeled at various component levels is critical to assessment and a central process of the personality system.

TRACKING ANXIETY—PATHWAYS OF THE DIATHESIS–STRESS

One can more fully understand symptom expressions and dysfunction at the various levels of the personality system with an appreciation for the way in which anxiety moves through a system. Anxiety is a central element of the personality system and has multiple expressions and processes. As reviewed in earlier chapters, trauma is a critical factor in the development of bionegativity in the personality system because of the disorganizing effect that it has. All of us have various diatheses or vulnerabilities in multiple personality subsystems. We can channel anxiety into physical or psychological expression, as well as relational and cultural pathways. These are unique for all of us, as individual as human personality and physical variation. Tracking anxiety is a critical aspect of a unified model and most important to assessment, as well as treatment. Anxiety can be channeled in many ways and expressed in various component processes of the four triangles. Assessment requires an understanding of the pathways and expression of the diathesis–stress. At each level of organization, we need to be able to understand the interrelationship of the way in which the system functions and what happens when anxiety becomes too great to modulate. Focusing on each of the triangular matrices assists us in observing the pathways of anxiety at these various systemic levels. Before proceeding, we need to examine briefly the nature of anxiety in the personality system.

The Nature of Anxiety

Anxiety is a physiological state that is associated with autonomic system arousal leading to a variety of changes in the neurobiological and cognitive–affective system. Most individuals describe anxiety as having some or all of the following physiological concomitants: increased heat rate, cardiac palpitations, tightness in the chest, dry mouth, flushing or blushing, light-headedness, sweating, and increased need to urinate or defecate. The surge of adrenaline involved in mobilizing anxiety is an evolutionary adaptation to prepare the organism for flight or fight when there is a severe threat to survival. Long-term activation of anxiety can have severe deleterious effects on an individual's functioning. There are also associated psychological components of anxiety such as a state of foreboding, called *hypervigilance*, that if severe can lead to a fragmentation of the self-system. Anxiety has many roots and is a multiple pathway phenomenon (Magnavita, 2000a). Anxiety can also be experienced nonconsciously and channeled by the individual into somatic pathways or defenses; into third members of a triadic configuration, as in scapegoating; or projected onto other groups, such as in genocide. The pathway that anxiety will follow is based on the diathesis of the particular matrix in which it is observed. Thus, the diathesis–stress represents the convergence of trauma or other forces that unduly stress the total personality system. Three essential categories of anxiety affect the human system:

1. *Existential anxiety.* This type of anxiety is a component of all humans and is related to mortality, isolation, aloneness, and freedom, all of which carry a cost. These are artifacts of the development of consciousness and have varying effects on the individual and larger systems, depending on factors such as individual awareness, family functioning, and culture. Existential anxiety may surge at critical stages or developmental transitions, brought on by leaving home, illness, death, loss, and so forth.

2. *Conflictual anxiety*. This type of anxiety is ubiquitous in the personality system. It can exist when there is an internal struggle between values and behavior (i.e., cognitive dissonance). It can also be generated from an internal lack of differentiation and integration of the intrapsychic–biological triangle, whereby affect is intolerable and defenses ill equipped to handle the stressor either over- or underregulate anxiety. Conflict anxiety can also emerge in the stress and demands of dyadic and larger-system interpersonal dynamics.

3. *Systemic anxiety*. This type of anxiety is stimulated in triadic or larger systems when the system is functioning ineffectively and unable to modulate the tensions inherent in human social systems. This type of anxiety can also be generated and transmitted generationally (Bowen, 1978). It can be seen in outbreaks of social pathologies, which can occasionally be lethal, as with the 1978 mass suicide of James Jones's followers in Jonestown, Guyana.

Each type of anxiety is present in all personality systems in various strengths. The important point is that anxiety is always present but only becomes a problem when reaching a certain level whereby a vulnerability or diathesis is stressed and the system's bionegativity increases to the point of dysfunction. More highly adaptive systems can handle higher levels of anxiety without becoming dysfunctional. Increasing empirical findings support the hypothesis that the personality system's integrity before a traumatic event is a strong predictor of whether the system will become chronically dysfunctional. The individual's innate ability to respond effectively to trauma is called *resilience*.

Intrapsychic–Biological Anxiety

At the intrapsychic–biological level of organization, anxiety can be channeled in a number of pathways (Davanloo, 1980). The channels of anxiety are means by which the intrapsychic–biological system attempts to regulate anxiety levels to maintain homeostasis to the degree possible.

- *Striated Muscle Pathway*. One such important pathway of anxiety observed and recorded by Davanloo (1980) is to the striated or voluntary muscles. In this case, anxiety is channeled most commonly to the lower back, neck, shoulders, and across the chest. Davanloo (1980) noted that an increase in activation of this channel results in sighing. This is an important observation that seems to bear out in clinical practice. When sighing increases, there is an increase in emotional activation. If this channel is an individual's habitual one, activation of anxiety will lead to the build up of substantial muscle tension and, when chronic, can lead to back problems.

- *Smooth Muscle Pathway.* Another common, and more deleterious, pathway of anxiety is to the smooth muscles or autonomic nervous system. When this is the primary channel, an individual often experiences a rise in activation of smooth muscle systems. Such individuals are likely to experience symptoms such as irritable bowel and other gastrointestinal disturbances such as constipation or stomach cramps when activated. Migraine headaches seem to be another expression of the diathesis–stress when anxiety is activated.

- *Cognitive–Perceptual Pathway.* Another pathway susceptible to the effects of anxiety for some individuals is cognitive and perceptual process. When this channel is used, an individual will demonstrate a disruption of thinking and perceptual distortion. An overload of anxiety will flood the intrapsychic–biological matrix and result in symptoms such as paranoid distortion and delusional thinking.

- *Personality Defense Pathway.* Often an individual's preferred anxiety pathway is through defensive organization. In these cases, the individual does not necessarily experience anxiety physiologically but demonstrates a rise in defensive response. Various workers have documented this pathway over the course of the last century. Individuals with this tendency often have a personality system that can be described as ego-syntonic.

Assessment Considerations

When conducting an assessment of the intrapsychic–biological system, clinician should identify the individual's preferred channels for anxiety. It is also important to remember that most individuals have multiple channels, but generally the tendency to use one channel is stronger when anxiety rises. When one channel becomes overloaded, a second, often more primitive pathway will open. For example, if an individual's preferred channel is to the personality defenses, when these are overloaded, they may then move to a smooth muscle or cognitive–perceptual pathway. Also, the anxiety may shift in its channel to one of the pathways within the remaining triangular matrices, described in the following sections. In well-functioning intrapsychic–biological systems, anxiety is generally experienced, tolerated, and channeled to higher order defenses. At the same time, there may also be a move toward establishing intimacy and closeness as another pathway.

Dyadic–Interpersonal Anxiety

When anxiety is not managed at the intrapsychic–biological matrix, it can find expression in dyadic channels. When the intrapsychic–biological channels cannot effectively modulate anxiety, the system will search for alternative pathways through which to seek stabilization.

- *Increased move toward fusion with another.* This pathway can often reduce anxiety at the dyadic level. Fusion is an attempt to move into another's personality system, resulting in a subsequent loss of self but engendering a feeling of pseudo-security. In the extreme, this is seen as a symbiotic relationship in which each member of the dyad needs the other to survive. In this way, the dyad attempts to keep overwhelming anxiety at bay, and this pathway is typically related to the separation–individuation phase of development. Each member seeks comfort in joining with the other, and one or both members give up their personality and elect to forego anything that would make the other feel disconnected or unique.
- *Increased move toward distancing and isolation.* Another interpersonal pathway of anxiety is toward distancing and isolation. When anxiety arises, there is increased movement away from the other. This may occur by one or both parties becoming increasingly distant until the two appear to be living parallel lives with little connection. This is often operative when there is too much anxiety in a dyad and little capacity for intimacy and closeness. This pathway may also occur when triadic pathways are operative.
- *Increased move toward intimacy and closeness.* Another, more functional channel of anxiety is when either individual in a dyad moves toward intimacy and closeness and finds reciprocation. In this case, anxiety is regulated by connection in relationship with the other, and empathy, understanding, validation, and acceptance of core emotion occurs.

Assessment Considerations

When making an assessment of the dyadic–interpersonal channels of anxiety, it is important to determine whether the preferred pathway is fusion, isolation, or intimacy and closeness. Fusion and isolation can be an oscillating process in some dyads. They may move toward fusion and then recoil in a repetitive process. In general, if the intrapsychic–biological system's preferred channels are autonomic nervous system or cognitive–perceptual, the dyadic channel will be either fusion or isolation distancing.

The attachment systems are also related to these preferred channels of anxiety. Those with secure attachment systems are likely to prefer intimacy and closeness as the preferred channel of anxiety. Those with preoccupied attachments seem to prefer the fusion channel, and those with fearful and dismissive systems prefer distancing and isolation. Another feature of dyadic–interpersonal channels of anxiety is that they can become fixed, so that all interpersonal process slips back to this pattern. When interpersonal patterns are fixed and rigid, they often contain high levels of anxiety. These interpersonal processes are often easily ferreted out when observing a dyad or listening to a history of relational conflict. To a degree, dominant–submissive, addict–enabler, parent–child, competent–incompetent, sick–healthy, and other asymmetrical patterns stabilize a dyad for a time, but the result is often a strong, hostile dependency.

Triadic–Relational Anxiety

Anxiety in the triadic–relational triangle has one basic process: to channel anxiety to a third person or nonhuman. As mentioned, when dyadic anxiety is not contained within the dyad, a preferred channel often becomes someone or something else. The most commonly seen pathways are as follows.

- *Pathway of anxiety to a child.* The most frequently observed pathway of anxiety seen in clinical practice when working with couples and families is when anxiety in a dyad is channeled to a child. In this case, the child becomes symptomatic as a way to express and contain the anxiety through triangulation. Maladaptive intrapsychic–biological processes in either or both members of a dyad may generate this anxiety, with multigenerational implications. Maladaptive processes and patterns from previous generations may be transmitted. For example, an uninvolved father who spends most of his time sitting in a recliner in front of the television provides a powerful model for a first-born son who later succeeds professionally but is passive at home. The son's marital dyad then suffers from his distance and passivity. This dyad endures the stress until it can no longer contain it through the preferred channels, and then the couples' child becomes symptomatic (triadic pathway), inviting the father to get out of his chair by facing his symptomatic son.
- *Pathway of anxiety to another adult.* Anxiety can also be channeled to another adult when a dyad is having difficulty containing its anxiety. This is a common channel of anxiety manifest in the high rate of extramarital affairs that are reported in the

literature. This channel of anxiety assists the dyad in containing anxiety that is generated by unresolved conflict in their relationship.

- *Pathway of anxiety to a nonhuman such as object or addiction.* Yet another triadic channel of anxiety is to use the pathway of a third object, which usually has some symbolic meaning related to the conflict. In some cases, the pathway is an addiction such as drugs, alcohol, food, or sex. The individual for all intents and purposes is having a "relationship" with the chemical or mood altering addictive cycle. One often hears alcoholics talk about alcohol as if it were a beloved partner. Almost any type of object can become the third corner of a triangle, such as a computer, boat, car, and so on. The point is that the object becomes overly imbued with meaning to the point of convergence of bionegativity.

Assessment Considerations

The triadic channel is ubiquitous and can occur over multiple generations. Members of these configurations are often highly invested in maintaining them, even though they prevent more adaptive functioning. They may be needed to contain a severely dysfunctional marriage that would have ended long before were it not for the triangulation. A triangular configuration may also mask another more destructive triangle. A marital relationship with a symptomatic child may be destabilized when an alcoholic stops drinking, because these interlocking triangles may have been essential to maintain the system. One key to assessment is to search for triadic channels of anxiety whenever there appears to be a highly symptomatic individual in what appears to be a "healthy" system.

Sociocultural–Familial Anxiety

The sociocultural–family pathways of anxiety are evident in various manifestations of anxiety in sociocultural processes.

- *Pathway of anxiety to a subculture.* A favored pathway of anxiety that occurs in many cultures is to channel anxiety into a subculture, which serves to bind the anxiety. This is evident, for example, when an individual, dyad, or family enters a cult or becomes captive to any group to which they lose their autonomous functions. We see this pathway taken by certain adolescents who seek stabilization of developmental or triadic anxiety in identifying with counterculture. This may serve to modulate the anxiety aroused during the phase of identity consolidation.

Adults, couples, and families are prone to seek out cults and other groups with which they can identify in an attempt to modulate anxiety arising from a complex, often chaotic world.

- *Pathway of anxiety to political and cultural dysfunction.* When the synergy among family systems and sociocultural and political forces build to a certain level, anxiety may be channeled on a large scale and in destructive ways. These events can be observed when there is a convergence of bionegativity. We have witnessed such events in many forms over the course of history, and there were remarkable examples such as the genocide of the past century. On a smaller scale, we can see social phenomena such as mass murder by high school students, a phenomenon unheard of before the 1990s. This pathway represents a convergence of multiple forces that can result in massive social, political, and cultural upheaval.

Assessment Considerations

When assessing the sociocultural–familial triangular processes, we must be concerned with the plethora of cultural and ethnic influences that are in motion at a given time. One has to understand the ways in which these powerful forces affect family and individual systems. We must also take into account how larger systems such as nations and world political struggles fuel and channel anxiety. Anxiety is bi-directional, with multiple channels in operation at various levels of the system. For example, the destruction of the World Trade Center on September 11, 2001, created a reverberation of anxiety at each level of triangular process. Individuals were affected as well as families and nations around the world. Major sociocultural and political reactions were set into motion. The impact of this event is likely to produce effects and have dramatic shifts for some time to come.

Now that we have reviewed the various channels of pathways of anxiety, we can examine more closely the processes and components important to assessment within and among each of the four triangles.

ASSESSING THE INTRAPSYCHIC–BIOLOGICAL COMPONENTS OF THE PERSONALITY SYSTEM

If we focus our lens on the *intrapsychic–biological matrix* of the personality system, we concern ourselves primarily with what is happening "within" an individual. We must nonetheless keep in mind that even at this level of conceptualization, we are concerned with the combination of biological elements and relational aspects of attachment and experience, which are the building blocks of the personality system. At the forefront of our thinking, we must remember, "the leg bone is connected to the foot bone" and so on, so as not to forget that the model is organically integrated in the personality system. Here I break the system into component parts for heuristic purposes.

An assessment of how the intrapsychic–biologic matrix operates is critical regardless of the modality or modalities of therapy selected, which I discuss in chapter 11, and should be carefully interwoven into the assessment process. Some of the most gifted therapists of the past century seemed to be able to read an individual or family personality system rapidly, often on a deep intuitive basis. Most of us, however, need a methodology and theory to guide our intuition. Intuition comes from theory and knowledge, but, more important, from clinical experience. Good therapists usually emerge after years of clinical experience that sharpen their intuition.

Neurobiological Substrate

The neurobiological substrate includes the various aspects of the nervous system and the action of the neurotransmitters. At this point in the development of our field, we are not able to take a direct reading of the neurobiological functions and, as in the psychological aspects of functioning, we rely on intuition and the current state of the art to make a determination as to what is occurring. There are new methods such as magnetic resonance imaging (MRI), functional MRI, positron emission topography, as well as other advances in technology that allow neuroscientists to have a better view of neurophysiogical function (Carter, 1998), but these are not yet available, nor would they be helpful at this stage of development, to the clinician. In the case of gross abnormalities, this technology is of course useful. A more readily available technology is neuropsychology, which advanced remarkably in the last quarter of the 20th century.

Mapping the Neurotransmitter System

Knowledgeable psychopharmacologists create maps of the neurobiological system when they do careful pharmacological intervention. This type of diagnostic dissection by pharmacology was pioneered by Klein (1967, 1970), who differentiated hysteric personality into what he termed the *hysteroid–dysphoric* and the *phobic–anxious* types. A contemporary version of this type of mapping is offered by Kramer (1993) in his book *Listening to Prozac*, in which he uses this approach to map the contours of the self and biological substrate. It is the case that most individuals respond differentially to psychoactive agents. The thoughtful pharmacologist administers a medication and carefully begins to map the terrain by the individual's response, selecting another medication if one is not successful, and in a sense reading the neurobiological system like an intuitive therapist maps the terrain of the intrapsychic system by observing how the patient responds to an intervention. With each intervention a more accurate holonic profile is developed.

Assessment Strategies

1. Create a family genogram to determine whether there is a history of biologically based disorders such as schizophrenia, schizoaffective illness, bipolar disorder, or other physical illness of a genetic nature.
2. Review the history of any previously prescribed psychoactive agents, their effectiveness, and any side effects noted.
3. Create a pharmacological map of the biological substrate. Although this type of assessment should be conducted by a medical professional trained in psychopharmacology, nomedical therapists should have a basic understanding of the major psychoactive agents, their uses, and their side effect profiles, so that information can be conveyed to the psychopharmacologists.

Attachment Matrix

Attachment theory has been a major contribution to understanding personality systems, especially the landmark work of John Bowlby (1969, 1973, 1980), who defined attachment theory as "a way of conceptualizing the propensity of human beings to make strong affectional bonds to others" (p. 201). Psychotherapy begins when the attachment system of the patient or multiple attachment systems of the couple or family is activated in the therapeutic process. An understanding of various types of attachment systems and identification of these often occurs for the skilled therapist at an intuitive level. Attachment theory has continued to gain prominence in the field. A more formal understanding of attachment systems allows systematic evaluation and strategy for employment of appropriate interventions. Bartholomew et al. (2001) wrote as follows:

> Attachment theory provides a useful framework for understanding personality pathology independent of any claims of continuity between childhood and adult attachment orientations. But the more exciting and controversial implication of the theory is that attachment patterns and associated patterns of adaptation established in the family of origin tend to be carried forward into adulthood. (p. 196)

This is an example of the *multigenerational transmission process* (MTI).

Bartholomew et al. (2001) suggested the use of four attachment patterns in adult relationships: (a) secure attachment, (b) preoccupied attachment,

(c) fearful attachment, and (d) dismissing attachment. There are other, more complex attachment schemas, such as that presented by Florsheim et al. (1996), and interested readers will find much written on this topic. Ainsworth (1979) described three patterns of attachment in children, and a fourth was offered by Main and her associates (Main & Cassidy, 1988):

1. *Anxious avoidant.* The infant shows anxiety when returning to the maternal attachment, avoiding eye contact and interaction (Ainsworth, 1979).
2. *Securely attached.* The infant seeks contact and proximity, becoming emotional at times but is capable of being soothed and reengaging in play (Ainsworth, 1979).
3. *Anxious resistant.* The infant demonstrates ambivalence, alternately seeking and rejecting contact and is not readily comforted (Ainsworth, 1979).
4. *Disorganized and disoriented.* The child demonstrates an attempt to control the parent, and there is a reversal of role in which the child may control or caretake the parent (Main & Cassidy, 1988).

Bowlby (1980) believed that the attachment system is retained in the personality. Drawing on the work of Bowlby, Mahoney (1991) made the following assertions from attachment theory that are useful to our mission:

1. At all ages, human beings exhibit their greatest happiness and well-being when they are confident that there are one or more trusted persons within psychological proximity who will come to their aid should difficulties arise. This trusted and available "attachment figure" can be construed as providing a secure base from which his or her companion can operate.
2. Although it is not confined to infancy or childhood, the need for a secure personal base in the form of an attachment figure is most evident and urgent during these early developmental eras.
3. The primary biological function of intimate emotional bonds is to provide such secure bases in and from which the individuals involved can explore their "working models" of self and intimate other, as well as the world they occupy.
4. Life span personality development involves the ongoing construction and reconstruction of these working models, reflecting a dynamic and generative tension between continuity (familiarity) and change (novelty).

5. A healthily functioning adult is not "compulsively self-reliant" and maximally autonomous; he or she is, instead, capable of trusting and relying on others, as well as providing a secure base for companions.

6. Private (and predominantly unconscious) models of self, others, and the world become increasingly firm (resistant to change) with the confirmation of experience, and such confirmation tends to accelerate as the infant, child, adolescent, and adult become more active and effective participants in selecting and creating their own environment.

7. The primary responsibilities of the psychotherapist are to provide a secure base that is safe, emotionally supportive, and respectful of the client's current experience. The main task of therapy is exploration, with the intent to understand and appraise old, unconscious stereotypes of self and world and to experiment with feeling, thinking, and acting in novel ways. (pp. 167–168)

The attachment system of a patient, when understood and captured, provides a helpful lens with which to frame ongoing difficulties in a way that is easily understood. The concept of attachment system is not unlike the psychodynamic of transference in that an individual often re-creates the early attachment experiences with the therapist and significant others. The attachment system can be viewed by the manner in which the patient establishes and maintains his or her attachment with the therapist. Bartholomew et al. (2001) stated that "attachment theory promotes the understanding of attachment as a process rather than a trait—the search for patterns in the person's attachment behaviors across relationships, consideration of the person's reactions to threats to relationships (real or imagined), and exploration of basic working models of self and others" (pp. 222–223). Adult to adult attachment styles are summarized as follows by Florsheim et al. (1996, pp. 84–85):

- *Preoccupied attachment.* An individual with an underlying feeling of unworthiness who looks to valued others for acceptance (Bartholomew & Horowitz, 1991).
- *Dismissive attachment style.* An individual with a basically "positive" view of him- or herself and a negative view of others who is avoids intimacy and vulnerability with an independent stance (Bartholomew & Horowitz, 1991; Main & Goldwyn, 1985).
- *Fearful–avoidant attachment style.* An individual with a negative view of him- or herself and others who avoids involvement to

reduce the chance of rejection and attack (Bartholomew & Horowitz, 1991).

- *Compulsive self-reliant attachment style.* An individual who needs to feel independent and self-reliant and avoids eliciting support and affection, not out of disdain but counterdependence (Bowlby, 1977; West & Sheldon, 1988).
- *Compulsive care-seeking attachment style.* An individual who compulsively seeks to confirm that there is access to a responsive attachment figure and feels ill equipped to care for oneself (West & Sheldon, 1988).
- *Angry–withdrawn attachment style.* An individual who displays anger and is defensive to the response or unavailability of another (West & Sheldon, 1988).
- *Obsessive–compulsive attachment style.* An individual who rigidly adheres to how things should be, putting work and being productive ahead of relationships (Pilkonis, 1988).
- *Interpersonal insensitive attachment style.* An individual who is not influenced by or is oblivious to the effect his or her actions have on others (Pilkonis, 1988).

Assessment Strategies for Attachment System

1. Conduct a developmental history to see whether a determination can be made about the likely attachment style.
2. Gather as much information as possible about the personality system and attachment style of major early attachment figures.
3. Determine the type and style of attachment that the patient has with current figures in his or her life.
4. Examine the attachment experience that the patient elicits and offers in the therapeutic alliance.
5. Notice the attachment style evident in dyadic and triadic configurations.

Affective/Cognitive–Anxiety–Defensive Matrix

As we have reviewed, the affective/cognitive–anxiety–defensive matrix represents the intrapsychic matrix of an individual. In the past, this matrix was conceptualized as an indication of an individual's intrapsychic "structure." This metaphor of structure to describe the manner in which the mind works and of consciousness is probably not accurate, however, based on current conceptualizations from neuroscience and system theory. "Consciousness . . . is not a *thing* or a *structure*, but a constantly changing, ongoing set of processes" (Grigsby & Stevens, 2000, p. 222). It is more consistent with contemporary thinking to conceptualize the intrapsychic domain as a process as opposed to something that has structure. Grigsby and Stevens (2000) wrote: "one's state is a *process* that has its origin in the nonlinear interactions and relationships of a large number of component processes and variables" (p. 165). As with any complex component system, one cannot separate the parts without losing something in the exercise. Academic and research scientists have traditionally attempted to isolate emotion and cognition in an attempt to study them respectively. Mahoney (1991) wrote of the difficulty in separating emotion from cognition: "The impossibility of segregating emotional processes from those involved in thinking and action has been recently highlighted by attempts to do just that—for example, in debates about the relative primacy of cognition versus affect in human experience" (p. 188).

Hartmann (1958, 1964), Horner (1994, 1995), Masterson (1988), and McWilliams (1994) are a few of the innovators who developed and refined strategies for intrapsychic clinical assessment.

Affective Domain (Emotion, Mood, and Anxiety)

The affect system of an individual is the seat of emotional experience and processing. Emotional experiencing is a key function of the personality system. Too much emotion, and the system can be flooded by ensuing anxiety; too little emotion, on the other hand, reduces the enjoyment of life and may rob the individual of motivational drive. Without an emotional guidance system, an individual is unable to derive pleasure from accomplishments or to interpret events in life in an accurate manner. Emotional availability is key to intimacy and closeness, as well as the capacity for nurturing and empathy. Negative consequences of the maladaptive emotional system can impair more attuned reactions and engender negative reactions that can elicit negative responses from others. This is obvious to most of us when working with a paranoid system. As we witness with personality systems in which emotional development is stunted, behavior toward others is often antisocial or asocial. When the emotional system is functioning adaptively, the individual is able to experience, label, articulate, and tolerate emotions without moving to action unless necessary for survival or adaptation. Conversely, when the emotional system is maladaptive, the individual is unable to guide behavioral and interpersonal responses effectively, often becoming trapped in emotional circuitry that is locked into defensive responding that impairs more attuned reactions.

A ubiquitous phenomenon of existence, anxiety is a state with which all human beings are familiar. When the emotional–defense system is not working adaptively, anxiety reactions predominate and may flood the system with paralyzing states of panic or seep into experience as generalized anxiety.

Of course, anxiety is a by-product of the fight-or-flight response and is necessary at an optimal level to prepare the system for action.

Assessment Strategies for the Affective Matrix

1. Determine the capacity for emotional experiencing by observing the congruence between activation of the emotional system and labeling (e.g., the patient cries yet declares he is not sad). Notice if feelings are activated when the patient enters into areas of vulnerability or cognitive–affectively "hot" zones.
2. Determine the capacity for emotional expression by observing and eliciting feelings when conducting the clinical interview.
3. Notice whether the patient is able and willing to disclose emotional aspects of him- or herself without becoming overly defensive.
4. Notice how the patient physiologically communicates feelings and whether the labeling of such feelings is congruent with communication (e.g., consider the patient who says "I am really angry" while smiling).
5. Catalogue the defenses elicited in emotion-laden communication.

Cognitive Domain (Beliefs, Schema, and Templates)

The cognitive domain is part of the intrapsychic matrix that retains the belief system and schema or template for how the relational world operates. As has been stated, the cognitive and affective components of this system cannot be separated and occur in a highly integrative manner. In clinical assessment, we attempt to elucidate an individual's core belief system and schema that have been internalized as a result of both positive and negative attachment experiences.

Assessment Strategies for Cognitive Domain

1. Attempts to elicit the belief—for example, the patient's expectation, attribution, or interpretation—that often underlies the interpersonal reaction or emotional response a patient is reporting.
2. Ask the patient to elaborate on what he or she is communicating to him- or herself when negative self-talk emerges.
3. See whether a cognitive link to a current attachment system with a significant attachment figure is evident and can be made. A particular set of beliefs or schema such as "I am too

needy" might be linked to the message delivered by a depressed mother that she doesn't have enough to give.

4. Notice how affirming communications are received and if the channel stays closed to maintain negative schema.

Defensive Operations

Included in the affective–cognitive matrix is the defensive operating system of an individual by which various defensive constellations are used depending on the patient and the maturity of the personality system to regulate anxiety. The level of anxiety within any system is in a constant state of fluctuation depending on the interpersonal experiences and unconscious activation of anxiety that may be stimulated when attachment systems or cognitive schema are activated. The activation of these central nodes of the intrapsychic network is brought into homeostatic balance through the use of defensive operations that contain or discharge anxiety. The various intrapsychic and interpersonal defense mechanisms have been covered in chapter 4. Defenses are not always effective in their role of managing and regulating anxiety. At times, the defenses cannot contain the affective stimulation, anxiety ensues, and, if not reorganized, the systems become overloaded and symptom formation occurs.

Assessment Strategies for the Defensive System

1. Conduct an analysis of defense and make a profile of the patient's defensive system or constellation in his or her current relationships and in the transference relationship. Ask for specific "hot" or emotionally laden episodes and encourage incident specificity.
2. Observe how defenses shift when focusing on a highly conflictual theme increases anxiety. Pay particular attention to rapid shifts to fewer and more primitive defense constellations. If this occurs, quickly reduce anxiety by having the patient focus on somatic experience, which serves to ground him or her.
3. Look for red-flag defenses (defenses that are primitive and very disruptive to self–other relationships and the stability of the intrapsychic–biological matrix) such as dissociation, projective identification, and acting out, and seek to reduce anxiety, and if observed, work at establishing a secure attachment.
4. Observe the feedback loop in couples and family progress to determine if there is a tendency to reactivate defenses that lead to rapid downward spiraling (i.e., more primitive defenses in an escalating pattern).

Anxiety

We have reviewed the primary channels or pathways that anxiety can take within the four triangles and three basic types, which we can further elaborate. A primary function of the affective–cognitive–defensive system is the regulation of anxiety. Anxiety is a central construct in psychopathology–bionegativity and personality theory. Various theoretical systems have proposed that anxiety emanates from different sources. Although there are many others, some of the main theoretical models in which the construct of anxiety has a central position include the following:

- *Psychobiological*. Anxiety emerges from activation of the flight–fight syndrome and the resultant increase in the activation of the endocrine system and hormones such as adrenaline. The stress of modern society inappropriately activates the more primitive flight–fight response when it is not required, causing undue stress on the system.
- *Psychodynamic—structural/drive*. Anxiety emerges from conflict in intrapsychic agencies, that is, the tension between the instinctual drives of the id for gratification and the conscience or the superego.
- *Psychodynamic–self psychological*. Anxiety results in the tension between, on one hand, the false self designed to maintain safety, and, on the other, the desire of the true self to seek expression.
- *Interpersonal*. Although there are some differences among interpersonal theorists as to the source(s) of anxiety, the prototypic view within the interpersonal perspective is that anxiety stems from feeling invalidated in some way by the other. This may entail perceiving or experiencing the other as not seeing self as self sees self (e.g., one sees himself or herself as capable but perceives other as seeing self as incapable) or, the more traditional Sullivanian (1953) perspective, perceiving and experiencing other as not valuing the self, as not seeing self as worthwhile, and so on.
- *Existential–humanistic*. Anxiety is present in all humans and is rooted in our consciousness about our mortality and creates death anxiety. Death anxiety is aroused during all developmental transitions characterized by greater separation and individuation. Anxiety is a by-product of the human condition, such as our aloneness, meaninglessness, and isolation. The challenge is not to avoid these but to master the critical issues that

are involved, such as making meaning in our lives and making intimate connections.

- *Family–systemic.* Anxiety is generated by the degree of tension among dyads and in triadic configurations when interpersonal conflict is not being appropriately managed.
- *Behavioral.* Anxiety is the result of conditioning by associating a feared stimulus with a neutral one.
- *Cognitive.* Anxiety stems from perceived or actual threat and danger. In the case of maladaptive anxiety, by virtue of the patient's irrational internal schema or beliefs, she or he perceives a stimulus situation as posing more of a threat or danger than is actually the case, and this gives rise to subjective anxiety (Beck, Emery, & Greenberg, 1985). Anxiety can also arise from internal values that contradict or are at odds with behavioral acts or expression. This type of anxiety is generated by "cognitive dissonance" (Festinger, 1957).
- *Trauma.* Anxiety emerges from the overwhelming impingement of trauma and the fragmentation of the self-system. The intense activation of overwhelming emotions can lead to severe states of fragmentation anxiety.

Which theory of anxiety is correct? "Anxiety has many roots and is best conceptualized as a multiple pathway phenomenon" (Magnavita, 2000a, p. 29). In other words, there are many origins of anxiety and a variety of expressions in the human psyche, at the interpersonal, triadic, and ecosystem levels. A multidimensional model of anxiety is required to gain a comprehensive understanding of the human personality system.

Intimacy–Closeness and Emotional Availability

There has recently been a groundswell of interest in the scientific study of intimacy and closeness (Mashek & Aron, 2004). Intimacy is the capacity to share oneself with another. Bradt (1980) wrote: "*Intimacy* involves a caring relationship without pretense, and revelation without risk of loss or gain from one another. It is giving and receiving, an exchange that enhances because it facilitates the awareness of selves, of differences and sameness" (p. 126). The cognitive–affective–defense matrix is directly linked to the interpersonal through the attachment system and the ability or capacity to develop and maintain intimate relationships as one matures. Intimacy in dyads is a circular process of mutual influence. Byng-Hall (1999) described the systemic process of mutual influence:

> The effects of any action thus circle back—either directly from the other persona within the dyad, or via other people—to affect how the

original actor behaves next time around in the cycle of interaction. Interactive cycles, which include both actions and verbal components, act as information feedback loops. These either discourage any deviation from the norm (negative feedback) and so maintain stability of the pattern, or they encourage and strengthen a new form of behavior (positive feedback), which encourages change and disruption of the previous pattern of interaction. (p. 631)

The chicken–egg conundrum. Which comes first, a lack of intimacy or a dysfunctioning personality system? As readers will already assume, there exists an exquisitely circular process that shapes the personality system and the capacity for intimacy and closeness. Intimacy requires a secure attachment system, an intrapsychic system with adequate defenses to modulate the anxiety that intimacy arouses in all of us as we allow ourselves to become more vulnerable. "The very act of entering psychotherapy will activate the patient's anxiety about intimacy . . . something they crave but also fear" (Magnavita, 1997a). To build the capacity for intimacy, there needs to be an interchange that ultimately alters the personality system by gradually differentiating and integrating the system.

Strategies for Assessing Capacity for Intimacy and Closeness

1. Assess the level of object relatedness, which is the capacity to establish mature relationships. As we have discussed, a rapid way to classify patients on object relatedness is to divide them between those who have issues with *attachment* (i.e., trust—lower functioning) and those that have issues with *intimacy and closeness* (i.e., higher functioning). A more sophisticated scale with substantial clinical utility, based on Kernberg's (1974) work and consistent with Bowen (1978), was adapted by Nichols (1988). I have reduced it even further to use as a rapid assessment tool. Each patient can be rated on a scale as follows: (a) no capacity for trusting others, (b) limited capacity to trust, (c) some capacity for intimacy and closeness, (d) capacity for emotional intimacy but not with sexual relatedness, and (e) full capacity for intimacy and closeness and sexual relatedness.
2. Assess the patient's ability to enter into a collaborative relationship.
3. Notice how interpersonal and intrapsychic defenses are mobilized when feelings of closeness or attachment (positive and negative) toward the therapist are aroused.

ASSESSING THE INTERPERSONAL–DYADIC MATRIX
(TWO PEOPLE) OF THE PERSONALITY SYSTEM

The interpersonal–dyadic matrix embodies the attachment, defensive system and offers a direct view of an individual's capacity for intimacy and closeness. This includes the ability to maintain integrity of the self with another without the loss of boundaries or overly relying on the fusion fantasy that can occurs in less differentiated individuals and couples. As Sullivan (1953) pointed out, all pathology is expressed interpersonally. Sullivan's work was a refreshing departure from the emphasis on the intrapsychic domain of those who preceded him. He was much more concerned with the evolving relational patterns. He did not believe that the therapist could ever remain neutral or detached but that he or she was a participant–observer in the process. The dyad is an excellent forum for viewing the interrelationships of personality systems and the feedback loops that often exaggerate processes, individually, dyadically, and triadically. When we consider the dyad, we also are guided by our interpersonal dyadic, which depicts the recreation of early, relational schema learned from attachment figures and then reenacted in current relationships, including the therapeutic dyad. This allows us to gather an enormous amount of valuable information about dyadic processes.

- *The therapeutic dyad.* This dyad is the one relied on by most therapeutic orientations for assessment and therapeutic process. The modality of individual therapy occurs in this mode. The therapist cocreates an intersubjective field with which to replay relational schema from past. This aspect of the dyadic representation is often the focus of therapeutic effort and includes the transference patterns, relational schema, cognitive beliefs and schema, or object relational representations, depending on one's therapeutic orientation.
- *Current dyadic relationships.* As we recall, the other element of the interpersonal–dyadic triangle are the relationships in which an individual is currently involved. If the treatment modality is individual therapy, then the patient often discusses his or her conflicts and dissatisfaction in these primary relationships. The therapist then begins to create a holonic picture of the patient's interpersonal level of functioning, capacity for relatedness, and repetitive maladaptive patterns. Because most individuals do not have a direct connection through awareness to these internalized interpersonal dyads (patient–mother, patient–father, patient–sibling, patient–relative, patient–

caretaker, and so on), the clinician does not have a direct view of these but can only co-construct a narrative by accessing this matrix through other channels. Thus the action of the original code or schematic representation may be pushed out of conscious awareness.

- *Past dyadic relationships.* The therapeutic action of most forms of therapy entail bringing to light and examining the past core relational experiences that have shaped an individual's personality system. These generally are the locus of traumatic relational or life events that have resulted in various dysfunctional developmental adaptations.

Dyadic Processes

One of the most innovative workers in the interpersonal or dyadic matrix is Lorna Smith Benjamin (1993), who expanded and integrated Sullivan's model with Leary (1957) and others. Her work on dyadic processes was reviewed earlier (chap. 4) and includes five primary interpersonal processes: (a) complementarity, (b) introjection, (c) similarity, (d) opposition, and (e) antithesis.

Rapid Downward Spiraling

One process that often occurs and can be witnessed in the more severely dysfunctional dyad is the rapid downward spiraling that is so familiar to those who practice couple therapy. This type of circular dyadic process occurs when one member of a dyad triggers the other's maladaptive defenses in an increasingly escalating manner, which creates a rapid spiral into more primitive modes of defensive responding. This is an example of a system in a positive feedback loop. The therapist needs rapidly to alter the process by having each member of the dyad listen and understand as opposed to react and defend. When couples report or exhibit this type of process and it cannot be adequately controlled, it is often necessary to use individual treatment modalities before resuming couples work.

ASSESSING THE RELATIONAL–TRIADIC MATRIX (TWO + PEOPLE) OF THE PERSONALITY SYSTEM

The relational classification of personality is an effort to account for the complex systemic action that occurs in personality systems. Currently, there are limited models of how dysfunctional families evolve over generations and the various types. Donaldson-Pressman and Pressman (1994) developed the concept of the narcissistic family. Studying families of individuals with severe psychiatric conditions, Doane and Diamond (1994) demonstrated how family typology expressed in patterns of attachment, and affective styles, are reflected in intergenerational patterns. In what they called "disconnected families" they state that: "Projection in disconnected families tends to encompass the whole personality of the child, who becomes a receptacle for the discarded, unwanted, and despised aspects of one or both parents, or of the parents' parents" (p. 114). As previously described, "The relational system views personality pathology as existing within a complex biopsychosocial system, not exclusively within the individual" (Magnavita, 2000a, p. 94). Dysfunctional personologic systems are defined as follows:

- A dysfunctional family system in which a preponderance of individuals have personality pathology, often observable over generations.
- A lineage of certain types of personality pathology associated with central family themes, dynamics, and triangles. (Magnavita, 2000a, p. 49)

Features of Dysfunctional Personologic Systems

- Impermeable or weak external boundaries that separate the family system from others
- Poor boundaries among family members
- Disturbed levels of communication and overreliance on primitive defenses
- Reversal of the parent–child relationship
- Need for family to revolve around narcissistic parent
- Poor emotional differentiation and regulation
- Emotional malnourishment
- Financial instability
- Multigenerational transmission process (Magnavita, 2000a, p. 54)

The processes and features of dysfunctional systems have certain characteristics and themes that may be typed and are useful in assessment.

Types of Dysfunctional Personologic Systems

Previously, 10 subtypes of dysfunctional personologic systems were elaborated (Magnavita, 2000a). These systems are ones that are more likely to produce family members with personality dysfunction. The following subtypes were initially formulated but are not meant to be comprehensive:

- The addictive dysfunctional personologic system (AdcDps)
- The narcissistic dysfunctional personologic system (NarDps)
- The covertly narcissistic dysfunctional personologic system (CNrDps)
- The psychotic dysfunctional personologic system (PscDps)
- The developmentally arrested dysfunctional personologic system (DevDps)
- The physically/sexually traumatizing dysfunctional personologic system (TraDps)
- The depressiogenic dysfunctional personologic system (DepDps)
- The chronically medically ill dysfunctional personologic system (MedDps)
- The paranoid dysfunctional personologic system (ParDps)
- The somatic dysfunctional personologic system (SomDps). (p. 60)

The various themes, communication styles, and relational issues are depicted in Table 6.1. A brief description of the 10 subtypes of *dysfunctional personologic systems* (*DPS*) follows:

1. *The addictive DPS*. This system revolves around addictive process. There is a reversed assumption that without substances, survival is threatened. Codependency is a substitute for intimacy. A positive feedback loop (as the substance use creates more chaos, substance use increases) produces marginally functioning systems: members may gravitate toward substances as a way to buttress fragile defense systems.

2. *The narcissistic DPS*. This system's major theme is false protection and avoidance of the vulnerable self. Donaldson-Pressman and Pressman (1994) described these families in their book *The Narcissistic Family: Diagnosis and Treatment*, which provides useful reading for many patients. In these families, public images must be maintained. Children's achievement that reflects favorably on the parents often becomes a substitute for core affirmation and validation.

3. *The covertly narcissistic DPS*. Another system identified by Donaldson-Pressman and Pressman (1994) is the covertly narcissistic family. This system, more subtle than the previous type, creates chronic feelings of not being understood or affirmed. There is pressure to compensate for deficits in members. Affirmation is provided for emotional caretaking, often taken on by children. This reversal is often seen in parent–

TABLE 6.1
Themes, Communications, and Relational Issues of Various Types of Dysfunctional Personologic Systems (DPSs)

Type of DPS	System Themes	Communications	Relational Issues
AdcDps	Addictive processes	Reversed assumption that without substances survival is threatened	Codependence as a substitute for intimacy
NarDps	False self-protection	Public images are to be maintained at all costs	Achievement substitutes for validation of person
CNrDps	Chronic empathic misalignment	Pressure to compensate for emotional deficits in members	Affirmation provided for emotional care taking
PscDps	Adaptation to chaos	We can never feel secure	Basic attachment is achieved by assuming care functions
DevDps	Inability to tolerate individuation	Separation is dangerous to family cohesion and survival	Differentiation—fusion
TraDps	Accommodation to chronic abuse patterns	Family members are objects to be dominated by "powerful" members	Trauma absorption—"Use and abuse" relationships
DepDps	Attempt to adapt to insufficient emotional resources	"Make do"—there will never be enough resources to meet needs	Distortion of family developmental processes
MedDps	Overdomination of family function with medical illness and processes	Chronic medical illness predominates all aspects of family communication	Exacerbation of pre-existing personality disturbances; relations revolve around illness
ParDps	"Us vs. them" dichotomy predominates	We must protect ourselves from intrusion by outsiders	Cohesion through sharing of paranoid view
SomDps	Substitution of somatic for emotional life	The only valid form of communication is somatic	Nurturing is elicited through illness

Note. From *Relational Therapy for Personality Disorders* (p. 131), by J. J. Magnavita, 2000, New York: John Wiley & Sons. Copyright 2000 by John Wiley & Sons. Reprinted with permission.

child interactions and, although subtle, is nonetheless pervasive and limits full development of the child.

4. *The psychotic DPS.* The theme of this system is adaptation to chaos. Family members struggle with feelings of insecurity and fragmentation. Autonomy is severely threatened and may be seen in fused relationships and, in some cases, shared psychosis. Basic attachment is attempted by assuming caretaking functions for disabled figures or by sharing psychotic behavior.

5. *The developmentally arrested DPS.* The theme of this system is inability to tolerate individuation. Separation is viewed as dangerous to family survival and cohesion. The relational dynamic is differentiation versus fusion. It should be noted that this system may be culturally determined and therefore not considered pathological (e.g., in some Asian or African American families).

6. *Physically or sexually traumatizing DPS.* The theme is this system is accommodation to chronic abuse patterns. Family members are viewed as objects to be dominated by the "powerful" members. Relational themes are "use and abuse" dynamics. Violence, emotional abuse, and neglect predominate family communication patterns.

7. *The depressiogenic DPS.* Insufficient emotional resources typify this system. There is typically a history of untreated affective disorder, influencing parenting style and attachment systems and marital function. In depressed systems, the quality of attachments does not provide a solid base for security and emotional growth (Diamond, Diamond, & Liddle, 2000). The dominant fear is that there are not enough resources to meet members' needs. Family development is stunted because of the chronic emotional insufficiency.

8. *The chronic medically ill DPS.* The theme in this system is the domination of family functions with the business of medical illness, which dictates family communication and relationships. There may be a history of genetic predisposition for chronic illness. The chronic stress of coping may lead to emotional disturbance, which, if left untreated, can consolidate into personality disturbance.

9. *The paranoid DPS.* The theme in this system is an "us versus them" dichotomy. Family members feel compelled to protect themselves from intrusion from outsiders or from other family members. Cohesion is maintained through a sharing of this paranoid view. Clinicians must be alert to the possibility that

the social milieu may engender this reaction, as in cases of subjugation or discrimination.

10. *The somatic DPS.* The theme of this system is the substitution of somatic for emotional expression. The only "valid" and safe form of affective communication is through somatic language and expression. Nurturing is elicited through "illness" and psychosomatic complaints. There is usually an extreme demand placed on primary care providers by these systems. "Among the most challenging patients presenting in medical contexts are those with somatoform symptoms (Watson & McDaniel, 2000, p. 1068)" (Magnavita, 2000c, pp. 439–441).

Assessment of Family Systems

Most clinicians rely on interview, history, genogram, and observing the family process for a multilevel assessment (Magnavita, 2000a). In addition, there are numerous assessment instruments that may be used to assess the family. Olson (1996) has developed a very useful assessment model based on a circumplex paradigm for couples and families. A review of these is beyond the scope of this volume. Interested readers can refer to *Family Assessment: A Guide to Methods & Measures* by Grotevant and Carlson (1989). These authors reminded us of the challenges:

> Attempting to review the domain of family assessment brings to mind the metaphor of the hydra from Greek mythology. The hydra was a nine-headed monster that Hercules was challenged to slay. But whenever anyone managed to cut off one of the hydra's heads, two new heads grew in its place. The state of affairs in the family assessment field evokes this metaphor because, like the hydra's heads, measure and specialized theories in family studies have proliferated rapidly and in an uncoordinated fashion. (p. 5)

An essential element of the family assessment includes a genogram, which is a visual depiction of the members of a system over generations.

The Family Genogram

The basic assessment process for any family can be enhanced by using the family genogram developed by McGoldrick and Gerson (1985). A family genogram of at least three generations allows the clinician to gather important historical, dynamic, and relational data and depict this information in a visual representation that can be referred to later. The family genogram, when combined with knowledge of systems, is a tremendously powerful tool of assessment. Also, it should be noted that conducting a family genogram is also a therapeutic intervention because it increases differentiation and awareness of processes and codes that are being transmitted or reenacted.

Key Elements of Family Assessment

Several key elements should be noted and explored when conducting a family assessment (Kaslow, 1996; Magnavita, 2000a; Mikesell, Lusterman, & McDaniel, 1995). These include the following:

1. Multigenerational transmission process (Bowen, 1976, 1978)
2. Fixed triangular cross-generational relationships (Guerin et al., 1996)
3. Family communication process (Olson, 1996)
4. Family process
5. Level of differentiation among family members (Bowen, 1976, 1978)
6. Family cohesion (Olson, 1996)
7. Family flexibility (Olson, 1996)
8. Developmental stage of family (Carter & McGoldrick, 1980)
9. Level of defensive functioning in the members of the family (see assessment of the intrapsychic–biological system)
10. Predominant attachment styles of family members
11. Level of or capacity for intimacy and closeness
12. Parental style and agreement or disagreement of basic parenting approach (Family assessment does not have to be conducted with the family. When these concepts are understood, one can see family process at work in individuals and couples.)
13. Nature and extent of dysfunctional triangular relationships (Guerin et al., 1996)

ASSESSING THE SOCIOCULTURAL MATRIX

An assessment of the sociocultural matrix of an individual, couple, or family is crucial for deriving an accurate understanding of the personality system of the patient and his or her family. The influences of the sociocultural, economic, and political matrix are of paramount importance when considering intervention.

Factors to be considered in assessing the sociocultural matrix:

1. Socioeconomic status of individual or family
2. Educational level

3. Ethnic background
4. Religious and spiritual beliefs
5. Resources available
6. Viability of social network
7. Connection to institutions such as church, school, and community
8. Capacity to access needed services in community
9. Available services in community

CREATING A HOLONIC MAP

In the final section of this chapter, I briefly discuss how to create a holonic map, taking into consideration the relationship among symptom expression, diathesis–stress, and genetic code formulation.

The Diathesis–Stress of Dysfunctioning and Functioning Personality Systems

We have reviewed the component systems of the total ecological system of personality. We can depict the personality process by assessing the integrity of various domain systems, preferred pathways of anxiety, as well as various diatheses within these systems vulnerable to stress. When personality systems are under undue stress that is having an impact on the system at any of the triangular matrices, the preferred diathesis of that component system can be overloaded and channel the anxiety into symptom formations, relational disturbances, or other expression. This channel can then reverberate at various levels of the personality system. If the intrapsychic–biological triangle has a vulnerability to depression that is activated and this continues, the dyadic, nuclear family, and extended family systems will be affected. The marriage may become unstable with the increased demands. The stress reverberates throughout the various systems and can create dysfunction in multiple systems. Conversely, the stress may be absorbed in subsystems, which are able to adapt and respond, mitigating the impact of the destabilization on vulnerable members of the system.

The Diathesis–Stress of Symptom Expression

The main premise of personality-guided therapy is that the personality system is the main determinant of the way in which symptom formation is expressed. Focusing on the symptom constellation, although important at the initial stage of treatment, should not be the goal of therapy. Only by understanding the personality system and the vulnerability to certain forms of expression of symptoms or interpersonal conflict can we effectively treat mental disorders. Fractionation of the clinical syndrome from the person and personality system results in artificial reductionism that misses the phenomenology of the patient's experience and the communicative function of the symptom formation.

Genetic Code Formulation

Another central aspect of assessment is to begin to formulate the genetic codes (see chap. 5) that are carried by individuals in their intrapsychic–biological processes and transferred multigenerationally through dyadic, triadic, family, and societal processes. The genetic code is the narrative that is co-constructed in the therapeutic matrix that explains the personality system dysfunction. This might relate to multigenerational patterns of dysfunction, experiences of trauma, or developmental injuries and how they have been encoded in the relational patterns as expressed in the dyadic and triadic processes and intrapsychic processes as carried in schematic representations.

Selection of Specific Assessment Instruments

There are numerous assessment instruments that have been developed to assess the various component systems of personality. Each of these offers data about the personality system. Clinical assessment instruments can be cost-effective and time efficient as well as costly and time-consuming. Selecting a specific clinical assessment instrument should be given consideration only after an initial evaluation in most cases. Indiscriminately administered clinical assessment instruments offer little in the way of useful information to the clinical treatment team. However, when an instrument or a battery is selected that is used to refine or clarify personality system processes, the value can be worth the expense and time required. For example, most patients don't require that a Rorschach be administered. However, if a clinician suspects that the pathway of anxiety is to the cognitive–perceptual zone, this information can be confirmatory and help in refining treatment planning. When conducting couples treatment with severely dysfunctional dyadic configurations, it is sometimes judicious to administer the Millon Clinical Multiaxial Inventory (MCMI) to derive a clearer picture of the personality configuration and how the interlocking configurations of the couple become habitual (Magnavita, in press-b). This then offers the clinician ideas about which characteristics are most important to focus on in the treatment.

SUMMARY AND CONCLUSIONS

This chapter offers a unified approach to assessment that examines processes and structure at the various levels of the personality system. Using the four triangles as lenses, we can witness the processes of personality function–dysfunction and adaptation–maladaptation in the way in which the system and subsystems channel anxiety in various pathways. Moving from our understanding of this unified model, specific methods and techniques of assessment may be selected to map the holonic system most accurately and parsimoniously. Assessment is not a matter of administering clinical instruments but of knowing the systemic processes well enough to know which are most warranted.

III
METHODS OF TREATMENT

This part of the volume is devoted to the methods of restructuring in the context of a unified personality-guided relational model. It is divided into four chapters, each of which is devoted to one method of restructuring. The four main categories of restructuring coincide with the four triangles described in chapter 2. An overview of the methods is presented in the Exhibit.

EXHIBIT 1
Main Categories of Restructuring, Methods, and the Systemic Level Targeted

---

Intrapsychic restructuring (IR)

System Level: *Intrapsychic–Biological Triangle*

1. Defensive restructuring: focus on defensive operations
2. Cognitive restructuring: focus on cognitive schema and beliefs
3. Affective restructuring: focus on affective process and experience
4. Cognitive–behavioral restructuring: focus on affective experience and learning
5. Neurobiological restructuring: focus on neurotransmitters and biobehavioral systems

Dyadic restructuring (DR)

System Level: *Interpersonal–Dyadic Triangle*

1. Expected–transactive restructuring: focus on expected relationship with therapist
2. Self–other restructuring: focus on real relationship with therapist
3. Relational restructuring: focus on relationship with other

(continued)

EXHIBIT 1   *(Continued)*

Triadic restructuring (TR)

Systemic Level: *Triadic–Relational Configuration*

1. Relational–triadic restructuring: focus on three-person relationships
2. Symbolic–relational restructuring: focus on individual or dyad not physically present

Mesosystem restructuring (MR)

System Level: *Sociocultural–Familial Triangle*

1. Ecosystem restructuring: focus on altering components of mesosystem

7

INTRAPSYCHIC RESTRUCTURING: WORKING IN THE INTRAPSYCHIC–BIOLOGICAL TRIANGLE

Intrapsychic restructuring (IR) is a group of treatment methods designed to reorganize the patient's intrapsychic system. The focus of therapeutic action is on the *intrapsychic–biological triangle* (see Figure 1.1, p. 16). In Millon's (1990) system, this method of restructuring is primarily related to the *pleasure–pain* polarity, in terms of how the affect system is organized and how it functions. The individual's affective system is shaped by pleasure–pain experiences in early attachments. Intrapsychic restructuring can occur in a variety of treatment modalities such as individual, group, couples, family, and ecological therapies. Typically, however, intrapsychic restructuring has been considered the domain of individual psychotherapy and is one of the most commonly used methods. A systemic relational model assumes that restructuring at the intrapsychic level is a normal part of the developmental progression. Thus, as a child progresses through development in optimal conditions, he or she will acquire an increasingly differentiated and stable intrapsychic system. This system responds with resilience to the negative forces that affect an individual, possessing capacities such as the ability to experience and regulate affect, as well as one's psychological mindedness (an understanding of one's own system), adaptive defensive functioning, and stable sense of self and identity. Conversely, when trauma, neglect, or other developmental insults and challenges are endured, the integrity of this personality system is compromised.

METHODS OF INTRAPSYCHIC RESTRUCTURING

Numerous intrapsychic restructuring methods have been developed over the last century. Clinicians from a variety of orientations and therapeutic schools have pioneered these methods, but all share a common focus on reorganizing and restructuring what occurs within the individual's personality system as opposed to what occurs between and among others. The primary methods of intrapsychic restructuring include the following: (a) *defensive restructuring*, (b) *cognitive restructuring*, (c) *affective restructuring*, (d) *cognitive–behavioral restructuring*, and (e) *neurobiological restructuring*. An overview of the variety of restructuring methods is presented in Figure 7.1 to orient the reader. The various methods of IR have a somewhat different focus in the intrapsychic–biological triangle, but all have a reorganizing effect on the personality system through differentiation and integration of its components (see Figure 7.1). The foci of the restructuring methods, for example, on defenses, on cognitive functioning, on affective elements, etc., are determined by the results of the assessment. The goal of most of these methods is to assist the individual in processing feelings and restructuring schema related to developmentally significant trauma.

Traumatic experiences form the nexus of unprocessed emotional reactions and associated internalized beliefs such as, "I must be unlovable to have been abused, neglected or emotionally mistreated in the manner that I was subjected to." Readers may refer to chapter 3 to review the foundational concepts and processes. Core traumata include the following:

- Incidents of physical or sexual abuse
- Emotional abuse and neglect
- Loss of attachment or inadequate attachment
- Narcissistic parental or adult use
- Environmental trauma, such as war, acts of nature, and so forth
- Severe environmental hardship, such as poverty
- Severe family dysfunction

Core trauma can be encapsulated in the cognitive–affective matrix and maintained in the individual's neurobiological system, which are later activated at unexpected times. These unmetabolized events and experiences form painful affective-laden configurations that may remain encapsulated but influence the overall integrity of the personality system. The forms of IR presented here serve to activate these complexes and in so doing may

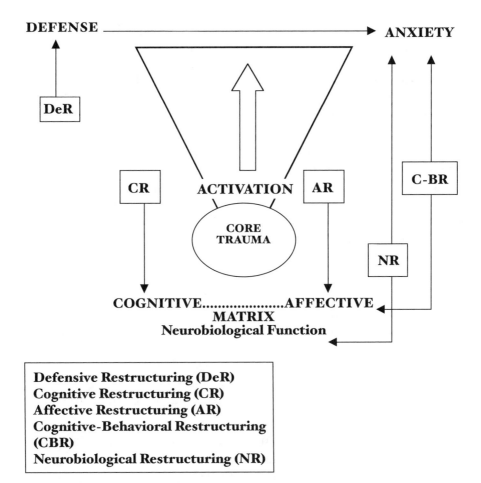

Figure 7.1. Foci of various methods of intrapsychic restructuring at the biological level.

afford the patient an opportunity to process and master these experiences. Conditions of intense or sustained core trauma have an impact on the personality system. The assessment of trauma requires an understanding of the developmental progression and nature of traumatic experience on human psychic functioning and personality organization.

DEFENSIVE RESTRUCTURING (DR)

Defensive restructuring, also called *defense analysis*, is a powerful method of modifying defenses and activating the affective–cognitive– neurobiological matrix. The study and elaboration of defensive functioning has been one of the hallmarks of 20th-century psychodynamic psychotherapy. Originally recognized by Freud and later elaborated by his followers, including Anna Freud (1966), Otto Fenichel (1945), and Melanie Klein (who developed the construct of projective identification, 1935/1964), defensive restructuring became a hallmark of psychoanalytic and psychodynamic treatment. Later workers, most notably Wilhelm Reich (1933) and Habib Davanloo (1980), advanced technical understanding of the importance of defensive functioning with the neurotic character or personality-disordered individual (Magnavita, 1997b). Empirical research shows strong support of the construct of defenses and the likelihood that there is a developmental progression to how they develop (Cramer, 1987; Perry & Cooper, 1989; Vaillant, 1971). Defensive restructuring basically concerns itself with the questions, "How are you acting right now?" or "How are you reacting in your relationship with others?" Fosha (2000b) described the following defensive strategies:

- Formal defenses that operate intrapsychically (e.g., repression, denial, minimization, isolation of affect, reaction formation)
- More primitive defenses that aim to manipulate reality (e.g., externalization, projection, somatization, introjection, projective identification)
- Defenses that affect the organization of the self (e.g., dissociation)
- Defenses that operate on relational contact (e.g., the barrier, the wall). (p. 84)

Grigsby and Stevens (2000), who provided an excellent illustration in a review of the neuropsychological evidence, noted that for personality to shift repeatedly, bringing behavior to awareness is necessary. They described the use of defensive restructuring with an individual with a passive–aggressive personality in the following passage:

> Successfully treating a passive–aggressive individual requires repeatedly drawing his or her attention to the habitual behavior and others' reaction to it, and to the discrepancy between his or her professed motives and rationalizations and the effect their behavior has on others. The behavior itself must become conscious, and the automaticity of the behavior must be disrupted, drawing into focus the discrepancy between these functional systems. Only then can the individual begin to take active control over the passive behavior, and the self-representation may begin to shift so that it comes to include the possibility that he or she might at times express aggression overtly. (p. 319)

Defensive restructuring is a set of powerful methods and techniques for a trained therapist. When applied in the correct dosage for the individual, it appears to destabilize the defensive functioning and allow affective responding to increase. This allows for the reorganization of the intrapsychic system at a higher level of adaptation. Defenses are called on when emotional capacity is low. As emotional capacity increases, the necessity of relying on defenses as a way of warding off emotional experience is reduced. The various types of DR, presented in the following section, can be distinguished by their varying modes of action and techniques, although there is a certain amount of overlap among them.

Types of DeR: Defensive–Affective–Cognitive and Neurobiological Processes

Defenses can be supported and strengthened or challenged and actively disrupted. The use of defensive restructuring can have an immediate impact on the individual's intrapsychic system, resulting in anxiety and the activation of regressive defenses. Clinicians should therefore use the technique only with appropriate training and under supervision of an experienced colleague. Less intensive use of defensive restructuring will mobilize anxiety but can be more carefully modulated. The patient's personality system is the main determinant in selecting a DeR technique. For example, using DSM–IV (American Psychiatric Association, 1994) terminology, someone with a narcissistic or borderline personality disorder may experience high levels of anxiety in response to the more or less benign process of identification of defenses, misperceiving this in a highly distorted way, and thus subjectively experiencing it as criticism or even attack. In contrast, a patient with a less severe type of personality disorder may indeed experience the more moderate level of anxiety designated in Exhibit 7.1. Therefore, the patient's individual personality system, or in dyads the level of differentiation between personality systems, must be taken into account. The types of defensive restructuring and the level of anxiety they mobilize are presented in Exhibit 7.1.

Identification and Cataloguing of Defenses

The therapist simply points out and "catalogues" defenses as they are observed in the interpersonal process with the therapist or in relation to

EXHIBIT 7.1
Types of Defensive Restructuring and Level of Anxiety Mobilized

Identification of defenses: moderate anxiety
Confrontation of defenses: high anxiety
Intensification of defenses: moderate anxiety
Affirmation and invitation to intimacy: low anxiety
Demonstration of defenses: low to moderate anxiety
Supporting defenses: low anxiety

significant others (Magnavita, 1997a). In doing so, the therapist increases the awareness of the defensive style that the patient has adopted. The identification of defenses is a fairly common method of psychotherapy. The systematic identification and explanation requires one to be familiar with the defenses listed in chapter 4. Each individual has a unique set of defenses that generally shifts under stress. In lower functioning individuals, the defense system can quickly become primitive, which may result in regression. In higher functioning individuals, the defenses may falter, but there is generally not the collapse of the defense systems or the major regression seen in those with lower functioning. Defenses can be pointed out in all modalities of treatment and lead to greater self-awareness. This type of restructuring does not generally exert a high degree of pressure on the patient to put them aside, as demonstrated in the following vignette:

TH: You tend to use a number of defenses in the relationships that you describe. These include a tendency to intellectualize, rationalize, suppress your feelings, and become tentative with others.

PT: Yes, I never put them all together in that way before.

TH: In what way do you think these have affected your relationships?

PT: My wife says that it is hard for her to know how I really feel about anything.

This type of restructuring has a psychoeducational emphasis and is used to increase awareness and gradually access emotion.

Confrontation of Defenses

A more intensive form of defensive restructuring requires a confrontation of the defenses by persistently pointing out how they disrupt the process of therapy as well as lead to less adaptive states of functioning. This method of IR was pioneered primarily by Ferenczi and Rank (1925), Fenichel (1945), Reich (1933), Perls (1969), and Davanloo (1980). Defenses are confronted with the invitation to relate to the therapist and significant others in a more direct, open, and emotionally based manner. Going a step beyond identification of defenses, once the patient's defense system is catalogued, it can be confronted more forcefully, and this might include toxic labeling (Magnavita, 1997a). The goal here is to disrupt an entrenched defensive pattern that is not responding to less intensive intervention. This type of disruption of defenses might be necessary for more entrenched and engrained personality systems. As Reich (1933) warned us, this can provoke a good deal of aggression toward the therapist, so it is necessary to be well grounded and supervised in this method before undertaking it. A confrontation of one's defenses goes a step beyond merely identifying them, also pointing out that they are self-defeating and self-sabotaging (Davanloo, 1980). Furthermore, it may be underscored that the defense system, as the patient is using it, interferes with the therapeutic process by keeping the therapist at bay and creating unnecessary emotional distance in the therapeutic relationship (Davanloo, 1980). As Davanloo (1980) and others (Firestone, 1997) have noted, this defensive system protects the individual from genuine emotional intimacy and closeness. Individuals who have experienced insults or losses in their primary attachment typically avoid emotional closeness. The defense system is organized to fend off potential harm or reinjury that is expected (cognitive and relational schema) to reoccur if others are allowed too close. The confrontation of defenses aims at disrupting the defenses and is thus a more forceful type of restructuring, as demonstrated in the following vignette:

TH: Are you aware that as you discuss your difficulties with me, you are looking out the window, rationalizing, and seem entirely disconnected from your feelings? If you continue in this pattern, it will be difficult for us to make any progress here.

PT: I have no idea what it is that you expect of me. This is the way I have always been.

TH: But now you declare that you are helpless to change these destructive defenses.

PT: I would like to but [becomes quiet and withdraws]—

TH: You declare that you want to, but you become withdrawn. These defenses—rationalizing, disconnecting from your feelings, detaching, withdrawing, becoming helpless—create a wall between you and me. What do you intend to do about the wall?

Actively confronting defenses in such a manner can have enormous impact in creating a disequilibrium in the intrapsychic system and in mobilizing powerful affects; When such confrontation is done effectively, it can be a major step in emotional processing that is a corrective experience.

Intensification of Defense

Another way to conduct defense analysis, pioneered by Perls (1969), is to have the patient exaggerate his or her defense. Asking the patient to assume a more strident stance in the use of his or her defense with the therapist or significant other. This is a type of paradoxical intervention that forces the system to bifurcate so that the other side of a polarity is brought to awareness. As the patient is encouraged to "own" his or her defensive responses, there is an increase in awareness and a likelihood that he or she will let go of the defensive posture. Also, underlying affective experience will be activated. Perls (1969) described many excellent technical interventions that are powerful means of defense restructuring. For example, when a patient is avoiding an area of focal conflict, instead of pointing out the defense of changing the subject, the therapist might ask the patient to state directly what he or she wishes. This is portrayed in the following vignette:

TH: You said last week that you wanted to discuss certain issues regarding your sexuality with me but we did not get to the subject.

PT: Well, there are some other things going on in my life . . .

TH: Can you tell me directly that you don't want to talk about this?

PT: Well, really I do. I planned to discuss this with you today.

TH: See if you can tell me directly that you won't.

PT: I won't talk to you about this.

TH: Now try again, but say it with conviction!

PT: I am not going to talk to you about this!

TH: Again.

PT: [*with more feeling*] I am not going to talk to you about this!

TH: OK, really let me know how you feel!

PT: I am not going to talk to you about this! [*Sadness breaks through, and the patient starts to sob.*]

PT: I never had a close relationship with either parent where I felt I could discuss intimate matters. They would always discourage me.

Affirmation and Invitation to Increase Intimacy With the Therapist

In this type of restructuring, the therapist affirms the patient's core self and feeling (Fosha, 2000b; Magnavita, 2001a) and invites him or her to closeness. Without pressuring the patient, the therapist offers the opportunity to relate in a more authentic way, emphasizing closeness—open, honest, and genuine communication from the patient. This is a method that side steps the defenses, as described by Fosha (2000b), in which the therapist uses affirmation of the patient and his or her accomplishments and offers an invitation into a deeper relational experience: "Paradoxically, removing the pressure often leads to therapeutic progress. When the patient feels that he does not *have* to proceed to an experience for which he is not yet ready, he will feel more control over it and therefore less anxious, and will have less of a need for defense" (p. 251). The therapist becomes like a coach who encourages the patient "to persist and affirming the value of trying to do so" (p. 251). When the patient can deepen the therapeutic relationship, the defensive system loosens its hold over the personality system. This is a gentler approach, as demonstrated in the following vignette:

TH: It seems very difficult for you to share your feelings with me. I am sure there are some very good reasons for you not wanting to do so, and we can wait until you are ready to go there.

PT: I am not sure I will ever be ready.

TH: It sounds like you have some very good reasons for not wanting me to get close to you.

PT: It is a very terrifying notion that you are inviting me to get close to you.

TH: I know that it is really hard, but I am here when you feel that you can face the terror with me.

PT: It is very sad to hear the way you are talking with me. No one has ever shown such patience. It seems like you are really here for me, not for your needs like it was with my father and mother. *[Sadness is mobilized and the patient becomes tearful.]*

TH: I guess you feel that we can face the terrifying aspects of this process together, in a way that you have never before experienced.

In this type of restructuring, defenses are more likely to melt rather than be disrupted (Fosha, 2000b).

Demonstration of Defensive Functioning

The therapist names the defensive operation and demonstrates how this is a defense against anxiety (Scharff & Scharff, 1991). An excellent way to conduct defense analysis, described by Scharff and Scharff, is to explain to an individual how his or her defensive operation is used to keep anxiety contained. This is particularly powerful in the "here-and-now" process of couples or family therapy. The therapist can point out the operation as it is occurring. For example, in a couples session, the husband was complaining about how his wife needed to be hospitalized because of her eating disorder and was talking about the research he had done and the evidence he had about her bulimia. She responded by describing how her husband does not provide any emotional support and how she doesn't feel loved. It became clear from their pattern of communication that he "lived in his head" and was a "fixer and problem solver" and that she was much more emotionally driven. Their communication endlessly missed the mark, frustrating them to the point that they were considering divorce. When the therapist pointed out this pattern, they realized that their communication pattern wasn't working and that their model for their marriage—she was sick and he was going to rehabilitate her—was flawed. Another example is provided in the following vignette:

TH: Are you aware that when your wife starts to talk about her depression, you start to tell her how to structure her day by becoming more active?

HUSBAND: Yes, now that you point that out; but I am only trying to help her.

TH: Yes, this is trying to be helpful, but is it possible that it is a way to avoid your own anxiety when it comes to the helplessness you feel in face of your wife's despair?

PT: Yes, I am used to having the answer and knowing what to do. Now that you point it out, I do feel helpless, and this makes me very anxious. I guess my attempt to fix it makes it difficult for me to listen to her.

TH: *[to wife]* Do you really want to tell him about the depth of your despair and what you think it is about?

WIFE: Yes, if he is willing to listen without trying to fix it.

TH: *[to husband]* What do you think?

HUSBAND: Yes, I want her to tell me, but I might become emotional myself.

TH: Well that would be quite all right.

The process of restructuring often has subtle differences, but essentially the therapist is attempting to reach emotional experience and validate and help the patient metabolize it.

Supporting Defenses

Finally, defenses can be supported while other methods of restructuring are incorporated. Thus, in a crisis, for example, the individual's defensive responding may be encouraged to assist the individual in navigating a particularly challenging phase of life. In fact, much of psychotherapy is supportive. Supporting defenses can be used to begin to create a more solid foundation in someone whose defensive functioning is at a lower level of organization. This type of defensive restructuring is a much more gradual one that has typically been the main method of supportive forms of psychotherapy. Supporting defenses can help create an attachment with the therapist for someone whose attachment experiences are limited. This can be seen in the following vignette:

PT: I think that they are all out to get me and I really needed to stand up for myself or be destroyed.

TH: Yes, it is really important to be able to stand up for yourself when you are in danger of being destroyed.

PT: What else can I do but react with anger when they want to attack me and put me down.

TH: Your desire to preserve your integrity must be maintained.

PT: Maybe I didn't need to react with such hostility to her insulting behavior.

TH: Well, we certainly can explore that, but the important thing is that you have a strong will to persevere in adverse situations.

The power of supporting defenses lies in the strengthening of the integrity of the intrapsychic system by trying to find elements of defensive functioning that have adaptive value without encouraging destructive behavior.

COGNITIVE RESTRUCTURING (CR)

Cognitive restructuring is a more recent method of psychotherapy, pioneered by Beck, Rush, Shaw, and Emery (1979) and Ellis and Harper (1961) and is based on an information-processing model. In a parallel development in the psychodynamic tradition, Davanloo (1980) developed another method of cognitive restructuring. Cognitive restructuring attempts to identify and modify attitudes, beliefs, and core schema that form part of the individual's cognitive–affective matrix. Whereas defensive restructuring works on the defensive response system of the intrapsychic–biological triangle, cognitive restructuring works at the level of the cognitive matrix vis-à-vis schemas, scripts, and internalized beliefs. Cognitive restructuring usually concerns itself with the question, "What are you thinking?" These beliefs form schema that guide internal information templates from which one's behavioral repertoire emanates. As Greenberg, Rice, and Elliott (1993) described, "The basic contribution of the schema concept is that it recognizes that humans internally represent objects or events by a configuration of features. Schemas include but go beyond purely propositional representations to encode regularities in categories that are both perceptual and conceptual" (pp. 46–47). From an object relational perspective, these include introjects (unchallenged beliefs about oneself based on treatment by major attachment figures) that guide and shape the individual's response system. This method of intrapsychic restructuring activates the cognitive–affective matrix by focusing on the cognitions first and then processing the affective components secondarily. There are three main types of cognitive restructuring, which have different origins and somewhat different therapeutic actions. Classical cognitive restructuring originated in the work of Aaron Beck and Albert Ellis. Another type of cognitive restructuring emanates from the work of Habib Davanloo, one of the pioneers of short-term dynamic therapy. The third type of cognitive restructuring, called *transactive restructuring*, originated primarily by Eric Berne (Berne, Steiner, & Dusay, 1973), has roots in transactional analysis and later evolved into redecision therapy (Joines & Stewart, 2002) and in Robert Firestone's (1997) voice therapy, which seeks to find the internalized voice that guides one's life.

Type I. Beckian: Classic Cognitive

This style of restructuring aims at altering the template that an individual has used to guide his or her response to relationships and life challenges. When an individual has experienced negative treatment from caregivers, these experiences are retained as part of the information processing system, forming schema that guide interpersonal interpretations and interactions and current relationships. This negative experience is incorporated into the covert–internal interpretational level. The following technical interventions have been described by Beck, Rush, Shaw, and Emery (1979, p. 14) and include challenging arbitrary inferences, selective abstraction, overgeneralization, magnification and minimization, personalization, and dichotomous thinking. In the Beckian model of cognitive restructuring, thoughts and beliefs that are dysfunctional are substituted with more adaptive ones that are not so limiting to the personality system. These techniques are intended to foster corrective effects on the meanings and interpretations patients give to interpersonal events, that is, other's actions and reactions (Anchin, 2003). Cognitive scientists believe that feelings emanate from thoughts, and if the thought system is altered, feelings will also be changed. The sequence of methods therefore considers cognitions first and the affect system second. This type of restructuring is portrayed in the following vignette:

PT: Last night when my wife and I were talking about our relationship, I started to become upset.

TH: What happened?

PT: I didn't want her to see me so weak.

TH: You believe that showing your feelings in an intimate way to your wife is a sign of weakness?

PT: Yes, men in my family were supposed to be the strong, silent type.

TH: So at some point in your life you were led to believe that showing feelings was not manly.

PT: It isn't!

TH: That sounds like a strong belief that you carry about men. I wonder where it came from?

PT: When I was a boy, whenever I hurt myself and cried, my father would become irate and say, "I'll give you something to cry about if you don't be quiet."

TH: So it seems that you developed a guiding belief about how men should behave from your father's harsh treatment of you. I wonder if this is no longer a useful guide for you as a man?

PT: I never really thought about how much it shaped my thinking and relationships.

Type II. Davanloovian: Cognitive–Dynamic

Davanloo (1980) pioneered another type of cognitive restructuring that has a somewhat different therapeutic action and focus than that of Beck et al. (1979). Davanloo's method uses the *biological intropsychic triangle of conflict* (impulse/feeling, defense, and anxiety) termed by Malan (1979) to orient the clinician and guide the restructuring process. He developed this technique for patients had what he termed "fragile ego," those who tend to rely on more primitive defenses and who have had trauma. Abbass (2001) summarized the method as follows:

> the therapeutic process involves examining situations of anxiety or defenses, focusing on the underlying feelings, reducing pressure if there are any signs of cognitive disruption and intellectually liking the feelings, anxiety and defenses. Gradually the patient will start to be able to express and experience emotions: the patient will feel grief about losses including the diagnosis [if schizophrenic], the treatment and loss of treatment providers in the past. (p. 144)

The Davanlovian method of cognitive restructuring consists of a structured series of examining the behavioral sequences in interpersonal relationships that are conflictual. In this method, the patient is asked to be incident specific and describe in detail the sequence of events that occurred. In progressing through the sequence, the therapist takes a psychoeducative stance, labeling and differentiating among the three corners of the triangle of conflict (feeling, anxiety, and defense). This method is easy to teach and can result in a gradual increase in the adaptive capacity of an individual. Abbass (2001) applied this type of restructuring to the treatment of patients with schizophrenia and achieved positive results (see chap. 12).

PT: I cut myself last night when my boyfriend went out with his buddies.

TH: Can you describe specifically what occurred? [*The therapist wants to have the patient describe in detail the interpersonal and behavioral sequence.*]

PT: He told me he would be going out and that's when it started.

TH: How did you react? *[The therapist uses the word "react" because she is looking for the behavioral sequence, not for an emotion, which might overwhelm a fragile patient.]*

PT: I started to scream at him that if he left he would be sorry.

TH: So your reaction to his telling you that he was leaving was to scream at him and threaten him. *[These are primitive and regressive defenses.]*

PT: Yes, I felt abandoned again by him!

TH: And then what happened?

PT: He left and I took some razor blades and cut myself.

TH: So when he said he was leaving this mobilized tremendous anxiety in you and the way you dealt with this anxiety was to cut yourself. *[The cutting is a defense that reduces the anxiety.]* OK, so what you describe is that you have what feels like intolerable feeling when you feel abandoned and the way you deal with this anxiety is to harm yourself.

PT: Yes I was enraged at him.

TH: Well yes, but rage is an emotion and cutting yourself is the way you defend against this unbearable emotion.

In this type of restructuring, the therapist is helping the patient build cognitive structure that can begin to mediate reactive patterns by systematically introducing the patient to her intrapsychic system and how it works. Thus, in a methodical way, the therapist differentiates anxiety, feeling, and defense so that the patient becomes increasingly familiar with reactive and nonmediated emotional states that cause overwhelming anxiety. The therapist continues to select a series of emotional incidents from the patient's current life experience to review in the same manner. With systematic review of numerous issues, ego structure is built as the individual gains the ability to predict intrapsychic response activation.

Type III. Transactive Cognitive Restructuring

This third type of cognitive restructuring elicits and examines the internalization of the communications of important attachments. Often the "voice" exists and guides behavior at an unconscious level. Firestone (1997) used a form of cognitive restructuring that consists of helping an individual identify the internalized "voice" that guides his or her behavior, a method that can often be very powerful. In a similar sense, transactional analysis uses a type of cognitive restructuring by deciphering and altering scripts that guide one's life and behavior (Stewart & Joines, 1987). Often in therapy, when the voice is operating, it may sound as if the patient's normal voice has changed tone. In one case, the parental voice becomes apparent through the harsh, critical tone that accompanies it. This type of restructuring is demonstrated in the following vignette:

PT: I was planning to go on vacation and then had second thoughts.

TH: What were you aware of?

PT: I started to ask myself, "Do you really need such an expensive vacation?" and "What will happen to the house if no one is there to watch it?" [Patient sounds harsh and condemning.]

TH: I noticed the tone of your voice became harsh and critical, which is not your normal way of talking.

PT: Oh, that's the way my father would get whenever my mother said she wanted to go on vacation.

TH: So you carry his voice inside you and use it to keep yourself in line the way your Dad used to do with your mother when she asked for anything.

PT: Yes, this has been my habit and has kept me from doing a lot of things.

TH: Maybe we could find something less restrictive and punitive to replace his voice.

PT: I think that would be a good idea. Maybe I could tell myself, I earned it and can afford to go and that taking vacation is healthy.

Using another approach from transactional analysis, the therapist can help patients find the underlying scripts that they use to guide their lives and help them examine and alter them.

When to Use Cognitive Restructuring

As one of the most empirically endorsed methods, cognitive restructuring is an excellent starting point for most patients. Classic cognitive restructuring is generally applicable to most clinical syndromes and has been used for the range of personality dysfunction. Most clinicians, even those who have not been formally trained in cognitive methods, naturally incorporate them into their approach. Cognitive–dynamic restructuring is most suitable for those whose personality system is fragile and needs to be restructured to pave the way for other methods that are more anxiety provoking. Transactive cognitive restructuring has a wide range of applicability and can be used by most clinicians, who are attentive to and adept at identifying scripts and internalized voices. All the methods described are generally excellent choices for lower functioning patients who cannot tolerate too much activation of anxiety.

AFFECTIVE RESTRUCTURING (AR)

Affective restructuring, also called *emotion restructuring*, emanates from the work of experiential therapy (Greenberg & Paivio, 1997; Greenberg & Safran, 1987), derived from short-term dynamic therapy (McCullough Vaillant, 1997), which emphasizes the centrality of "core emotional experiencing" (Fosha, 2000b). Affective restructuring is the process by which emotion is experienced, felt, labeled, and communicated interpersonally. Affective restructuring generally concerns itself with the question, "How are you feeling?" or "How do you experience your feeling?" Historically, emotional or affective restructuring emanates from the work of Rogers (1951) and Perls (1969), who developed different approaches to accessing and processing core emotion. Today, this would be called "emotional intelligence" (Goleman, 1994) and is an essential aspect of effective interpersonal relationships. Goleman identified key ingredients for attaining emotional intelligence:

1. Identifying and labeling feelings
2. Expressing feelings
3. Assessing the intensity of feelings
4. Managing feelings
5. Delaying gratification
6. Controlling impulses
7. Reducing stress
8. Knowing the difference between feelings and actions (p. 301)

Following the Affect

Many contemporary clinicians and theorists are convinced that following the affect is the key to effective psychotherapy. When the therapist follows the affect and looks for areas in which there is affective resonance, therapy is generally more satisfying for the patient and therapist. For therapists, becoming a master of affect systems will attune the therapist to attractor states and processes that are maladaptive. These are the "hot spots" or emotional nexus in the various component subsystems. Metabolization of affects can strengthen the patient's functioning, and the development of such mastery can strength the personality system by allowing a greater tolerance and range of emotion. Patients generally don't recognize or acknowledge the power of their emotions and are often unaware of the benefit of full emotional processing of conflictual zones in their experience. The first sign of affect is usually seen nonverbally and the therapist is often aware of this before the patient. Emotion for many people has associated shame and is therefore avoided. Dealing directly with clear communication about what the therapist senses and observes is refreshing for most patients, who are unaccustomed to being affirmed in their everyday lives. At first they may appear uncomfortable, but with explanation about the importance of the "emotional guidance system," they become appreciative about the attention paid to their affect system.

Processes of Affective Restructuring

Within the broad category of affective techniques are various processes to restructure affect. These include processes aimed at (a) amplification of affect, (b) differentiation of affect, (c) integration of affect, and (d) metabolization of affect.

Amplification of Affect

Affective arousal is usually quite high at the onset of psychotherapy as the entry into the therapeutic matrix immediately activates anxiety due to the expected relational system that the patient has as his or her template. The therapist should amplify underlying affect as soon as there is a strong therapeutic alliance and the patient can tolerate this activation. The amplification of affect can be achieved in many ways. Patients can be asked to focus on what they physically experience in their viscera. The therapist can keep the patient focused on painful areas that are more likely affect laden and with sustained focus will lead to activation of emotion. This is demonstrated in the following vignette:

PT: When I received the divorce papers I was really not happy.

TH: What were you aware of physically when you received them?

PT: Oh, I thought it was finally over.

TH: I notice as you are talking that there is a certain look of pain on your face.

PT: I am not aware of any.

TH: See if you can take some time and focus on what you are experiencing.

PT: There is tightness in my chest.

TH: What is underneath the tightness?

PT: There are some other feelings [eyes start to water].

TH: It seems there are some tears in your eyes. What would it be like if you really let yourself contact that sadness?

PT: *[Starts to cry.]* I am not sure I can let myself.

TH: How deep does it go?

PT: I think it goes way down to the bottom.

TH: It sounds like there is a tremendous amount of sadness if you allow yourself to feel it.

PT: Starts to cry and then sob.

TH: There is a deep grief inside of you that you are contacting.

Differentiation of Affect

Differentiation of affect is another essential process of affective restructuring. Reflecting nonverbal manifestation and labeling of affect are ways to assist in the differentiation of emotion. When the therapist observes affect, the patient is often unaware of emotional experience. Labeling the various core emotions can emotionally differentiate the patient's affective experience. Emotional constellations are often a tangle of diffuse emotional experience mixed with anxiety and defensive operations. The first order in differentiation of affective experience is the differentiation of anxiety and defense. The patient must learn to recognize the physiological components of anxiety (e.g., sweaty palms, dry mouth, rapid heart beat, apprehensiveness). For example, although a patient may state that he or she was angry when describing this, the actual visceral components are describing anxiety. This is a common manifestation of low emotional differentiation. Once established, anxiety then can be monitored as it ebbs and flows during the therapeutic process. Once anxiety is established and grounded to the physiological components, the therapist can begin to untangle the complex of feeling. This is demonstrated in the following clinical vignette:

TH: How are you feeling right now?

PT: I am confused about what I feel.

TH: What do you notice in your body?

PT: Well, there is a certain degree of anxiousness, and I am thinking about the death of my sister years ago.

TH: What else besides the anxiety?

PT: There is a pain.

TH: Can you describe the pain?

PT: It feels like heaviness in my chest.

TH: You look very sad right now.

PT: I am. I really never said goodbye to my sister. I didn't go to her funeral.

TH: I wonder if there are other feelings that go into the anxiety besides the sadness.

PT: *[The patient makes fists.]* Well I suppose there are.

TH: Your hands are in fists. I wonder if there is some anger there as well.

PT: Yes, I think I was so mad I could not go to her funeral.

TH: How do you experience the anger right now?

PT: It feels like a hot welling up of lava in a volcano.

TH: It sounds like a massive rage coming to the surface.

PT: Yes, I am furious but I shouldn't be because she died.

TH: It sounds like you feel guilty.

PT: Yes, I do. I really loved her and was furious that she left me with my parents without anybody to talk to. They were both alcoholics.

Integration of Affect

Affect resulting from conflict may also benefit from being integrated, especially when it is competing emotions that are in conflict. Playing out polarities is a useful technique to integrate affect. The therapist either has the patient literally play out polar positions using the two-chair technique pioneered by Perls (1969) or does so without the physical movement from chair to chair. This is essentially a dialectic process in which each side of a polarity is voiced and then a third, more integrated position is achieved. Once affect is amplified, the affective states associated with various sides of the conflict can be brought to the surface, and splits can be mended. This is demonstrated in the following clinical vignette:

PT: I should not continue with school. There are other people who could take my place and benefit more from going.

TH: It sounds as if part of you wants to go and part wants to dropout, and you are feeling guilty about this.

PT: I think I should just drop out; others deserve to be there.

TH: Can you let the part of you that wants to drop out speak?

PT: Yes. You have no right to go to school. You are not smart enough, and you are the only one in your family who has ever tried. You take time away from others when you go to school.

TH: It sounds like there is an angry tone in your voice.

PT: I am angry.

TH: Now can you let the other side talk.

PT: You really love school and believe it will add a lot to your life in the future. It makes you feel like you're smart and capable and deserve something.

TH: It sounds like a part of you is feeling really guilty for going beyond your family and another part is really pleased with your accomplishments.

PT: Yeah, my family never encouraged me, and I guess I am angry about that. It seems like they wanted to hold me back because they are so miserable.

TH: It sounds like holding yourself back is a way of staying attached and not threatening the system.

Metabolization of Affect

Painful affect when not felt can result in destructive and maladaptive behavior. The overall goal of therapy is metabolization—literally the digestion, absorption, and accretion of the by-products of feelings patients have kept at bay. For full metabolization of affect to occur, there must be activation of the cognitions associated with this affective constellation. The cognitive component must be connected to the affective component in such a way that a narrative is formed, which includes the genesis and associated schematic representations that are dysfunctional and can now be restructured. Thus, it is often the case in states of pathological grief over unresolved loss and reactive sadism (i.e., will to harm those who have harmed us), and associated guilt, shame, and grief over traumatic experience, that the memories and affective responses are encapsulated. When affective resonance is created and emotional capacity increases, intense feelings may begin to emerge and must be experienced. Pathological grief and traumatic experience are affective constellations that benefit from metabolization, but it may require multiple episodes of affective restructuring to fully metabolize core trauma and unresolved loss. When the patient has fully metabolized the affect associated with an intensely painful experience, he or she has identified and deeply experienced the full range of painful affects associated with the unresolved loss or trauma. Through cognitive processing of those feelings, the patient has developed a clearer understanding about their bases, translated these insights into overt actions if necessary, and experienced resolution of the core trauma. This is demonstrated in the following clinical vignette:

PT: I can't remember where my father was buried and whether I attended the funeral.

TH: I notice you have a look of pain on your face. You say that you don't remember where he was buried or even if you attended his funeral.

[A phase of work ensues focusing on activating his grief.]

Next Session

PT: I spent a day searching for my father's grave at the cemetery where my mother said he was buried. I finally found the grave and sat there for a long while.

TH: What did you say to him?

PT: I told him I was sorry. *[Patient starts sobbing in deep grief.]*

TH: There is a deep grief but also guilt. Where is the guilt from?

PT: I was so angry with him for abusing me when I was a kid. When he died I didn't want to deal with all my mixed feelings toward him.

TH: So you filed all that grief and guilt away and never went through a state of mourning.

PT: Yes, I feel like I am doing that now, almost 20 years later.

COGNITIVE–BEHAVIORAL RESTRUCTURING (C-BR)

Cognitive–behavioral restructuring uses methods of exposure to extinguish the connection between thoughts and painful feelings and modify the intrapsychic system. C-BR shares many features with affective restructuring techniques, although the mode of action differs. These methods are primarily based on classical and operant conditioning paradigms. In a classical conditioning paradigm, traumatic events are often powerful learning experiences that pair intense emotional reactions with stimulus features of the event that often become generalized. In the operant conditioning paradigm, certain bionegative patterns may be reinforced and positive ones punished. In treatment, the introduction of feared stimuli to the intrapsychic system can be achieved either in a gradual manner or through flooding. The main pioneers of this approach are Thomas Stampfl (Stampfl & Lewis, 1973), who developed implosive therapy, and Joseph Wolpe (1958, 1973), who developed systematic desensitization.

Implosive therapy is a method by which a patient's intrapsychic system is flooded so that the individual may face frightening memories and thoughts. Systematic desensitization is a more gradual approach to extinguish anxiety related to feared stimuli. Systematic desensitization uses relaxation training while introducing successive gradations of feared stimuli until the anxiety and fear is extinguished. Francine Shapiro (1995) developed an innovative method of C-BR called *eye movement desensitization reprocessing* (EMDR), which uses rapid eye movement to access emotional states related to traumatic events and to extinguish stimulus–response associations. Techniques and methods of *dialectic behavioral therapy* (DBT), developed by Marsha Linehan (1993), also use techniques of restructuring to modify conditioning paradigms. Linehan uses various cognitive–behavioral techniques to build more adaptive self-soothing strategies and extinguish bionegative ones such as parasuicidal behavior. Another similar type of technique of restructuring was developed early in the 20th century by Ferenczi and Rank (1925) and is used in contemporary short-term dynamic psychotherapy (Magnavita, 1993a, 1997a). Ferenczi developed a technique similar in some ways to what Stampfl later developed that uses forced fantasy to desensitize the patient to his or her neurotic fears. McCullough (1998) referred to this as an *affect phobia* and suggested that the affective component actually becomes the feared state that is avoided. Patients are asked to elaborate on their fantasy without censoring, and in doing so the emotional arousal and anxiety that accompanied these incomplete fantasies could be mastered. Techniques of C-BR are varied, and many, such as those described here, require advanced training because they can unleash powerful forces that may flood the patient. Readers should refer to these works to gain a deeper appreciation of these powerful restructuring interventions. The use of forced fantasy as a means of restructuring is demonstrated in the following vignette:

PT: I really felt like I was going to lose control last evening when my son came home late and drunk.

TH: In fantasy, could you describe what would have occurred if you had lost control?

PT: I was afraid that I would start screaming at him, and that would not be the worst.

TH: What further would have happened?

PT: I might have lost it physically and gone after him.

TH: Can you describe what you would have done?

PT: I would have punched him in the face as hard as I could!

TH: And then, if you continued to be in this type of violent state?

PT: I am afraid I might not have stopped!

TH: What would have happened in this case?

PT: I am afraid I might have killed him. *[Patient starts crying.]*

TH: You have a lot of sadness.

PT: I feel so guilty about my rage toward him. I really care about him, but his behavior makes me furious. I tend to avoid my feelings until I feel like I will explode.

TH: This is a complex of painful feelings that you try to contain.

PT: I remember that my father used to be physically abusive to me when I was a teenager, so I left home early, when I was 15.

TH: Can you tell me more about your feelings then?

[Through exposure to and expression of the affect that is elicited through forced fantasy, this type of restructuring reduces the patient's anxiety related to intense feelings toward his son and, as is often the case, allows the patient to access other painful experiences that have not yet been metabolized.]

Forced fantasy can also be a powerful method for mobilizing pathological grief processes, as demonstrated in the following clinical vignette:

[The focus of the session is on the conflicted relationship with the patient's father.]

PT: I am worried about my father's health.

TH: What are your worries?

PT: Well, you know, the ultimate loss.

TH: Have you imagined your father's death?

PT: Yes, but I don't like to think about this.

TH: Have you ever thought about what his funeral will be like?

[Asking patients to describe their fantasies can be a powerful way to mobilize grief.]

PT: There would be a lot of people there. Everyone thinks he is such a great guy.

TH: *[After inquiring about the nature of the funeral, the therapist further explores the fantasy.]* What would he look like in the coffin?

PT: I imagine him in the blue suit that he always wore to his office and looking peaceful.

TH: What would your goodbye to him be?

PT: I would *[starts to sob]* tell him that I am angry and wish we had had a better relationship.

TH: So, there is much mixed feeling toward him?

PT: Yes, I am angry and sad. I also loved him in spite of his treatment of me.

[Patient does a phase of grieving and metabolizing his feelings.]

PT: *[The patient spontaneously shifts the focus to his mother.]* I did not go through a grief process when my mother died. I never said goodbye to her. I think I was numb when she died so suddenly.

TH: It seems that you bypassed your grief over your mother's death by becoming numb. What would your goodbye to her be if you were standing at her coffin? *[The focus becomes mobilizing the pathological grief over the loss of his mother.]*

These same affective processes can also be activated using eye movement desensitization reprocessing and other techniques from a variety of C-BR methods.

NEUROBIOLOGICAL RESTRUCTURING (NR)

The last of the intrapsychic restructuring methods is NR, which acts directly on the neurochemical reactions at the level of neurotransmitter action. Physicians have commonly used neuroleptic medication to treat Axis I clinical syndromes, and more recently there has been progress in using psychopharmacological agents to treat Axis II, or personality disorders (Grossman, 2004). Neurobiological restructuring enhances the functioning of the patient's neurophysiological system and thus affects the intrapsychic–neurobiological level at a microscopic level of action. Treating the various clinical syndromes, such as anxiety, depression, sleep disturbances, and so forth, enables the personality to function at a higher level of adaptation, which can in turn recalibrate faltering neurobiological functions. Increasing evidence suggests that neurobiological restructuring also occurs through the process of psychotherapy. Neuroscientist LeDoux (1995) suggested that "the role of therapy may be to allow the cortex to establish more effective and efficient synaptic links with the amygdala" (p. 225). The amygdala and hippocampus have been implicated, along with various other structures, in aversive memory maintenance and fear conditioning (Charney, 2004).

SELECTION AND APPLICATION OF INTRAPSYCHIC RESTRUCTURING METHODS

The choice and blending of various methods of intrapsychic restructuring methods should be based on a systematic assessment of the individual's personality system. The clinician should complete an assessment of the patient's level of adaptive functioning. This requires knowledge of defensive functions and a flexibility of the patient's personality system. Patients who are functioning at a low level of adaptation generally benefit from CR and NR, and higher functioning patients can more readily benefit from AR. The more intensive types of DR should generally be reserved for highly syntonic patients who will not benefit from other approaches (patients whom Reich [1933] aptly described as "character armored"). C-BR as developed by Linehan (1993) is highly applicable to borderline conditions, and eye movement desensitization reprocessing seems to have a wide range of applications (Shapiro, 1995, 2001). All approaches, however, require training and experience under supervision before applying them to treatment. Readers are encouraged to read the primary texts on these approaches.

SUMMARY AND CONCLUSIONS

This chapter provides an overview of the main types of intrapsychic restructuring. The approaches to treatment have differential impact on the intrapsychic–neurobiological triangle. The primary types of IR include defensive restructuring, cognitive restructuring, affective restructuring, cognitive–behavioral restructuring, and neurobiological restructuring. With the exception of NR, these methods result in varying degrees of activation of the cognitive–affective matrix and of unmetabolized affect and schema that are related to core traumata.

8

DYADIC RESTRUCTURING: WORKING IN THE INTERPERSONAL–DYADIC TRIANGLE

Dyadic restructuring (DR) refers to restructuring that occurs in the *interpersonal–dyadic triangle* (see Figure 1.1, p. 16). We are shifting the focus from the intrapsychic domain discussed in the previous chapter to the interpersonal domain, which is an intermediate level of magnification of the personality system. In Millon's (Millon & Davis, 1996) system, this method of restructuring refers primarily to his dimension of *self–object/ self–other*. Dyadic restructuring is a process in which a two-person system is the locus of intervention. This method is commonly used when the therapeutic focus is the therapeutic dyad—a couple, a parent–child subsystem, or another two-person unit is the focus of the restructuring. It is also an important method used in family and group therapy when dyadic interaction is the focus of intervention. Dyadic restructuring occurs when the interaction between two individuals, in group or family therapy, is the focus of intervention, as in resolving a conflict with the remainder of the group bearing witness.

The therapeutic unit in DR is a dyadic relationship, not the individual, as in IR methods. DR is an excellent vehicle to identify interpersonal styles, patterns, adaptations, and communication patterns. While involved in a relational transaction, it is difficult for people to have a clear perspective on the process. When facilitated by the therapist, DR offers a clearer perspective than what would occur in a therapeutic dyad. These different foci, patient–therapist or patient dyad, represent two variations of dyadic restructuring.

Dyadic restructuring is based on the work of Murray Bowen (1976), a pioneering theoretician in the application of systemic theory, although he eschewed the notion that his was a general system theory (von Bertalanffy, 1968). The main goals of dyadic restructuring are increased *emotional differentiation* and *self-differentiation*. In the work of increasing differentiation, old styles of adaptation can be jettisoned, and new, more functional ones adopted. Reactive downward spirals of communication are less likely to occur. Also, patterns of the dyad's interpersonal relationship are brought to the patient's awareness; the origins of these patterns are understood and their limitations discussed. Intrapsychic restructuring techniques and methods can then be used to metabolize the affect and restructure beliefs. In dyadic restructuring, the therapeutic task is to enhance and encourage the members of the dyad to listen to and respect the other, and to learn to develop empathic responding, which will deepen intimacy while restructuring the individual defense systems of both people. This includes appropriate boundary setting and owning of projections that go along with blaming and trying to change the other, which is common in dysfunctional dyads. As emotional capacity increases, defensive responding diminishes and more intimate communication ensues.

THE INTERPERSONAL SYSTEM

Personality systems are expressed interpersonally and can be observed as transactions and processes among people. The therapist can observe the interpersonal transaction in "current" or "expected" corners and in these observe derivatives from the patients' early relational matrices that have significantly shaped their present-day interpersonal–dyadic triangle. These include the following:

- *Early relational matrix.* The early relational matrix *cannot be directly observed* but primes the pump of personality organization. Early experiences with attachments—positive, negative, or "good enough"—will begin the process of structuring the personality components of the intrapsychic–biological triangle. These then coalesce into cognitive and relational schema and defensive preferences that shape the person's responses, expectations, reactions, and capacity for current and future relational experiences.
- *Current relational matrix.* The current relational matrix includes the dyadic configurations that shape and reinforce personality

types and styles. Interpersonal patterns that are evident in all personalities *can be observed* in this corner, in the characteristic way that people relate to others. Thus, using two of Millon's (Millon & Davis, 1996) key constructs, the therapist can determine whether an individual is active or passive or self or other oriented. A particular pattern of behavior then emerges based in part on the matrix that has been incorporated from early relational experiences. Even though there is a guiding relational schema, individuals may have multiple schemas or scripts (Joines & Steward, 2002), depending on the social context within which the individual is observed, and it is thus necessary to consider the context in which the individual is functioning.

- *Expected relational matrix.* The expected relational matrix has to do with the core schemas that are stored in the psychobiological system and are projected onto others. The expected relationship *can be observed as well as experienced* in the relationship the patient develops with the therapist. This process is often outside of awareness and contains much unconscious process; it is what psychodynamic theorists have termed *transference*, and cognitivists, *schema.* The process relates to the patient's expectations and assumptions with regard to how he or she will be received and reacted to in an interpersonal transaction. Thus, a person with early experience of being unable to trust expects the other to act untrustworthy, regardless of how trustworthy the other actually is (Magnavita, 2002a, pp. 402–403).

Various mechanisms and processes are involved in maintaining dyadic configurations, some important examples of which I review in the following section.

TRANSMITTING, INCORPORATING, AND REPEATING INTERPERSONAL PROCESSES

Interpersonal processes are learned and replicate themselves across generations through various mechanisms. How is it that the therapist can clearly observe what appear to be copies of dynamic processes from another generation and repetitions of themes and dynamics that often are not evident to participants? Benjamin (1993) suggested that most interpersonal patterns are expressed in three primary patterns: (a) recapitulated simply by continuing them; (b) copied through identification with past figures; and (c) introjected, when individuals treat themselves the way they were previously treated (Benjamin, 2003).

The Process of Projection, Introjection, and Internalization

Projection and introjection can be understood as mechanisms of defense, but object relations theorists suggest that the way in which these processes operate shapes and consolidates various relational patterns. Projection is a process by which one's undesirable elements are transmitted, or superimposed, on another. "The individual thus attempts to master painful feelings by getting rid of them and placing them in a 'bad' outside object. In addition, in projective identification, the individual frequently behaves in such a manner as to actually induce the unwanted aspect of the self into the object (e.g., making the object angry)" (Glickauf-Hughes & Wells, 1995, pp. 199–200). Introjection is the process by which this template is absorbed without being assimilated and metabolized. This is often the case when parental attachments are undifferentiated and children are unable to fend off the projection, internalizing without assimilating accurate aspects and discarding inaccurate aspects. As the level of maturity decreases in dyadic configurations, much of what occurs in interpersonal dyads in projective. We constantly project unowned aspects of ourselves onto those in the relational matrix. By assuming another's projection, as if it represented core parts of our self, we maintain attached to the figure from whom the projection originated. Paolino and McCrady (1978) described this process in dyadic relationships:

> To the extent that the partners are deeply involved in this emotional interaction—that is to say, to the extent that each of them enters the interaction in terms of a relatively undifferentiated self, the emotional currents at play have a definite interpersonal effect. Such currents of emotion may, for example, be conveyed through the projection of one partner to the other. To the extent that the second partner is enmeshed in the underlying emotional matrix, the projective elements tend to be internalized and introjected by the first. (pp. 50–51)

These introjected elements of the individual personality system are absorbed in attachments to the parental system. These patterns can also be understood in the modeling and reinforcement of patterns of interaction observed in parental attachments.

Modeling, Reinforcement, and Shaping of Behavioral Response Systems

Interpersonal patterns of behavior are also influenced by behavioral contingency systems of rewards, negative reinforcement, and punishment. Transactions that occur in dyads also fall under the influence of behavioral principles, which offer another perspective on how negative behavioral sequences are ultimately reinforced. We analyze the sequence of behavioral interactions when we ask patients to describe their interpersonal reactions. We change dynamics by creating awareness, disrupting old patterns, and reinforcing new patterns.

TYPES OF DYADIC RESTRUCTURING (DR)

There are three major types of dyadic restructuring, which have somewhat different foci and therapeutic action within a dyadic configuration. When the focus is the expected relationship with the therapist, it is called *expected–transactive restructuring*; when the emphasis is on the real relationship with the therapist, it has been termed "*self–other restructuring*" (McCullough Vaillant, 1997), which is particularly concerned with managing the intersubjective space (Safran & Muran, 2000). If, on the other hand, the focus of the restructuring is on a dyad other than the therapist–patient, it is termed *relational–dyadic restructuring*. This form of dyadic restructuring emerged from the work of Bowen (1976), Minuchin (1974), and other systems theorists.

Expected–Transactive Restructuring

In the classic comparison of three types of psychotherapy, conducted on the same patient, by three luminaries in psychotherapy, Rogers, Perls, and Ellis (1965), the viewer immediately witnesses the immediate emergence of the expected–transactive relationship with Rogers and then Perls. The patient, Gloria, in her first communication to both therapists, describes how she expects Rogers and then Perls to be "harsh and critical" and later in the interviews links this to her relationship with her father who treated her in this fashion. These interviews demonstrate how a person can immediately bring to bear his or her relational schema and project it onto another. This tendency for us to project our relational experiences and expectancies on others is one of the cornerstones of psychoanalysis and represented a major theoretical and clinical breakthrough. Freud called this process "transference," of course, and described specific sets of conditions for how it develops. After a century of clinical observation, however, it appears that this transference is a much more ubiquitous mechanism of dyadic relationships. In contemporary terms, this transference really, then, is the expectancies that we bring to new relationships and our attempts to influence these relationships so that they will meet our expectancies. These processes are well documented by interpersonal theorists and researchers (Anchin & Kiesler, 1982; Weissman, Markowitz, & Klerman, 2000).

Expected–transactive restructuring is a set of methods that attempts to alter these relational schemata. Levenson (2004) called the process in this domain the *cyclical maladaptive cycle* (CMP), from the work of Binder and Strupp (1991), and provided useful modes of expected–transactive restructuring. She used four categories to organize the data from the patient system: (a) acts of the self, (b) expectations of others' reactions, (c) acts of others toward the self, and (d) acts of the self toward the self. She suggested the following technical interventions:

- Ask for details (actions) describing social interchanges.
- Explore the interpersonal context related to symptoms.
- Obtain data for CMP.
- Link patient's action to the complementary action of others in a coherent narrative. (p. 269)

Other techniques include intrapsychic restructuring, such as cognitive restructuring and defensive restructuring, using the therapeutic relationship as the matrix within which these operations are conducted. In this manner, the therapy functions primarily at the past and expected relational matrix of the interpersonal–dyadic triangle. This is demonstrated in the following vignette:

PT: It was very difficult for me to come here to see you.

TH: What was difficult about it?

PT: What I want to talk about is very difficult, and I am not used to discussing this with other people.

TH: It sounds as if you might have some shame or embarrassment about talking to me about your concerns.

PT: I suppose I expect that you will react in a disinterested or bored way or, worse yet, or laugh at me.

TH: When did you have these thoughts and feelings about me?

PT: Actually, before I made the initial appointment with you.

TH: You actually had these thoughts before you even talked with me?

PT: Yes, I guess this is a problem that I didn't realize was connected to the way my mother was with me.

TH: How was she with you?

PT: Whenever I had anything personal to talk about, she seemed disinterested, or at other times, she would make fun of me and say I was a baby.

TH: So you expected that I would treat you in a similar fashion as your mother?

PT: Yes. Now that we are discussing it, I guess I carried this around in all my relationships.

TH: So you carried an expectation that you would receive a bored, disinterested, or shaming reaction?

PT: Yes, and I think that this has made it hard for me to get real close to anyone.

TH: What are the reasons that you are here today?

PT: I didn't think of it before, but I guess it is all part of the same package. I am here because I am having problems in my marriage letting my husband get close to me.

Expected–transactive restructuring is based on Freud's discovery of transference. Comparing the expectancies in the relationship with the therapist to current interpersonal and past relational experience can enhance the restructuring process.

Self–Other Restructuring

The focus of "self–other restructuring" aptly coined by McCullough Vaillant (1997) is the differentiation of self from therapist, typically when there is a low level of differentiation in the patient system. This method of dyadic restructuring describes a number of similar methods that have been developed over the last century to treat the more difficult "self" disorders, as Kohut (1971, 1984) labeled them. In current-day nomenclature, self disorders are narcissistic disorders of varying degrees of severity. "Restructuring or self–other representations means that the therapist helps the patient regulate the degree of aversiveness or inhibition that has been associated with attachment, that is, experience of self, others, or both (McCullough Vaillant, 1997, p. 36). Self–other restructuring was pioneered primarily by Sullivan (1953), Rogers (1951), and Kohut (1971, 1977) and is especially concerned with empathic attunement to damaged zones of the self. Sullivan advanced the field with his conceptualization of therapy as a process of "participant observation" whereby there is a process of mutual influence and co-construction of the dyadic configuration that cannot be conceptualized merely as transference. Originally, however, one can trace the early roots of relational therapy from which this method emanated to the work of Sandor Ferenczi (Magnavita, 2000b). Ferenczi was the earliest psychotherapist to stress the real personality of the therapist and the fact that a therapist must never be ashamed to admit his or her mistakes to the patient (Rachman, 1997). Rachman suggested that Rogers was influenced by Ferenczi's work. Ferenczi also introduced the use of empathy and self-disclosure as vital tools of restructuring, as some contemporary pioneers such as Fosha (2000b) demonstrate.

Self–other restructuring is primarily concerned with the intersubjective space co-constructed between patient and therapist (Muran & Safran, 2002) and emphasizes identification of ruptures of the therapeutic alliance and mending these as they occur. "Therapists are always directing their attention back and forth or alternating their attention between the patient's inner experience and their own inner experience" (Muran & Safran, 2002). McCullough Vaillant (1997), comparing the differences among the more technical intrapsychic restructuring methods presented in the previous chapter, described "self–other restructuring" as follows: "In the restructuring of the inner representations of self and others, however, *the therapist stance becomes the intervention*. The therapist stance itself is the healing connection" (p. 319). As Muran and Safran (2002) described it, "a central tenet of our relational perspective is the recognition that there is an ongoing reciprocal relationship between self-states of one person and those of the other in dyadic interaction" (p. 255). They proposed that "change is essentially understood as involving the parallel processes of increasing immediate awareness of self and other and providing a new interpersonal experience" (p. 255). Jordan's (1997, 2004) relational model also emphasizes primarily connection and the role of mutual empathy as vital to the therapeutic process. Various styles and approaches for conducting this type of dyadic restructuring between the patient and therapist have been described, including the work of K. A. Frank (1999, 2002), whose concentration on intrasession enactments is synchronous with self–other restructuring; the incisive work of Aron (1996); and the interpersonal communications approach developed by Kiesler (1982, 1988, 1996), in which metacommunication about the relationship between patient and therapist is an ongoing intervention priority throughout the treatment process. Readers should refer to McCullough Vaillant's (1997) volume for specific techniques. Of particular concern with this type of restructuring is the "real" relationship between patient and therapist that, in a sense, attempts to allow the patient to teach the therapist what is needed. Much of this type of restructuring is concerned with mending the inevitable therapeutic misalliances that occur, especially with patients whose attachment experiences are less than optimal and when establishing trust is a major challenge. This is demonstrated in the following vignette:

> **PT:** I almost did not return for treatment because when I paged you a few days ago, you did not respond.
>
> **TH:** I wasn't aware that you paged me. The page did not come through. I am sorry that I wasn't available when you needed me to respond.
>
> **PT:** I feel like I am too much for you to have to deal with and that you would rather that I go away.
>
> **TH:** No, that is not the case, but sometimes it is hard for me to be as available as you need.

PT: It seems that no one will ever be concerned with what I need.

TH: Well I can understand how you feel this way after me not responding to your page, which you thought I did purposely. I am sorry
and would not have ignored your page if it had come through.

McCullough Vaillant (1997) suggests that self–other restructuring
should be the primary method used with patients experiencing greater disturbance who would be injured by other, more technical forms of restructuring.
Kohut (1971, 1977) developed his self-psychological approach because of
the ineffectiveness of traditional methods with patients who have self-
disorders. McCullough Vaillant's (1997) observation that the stance is the
critical aspect of this type of restructuring is supported by the work of many
other relationally oriented therapists, such as Jordan (2004). Trujillo (2002)
also developed a similar form of restructuring in his work with narcissistic
disturbances. He described his model as follows:

> The paradigmatic intervention for self-problems is empathic under-
> standing and empathic interpretation. In this realm, empathy involves
> an accurate grasp, both cognitive and affective, of what others experi-
> ence. This commitment to empathic understanding creates a supportive
> milieu in which the patient can either bask in the utilization of the
> therapist as an optimum self-object, or bitterly, but safely, complain
> about the therapist's failure while benefiting from the healing effects
> of resolving the damage caused by the failure. (pp. 350–351)

Fosha (2002) described similar elements of this method: "The dyadic
regulatory processes are involved in the optimal transformation of both
relatedness and emotion, and thus the self. As with emotion, adaptation is
a central concept in understanding" (p. 316). These restructuring processes
are designed to facilitate the patient's deep experiencing and full expression
of his or her core emotion and experience of the therapist and their relational
process, while incorporating the therapist's verbal expressions of his or her
empathic experience of the patient and their relationship. Fosha described
the process of restructuring as follows:

1. the experience and expression of core emotion;
2. the dyadic regulation of affective states, where the experiential
   focus is the relational process;
3. the empathic reflection of the self, where the focus of both
   partners is on the experience of the self (of the patient);
4. somatic focusing, where the experiential focus is on the
   body; and
5. the activation of metatherapeutic processes, where the focus
   is on the very experience of transformation itself. (p. 312)

One might say the goal of self–other restructuring is to allow the patient to teach us how to be an effective therapist for the patient. This becomes a matter of close monitoring (the moment-by-moment experience) of the therapeutic relationship and intersubjective experience.

Muran and Safran (2002) in their relational theory of change relied almost solely on this type of dyadic restructuring:

> Change is essentially understood as involving the parallel processes of increasing immediate awareness of self and other and providing a new interpersonal experience. By increasing the patient's immediate awareness of the processes that mediate a dysfunctional interpersonal pattern, change suggests not simply a correction of a distortion, but an elaboration and clarification of the patient's self-definition, in other words, expanding one's awareness of who one is in a particular interpersonal transaction. (p. 255)

This type of dyadic restructuring can be considered more process oriented than technical. When we compare the techniques with those of IR, one can see that fewer actual techniques are offered. Muran and Safran (2002) described their principles of metacommunication as including the following: (a) start where you are; (b) focus on the here and now; (c) focus on the concrete and specific; (d) explore with skillful tentativeness; (e) establish a sense of collaboration and we-ness; (f) emphasize one's own subjectivity; (g) gauge intuitive sense of relatedness; (h) attend to patients' responsiveness to all interventions; (i) recognize that the situation is constantly changing; (j) expect resolution attempts to lead to more ruptures and expect to revisit ruptures; (k) accept responsibility; and (l) judiciously disclose and explore one's own experience.

With regard to child or adolescent therapy, Greenspan (1997a) advanced a developmentally oriented approach that can be used with both children and adults and focuses on the attachment system. A major component of this developmental psychotherapy approach is the process that "involves the *role of relationships and affective interactions* in facilitating a child's intellectual and emotional growth" (Greenspan, 2002, p. 15). His restructuring method seeks "to help the child learn how to attend and to become engaged or connected, and to be calm and regulated at the same time" (p. 445). Thus, the real relationship between the therapist and child or adolescent is emphasized.

Most forms of child therapy and play therapy use the paradigm of creating and modifying attachment systems by actively engaging the child in the relational space. Bleiberg (2001, 2004) also developed a relational approach consistent with a unified model where he blends individual, family, and psychopharmacological intervention. "At the heart of this treatment model is the concept of mentalization or reflective function. Mentalization refers to the biologically prepared capacity to interpret, represent, and respond to human behavior (that of self and others) in meaningful terms" (p. 468). Self–other restructuring is a main treatment method, but others are discussed in the following chapter, including historical and generational patterns.

Relational–Dyadic Restructuring

The focus of dyadic restructuring can occur in current relationships between partners, parent–child dyads, and so on and is usually done in a couples modality or in a group, when the dyadic relationship of two group members are the focus of intervention. Relational–dyadic restructuring emphasizes the use of adaptive communication skills, such as the ability to listen and respond to another without using projection. Solomon (1989) and Solomon and Lynn (2002) developed relational restructuring techniques for couples that are especially useful for those with personality dysfunction. Magnavita (2000a) presents various types of restructuring dyadic relationships. Yalom's (1985) approach to group therapy is the prototype of interpersonal process-oriented group treatment, and his volume *The Theory and Practice of Group Psychotherapy* details procedures for therapeutically restructuring the maladaptive interpersonal patterns that group members play out in relation to one another—both dyadically and in larger (i.e., 2+) relational configurations—as well as in relation to the therapist. Much of relational restructuring emphasizes the intimacy-closeness dimension, which is similar to the intersubjective therapeutic space.

During the course of relational restructuring, patterns of interpersonal behavior are brought to the awareness of the dyad, and defensive operations may be pointed out. The goal is to increase the capacity for intimacy and closeness. This requires the concomitant increase in emotional differentiation, that is, the ability to acknowledge, label, and express feelings.

> **HUSBAND:** I really am doing everything I can to demonstrate my love for you, but you aren't responding!
>
> **WIFE:** Whenever you offer me something, it really feels like you want something in return. I am trying to find my feelings for you, but I don't know if I really have them anymore.
>
> **HUSBAND:** I am really trying my best to make you feel loved.
>
> **WIFE:** I feel really badly that I can't return any feeling to you right now.

HUSBAND: All that I get from you is dismissed.

WIFE: I know my coldness is there.

TH: It seems that when you approach Nancy and try to give her some affection, she experiences it as if you are poking her. Nancy, it appears that the more you experience the poking, the colder and more dismissive you become.

WIFE: Yes, it's as if he is trying to chip through my ice with an ice pick, but it makes me withdraw.

TH: Maybe there is another model that would be more effective, like trying to melt the ice, but, Nancy, you have to be in charge of controlling the temperature of the deep freeze you give Bob.

WIFE: Maybe, Bob, if you didn't approach me with such impatience about what is happening, I would feel freer to respond without the ice.

ESTABLISHING THE PSYCHOTHERAPEUTIC FOCUS

The therapist has a number of ways to approach the process of dyadic restructuring using the dyadic–interpersonal triangle as the guide. Furthermore, all restructuring takes place via this triangle, because this is also the triangle for the therapeutic relationship, as well as corrective–social experiences in current relationships. If the patient is being seen in the modality of couples, family, or group therapy, dyadic interactions will be a major part of the therapeutic process. These can be observed as they occur in the "here and now" and are *current relationships in process.* In group and family therapy, others in addition to the therapist bear witness and give feedback to the transactional patterns. Once patterns of transaction are observed and brought to awareness, an invitation to explore the roots of these and link the patterns to early relational and attachment experiences is the main goal of restructuring. This then allows for the identification and metabolization of repressed emotion. Pattern recognition is one of the central features of psychotherapy and requires familiarity with a theoretical model to contextualize the patterns. They can present in a variety of ways, and it is imperative that the therapist develops an ability to interpret them. Examples include the following:

- *Patterns of reenactment.* When relational experiences have been associated with negative affects, they seek expression. If the patient experienced trauma prior to the development of language, which might allow for a verbal-symbolic encoding, non-language modes of expression remain the only channel of communication. Reenactment is also likely when there has been severe dissociation of traumatic events. In one example, a woman in treatment for severe anxiety would become so enraged when fighting with her husband that she would repeatedly punch herself in the head. When this behavioral sequence was closely tracked, she contacted a feeling of deep shame and then recalled her father punching her in the head when he was angry with her. Another women who had been severely abused by a sociopathic father was made aware of her pattern of finding antisocial men and encouraging abusive treatment by taunting and provoking them about their manhood. Because she was under strict injunction from her father not to speak of her abuse or her family would be killed, she could only keep herself aware of the pattern by these reenactment patterns. When she fully understood and could verbalize her experience without her fear of annihilation, she gave up the reenactment. Often the specific aspects of reenactments, such as occur in abusive relationships, are an expression of what happened in the past. Specific details should be requested, when appropriate, when these patterns come to light. Reenactment is both a defense against painful feelings and an attempt to form and express a narrative of the traumatic relationship.

- *Transference patterns.* Transference patterns are the hallmark of psychodynamic psychotherapy and evident in all human relationships. These are the projected expectations about how one expects to be treated and include cognitive and relational schemas. Most therapists are knowledgeable about interpreting these patterns and link them to similar patterns with major attachment figures. It was once believed that for the transference to be enacted, the therapist had to remain neutral and abstinent; it is now well accepted, however, that people project onto others all the time and that a major part of any therapy is owning one's projections.

- *Symptomatic expression.* The unique expression of symptomatic configurations is evidence that the personality system is not adequately handling the level of anxiety or that overwhelming stress has occurred. One of the assumptions of personality-guided therapy is that the symptoms are not random but unique expressions of the biopsychosocial matrix and how it reacts under stress. For example, a patient with a chronic sleep disturbance as therapy progressed became aware of the terror in which she lived growing up with a chronically mentally ill father and alcoholic mother. She recalled how she always had to sleep with one eye open so that she could be prepared for the next catastrophe. Another patient had chronic stomach spasms that were unexplained until she remembered during the course of therapy that she was often starving as a young girl and experienced gross neglect that went undetected by the community. This is not an uncommon occurrence in some people with covertly narcissistic dysfunctional personality system or in those with addictive dysfunctional personality system, as well as other types.

- *Profiling attachment systems.* The therapist should also elucidate the type of attachment behavior that the patient uses in his or her dyadic relationships. A patient showed a marked reaction, becoming very anxious and frightened, when her husband announced that he had a business trip planned. She had tried various strategies in the past to keep him from going. As she focused on her reaction, she recalled that her parents had left her for long periods when she was a child and described feeling terrified and worried about what would become of her if they did not return. This was framed to her as evidence of an insecure attachment and that her behavior was an attempt to strengthen her attachment system.

- *Repetitive maladaptive patterns.* An important expression of problems within the personality system can be observed when there are repetitive patterns of interaction that are not functional but continue to occur despite their lack of adaptive value. Underlying these patterns may be more complex symbolic expressions, including identification with an attachment figure that is kept alive by the behavior. In one case, a father who had treated his son harshly recalled that his own father made him move a stonewall 3 feet for no reason other than to teach him self-discipline. He understood this treatment as being a form of paternal love but denied the sadistic elements of this attachment and carried them on in a lesser version to his son.

To reiterate a central assumption, much of what occurs in personality-guided therapy is pattern recognition. The therapeutic task is to identify and to develop awareness about the individual's interpersonal system and concomitant relational, cognitive, and affective subsystems that compare these and to explore their ramifications, both positive and negative. This process of co-constructing a narrative with a patient was pioneered by Freud and remains a central aspect of all therapeutic approaches.

Providing a Container for the Affects

One of the main elements in dyadic restructuring is to provide a container for the conflicts and primitive affects that are expressed in the dyadic matrix (Scharff & Scharff, 1991). These include the core emotions and secondary ones, such as envy, jealousy, and anxiety. By doing so, the therapist allows for the expression and acceptance of the other as a unique individual with his or her own set of needs and identity. Therefore, the therapeutic setting must be sufficient to withstand the force that the dyad is trying to manage. Schnarch (1991) used the metaphor of a crucible, as did Whitaker (1986; Whitaker & Keith, 1981) when working with families. For intensive couples work he has developed for sexual dysfunction, but it is also apt for what occurs in dyadic restructuring:

> The crucible participates in the metamorphosis of the ingredients by *containing* the reaction so that the qualitative changes can occur. The crucible must have a lower coefficient of reactivity (e.g., a higher melting point) than the ingredients placed in it; moreover, its degree of inertness must be higher than that required for the intended reaction. Said differently, the crucible must be nonreactive to the specific ingredients it will contain as well as to the process itself. Depending on the nature of these two variables and their unique interaction, a particular crucible might be appropriate for some use and not for others. (Schnarch, 1991, p. 159)

The crucible is the therapeutic context and relationship that holds the energy released by that same context and relationship. Bion (1977) wrote of the function of containment and the maternal–infant attachment as being the container and the contained. The mother transforms undifferentiated emotion into coherent emotions. The therapist must be involved but differentiated.

> The therapist's capacity to be nonreactive while remaining highly involved is another manifestation of a high degree of differentiation. From this perspective, it becomes obvious that therapists cannot help the patient achieve a higher degree of differentiation than they themselves have reached. (Schnarch, 1991, p. 160)

Of course, differentiation is a lifelong process, and this should not discourage young therapists to avoid the challenge of conducting therapy when they themselves are not yet highly differentiated. One benefit of doing personality-guided relational therapy is that, as is the case with most other approaches, with time and experience one often gains greater personal maturity.

THE MARITAL DYAD AS A PERSONALITY SYSTEM

The marital dyad remains one of the essential subsystems, which becomes in effect a crucible, of adult personality development. It is often the focus of treatment for those seeking psychotherapy.

Winnicott (e.g., Winnicott et al., 1989) is often noted as saying that "there is no such thing as an infant, only an infant–mother dyad." To a lesser degree, this can be said about marital personality systems; individuals cannot be fully understood outside the dynamic interaction of the marital relationship. This observation becomes more evident the longer the marriage endures. Solomon (1989) described this system as follows: "The partners' individual behavior is shaped not only by temperament, personality characteristics and early history, but also by the *mutual self* or *joint personality* that emerges from marital interaction" (p. 27). Even if not the focus of treatment, the marital unit is a powerful system that responds to and reinforces or undermines changes made in various members of family systems, in other modalities of treatment. Carter and McGoldrick (1980) considered the joining of families through marriage an essential component of the family life cycle. In most societies, marriage remains one of the primary institutionalized relational subsystems and it is therefore crucial for therapists to consider, even those not formally trained in marital and family therapy. In her excellent volume *Narcissism and Intimacy: Love and Marriage in the Age of Confusion*, Solomon (1989) discussed a number of modern myths about marriage: (a) the myth of entitlement, (b) the myth of autonomy, (c) the myth of romantic love, (d) the myth that benefits of marriage are greater for men, (e) the myth of the decline of marriage, (f) gender myths about what is normative, (g) the myth that women's liberation has lead to social decline, and (h) the myth of the positive divorce (pp. 9–10). Solomon proposed that these myths lead to narcissistic expectations that are unrealistic and destructive. It is worthwhile for therapists to examine their own attitudes about these myths and to explore the couple and family's notions. Solomon also commented on the complexity of the systemic issues involved in the marital pairing:

> Each partner brings into the marriage a personal world view of how things ought to be as well as a developmental history that programs the interpersonal roles of husband, wife, parent, children, friends, and community interaction. These are not experienced as personal values, beliefs and ways of seeing the world, but as truth and reality. (p. 21)

The viability of marriage is exquisitely related to a number of experiences along the developmental progression, as well as to the level of differentiation of each member of the dyad and to the marital containment that allows for greater differentiation and maturity to develop without threatening the foundation of the marriage. Solomon described the challenge and systemic influences:

> Marriage embraces two individual subsystems that combine to form a new family system. The task of the spouses is to devise, consciously and unconsciously, a mutual working system that allows them to function comfortably without completely sacrificing the values and ideals they brought into the marriage. A new social order with its own structure and language develops through a process of trial and error. Partners influence each other and members of their respective birth families and are in turn influenced by their relatives-in-law. (p. 23)

Healthy marital dyads enhance the personality functioning of each partner in a circular process. When the level of emotional and self–other differentiation in the couple decreases, there is more likelihood of severe bionegativity that has a significant impact on the couple's relationship. The undifferentiated self seeks to fuse with another in an attempt to be complete or whole.

The Fusion Fantasy

Individuals at lower levels of differentiation are more likely to be driven by the fusion fantasy, which is a natural part of falling in love but can be the seeds of destruction if it does not evolve into more mature love. A wish to merge with another represents an unsuccessful attempt at intimacy and closeness, similar to Bowen's notions of what occurs with individuals at lower levels of differentiation. In one case, an attorney and his wife fell in love writing letters and talking on the phone, as they shared attitudes, religious values, and hopes for the future. When they met after 6 months, they found the attraction "real in a physical way" and proceeded to marry shortly afterward. Quickly establishing themselves in a community and having five children seemed like the attainment of their longings. However, the wife experienced a marital crisis and walked away from the marriage, seeking freedom and independence. During a course of couples and individual therapy, she became aware of how she had lost herself in the marriage to the point that she could no longer stand her husband and was repulsed by his presence. The fusion fantasy is powerful in undifferentiated individuals and requires much restructuring of the couple to create a more mutual and mature marital relationship.

Downward Spiraling of Dyad

A problem with many marital and couple relationships is a tendency to trigger one another's primitive defenses, creating a downward spiral in which the couple's communication pattern becomes increasingly regressive (Magnavita, 2000a). As anxiety increases, usually because of fear of intimacy and closeness, more defenses are used in the intrapsychic configuration; as the defenses become increasingly more primitive, they trigger in kind regression in the partner. Most couples' therapists have witnessed these displays of regressive downward spiraling, and in some couples it may occur so rapidly that violence results. Some of these couples reconstitute in amazingly trajectories, often repressing the impact that their brutal interactions have on others. The discharge of anxiety in these episodes is enormous and thus in some manner reinforcing as the discharge of built-up anxiety is quite uncomfortable. Solomon (1989) commented on working with these dyads:

> It is a challenge, as every therapist knows, to help those who utilize primitive defenses. In conjoint therapy, the process may include allowing the partner or therapist to take on projections in collusive patterns that invariably arise, asking how the difficulty is usually played out in the real environment outside of treatment, directly examining with the couple how the usual reaction of each provokes vulnerable areas within the other.
>
> Within the atmosphere of a containing therapeutic environment, the therapist may stop the process when things warm up, tell the partners that they are getting to the heart of something that hurts them both a great deal, and suggest that they try to stay with what they feel as they speak and listen to each other. (p. 159)

Symptomatic Expression

The manners in which symptoms are expressed in a dysfunctional dyad are multitudinous, and yet common themes are seen in clinical practice. Dysfunctional marital systems have a major impact on the partners and, if not addressed or deflected in triangular configurations, will find other pathways of disguised expression. Some of the common forms include extramarital affairs, parent–child problems, a partner's increased clinical symptomatology, and fueling of addictive processes.

Extramarital Affairs

A common form of expression of dysfunction in a marital dyad is an extramarital affair, which is fairly commonplace in clinical practice and in contemporary society. Unstable dyads often seek a third party, which will be discussed in more detail in the following chapter devoted to triadic restructuring. Dyads can quickly move into triads when there is opportunity. Solomon describes this process as follows:

> They are symptoms of underlying problems or attempts to deny such problems. An affair is an emotionally charged series of events among husband, wife, and a third party enlisted to complete the triangle. Affairs have a variety of causes, but for the most part they are representations of underlying narcissistic needs. An affair may function as a distance regulator, as an instrument of revenge, as the expression of a need for an affirming other, as a way to convince oneself of one's attractiveness, sexual potency or lovableness, or as the expression of a desire to play. (p. 114)

Parent–Child Problems

Parent–child problems are another common expression of dysfunctional dyads. Here the channel of the anxiety becomes the child. When this channel becomes predominant, the impact on the child's development is severely compromised. Pawl and St. John (2002) described this personality system process as follows:

> Often, the parent–child dyads and triads we treat are in the clutches of this more fundamental and pervasive kind of repetition of harm— a repetition that results not from repression, but from disassociation; not from forgetting painful thoughts and experiences, but from building a personality structure around surviving intolerable experiences that precludes the capacity to remember. These structures shape the way the world is seen and experienced. (p. 91)

These processes, which include multigenerational transmission effects, are covered in more detail in the following chapter.

Increased Clinical Symptomatology of a Partner

When a dyad is functioning poorly, another route of expression can be the bearing of symptoms in one member of the dyad and relative symptom absence in the other. This may, for example, take on a somatic pathway and result in migraine headache or irritable bowels. In other cases, it might result in depression or panic.

Exaggerated Characterological Patterns

An unstable dyad can also be stabilized by the exaggeration of characterological patterns of one or both members of the dyad, as when repetitive maladaptive patterns become increasingly destructive or entrenched.

Fueling of Addictive Processes

In some dysfunctional couples, there is a tendency to use addictive processes as a way to stabilize the marital dyad. This can take many forms—substance abuse, gambling, computer addiction, and so forth. Often times, latent addictions become prominent when the marriage is overly stressed for an extended period of time. In one couple, the wife developed an increasing dependency on gambling and was spending longer periods of time at the casino. Her husband participated by encouraging her and accompanying her, even though he did not gamble. He was aware that he used this as a distraction, and essentially dropped her off and would find a quiet place to read until she lost her money or became tired. He said that he did not enjoy spending time with her and would leave but for his children.

Dyadic Restructuring and the Severely Dysfunctional Couple

Nowhere is the clinician more challenged than when both members of a severely dysfunctional relationship also show profound disturbance in their individual personality systems. This is often the case when both members of a couple are functioning at or below the borderline level of organization. Often there are combinations, such as the narcissistic–borderline couple, that therapists see in clinical practice and that are identified in the literature (Solomon, 1998; Lachkar, 1992, 1998, 2004). As discussed previously, there is some advantage to one therapist undertaking treatment of these couples by using mixed modalities. Glick and Loraas (2001) described their experience using one therapist with these borderline couples:

> In our experience with large numbers of inpatients as well as very impaired outpatients, the family therapist preferably should do the individual therapy. The rationale is that there is more to be gained than lost by employing one instead of two therapists. Due to the severity of the illness and the impression that many patients and families of [borderline personality disorder] have regarding therapy, patients often have difficulty trusting therapists. It is our belief that once a patient finds a therapist he or she can trust, it usually is too hard for the patient to transfer to another therapist (but hard data on this belief are lacking). (p. 144)

Although there is much merit in the same therapist offering multiple modalities, this may not be appropriate for some patients.

> Methods of dyadic restructuring have not been widely applied to working with couples that have severe personality dysfunction although the tide may be turning (Solomon, 1998). Most therapists have been loath to have two individuals, especially with severe personality dysfunction, in their office together. Therapists who have received their primary train-

ing in intrapsychic methods of restructuring often resist doing intensive couples therapy because of the intensity of responses that can occur and the difficulty of managing multiple, often intense alliances. It is essential that the therapist be grounded theoretically, technically, and personally before embarking on such work. This type of work often has enormous impact, however, and can be a highly efficient method of restructuring that can reverberate in the larger system and through the multigenerational transmission process.

One of the first and most important aspects of working with severely disturbed couples is conducting a careful assessment. Therapists should also be clear about providing a clear explanation of the treatment format, how flexible he or she will be, and what the expectations are. In an informal survey I conducted with clinical patients treated over the course of the last 15 years, the feedback received doing this type of work was positive. An important aspect of working with severely disordered couples is using both individual and marital therapy with the same therapist. Many patients reported that the advantage of working with one therapist with different modalities is that he or she has knowledge of both partners and that this benefits them and can accelerate the treatment.

Relational Resilience in Dyads

In distinct contrast to the severely dysfunctional couple, there also exist couples in which the partners jointly transmute their significant individual issues into genuine healing and relational strength. Dyadic relationships can also have a resiliency when there is a type of pairing that serves to enhance the functioning of both individuals in the dyad. Most therapists have met and worked with couples from horrendous backgrounds who have used their relationship to heal and mature. Solomon (1989) called this the "healing nature of a functional relationship":

> Sometimes two people with serious vulnerabilities to injury succeed in serving in a capacity for each other that promotes the well-being of both. In a loving relationship it is possible for the partners to develop a mutual interplay and reciprocity that, while imperfect and subject to the usual stresses of living together, provides a reparative function. Each legitimizes his or her own residue of child-like needs by caring for the other. . . . It is not the stress of life but the ability to see the relationship as a haven in a difficult world that defines marital satisfaction. (p. 38)

CENTRAL ASPECTS OF DYADIC RESTRUCTURING

Following are a number of central considerations to bear in mind when undertaking restructuring with couples. In actual practice, all of these considerations pertain to the process of restructuring the dyad and are thoroughly interactive, but they are necessarily discussed separately to highlight salient issues in each area.

Providing a Sufficient Holding Environment for the Couple

The therapist is responsible for providing a sufficient holding environment for the couple to do the work of emotional differentiation and self-development. The format of treatment becomes a viable part of the overall treatment package. In many cases, the flexible use of treatment modalities can accelerate the course of treatment. Usually even the most disturbed couples can benefit from working intensively with one therapist. At other times, it is necessary to use another therapist to provide a sufficient container. Often the benefit of two therapists is that both can share in the intensity of the projected affects that one therapist alone might find unmanageable. For many of these couples, there may be a strong suicidal level of adaptation in which the therapist is continually examining his or her efforts in the context of an eventual suicide. Strong homicidal impulses may also dominate the clinical picture, and the therapist might fear that acting out will occur with catastrophic results. In one case reported in the news, a patient in treatment acted on his homicidal impulses, killing three coworkers. It is unfortunate that the prediction of violence is not scientific, and the expectations of society and the legal system are often unrealistic. Many therapists now refuse to see more disturbed patients with a propensity for acting out because of the difficulty in providing a container for the process, in part fueled by fears of reprisal should an inevitable violent or suicidal act occur. Yet some patients carry violent impulses and have dysfunctional personality systems, and they need treatment desperately.

Emotional Differentiation and Affective Regulation

Those who are poorly differentiated emotionally are "trapped within a feeling world" (Bowen, 1976, p. 67). Later, Goleman (1994) used the concept of emotional intelligence that accounts for a high or low level of emotional differentiation. As discussed in chapter 7, emotional differentiation and affective regulation are central aspects of intrapsychic restructuring and are also central concerns in dyadic restructuring. As Bowen established in his work, emotional differentiation goes hand-in-hand with differentiation of the self. The higher the adaptive capacity of the intrapsychic personality system, the greater tolerance one has for emotional experiencing and tolerance of emotion in dyadic relationships. Paolino and McCrady (1978) described this process specifically as it applies to the marital dyad, although we may note that it pertains to any dyadic system of significance in the participants' lives:

> When identities are more stable and well defined, strong emotion can be experienced without a sense of flooding of the self or endangering of the maintenance of a sense of identity. Situations of intense emotional involvement are inherently difficult for individuals with poor individua-tion. They tend to avoid such emotional situations by forms of distancing or schizoid withdrawal, or by a relative diffusion of a sense of identity, which may result in the phenomena of depersonalization or overwhelm-ing anxiety. Individuals with well-differentiated identity, on the other hand, can operate relatively comfortably in situations of intense emo-tional involvement, with the confidence that such involvement does not impair their ability to remain in contact with reality and to objec-tively discern that reality from the fantasies and feelings that may be stirred up by emotional involvement. (p. 48)

When the level of emotional differentiation is poor, it is difficult for dyadic relationships to be successful; high reactivity, mutual projection, and emotional flooding predominate and generally lead to triangulation of others, as described in the following chapter.

Differentiation of the Self

Bowen (1976, 1978) considered his concept of "differentiation of self" a cornerstone of his theoretical model. Accordingly, all people can be placed on a continuum, with individuals at one end being fused between emotional and intellectual systems. They tend to be dominated by their emotional system and more easily become dysfunctional under stress. At the opposite end of the continuum are those who have achieved a relative separation between their emotional and intellectual functions. In the extreme, we would describe this as the defense of isolation of affect, but here Bowen referred to a more integrative emotional–cognitive system.

Bowen (1976) described the lowest level of differentiation as an "undif-ferentiated family ego mass" (p. 69). These individuals "are totally relation-ship oriented. So much energy goes into seeking love and approval and keeping the relationship in some kind of harmony, there is no energy for life-directed goals" (pp. 69–70). Each member of the dyad is likely to be reactive, and "it is relatively impossible for the poorly differentiated individ-ual to take responsibility for his own functioning and feelings without blaming the other for his unhappiness and suffering" (Paolino & McCrady, 1978, p. 49). When self-differentiation is at lower levels, boundary issues predominate. Dyadic relationships may be experienced as engulfing or aban-doning. The ability to regulate distance from others is faulty, and thus the individual may oscillate between the polarities of feeling engulfed and abandoned. In extreme cases, there may even be evidence of symbiotic attachment or fusion with another so that the two selves are so intertwined that they are virtually indistinguishable.

When the level of differentiation is high, there is less likelihood of an individual being emotionally reactive, and a harmony exists between cognitive and affective functioning so that each aspect is brought to bear when difficulties arise. Individuals with higher levels of differentiation can tolerate and enjoy both aloneness and emotional closeness and intimacy. They neither fuse nor detach as a way of regulating distance but can appropriately enjoy both separateness and connection. They are able to regulate flexibly the emotional space between themselves and others. There is an ability to regress and let oneself experience merger during sex and other peak experience with an easy return to self-cohesion. These characteristics allow for more mature dyadic relationships and less of a tendency to triangulate others when anxiety arises, because they are able to bear and tolerate their own dysphoric affects when life brings the inevitable losses and injuries.

Enhanced Communication

One of the essential goals of dyadic restructuring is enhanced communication. This remains a major challenge for the therapist when working with couples, especially those whose defenses are primitive and whose affect regulation is poor. Communication is a cornerstone of a functional relationship. Couples that communicate poorly have little to rely on when attempting to resolve inevitable conflicts. Most therapeutic approaches that focus on the dyad have emphasized various aspects of the communication process, such as the use of "I statements" rather than "You statements," the latter often being preludes to projection. One of these approaches, *Relationship Enhancement Therapy* (Harman & Waldo, 2001), primarily emphasizes the centrality of structured communication training for the therapist doing dyadic restructuring. The authors outlined the five features of communication that the expresser needs to follow:

1. State the problem from a subjective stance, such as, "It seems to me," or "From my point of view."
2. Disclose the feelings or emotions associated with the situations.
3. Offer specific examples of events or behaviors related to the problem while avoiding making generalized statements, particularly generalized statements about the listener's character (i.e., "I thought you would get here at five o'clock and you did not come until six" instead of "You are inconsiderate and irresponsible").

4. Tell the listener what the expresser is describing, what matters to the expresser, [and] what the issues raised say or mean about the positive qualities preferred in the relationship.
5. Make requests of the listener, informing the listener about behavioral changes that could move the relationship in the direction the expresser desires. (p. 223)

The listener is instructed to focus on what his or her partner is communicating and not on associated feelings and thoughts. Summarizing and paraphrasing what the expresser is communicating achieves this.

DIFFERENTIATION, IDENTITY, PERSONALITY ORGANIZATION, AND DYADIC FUNCTIONING

There is coherence among an individual's level of differentiation, identity, personality organization, and ability to function successfully in a stable dyadic relationship, such as a marriage or long-term partnership. An individual with a mature sense of identity has attained a higher level of differentiation than someone who has a diffuse or unstable sense of self. Paolino and McCrady (1978) described the individual with a secure sense of self as being

> capable of not only tolerating differences between himself and others, but of accepting and valuing this separateness and difference. Rather than being caught on the horns of the dilemma of rigidly blocking out or submissively swallowing the viewpoints of the important figures around him, he is free to listen, to sample and taste, to learn what is to be learned and to make use of what is helpful and constructive in the pursuance of his own interests and objectives. He has no need to force agreement from others since he can tolerate the fact that they may not agree with or endorse his own point of view. (p. 34)

Dyadic Functioning

The capacity to function within a dyadic configuration is a central capacity required to maintain the relational matrix, which includes marriage, partnerships, parent–child relationships, friendships, and work relationships. New relationships will be "contaminated" (Paolino & McCrady, 1978, p. 46) by the impact of "the personality organization of each partner and their intermeshing" (p. 47). The interrelationship among the various components of the relational system can either improve or take away from the functioning of the dyad. Paolino and McCrady (1978) described this process as follows:

> if the personalities which enter the marital relationship are relatively individuated and differentiated, the potentiality exists for positive and

constructive identifications that enhance and enrich the personality structure of each partner. Where the personalities are dominated by pathogenic configurations, however, the intermeshing internalizations in such a couple will take place in terms of the organization of such pathological introjects. (p. 47)

When the personality organization and structure of individuals in a dyad are fairly well differentiated and intimacy and closeness are not too anxiety provoking, the personality system of the dyad will enhance development. Again, Paolino and McCrady's (1978) elaboration of this idea is couched in terms of the marital relationship, but it can be seen to have varying degrees of relevance to other dyads, particularly those formed between other family members (e.g., sibling dyads), friends, and close co-workers:

> As the person with a well-differentiated and individuated identity enters into a relationship as close and intimately interdependent as the marital relationship, he/she is able to enter into, share, and participate freely in the emotional life that takes place between and around the marital partners. The less the degree of individuation or of differentiation of self, however, the more emotion tends to spill over and be communicated to the other member of the dyad in a way which influences the functioning of that other member. Within this complex of implicit and relatively unconscious emotional influences, a pattern tends to establish itself in which one of the partners begins to function with a facade of exaggerated strength and assertion, while the other partner shifts to a position of compliance, submissiveness, and giving-in to the influence and domination of the more adequate partner. Within this emotional matrix there is a phenomenological shift in which one partner seems to attain a degree of hyperadequacy and the confirming of pseudoidentity, while the other partner seems to lose identity and become a relative nonentity. (p. 47)

Within the therapeutic relationship, Fosha (2001) described the process: "Dyadically regulated affects can be fully experienced, and the patient benefits from their intrinsic adaptive properties" (p. 232).

Kernberg's Continuum of Relationship Capacity

The capacity to form and maintain interpersonal relationships is a central function of the interpersonal–dyadic triangle. A previous chapter referred to the work of Nichols (1988), based on Kernberg's model (1974), that describes a continuum of attachment–intimacy and closeness in romantic-love relationships. The more mature the personality system of an individual, the greater capacity for intimacy and closeness. Nichols described the following configurations:

1. almost total incapacity for establishing genital and tender relationships
2. sexual promiscuity and or polymorphous perversity
3. primitive idealization of the loved one, with clinging dependency and some capacity for genital gratification
4. the capacity for establishing stable and deep relationships without the capacity for full sexual gratification
5. normal integration of genitality with the capacity for tenderness and a stable deep relationship. (p. 487)

According to Kernberg (1974), the level of interpersonal maturity is a reflection of the organization of the personality system and is negatively correlated with the "extent to which there has been a failure of the process of differentiation and individuation of the self" (Paolino & McCrady, 1978, p. 42).

Strategies and Techniques of Dyadic Restructuring

Dyadic restructuring has a variety of clearly articulated strategies that serve to alter the recursive transactive patterns evident in interpersonal configurations (Millon & Davis, 1996). Anchin and Kiesler (1982) offered a variety of well-articulated approaches to utilizing and systematically intervening in the patient–therapist relationship to effect self–other restructuring. We can address dysfunctions in the realm of interpersonal conduct by using any number of family (Gurman, 1992) or group (Yalom, 1985) therapeutic methods, as well as a series of recently evolved and explicitly formulated interpersonal techniques (Anchin & Kiesler, 1982, along with the McCullough Vaillant, 1997, and Muran & Safran, 2002 volumes cited earlier in this chapter). Additional well-articulated strategies for guiding self–other restructuring include those of Strupp and Binder (1984), Cashdan (1988), and Levenson (1995, 2004). With regard to undertaking relational–dyadic restructuring in marital and couple dyads, the literature contains a voluminous array of well-articulated strategies (Donovan, 1999; Gurman, 1992; Jacobson & Christensen, 1996; Jacobson & Gurman, 2002; Johnson & Greenberg, 1995).

Identification of Interpersonal Styles

The identification of interpersonal styles is a useful diagnostic step that in turn points to specific strategies and interventions for dyadic restructuring developed by the interpersonal school of psychotherapy (Anchin & Kiesler, 1982; Benjamin, 1993; Kiesler, 1988). When applied to the dyad, whether in marital, family, or group therapy, the therapist can create a vital aspect of the holonic map of interpersonal processes that need to be restructured.

In one case of a couple on the verge of a divorce after a gradual distancing that occurred over many years, it was pointed out to the couple that their interpersonal model was not working, and if they continued to rely on it, they would ultimately divorce. As they were made aware, their particular style of interacting was organized around a dominant–submissive interpersonal pattern. Instead of providing emotional intimacy and closeness, when either member of the couple reacted to conflict, the wife would become dismissive of her spouse, which would intensify his core theme of emotional abandonment. When he would react with anger, she would dismissively negate his feelings and say she would not tolerate and could not respect someone so weak. He then would take a submissive position, withdraw, and fume until he exploded at another family member in an impotent rage.

SUMMARY AND CONCLUSIONS

All psychotherapy is essentially an interpersonal process regardless of the theoretical model or techniques one uses. Personality-guided relational therapy accepts this as a fundamental principle. Over the course of the last century, the developments of dyadic methods of restructuring have been a major advancement in the field of psychotherapy. There are primarily two basic methods of dyadic restructuring, one that emanates from systemic theory and family therapy, termed *relational–dyadic restructuring*, and the other based on empathic attunement in the therapeutic dyad that emphasizes the process, finding the correct therapeutic stance, and mending inevitable therapeutic misalliances that are particularly characteristic of working with more disturbed or self-disordered patients.

9

TRIADIC RESTRUCTURING: WORKING IN THE RELATIONAL–TRIADIC MATRIX

Triadic restructuring (TR) refers to a method that emphasizes the alteration of processes that occur in a three-person system or multiple overlapping triangular configurations that occur in larger systems and are often multigenerational. This is depicted in Figure 9.1, the *relational–triadic configuration* (see also Figure 1.1, p. 16), which represents the triangular nature of relationships. In Millon's (1990) system, this method of restructuring is most aligned with the *active–passive* polarity. Although his system depicts the polarities within an individual, to some degree the active–passive polarity determines the position one takes interpersonally and in triadic configurations. Although largely carried out in the context of family therapy, triadic restructuring occurs and is a by-product of both intrapsychic, as well as dyadic restructuring. As an individual gains higher levels of differentiation, the dyadic and triadic systems in which they function are restructured. Therefore, even if a clinician primarily conducts individual psychotherapy, knowledge of the triadic system will enhance his or her skills.

Triadic restructuring was primarily pioneered by Murray Bowen (1976), who developed a cohesive model of systemic functioning, and Salvadore Minuchin (1974), who pioneered a type of structural family therapy that worked in the relational system. Describing the systemic family perspective,

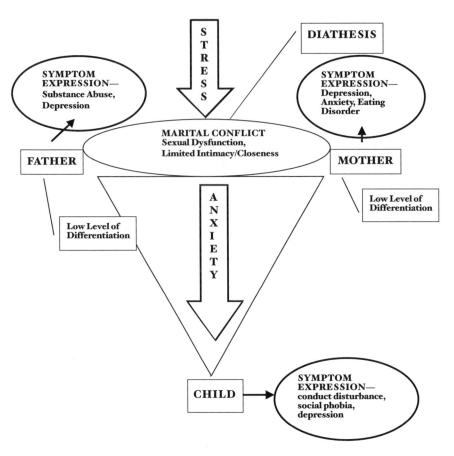

Figure 9.1. The diathesis–stress model and the expression of symptoms in the dyad and triadic–relational configuration.

Minuchin (1974) wrote, "the family therapist does not conceive of an 'essential' personality, remaining unchanged throughout the vicissitudes of different contexts and circumstances. . . . His concept of the site of pathology is much broader, and so are the possibilities for intervention" (p. 4). Minuchin was a broad integrative theorist whose model was groundbreaking. He was intuitively aware of the triangular nature of interpersonal relationships (unstable dyadic configurations tend to form three-party triangles) depicted in the interpersonal–dyadic triangle:

> The individual's present is his past plus his current circumstances. Part of his past will always survive, contained and modified by current interactions. Both his past and his unique qualities are part of his social context, which they influence as the context influences him. (p. 14)

TRIADIC PROCESSES AND FAMILY STRUCTURE

One of the main functions of triangular relationships is defensive (Guerin et al., 1996). Essentially triangular relationships occur when there is too much unmetabolized anxiety in a dyadic relationship, which seeks equilibrium by engaging a third individual, usually a vulnerable person. Bowen (1976) believed that relational triangles are the basic building blocks of any relational system, including marriages and families. Steinglass (1978) described how a dyadic configuration moves to the triadic: "Although two-person systems may exhibit relative stability during periods of calm, at times of stress the two-person system is highly unstable, and the tendency of such a dyad is to attempt to involve or incorporate a third person, thereby establishing a triangle" (p. 332). As discussed in previous chapters, dysfunction can be expressed in various ways. Early systemic theorists noted that the pathway is often relational, which provided a major insight into how human systems function. The third person in a triadic relationship is often the one who becomes visibly symptomatic, although this is often diversionary. Minuchin (1974) described his structural family approach, to which many elements of personality-guided relationship therapy pay homage, as

> a body of theory and techniques that approaches the individual in his social context. Therapy based on this framework is directed toward changing the organization of the family. When the structure of the family group is transformed, the positions of members in that group are altered accordingly. As a result, each individual's experience changes. ... A therapist working within the framework of structural family therapy, however, can be compared to a technician with a zoom lens. He can zoom in for a closeup whenever he wishes to study the intrapsychic field, but he can also observe a broader focus. (pp. 2–3)

Minuchin was aware of the necessity to view the family system at different levels of magnification, which offers different but fundamentally compatible views of the same process. Triadic configurations do not emerge out of the current relational matrix but are anchored in past developmental progressions and generational influences. For triangulation to occur, there must exist a low level of differentiation among a dyad, who then spill the anxiety they cannot bear into a vulnerable third party, who absorbs and expresses (albeit in a disguised way) the conflict, which then often serves to join the dyad in a shared task.

DEVELOPMENTAL PROGRESSION

Marital relationships are one of the central dyadic configurations in families. Much of what the personality-guided clinician sees in clinical practice is the effect on the marital subsystem from stressors within and without the marital matrix. Marital relationships and longer term partnerships are sensitive barometers of the personality systems that make up the dyad and reflect the triadic configurations from which both members emerge. As Nichols (1988) noted,

> marriage as a whole is different from the sum of its parts. Marriage is not understandable merely through summarizing the attributes or characteristics of the individual marital partners. To describe Jack as an individual and Mary as an individual is not the same as describing the pair of them in relationship and interaction. Summing up the parts does not provide the whole picture, that can be done only looking at the picture as a whole.
>
> To use an analogy, a house is made of nails, lumber, electrical wiring, and other materials, but to say that one's house is composed of so many nails, so much lumber, and so on does not describe the house. Rather, it is necessary not to look at the parts and sum them up but to pay attention to "the pattern which connects" (Bateson, 1980, p. 3) in order to appreciate the structure. (pp. 46–47)

These marital dyads form the basic subsystem from which families grow. When marital dyads are unstable and have more tension than the individual personality system of each partner can handle, a third figure is often sought to stabilize the dyad and keep the anxiety within tolerable bounds. Guerin et al. (1996) described the following possible configurations that might result, dividing them between *extramarital* and *intrafamilial* *triangles*.

Extrafamilial Triangular Configuration (Guerin et al., 1996)

- *Extramarital affairs triangles* are attempts to deal with anxiety and tension by externalizing the process to a third party. Although temporary, this often serves to reduce the tension and stabilize a marriage. When discovered, an affair becomes a central therapeutic issue that needs to be addressed and discontinued before the marital relationship can repair.
- *Social network triangles* involve social groups outside the family that unduly influence an individual and become a third "party" in the dyad. In one couple, the "boys" down at the local bar were the main network for a man in a conflicted marriage. Social clubs and community activities can also serve this function. Many also believe alcohol, drugs, or any addiction can serve the same function as a third person does.
- *Occupational triangles* are present when there is an intense emotional attachment that is resented by the spouse and absorbs a

significant amount of tension from the marriage. The individual may have abandoned family life for the work family, where emotional needs are met instead of in the primary relationship.

Intrafamilial Triangular Configurations (Guerin et al., 1996)

- *In-law triangles* exist when an individual has not made a shift from the family of origin to his or her relationship. In this triangular configuration, individuals seek to maintain overly reactive emotional links with their family of origin and place secondary importance in their marital relationship. There is a blurring of boundaries with the primary relationship system and an overinvestment in the family of origin at the cost of the nuclear family. A man may go and visit his mother every morning for coffee, ignoring his wife and children in the process; loyalty or idealization of a parent might be maintained so that the spouse is always second best to Mom or Dad; a parent may be demanding or controlling and expect the triangulated individual to remain faithful.
- *Triangles with children* "are ready made" (Guerin et al., 1996, p. 187). Children are easy targets for projection and vulnerable to triangulation because of their underdeveloped emotional systems. Often where there is a symptomatic child there is one or more triangular configurations such as husband–wife–child, grandparent–parent–child, and parent–aunt/uncle–child. Sometimes these cross three generational boundaries.
- *Spouse and sibling triangles* exist when an individual is overly invested in a sibling or sibling subsystem (two or more siblings). For example, a man is always bailing his younger sister out of trouble by giving her money and spending excessive time and energy extracting her from bad situations.
- *Primary parental triangles* of each spouse refer to the position each spouse has been in with his or her own parents. Any sensitivity or emotional reactivity that has been cultivated in a primary family of origin triangle is brought to the new relationship. A rebellious daughter may react to her husband's suggestion that she not drive so erratically by speeding up (Magnavita, 2002a, pp. 353–354).

Families restructure and reorganize themselves as development progresses through the family life cycle, with ever-changing demands on its members for increased differentiation and patterns of communication. Minuchin (1974) described this process as follows:

The birth of a child marks a radical change in the family organization. The spouses' functions must differentiate to meet the infant's demands for care and nurturance and to handle the constraints thus imposed on the parents' time. The physical and emotional commitment to the child usually requires a change in the spouses' transactional patterns. A new set of subsystems appears in the family organization, with children and parents having different functions. This period also requires a renegotiation of boundaries with the extended family and the extrafamilial. Grandparents, aunts, and uncles may enter to support, guide, or organize the new functions in the family. Or the boundary around the nuclear family may be strengthened. (p. 18)

This developmental progression leads to a continual process of adaptation and restructuring. Triadic restructuring attempts to intervene in this process and take advantage of natural opportunities for change or when crises create disequilibria. As the family members make the transition from one stage of development to another, the family system is generally in an increased state of disequilibria before homeostasis is reestablished and another level of functioning achieved.

AFFECT, ANXIETY, AND DEFENSE SYSTEMS IN FAMILY PROCESS

As in the *intrapsychic–biological* and the *interpersonal–dyadic* triangles, affect is crucial to the *relational–triadic* configuration, a point emphasized by early systemic theorists such as Ackerman (1958) and summarized by Paolino and McCrady (1978) as follows:

One important aspect of the unitary organization of the family system is the flow of emotion that takes place within it and the intimate exchange of emotional influences, which form a sort of emotional contagion (Ackerman, 1958). There are countless examples of the ways in which one family member will manage to be preserved from pathogenic effects of emotional involvements, but at the expense of one or more members of the family. Or the outbreak of symptoms in one member may serve as a protective device which allows other members of the family to maintain an adequate level of functioning. There are family systems in which, when stress impinges on the family systems from certain directions, there is an outbreak or exacerbation of pathology in one or another of the members, or in the whole family itself, embracing all of its members. (pp. 54–55)

The diathesis–stress paradigm, when applied to triangular configurations, posits that the expression of dysfunction will be based on the family system or subsystems that are most vulnerable, as is often the case in complex clinical syndromes (see Figure 9.1). This can explain the various pathways that relational anxiety may take—in symptoms, character patterns, and addictive process, as discussed in chapter 8. Figure 9.1 uses the diathesis–stress model to understand how symptom formations can occur at the *dyadic* and *triadic* levels. In the example depicted, mother and father both have a low level of differentiation; when stress arises, this is likely to lead to dysfunction in the marital dyad, expressed, in this example, as sexual dysfunction and marital conflict. The marital conflict is multifactorial and includes the likelihood, because of each of them having a low level of differentiation, that increased conflict will arouse anxiety that cannot be contained. Some of this anxiety is then transmitted to their son, who absorbs and expresses the anxiety based on the unique functioning of his individual personality system, which is unlikely to have adequately functioning intrapsychic defenses. He therefore will develop his own symptom constellation, which might include conduct disturbance, social phobia, and other clinical expression consistent with the type of family and genetic endowment that influences his vulnerability to certain symptom formations. Each of the parents has his or her own unique expression of symptom disturbances based on the integrity of their intrapsychic functioning.

Each member of this triad might also express chronic stress in his or her personality system and may additionally exhibit personality dysfunction. In severe cases in which there are long-standing patterns of dysfunction, the family may exhibit signs of a dysfunctional personologic system with generational implications as well. Satir (1972) described three of the most common injunctions that dysfunctional families engender among their members: *don't feel, don't trust,* and *don't talk about it.* Continuing with our example, there may be a history over generations of unresolved conflict that continues to influence the current generation. This might include family themes of addiction, false self-protection, chronic empathic misalignment, adaptation to chaos, and so forth, as represented in Table 6.1.

Styles of Emotional Parenting and Triadic Process

Goleman (1995), in reviewing the literature, described three of the most common parenting styles that lead to problems in affect systems:

- *Ignoring feelings altogether.* Such parents treat a child's emotional upset as trivial or a bother, something that will blow over. They fail to use emotional moments as a chance to get closer to the child or to help the child learn lessons in emotional competence.

TABLE 9.1
Themes, Communications, and Relational Issues of Various
Types of Dysfunctional Personologic Systems (DPSs)

Type of DPS	System Themes	Communications	Relational Issues
AdcDps	Addictive processes	Reversed assumption that without substances survival is threatened	Co-dependence as a substitute for intimacy
NarDps	False self-protection	Public images are to be maintained at all costs	Achievement substitutes for validation of person
CNrDps	Chronic empathic misalignment	Pressure to compensate for emotional deficits in members	Affirmation provided for emotional care taking
PscDps	Adaptation to chaos	We can never feel secure	Basic attachment is achieved by assuming care functions
DevDps	Inability to tolerate individuation	Separation is dangerous to family cohesion and survival	Differentiation—fusion
TraDps	Accommodation to chronic abuse patterns	Family members are objects to be dominated by "powerful" members	Trauma absorption—"Use and abuse" relationships
DepDps	Attempt to adapt to insufficient emotional resources	"Make do"—there will never be enough resources to meet needs	Distortion of family developmental processes
MedDps	Overdomination of family function with medical illness and processes	Chronic medical illness predominates all aspects of family communication	Exacerbation of pre-existing personality disturbances. Relations revolve around illness
ParDps	"Us vs. them" dichotomy predominates	We must protect ourselves from intrusion by outsiders	Cohesion through sharing of paranoid view
SomDps	Substitution of somatic for emotional life	The only valid form of communication is somatic	Nurturing is elicited through illness

Note. From *Relational Therapy for Personality Disorders* (p. 131), by J. J. Magnavita, 2000, New York: John Wiley & Sons. Copyright 2000 by John Wiley & Sons. Reprinted with permission.

- *Being too laissez-faire.* These parents notice how a child feels, but hold that however a child handles the emotional storm is fine—even, for example, if a child resorts to hitting. Like those who ignore a child's feelings, these parents rarely step in to try to show their child an alternative emotional response. They try to soothe all upsets, and will, for instance, use bargaining and bribes to get their child to stop being sad or angry.
- *Being contemptuous, showing no respect for how the child feels.* Such parents are typically disapproving, harsh in both their criticisms and their punishments. They might, for instance, forbid any display of the child's anger at all and become punitive at the least sign of irritability in the child. There are the parents who angrily yell at a child who is trying to tell his side of the story, "Don't you talk back to me!" (pp. 190–191)

NATURAL MOVEMENT FROM DYADIC TO THE TRIADIC

In most developmental progressions, individuals leave their families of origin, marry or establish long-term partnerships, and have children. Meissner (1978) described this shift:

> The arrival of the first child is an event of singular importance in the history of any marriage and marks a decisive turning point in its psychological development. The equilibrium between husband and wife is shifted from the dyadic balance to a triadic configuration. This shift cannot take place without some degree of psychological tension and upheaval (Blanck and Blanck, 1968). The balance of love and hate within this triad is largely determined by the attitudes of the parents, although from the very beginning the interaction is reciprocal. The parents may carry into this new psychological situation residues deriving from experience in their own families of origin. Consequently, they may reproduce patterns of interaction previously experienced in that context, or may shift to a polar opposite set of attitudes as a rebellion against and rejection of those childhood experiences. (p. 76)

The homeostatic balance is disturbed with each new child.

> In this sense it is appropriate to think of the grouping of mother and father with each individual child as forming a triangular configuration which is distinct from the triangular involvement of the parents with each other child. The overlapping and interaction of these respective triads within the family system form a dynamic matrix within which the family emotional processes play themselves out. (p. 77)

In clinical practice it is common to have couples and individuals enter treatment with a spectrum of complaints following the birth of a child or when children are young. A common pattern has been for the male to enter into an extramarital relationship, essentially explaining that he has been neglected as his spouse's energy has been redirected to the demands of an infant.

Emotional Cutoff of Family Subsystems or Members

"The concept of emotional cutoff describes the way people commonly deal with unresolved fusion to their families of origin, namely, by insulating themselves or cutting themselves off emotionally from the parental subsystem" (Kerr, 1981, p. 349). Emotional cutoffs are a way in which the multigenerational transmission process is fueled. Kerr (1981) stated:

> Emotional cutoff is an interesting paradox in that it at one and the same time *reflects* a problem, "*solves*" a problem, and *creates* a problem. It reflects the problem of the underlying fusion between the generations. It "solves" a problem in that, by avoiding emotional contact, it reduced anxiety of the moment. It creates a problem in that it isolated and alienates people from each other, people who could *benefit* from contact with each other if they could deal with each other better. (pp. 249–250)

Although emotional cutoffs reveal and create problems, it may be necessary in some family systems for individuals or subsystems to cut off other members, especially in cases of severe emotional, sexual, or physical abuse that occur primarily in people with the physically/sexually traumatized dysfunctional personologic system or in people with the paranoid dysfunctional personologic system.

Multigenerational Transmission Process

As noted in the previous chapter, interpersonal styles can be transmitted through dynamic interpersonal processes of projection and introjection, as well as through modeling and the shaping of response systems through positive and negative reinforcement and punishment. "As Skynner (1976) and others (e.g., Davis, 1983) have noted, children internalize a model of each parent, a model of the affective interaction between spouses, and a model of the parents as a system" (Nichols, 1988, p. 57). In contemporary parlance, children develop *relational schema* by witnessing the interaction of parental figures. Families also transmit conflict and unresolved issues through the multigenerational transmission process. Kerr (1981) described this family projection process as follows:

> The concept of a family projection process describes the way the undifferentiation of the parents is transmitted to their children. The result of this transmission is that the capacity for differentiation in the children

generally approximates closely that of their parents. Since the process does focus unevenly on the various children, it is possible for some children to grow up with slightly less capacity for differentiation than the parents, others with the same capacity, and still others with somewhat more ability to maintain differentiation in an emotional system. (p. 245)

An atavistic residue of previous processes, both positive and negative, is evident in subsequent generations. Dysfunctional personologic systems show these effects when, for instance, in an alcoholic family system, a generation of active addictive process is avoided only to emerge in a virulent form in the subsequent generation. Each generation show the effects "of an endless chain of influence linking the developmental experience of each generation to that of its immediate and distant ancestors" (Terkelsen, 1980, p. 43).

The evidence of this multigenerational transmission process is seen by most clinicians, regardless of their theoretical orientation, in cases of family members who discover significant parallels in their lives with those of others from the extended family network and in the recurrent roles that individuals are assigned and volunteer for, such as the "black sheep," "savior," and so forth.

Positive and Negative Feedback Loops

Oftentimes, negative feedback loops become an important process for maintaining dysfunctional adaptations. Negative feedback loops have been identified by pioneers in the field of cybernetics (Maruyama, 1963). A negative feedback loop dampens, that is, reduces and suppresses, a process, and hence is an equilibrium-maintaining process, whereas a positive feedback loop, by definition, amplifies the processes occurring among the variables under consideration (Anchin, 2003, pp. 340–342). As a behavior is emitted, a pattern of correcting the response ensues, which has the effect of either dampening or amplifying the response. An example is of an adolescent who, in a normal phase of increased drive to individuate, begins to act out against the overly controlling parental subsystem, which responds with increasingly ineffective constraint that exacerbates the situation.

Dysfunctional Personologic Systems

Two of the common features of dysfunctional families are the lack of differentiation and problems with emotional process and response. "One of the most striking features of families composed of such poorly differentiated individuals is the extent to which emotional stirring in one family member plays upon the emotional functioning of other family members. If there is emotional upheaval, there tends to be a communication of emotion which influences the functioning of other family members" (Meissner, 1978, p. 35). This reactivity is a hallmark of lower functioning and undifferentiated systems. Dysfunctional personologic systems are cases of extreme bionegativity that become entrenched in a positive feedback loop in which repetition of the same responses, sometimes over generations, continue to worsen the participants' ability to function effectively. The clinician should attempt to assess for the presence of multigenerational themes that have negatively affected the personality development of its members. Attempts should be made to engage these families in treatment by carefully establishing their power hierarchies and working closely with individuals and subsystems to create an initial therapeutic alliance.

TRIADIC RESTRUCTURING STRATEGIES AND SUBTYPES

We can conceptualize triadic restructuring as a method that emphasizes processes among groups of three people, or among multiple triangular configurations as might occur in complex systems or in a multigenerational process. It is not necessary, however, to have the triad in the consulting room. Bowen (1976) was adamant that triadic restructuring can occur with one individual only. The emphasis, then, is the explication of processes that occur within triangular relationships so that these can be altered. Bowen believed that if an individual worked toward greater differentiation from the family of origin and was successful in this work, he or she could alter entrenched patterns.

Triadic restructuring has two basic formats: *relational triadic restructuring*, which is concerned with the processes that occur *in vivo* in triangular relational subsystems, and *symbolic triadic restructuring*, which occurs when the triangulated figures are deceased or unavailable for *in vivo* work. Guerin and Chabot (1997) describe an example of this process as follows:

> Triangulation is the emotional process that goes on among three people who make up the triangle. For example, . . . the father might desire a connection with his son and resent his wife's monopoly of the boy's affections: the mother may be angry at the father's distance from her and compensate by substituting closeness with her son. The child, in turn, may resent his father's inattention and criticism and may move toward his mother but, at the same time, be anxious about his overly close relationship with her. As the emotional process of triangulation moves around the triangle, it can produce change in the structure. For example, the father may try to reduce his loneliness by moving toward his son or his wife, or the son may try to avoid fusion with his mother by distancing toward his peers, causing his parents to draw together in their concern for him. (p. 245)

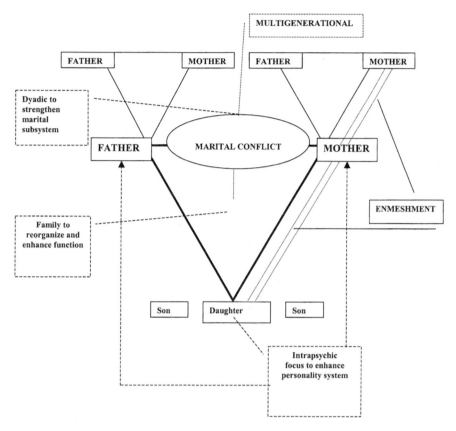

Figure 9.2. Foci and strategies of relational triadic restructuring.

Various strategies of relational triadic restructuring can be incorporated at each systemic level, from the individual, to the dyad, triad, or larger system (see Figure 9.2). In the *triadic–relational configuration* in Figure 9.2, two additional triangles at the top represent mutigenerational processes in operation. The larger triangle represents the system of treatment focus, a father–mother dyad and three children, two boys and a girl. The girl is triangulated with the parents and has an enmeshed[1] relationship with the mother that is diverting anxiety from the dyad. The maternal grandmother is also triangulated with the mother.

One can conceptualize a number of triadic restructuring interventions that would theoretically be capable of altering the system. A clinician might select various approaches based on our assessment and the flexibility and

---

[1]*Enmeshed* refers to a dyad or triad where there is a low level of self/other and emotional differentiation, what Bowen (1976) refers to as an *undifferentiated ego mass*.

motivation of the various systems and subsystems within the family unit. If the parents are concerned about their daughter but not motivated for treatment, one might consider focusing on the daughter. Conversely, if the daughter is highly resistant, either parent might be amenable. A focus of intervention might use an array of restructuring methods, but the guiding principle is detriangulation. One might also focus on the couple as a way to strengthen that subsystem or conduct the process with the nuclear family. Also, one might involve the entire family in multigenerational therapy to restructure the larger system.

SUBTYPES OF TRIADIC RESTRUCTURING

In the following sections, two subtypes of triadic restructuring are presented. The first, *relational restructuring*, refers to the processes that occur when working with groups larger than dyads. The second subtype, *symbolic restructuring*, entails a symbolic elaboration and restructuring of triadic representational systems, useful when attachment figures are deceased or unavailable.

Relational Triadic Restructuring

Relational triadic restructuring refers to processes and techniques that work with any system larger than the dyad, such as a triad or larger family, group, or social system. Relational triadic restructuring occurs in these systems as the process unfolds. These techniques have been developed by Bowen (1978), Haley (1987), Minuchin (1974), Whitaker (Whitaker & Keith, 1981), Satir (1967), and others. The variety of techniques offered by these seminal clinical theorists are beyond the scope of this volume. Readers are referred to their original works and many other excellent volumes in the field of family therapy to gain an appreciation for the variety of innovative approaches.

Minuchin (1974) understood that triangles undermine the hierarchy of family systems and often exist when generational boundaries have been breached. Figure 9.2 depicts the elevation of the son to a position of emotional equality with the mother and a distancing of the father, who is relegated to a peripheral position. This is a highly troubled triangular configuration as the forces are especially powerful and often there is much anger that is not being expressed in the marital dyad. If this situation has been going on for an extended period of time, the emotional development of the son will likely be highly compromised. He may develop symptoms of school phobia to remain home and run interference or contrarily may begin acting out to try to reconfigure the triangle. This is what psychodynamic therapists refer to as winning the oedipal struggle but at great costs.

Triadic restructuring will be indicated in the early period of contact with this family. An evident emotional process makes it clear that the father has allowed himself to be marginalized, and this may even be a retaliatory action against his wife. The following vignette demonstrates a phase of triadic restructuring with this family:

TH: So what is it that brings you to see me?

M: We have been having problems getting John [son] to go to school.

TH: What is your view of the problem, Mr. Houston?

SON: [responding for father] I don't think it is really a problem. I have really bad allergies and it gets worse when I go to school sometimes. I am planning to go tomorrow.

TH: I notice you answer for your dad. Mr. Houston, what is your take on this situation?

M: [as her husband begins to speak, Mrs. Houston cuts him off] Well, he is right, you know, his allergies do get worse when he goes to school. He really wants to, but it is hard for him when he isn't feeling well. He stays home and reads, so it's not like he is out running around unsupervised.

TH: Well, I really did want to hear what you have to say, Mr. Houston, but it seems that you are outgunned here.

F: Yes I am! I haven't a clue about what is going on with him. All I know is that when I leave for work, he's there and when I get home, he's there.

TH: Have you tried to get him to go to school?

M: Oh no! He doesn't get involved. He just sits in his armchair watching television every night after work. He winds up sleeping in the chair for the night.

F: Well, there isn't any room in the bed.

TH: No room in the bed?

M: Oh, don't bring that up.

F: I think it is important that the doctor knows he sleeps in your bed every night.

TH: You said "your bed" to your wife?

F:	We haven't shared the same bed for as long as I can remember.
M:	Oh, you are the one who likes to sleep in that chair of yours, like Archey Bunker!
TH:	I would like to ask your son to leave so we could discuss some adult issues that are not appropriate for him. Is that OK, Dad and Mom? [*The therapist makes a structural intervention that demarcates a clear boundary between the parental and child subsystems.*]
M & F:	Yes.
TH:	John, could you please have a seat in the waiting room while we talk?
SON:	OK.
	[*The focus then resumes on the dyad to enhance communication.*]
TH:	It sounds like there are a lot of negative feelings that have been brewing between the two of you?
WIFE:	Our marriage is a joke.
HUSBAND:	Your life revolves around that kid.
TH:	You say that with venom.
HUSBAND:	You bet I'm angry. He rules the roost.
WIFE:	If you would get out of your chair and get involved, it might be different.
TH:	It sounds like the marriage has been suffering for a long time. I wonder if we might make this the focus of a few sessions, and then we can bring your son back into the sessions at a later time?
WIFE:	Well, we didn't come for marital therapy but it's either that or a divorce.
HUSBAND:	You are not the only one who might be better off if we called it quits. [*The focus is now on the disturbance in the couple in which their son has been triangulated. There are clearly multiple pathways that one could follow to further the triadic restructuring here, including working with the parents around coparenting while the son is present, all the while restructuring the family system by blocking communication from the son that would maintain his position.*]

Triadic relational restructuring may also be conducted in group therapy sessions in much the same way when triangular configurations have developed. Such configurations also reflect problematic relationships that recapitulate family of origin problems. Group members can be coached to role-play family members and depict the triangles in which they are caught, helping the person externalize and understand them.

Symbolic Triadic Restructuring

Symbolic triadic restructuring occurs in subsystems with one or two individuals and uses the triangular formulations to assist the individual or dyad in a symbolic working through of triangular relationships for which other participants in the configuration cannot be present. This is often necessary when important members of triadic configurations are deceased or unavailable. The following case of a man "chained" to his dead father and caught in shared unhappiness with his mother demonstrates this type of restructuring.

> **PT:** I have been unable to make any decisions about what to do with the farm. I have been sitting and ruminating, what would my father have me do?
>
> **TH:** So you are unable to do anything with the farm?
>
> **PT:** I don't think of it as my farm. He bought it and made it what it is!
>
> **TH:** But you worked like a slave since you were 15 to make it possible!
>
> **PT:** I know, but he won't be happy if I don't do it the way he would have.
>
> **TH:** So you are chained to the grave of your dead father, and he continues to rule you as he did when he was alive!
>
> **PT:** Yes, this is the case. I never thought of it in that way. It is almost like I am waiting for him to return and take charge. My mother also complained to me about his focus on the farm. She was very unhappy and lived a life I feel sorrow for. She used to confide in me because of his emotional unavailability. It was the farm first, the wife and the kids second and third.
>
> **TH:** You were caught and still remain in the triangle with them.
>
> **PT:** She used to complain all the time but never went against his vision of the farm as the be all and end all. I was so unhappy as a child being her confidante and always trying to gain his approval by doing whatever he wanted of me to further his farm. I guess I felt a kind of closeness with her and had of feeling of being special, but she was part of the problem. I always felt sorry for her but now I am angry at what she didn't do.

TH: She seemed to enable him and his behavior and used you as an emotional outlet.

PT: I think I continue this pattern in my relationships with women who I look to care for because they are so unhappy. I guess I want to rescue them like I was unable to do with my mother.

TH: Rescue from what?

PT: My father and her unhappiness with the marriage and the farm.

TH: It sounds as if this triangle that you are caught in had and continues to have a major hold on you.

PT: I would really like to cut the chain. I think I might go to his grave today to see that he is not coming back and I can run the place the way I see fit.

GOALS AND APPROACHES OF TRIADIC RESTRUCTURING

The basic goal of triadic restructuring is to alter process, hierarchy, and communication style in the family system in an attempt to engender second-order change (i.e., structural and functional transformation of the entire system; Mahoney, 1991) as opposed to first-order change (i.e., minor system modifications of parts of system; Watzlawick, Weakland, & Fisch, 1974), and to address the patterns of circular causality that occur (Nichols, 1988). To achieve such change, communication patterns within a system need to be reorganized, the family boundaries need to be clarified if diffused or loosened if artificially rigid, and the hierarchy needs to be rearranged to a more functional structure. For these key, overarching systemic changes to be achieved, certain conditions must also exist or be therapeutically attended to. "For the treatment process to work, the family must have some ability to regulate affect, tolerate anxiety, control projection, and not denigrate treatment" (Glick & Loraas, 2001, p. 148).

The initial goals in the restructuring process are to establish an alliance and conduct an assessment. These initial goals include the following:

- Accept the system at the point at which members meet you.
- Engage; develop a therapeutic alliance.
- Assess the type, degree, and level of functioning of the system as well as the individuals.
- Address safety issues—emotional, physical and sexual abuse patterns.
- Identify key individuals or subsystems that may be amenable or ready for change.

- Enlarge or limit the focus of treatment on the basis of the stage of change and degree of readiness.
- Use psychometric instruments to gather more data and corroborate impressions.
- When the time is right, surprise the system by shifting the frame and offering a consultation to an individual or a subsystem. (Magnavita, 2000a, pp. 121–122)

In addition to the initial goals, there are broader goals to which one should attune as the process unfolds.

Broad-Spectrum Treatment Goals

The treatment goals vary from family to family, and from system to system, on the basis of the assessment and presenting complaints. The general goals of triadic restructuring include

1. Improved communication
2. Enhanced emotional capacity
3. Creation of functional family hierarchies
4. Development of higher order defenses
5. Enhanced capacity for intimacy or developing capacities for attachment
6. Improved problem-solving capacity
7. Greater tolerance for anxiety without compromising family functions (Magnavita, 2000a)
8. Ability to flexibly navigate life cycle transition periods and reconfigure on the basis of new demand features of phase of development

Meissner (1978) described the complexity of shifting from one system to another as broad-spectrum treatment goals are pursued within the family:

> When the discussion shifts from the marital couple to the family unit, there is a moving to a new level of sociological and interpersonal organization. The emotional matrix compounded out of the interacting personalities of the husband and wife becomes the basis out of which an entirely new and considerably more complex form of emotional interaction is elaborated as new members are added to the family unit. (p. 53)

When the family is unable to work together, other restructuring methods should be used to increase functional capacities of the members and dyadic configurations. The goal of triadic restructuring is to enhance systematically the level and functioning of adaptation at each level, from the individual, to subgroups within the family, to the entire family. Changes at any level of the family system will reverberate at other levels. As we have seen, intrapsychic restructuring enhances the functioning of the individual personality system, so individuals will relate in a healthier fashion within dyads and triads, thus changing their dynamics. Various common goals of restructuring dyads actually proceed through focusing on the dysfunctional triangular configuration, including the strategies that follow.

Detriangulating an Extramarital Triad

Extramarital relationships are a common expression of a dysfunction in the primary partnership. These extramarital relationships are often the reason that families and couples seek treatment. Often the extramarital relationship is a "secret" that is guarded to prevent the anxiety that would result from destabilization. Lusterman (1995, p. 267) delineated three treatment phases for infidelity: (a) restoration of trust, (b) examination of predisposing factors, and (c) rapprochement. Gordon and Baucom (1999) presented another clinically rich approach to treating marital infidelity in which they conceptualized affairs as interpersonal trauma using a multitheoretical model.

Detriangulating a Child

In dysfunctional personologic systems, triangular relationships may be used to create an artificial presentation of harmony between adult partners. The first step in addressing the marital issues is to detriangulate the child from the spousal subsystem because of the bionegative or pathogenic effects on the child:

> In triangulation, each parent demands that the child side with him against the other parent. Whenever the child sides with one, he is automatically defined as attacking the other. In a highly dysfunctional structure, the child is paralyzed. Every movement he makes is defined by one parent as an attack. (Minuchin, 1974, p. 102)

In other cases the child is used by the spousal subsystem to deflect or detour their problems by attacking the child and supporting deviant behavior. "The parents' detouring may take the form of attacking the child, defining him as the source of family problems because he is bad. In other families, the parents may define the child as sick and weak, and then unite to protect him" (Minuchin, 1974, p. 102). In cases like these, it is often necessary to detriangulate the child as soon as is expedient, and there can be considerable energy expended to maintain the process. In one case of a triangulated 12-year-old boy, the mother spent most of her time searching for a cause for her son's poor performance at school. He was taken to a variety of attention-deficit specialists, psychiatrists, psychopharmacologists, biofeedback specialists, and many others. The boy was determined through testing to be in the borderline range of intelligence, but the mother would not accept this, and the father had rejected him in part because of his overly close attachment to her. She preferred having her son sleep with her to her husband. The bottom line was that this very troubled marriage continually bordered on divorce, but because of both parents' personality dysfunction, this solution was never allowed. Instead, they wound up living in different states as a way to maintain the system, but their son continued to suffer the effects of their dysfunction.

Minuchin gives an example of strategies for subsystem restructuring in the following case of a conflict-avoiding transactional pattern:

> In one case, for instance, where the identified patient is a fifteen-year-old suffering from psychogenic vomiting, the therapist takes on the medical responsibility for her symptom. She is not to discuss it with her parents at all. She can talk about it only with him. He thus places himself as a barrier between the girl and her parents, in a maneuver that promotes her autonomy and also promotes closeness between the parents. (p. 103)

When detriangulating a child, it is often necessary to increase the father's functional parenting capacity. Meissner (1978) described a common presentation: "Fathers of disturbed children are frequently found to be domineering, authoritarian, hypercritical—or else passive, ineffectual, unable to cope with family responsibility, and often engaged in passive–aggressive undercutting of the mother's authority" (p. 55). This often requires a dual-pronged therapeutic approach, strengthening the father's parenting skills and helping him be clearer about his conflict with his spouse. In these situations, the mother's role is that she is often overprotective and in so doing looks to have her needs for affirmation met. Changing the transaction and emotional process inevitably means that the marital dyad needs to be strengthened so that issues are communicated directly and faced.

Resolving Multigenerational Conflict

Creating an awareness of and solving multigenerational conflict can allow subsequent generations to live in greater harmony. It is often useful and therapeutic to bring in members from other generations when multigenerational conflict is entrenched. A few consultations may be useful in gathering information and adding an important dimension to the family system's functioning across the generations. Another useful method that can help with this process is to have the patient bring in family albums and pictures to derive additional information. As audiovisual technology has become more commonplace, videotapes of family events can also be useful in identifying and resolving generational issues. Using these techniques, I have often been able to confirm hunches about attachment styles, boundary issues, and the presence of psychiatric and characterological problems. Letters can also be another valuable source of family information. The style and content as well as the covert messages can be explored and placed in the proper perspective. When possible, conducting multigenerational family therapy is one of the most powerful experiences for all involved. Breakthroughs can be achieved when the family healing potential is mobilized. In other cases, significant information is gathered to advance treatment even if the generational focus does not pan out with the members present. In one case, the elderly parents of a 45-year-old woman with lifetime personality problems were invited to a consultation. During the session, the parents proclaimed that they would help their daughter in any way possible and then failed to show up for the next session, choosing to go to the mountains instead. This confirmed the patient's impression that they said one thing and did another. Most of her life, they had professed strong family values while colluding in the father's abuse of their daughter. The degree with which she remained triangulated with her parents required years of therapy to affect, because it was instilled in her from an early age to "honor your parents"—and she did despite what they had done to her.

Reorganizing Dysfunctional Triads

Dysfunctional triads often respond to attempts to reorganize the basic process. In some cases, reorganization can take place by setting boundaries that are poorly operating among or within generations. In one case, a recently divorced mother of three came to her first session with her mother, who did most of the talking for the identified patient. The patient's mother decided it was important that she return for future sessions to make sure her daughter reported the information about what was happening in her life and family. The identified patient accepted this as a typical controlling function by her mother. The therapist made it clear that it would be helpful for the patient to come herself and for the mother to make a separate appointment if she wanted to discuss the situation. The identified patient was greatly relieved at the next session, which she attended alone, and reported a pattern of lifelong maternal intrusiveness and boundary violations.

Creating a More Functional Family Hierarchy

An important method of triadic restructuring entails realigning the family hierarchy to a more functional and adaptive one. In some families, the nuclear constellation is intruded on or ruled by members from previous generations or by children who hold power relinquished from parental dyads. In other families, the nuclear constellations need to be restructured by creating clearer generational boundaries and an awareness of the negative impact of multigenerational transmission.

Strengthening the Parental Subsystem

Whether a single- or dual-parent system, the parental subsystem of dysfunctional families endures a great deal of stress and strain. Whenever possible, the therapist should offer support aimed at more adaptive functioning. Underscoring and accepting the demands of child rearing can be palliative, especially in cases with extra burdens (e.g., dysfunctional or missing parental or spousal figures, physical or psychiatric illness). Modeling effective parenting techniques and communication styles can be useful to a strained parental subsystem. Understanding, clarifying, and stopping multigenerational themes are also useful in reducing emotional burdens that arise from difficult situations such as caring for an abusive parental figure or dealing with excessive emotional or physical demands from the extended family.

Redistributing Family Power to the Most Appropriate Individual

Often the symptomatic individual in a triad holds more power than is appropriate. Whenever possible, the power in a triadic configuration should be redistributed to the essential dyad and hierarchy established. This is the case for the spectrum of triangular configurations. The therapist can do so in many ways, some physical and others symbolic. In some cases, the symptomatic individual can be excused from treatment, especially when he or she appears the most resistant in the family system. The focus can then be on the subsystem that is experiencing more pain.

Identifying and Educating the Family About Processes That Maintain Triangular Relations

Explaining how triangular processes work can be helpful to those caught in triangular configurations. Most people readily understand the concepts. An explanation of how anxiety is channeled from a dyad to a third stabilizing party should be given to the family so that all participants can begin the process of enhancing communication and emotional containment within appropriate dyads.

Containing Emotional Reactions by Modeling
Tolerance and Acceptance of Feeling and Thoughts

A useful method of triadic restructuring is for the therapist to model the acceptance of feelings and thoughts offered in the treatment process. Being able to express oneself freely is essential to the increased differentiation required in relationships based on respect and attunement to the emotional process of all participants. Tolerance and acceptance foster differentiation by making it safe to express oneself. Encouraging revelation and discussion of dreams can also be an effective exercise to build trust and interest in others.

Core Affective Exchange

Core affective exchange as a process of relational restructuring was introduced by Scharff and Scharff (1991, p. 179) and refers to a method of focusing communication on the "here and now" process as opposed to the "there and then" of what happened outside of the session. "If we choose to work in the here and now, we might explore an event in the therapy hour, such as a dirty look, an argument in the room, or the family's difficulty in talking about anything meaningful" (Scharff & Scharff, 1991, p. 179). What is attempted is to focus the family on the "core affective exchange—the golden moments for understanding and change" (p. 180).

Regulating and Shifting Triadic Systemic Anxiety

An important aspect of triadic restructuring, regardless of the techniques used, is the ability to assess the level of anxiety in a family or other group and then modulate it without flooding the system. This is easier said than done. One must be ever vigilant to the channels of anxiety as the process of therapy unfolds. A sufficient level of anxiety must be present to destabilize homeostatic and entrenched patterns and processes, which often requires a careful increase in anxiety to the point that the system becomes disrupted. The therapist may then address the emotional residue of the destabilization. For example, a woman entered therapy after a number of unsuccessful initial attempts to address issues with her son. The main issue, however, was the relationship with the husband, whom she said would not enter treatment. She described her chronic relational difficulties, both marital and parent–child, and her attempts to resolve them with her husband. She said the situation was hopeless, because he would not come to treatment. The therapist asked the patient about divorce, and she recoiled at the mention of the word. She became more comfortable, and in the next session she playfully spelled "divorce" when asked what she would do if her husband refused her invitation to participate. She then transmitted this anxiety to him, and he attended the next session and then entered a successful course of treatment. At times, anxiety has to be raised almost to the point where it seems intolerable to the patient, couple, or triad. Knowing which systems can tolerate this and which require decreased anxiety is often murky, however.

Dysfunctional Personologic Systems With Extreme Deficits in Structure and Process

Family systems that suffer primarily from deficits in structure and process usually need to be stabilized and to have their anxiety lessened. Families that include highly impaired members often experience extreme biological vulnerabilities and difficulties with attachment, expressed as an impaired ability to trust. These individuals must have their most pressing needs attended to without mobilizing undue anxiety.

Ongoing anxiety is often a part of the chronic dysfunctional family process. When it is beyond the family's capacity to manage the anxiety effectively, positive feedback loops arise, leading to more dysfunction and increasingly ineffective attempts to deal with the anxiety, such as addiction, hypochondriasis, self-injurious behavior, and so forth. The therapist's most important function is to provide a container for the anxiety and to assist in the development of more effective coping and self-soothing strategies. These deficits are often evident in evaluation of the family members' individual personality systems as well as in the extremely impoverished communication and chaotic family organization.

Dysfunctional Personologic Systems With Primary Conflict in Process and Limited Structure Deficit

Families that suffer primarily from conflict may better tolerate anxiety, and thus anxiety levels can be raised more rapidly to accelerate treatment. Compared with those who have attachment disturbances, these family systems do not exhibit major developmental dysfunction but are struggling more with conflicts related to intimacy and closeness. Anxiety may be required to jolt the system out of entrenched homeostatic patterns that provide a buffer for normal anxiety associated with growth and development, loss of structure, roles, and meaning systems, which naturally evolve over time.

SUMMARY AND CONCLUSIONS

Triadic restructuring is a method for working with triangular relationships in their various forms. These triadic relational configurations are engendered when unstable dyads seek stabilization by drawing in a third, usually vulnerable party, who often becomes the symptom bearer of the triad, or through establishing an extramarital affair. Often this third person is the ostensible reason that treatment is sought. Triadic restructuring has its roots in family system theory of the prior century and remains a vital approach with a wide array of technical interventions that can be used to transform personality systems. The processes of triangulation are affected by multigenerational transmission, which carries unresolved relational dynamics and themes from one generation to the next through interpersonal and emotional projective processes. Two primary methods of triadic restructuring, *relational triadic restructuring* and *symbolic relational restructuring*, account for most of the innovative technical advances that clinical theorists have offered.

10

MESOSYSTEM RESTRUCTURING AND THE TOTAL ECOLOGICAL SYSTEM

This chapter considers *mesosystem restructuring* (MR). The mesosystem's view of the patient's personality system includes sociocultural factors, family systems, and individual personality systems, as represented in Figure 10.1 (see also Figure 1.1, p. 16). The total ecological system includes these factors as well as the environment or ecosystem in which personality systems are embedded, including the actual physical environment that a family or individual inhabits.

Mesosystem restructuring is the method of choice when working with dysfunctional systems that are clearly embedded in larger sociocultural institutions and structures and that are adding to or creating the bionegativity (i.e., working with those who have been the victims of poverty, racism, natural disasters, genocide, or war). In these situations, the larger sociopolitical structures and potential resources must be assessed and be a focus of the restructuring. Also, MR is highly indicated for entrenched and refractory patient systems. For example, a patient with chronic psychiatric illness who was being treated in a community mental health center while living in his or her supervised living facility and was threatening to the staff was appropriate to consider for MR. In this case the clinician was called in as a consultant to address the multiple systemic issues, such as staff fear and inconsistency in dealing with this patient.

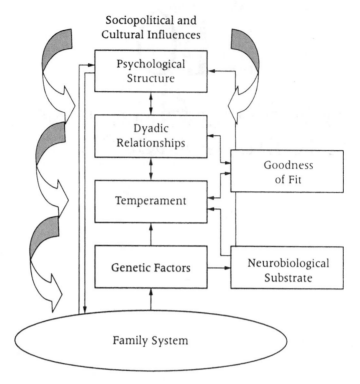

Sociopolitical and
Cultural Influences

Psychological
Structure

Dyadic
Relationships

Temperament

Genetic Factors

Goodness
of Fit

Neurobiological
Substrate

Family System

Figure 10.1. The systemic interrelationships among the modular components of personality. From *Theories of Personality: Contemporary Approaches to the Science of Personality,* by J. J. Magnavita, 2002, New York: John Wiley & Sons. Copyright 2002 by John Wiley & Sons. Reprinted with permission.

The premise of this volume is that human personality and psychopathology is best understood as a complex system, which therefore must incorporate explicit consideration of the total ecological system. This is not new to psychology and social science. As Erich Fromm (1970) wrote,

> Man is a system—like an ecological or political system, the system of the body or of the cell, or a system of society or an organization. In analyzing the system "man," we understand that we are dealing with a system of forces, and not with a mechanical structure of behavior particles. Like any system, the system "man" has great coherence within itself and shows great resistance to change; furthermore, the change of one item that is allegedly "the cause" of another undesirable item will not produce any change in the system as a whole. (p. 63)

Although most systemic thinkers would not agree with his later conclusion, asserting that change in one item does not reverberate throughout the system, Fromm (1955) valuably expanded the realm of psychoanalytic thought from the domain of the intrapsychic and interpersonal to an examination of the impact of society on shaping "human nature." In *Civilization and Its Discontents*, Freud (1939) was aware of the mesosystem but viewed it through a more individual lens. In contrast, Fromm looked at it from more of a sociological perspective—from the broader system to the individual system. He questioned sociology's then-dominant concept of cultural relativism and looked to dysfunction in the social system as a major contributor to personality system dysfunction. He believed that society itself could be the problem and that "there can be a society which is *not* sane" (p. 12). He discussed the concept of "social character," which is shaped by the mesosystem, and described the interrelationship of the family system in this process:

> The structure of society and the function of the individual in the social structure may be considered to determine the content of the social character. The family on the other hand may be considered to be the *psychic agency of society*, the institution which has the function of transmitting the requirements of society to the growing child. The family fulfills this function in two ways. First, and this is the most important factor, by the influence the character of the parents has on the character formation of the growing child. Since the character of most parents is an expression of the social character, they transmit in this way the essential features of the socially desirable character structure to the child. The parents' love and happiness are communicated to the child as well as their anxiety or hostility. In addition to the character of the parents, the methods of childhood training which are customary in a culture also have the function of molding the character of the child in a socially desirable way. (p. 82)

Bronfenbrenner (1979) defined the mesosystem thus: "The ecological environment is conceived as a set of nested structures, each inside the next, like a set of Russian dolls" (p. 3). He begins his book *The Ecology of Human Development* with this observation: "a person's development is profoundly affected by events occurring in settings in which the person is not even present" (p. 3). A major thesis of his work is "that human abilities and their realization depend in significant degree on the larger social and institutional context of individual activity" (p. xv). He then gave an example of how economic factors influence mental health and used the example of how a child's development is affected by conditions of parental employment in industrialized nations.

Other factors, such as physical environment, affect human personality as well. We know, for example, that certain personality adaptations are related to climate and ease of survival and even describe a national character. Warm climates seem to encourage phlegmatic personalities or, in the current argot, less "Type A" behavior. Edward Sapir, an eminent cultural anthropologist who strongly influenced Harry Stack Sullivan's interpersonal model, noted these cultural differences in socialization: "Thus Eskimo culture, contrasted with most North American Indian cultures, is extraverted; Hindu culture on the whole corresponds to the world of the thinking introvert; the culture of the United States is definitely extraverted in character, with a greater emphasis on thinking and intuition than on feeling; and sensational evaluations are more clearly evident in the cultures of the Mediterranean than those of northern Europe" (Sapir, 1963, p. 563). One might argue that this is the domain of anthropology, sociobiology, evolutionary psychology, and sociology, which they indeed are, but there are important reasons for understanding the influence of these factors on the personality system. The context in which personality is expressed is vital to our understanding of personality expression and adaptation. Sapir writes:

> A personality is carved out by the subtle interaction of those systems of ideas which are characteristic of the culture as a whole, as well as of those systems of ideas which get established for the individual through more special types of participation, with the physical and psychological needs of the individual organism, which cannot take over any of the cultural material that is offered in its original form but works over more or less completely, so that it integrates with those needs. The more closely we study this interaction, the more difficult it becomes to distinguish society as a cultural and psychological unit from the individual who is thought of as a member of the society to whose culture he is required to adjust. (Sapir, 1963, 518–519)

The power of the context, such as sociocultural, political, and environmental, by which personality is shaped, expressed, and maintained should not be underestimated. An example brought to my attention was of the sniper who was randomly killing people in the Washington, DC, area in October 2002. Clearly, his behavior was considered aberrant and his personality system dysfunctional. The public was outraged by the senseless, random killings. In contrast, an article in the *New York Times Magazine* (November 10, 2002) described a member of the Special Forces who led an assault on some suspected Afghan insurgents locked in a hospital who were subsequently killed. He described feeling no remorse for the people he had killed. We understand his behavior as being appropriate to the context of what is expected and sanctioned during war. The context had changed; one man who behaves psychopathically is condemned and the other is just doing his job.

In this example, the important corner of the triangle is the sociocultural one for the Special Forces soldier who is acting under the authority of the "dominant," that is, Western sociocultural system and its military–political subsystem. The sniper, on the other hand, is probably acting from a disordered personality system and likely a dysfunctional family system as well. The sociocultural influences we can only speculate about. This man reportedly, like our Special Forces solider, was also a member of the military system and had served in the Gulf War with commendation. How these domain systems interacted to produce such a monstrous expression is unclear, but what seems evident is that some combination of these produced this individual's personality system.

Other psychological theorists have focused on the mesosystem in their work and have used other terms, the most common being the *molar system*, as used in the writings of Rotter (1954) in his classic work *Social Learning and Clinical Psychology*, and later in Rotter, Chance, and Phares (1972) in *Applications of a Social Learning Theory of Personality*.

CRITICAL DOMAINS THAT DEFINE THE MESOSYSTEM

We can only attempt to approach an understanding of human personality systems and the ways in which change can be effected by having knowledge of the multiple domains of influence. When we ignore domains, we lose perspective, and, in turn, we lose flexibility in developing intervention strategies. Moreover, a unified theory requires an understanding of how domains are interconnected (Bronfenbrenner, 1979). "The interconnectedness is seen as applying not only within settings but with equal force and consequence to linkages between settings, both those in which the developing person actually participates and those that he may never enter but which events occur that affect what happens in the person's immediate environment" (pp. 7–8). Small perturbations in systems can reverberate and result in states of chaos and reorganization in new ways. A compelling, real-world illustration of the effects and contributions of multiple influences can be observed in the subsystems that coalesced and led to the massive destruction on September 11, 2001, when 19 terrorists took down the World Trade Center. The effects of this singular event continue to reverberate through and exert profound influence on multiple subsystems on a global scale.

Indeed, over the course of this volume, the reader may have come to appreciate the interconnectedness of the domains that unite various disciplines. Within this broad ecological system, personality systems must be understood in the context of the mesosystem in which personality is expressed and can be observed. One can never hope to create a holonic representation of a system without paying some attention to the critical domains of the mesosystem and their place in the overall ecological field. It is far beyond the scope of this volume to present an in-depth presentation of the array of systems that are essential elements of the personality matrix. An understanding of key domains composing the mesosystem is essential, however. Interested readers should refer to the volume *Sociogenesis Reexam-*

ined (De Graaf & Maier, 1994) for an in-depth review of the mesosystem relationships and domains.

Societal Factors

Societal factors and influences operate as essential determinants of behavior. The vast discipline of sociology is devoted to the study of human society in its multiple dimensions. For better or worse, human adaptation has evolved in its present form in broad variations of social customs and political systems. Eric Erikson (1968) realized the importance of biological systems but emphasized the social system:

> The first of these—first because studied originally through Freud's transfer of biology and physiological modes of thought to psychology—is the *biological process*, by which an organism comes to be a hierarchic organization of organ systems living out its life cycle. The second is the *social process*, by which organisms come to be organized in groups which are geographically, historically, and culturally defined. (p. 73)

Can societies be dysfunctional? Lachkar (2004) asked pertinent questions in her excellent volume *The Narcissistic/Borderline Couple: New Approaches to Marital Therapy* and then explored the ramifications of toxic or bionegative sociocultural systems. She asked, "Where do pathology and culture interface? How much is cultural and how much is [individual–dyadic–triadic] pathological? Where do the boundaries between aggression, cruelty, and cultural tradition interface?" (p. 133). For instance, "Men who violate women's rights under the banner of 'cultural differences' claim such behavior is an inherent component of their culture or society" (p. 141). Fromm (1955), in his landmark book *Sane Society*, challenged the predominant clinical relativism of his thesis that societies could indeed be insane. He wrote:

> What is so deceptive about the state of mind of members of a society is the "consensual validation" of their concepts. It is naively assumed that the fact that the majority of people share certain ideas or feelings proves the validity of these ideas and feelings. Nothing is further from the truth. Consensual validation as such has no bearing whatsoever on reason or mental heath. Just as there is a *"folie a deux"* there is a *"folie a millions."* The fact that millions of people share the same vices does not make these vices virtues, the fact that they share so many errors does not make the errors truths, and the fact that millions of people share the same forms of mental pathology does not make people sane. (pp. 14–15)

We see evidence of this in some cultures where socially sanctioned repression of women and children, as well as devaluing of education and culture, has become part of the social mores. Lackhar (2004) described this phenomenon and the bionegativity that undergirds it in various domains of the mesosystem: "Societies or religious groups that cannot find healthy ways to deal with aggression or dependency needs hide under the rubric of religion to assuage their shame or guilt, a 'toilet receptacle' to mask their torrid rage" (p. 141). In some of these systems, there has been a downward spiral into genocide and mass murder that may be a result of multiple negative feedback processes in operation.

Political Systems

Political factors are central shapers of personality systems over short spans of human development. The impact of these forces can be seen in many examples during the 20th century. The Holocaust, genocide in Africa, Serbia, and Cambodia—these are examples of major political upheavals that have shaped, or will shape, the personality development of generations to come. Fromm (1970) was attuned to the political and social factors that shape the personality systems of humankind:

> In terms of its psycho-social foundations, the patriarchal social structure is closely bound up with the class character of present-day society. The society is based, to an important degree, on specific psychic attitudes that are partially rooted in unconscious drives; these psychic attitudes effectively complement the external coerciveness of the governmental apparatus. The patriarchal family is one of the most important loci for producing the psychic attitudes that operate to maintain the stability of class society. ... We are dealing here with an emotional complex that might well be called the "patricentric" complex. Characteristically, it includes the following elements: affective dependence on fatherly authority, involving a mixture of anxiety, love and hate; identification with paternal authority vis-à-vis weaker ones; a strong and strict super-ego whose principle is that duty is more important than happiness; guilt feelings, reproduced over and over again by the discrepancy between the demands of the superego and those of reality, whose effort is to keep people docile to authority. (p. 97)

Religious Systems and Institutions

Religion has substantial influence on the shaping of morals and character. Religious training leaves an indelible mark on the personality of many individuals and organizes and shapes family systems, communities, and countries. One can recognize both the positive and negative influences that organized religion has on the development of humankind. In our own time, for example, we have seen a major crisis within the Catholic Church that has shaken its foundation, and we have seen the Taliban subvert the rights of women and other Afghanis in the name of religion. These are but two examples in which a trusted religious institution is seen to be attuned not to the advancement of human functioning but to other agendas. By the same token, religion and prayer can offer comfort and solace to people in times of emotional pain and grief, as is evident on a small scale after the death of a loved one and on a large scale in the aftermath of an event such as September 11.

Scientific and Medical Developments

As with religion, another defining feature of contemporary societies is the impact that science has on the evolution of humankind. The advances in science during the 20th century were greater than in all previous history combined, yet scientific developments create increasing philosophical and ethical challenges to humans. The discoveries of the last century have substantially altered the social systems of the world. The ability to sustain life, transplantation of human organs, human cloning, space travel, rapid transportation, and communication have created enormous change.

Economic Factors

Economic factors exert a tremendous influence on the development of personality systems. When we consider Maslow's (1962) hierarchy of needs, one can see that not having one's basic needs met has a tremendous impact. When needs are met, the opportunity to develop beyond one's ancestors is enormous, as is the potential to become driven by material comfort and acquisition. In his book *Sane Society,* Fromm (1955) questioned Western cultural values and their relationship to mental health, and although his observations were made some 50 years ago, their pertinence clearly endures:

> We find that the countries in Europe which are among the most demo-cratic, peaceful and prosperous ones, and the United States, the most prosperous country in the world, show the most severe symptoms of mental disturbance. The aim of the whole socio-economic development of the Western world is that of the materially comfortable life, relatively equal distribution of wealth, stable democracy and peace, and the very countries which have come closest to this aim show the most severe signs of mental unbalance. (p. 10)

Cultural Factors

Culture has evolved in various forms since humans emerged from the primordial pool and began to develop incrementally. Culture and personality systems cannot be separated; they continue to shape one another in a constant feedback loop (De Graaf & Maier, 1994). The importance of cultural factors in the development and organization of personality was a major advance for the sister sciences of personality theory, psychopathology, and psychotherapy. Karen Horney, Harry Stack Sullivan, and Erik Erickson all emphasized the critical influence of cultural and social factors during the middle half of the last century of scientific psychology. In particular, Sullivan's interpersonal model had a strong cultural bias. He was convinced that psychiatry was not served well by its reliance on the medical model and tried throughout his career to provided an interdisciplinary alliance with the social sciences, which he believed was vital to achieve a comprehensive understanding of human personality.

Cultural Transposition

With our new technologies, advanced communication capabilities, and high level of immigration, cultural shift is a worldwide phenomenon in the new millennium, something that has come to be known as "globalization." As Edward Sapir wrote, "It is a dangerous thing for the individual to give up his identification with such cultural patterns as have come to symbolize for him his own personality integration" (Sapir, 1963, pp. 519–520). Pipher (2002) investigated this phenomenon in her book *The Middle of Everywhere: The World's Refugees Come to Our Town*, observing, "One of the main points of this book is that identity is no longer based on territory. The world community is small and interconnected" (p. xvii). Pipher also noted the complex interrelationship at work when individuals leave their homeland and embrace a new country and culture. She attributes the success of many of those she studied to 12 resilience factors:

1. Future orientation
2. Energy and good health
3. The ability to pay attention
4. Ambition and initiative
5. Verbal expressiveness
6. Positive mental health
7. The ability to calm down
8. Flexibility
9. Intentionality
10. Lovability
11. The ability to love new people
12. Good moral character (pp. 69–70)

Readers who are conversant with psychoanalytic developments will quickly identify these resiliency factors as what others have called "ego adaptive capacities." Regardless of the terminology, it is clear that adjustment is determined by an interaction of the four domains characterized by the progression of embedded triangular configurations and their functional aspects. The individual personality, dyadic, and family systems are the molecules of the sociocultural system, each influencing and shaping the other through complex feedback (i.e., positive and negative loops) processes.

The increase in globalization has a direct influence on psychological functioning, as Arnett (2002) noted: "The central psychological consequences of globalization is that it results in transformations in identity, that is, in how people think about themselves in relations to the social environment" (p. 777). Arnett described four trends that result from the ever-increasing trend toward globalization: (1) most adolescents "develop a *bicultural identity*, in which part of their identity is rooted in their local culture and another part stems from an awareness of their relations to the global culture"; (2) "the pervasiveness of *identity confusion* may be increasing among young people in non-Western cultures"; (3) "in every society there are people who choose to form *self-selected cultures* with like-minded persons who wish to have an identity that is unattained by global culture and its values"; and (4) "identity explorations in love and work are increasingly stretching beyond the adolescent years (roughly from ages 10–18 years) into the postadolescent period of *emerging adulthood* (roughly from ages 18 to 25 years)" (p. 777). Marginalization may increase as a result of this identity confusion, the consequence of rejecting one's own local culture and not feeling part of a global culture. "Identity confusion among young people may be reflected in problems such as depression, suicide, and substance use" (p. 779). The necessity of viewing human functioning as part of the personality system with its associated global influences will become more important with time. "For individuals, diversity of identity will only grow as globalization results in increasingly complex bicultural, multicultural, and hybrid identities" (Arnett, 2002, p. 782).

Popular Culture

One can witness the effects of popular culture, on our selves and those around us, in our response to phenomena from subcultures and how these shape the greater cultural milieu. A television show such as the currently popular *The Sopranos* has resulted in an increased interest in the process of psychotherapy (see Gabbard, 2002). Many social theorists (e.g., Fromm, 1955) have implicated popular culture as a toxic aspect of contemporary Western culture. Western societies' tendency to export their popular cultures, with its sex, violence, substance abuse, and materialism, to other societies has been a major point of criticism throughout the world. Within U.S. society, popular culture has influenced everything from eating habits to the ascendance of agribusiness and its by-products—obesity, fast-food diets, and increased incidence of diabetes (Schlosser, 2001).

Western values are embedded in aspects of popular culture (e.g., hairstyles, clothing such as jeans, rock music, etc.) and the value placed on experiencing and freely expressing the self implicit therein. A recent TV documentary, for example, on Paul McCartney's recent trip to Russia discussed the significant effect that the Beatles had on imparting liberating values to Russian youth. Some members of the Russian intelligentsia interviewed in the documentary suggested that this played a distinct role in eroding the Soviet Union and bringing down the Iron Curtain (thus illuminating the systemic interplay among individual, society, culture, and the political system).

Technology and Computer Science

The impact of technology on humans is immense and rapidly changing the fabric of society. Within the last 50 years, the technological advances have begun to change the way in which we conceive reality. The impact of the discovery and evolution of computers within a period of 50 years has led to exponential changes in Western and world cultures. One aspect of this advance, the development of the Internet, has created an information explosion, providing access to just about anything one can imagine. Along with many of the positive benefits, we have also seen the development of new forms of addiction and psychopathological adaptations.

Clinical Conditions and Morphological Expression

Psychopathological expressions, sometimes severe, emerge from the mesosystem matrix. Over the course of evolution, there have been waves of these types of pathologies fueled by socioeconomic and political factors. During the later part of the 19th century, "hysteria" was the expression of a matrix of factors, such as sexual repression and child sexual abuse, that comprised a unique condition documented by Charcot in his photographs. In the late 19th century, fugue states were said to be another emergent disorder, one that many think was fueled by a lack of social and economic opportunities for young men, who seemed most prone to losing years wandering around with no clear recall. More recent is the emergence of apotemnophilia, a new outbreak of dysfunction in which "healthy" individuals seek elective amputations. This gruesome syndrome seems to by fueled by social reinforcement available on an Internet listserve with 1,400 subscribers (Elliott, 2000). There are surgeons who have agreed to amputate healthy limbs for individuals who believe their identity is that of an amputee. Popular culture has a powerful effect in shaping and hatching disturbances at various levels of the personality system. An understanding of these phenomena requires some form of conceptualization of the processes that occur in the sociocultural–familial triangle.

A Convergence of Social Factors and the Development of Eating Disorders

The rise of eating disorders in Western societies is a clear example of the importance of cultural factors in the development and prevalence of eating disorders, a condition that 50 years ago did not exist at such high rates. Levine et al. (2001) reports that 10% of adolescent girls suffer from eating disorders. Eating disorders represent a clinical syndrome that demonstrates the powerful impact of multiple domain systems that converge and seek expression in behaviors that may become life-threatening. Much of the fuel for eating disorders lies in our notions about attractiveness that are biologically and culturally shaped (Barber, 2002). According to Barber:

> Anorexia is not a very common problem, striking about 1 percent of young Swedish and American women (although other eating disorders such as bulimia are much more common). Yet the fact that living up to the prevailing standard of attractiveness can be confused with a fatal illness shows just how extreme the slender standard is in economically developed countries. (p. 232)

Barber extracted this thesis from the work of the evolutionary psychologist Judith Anderson (Anderson, Crawford, Nadeau, & Lindberg, 1992), who proposed that body weight and physical attractiveness in women has been shaped by women's "perceived importance of their work, property ownership, and political influence" (Barber, 2002, p. 234).

FOUR IMPORTANT ELEMENTS OF MESOSYSTEMS

Increased understanding of the functioning of the mesosystem can be achieved by examining its structure, organization, and function. Examining and explicating the structure, organization, function, and form of complex systems allows the clinical scientist to understand where there are extant problems that create bionegativity in various domains and components of the system. These are briefly reviewed as follows.

1. Structure

An element of a complex system includes its structure, which can be identified in the hierarchy and boundary lines that exist within it. Structure includes features or form, as well as the function of the system, such as the number of members and physical aspects of the system and the philosophy or teachings. A church, school, or community institution generally has a physical presence or is symbolically represented in some fashion that indicates the structural features of the system. Structure also includes the language and system of symbols used by a system.

2. Organization

The second feature of a system is the way in which it is organized; this can include covert organization and overt organization. Organization includes the various roles, expectations, and principles by which a system is guided. Essentially, organization is expressed in patterns that we can recognize. Using our personality-guided relational constructs—namely, the four triangles—we can look at organization at various systemic levels, as they express various patterns. Sapir commented that

> the difference between individual and social behavior, [is] not in terms of kind or essence, but in terms of organization. To say that the human being behaves individually at one moment and socially at another is as absurd as to declare that matter follows the laws of chemistry at a certain time and succumbs to the supposedly different laws of atomic physics at another, for matter is always obeying certain mechanical laws which are at one and the same time both physical and chemical according to the manner in which we choose to define its organization. (Sapir, 1963, p. 545)

Sapir taught that "all cultural behavior is patterned" (p. 546) and that the organization of a system is revealed in these patterns.

3. Process

The third element of a system includes the processes by which it is regulated. The processes that guide the transactions in a given system bind every system. This includes the ways in which subsystems interrelate and patterns and rules of communication, as well as how components affect other components. The process is regulated by the positive and negative feedback loops.

4. Function

The fourth element of a complex system is that its function drives the interrelationships of its components, organization, and structure. Millon and Davis (1996) described this as follows: "For a system to do its work, it must contain various structural elements, each of which is physically differentiated toward some functional purpose essential to the operation of the whole" (p. 10). Each system has a purpose. Anchin (2003) wrote of the teleological nature of systems: "living systems are fundamentally purposive (i.e., goal-oriented) in nature" (p. 336). Generally, the basic function of any personality system is survival, but in cases where bionegative forces are in operation, the system can head toward self-destruction or annihilation; consider the mass suicide at Jonestown, Guyana, and the self-destructive patterns of individuals in our own and other cultures (Magnavita, 2002a).

BRINGING ATTENTION TO AND DEVELOPING AWARENESS OF THE MESOSYSTEM

To alter patterns and change behavior, it is important to be aware of the arena in which we function. West (2001) described the interrelationships of the mesosystem as follows: "Culture is as much a structure as the economy or politics; it is rooted in institutions such as families, schools, churches, synagogues, mosques, and communication industries (television, radio, video, music)" (p. 19). Just as psychoanalysis shined the light of inquiry on unconscious mental processes, so do ecological psychology and sociogenesis shine the light on the mesosystem. The mesosystem is a crucial source of influence relative to the virtually unconscious nature of the more or less clearly organized forms of behavior. Sapir believed that much social behavior was unconsciously driven:

> No matter where we turn in the field of social behavior, men and women do what they do, and cannot help but do, not merely because they are built thus and so, or possess such and such differences of personality, or must needs adapt to their immediate environment in such and such a way in order to survive at all, but largely because they have found it easiest and aesthetically most satisfactory to pattern their conduct in accordance with more or less clearly organized forms of behavior which no one is individually responsible for, which are not clearly grasped in their true nature, and which one might almost say are as self-evidently imputed to the nature of things as the three dimensions are imputed to space. (Sapir, 1963, p. 558)

RESTRUCTURING DYSFUNCTIONAL AND DESTRUCTIVE MESOSYSTEMS

Restructuring destructive elements of mesosystems is the most challenging task that faces the international community of social scientists. Lakhar (2004), among others, offered some of the following abbreviated suggestions:

- Learn the fundamental dynamics of the culture; mirror and reflect.
- Know something about the foods, holidays, and traditions.
- Be empathic to cultural differences, not to aggression.
- Be aware of differences between the individual and the group.
- Find pathology within the culture.
- Find pathology within the individual.
- Find pathology within the government. (p. 144)

Note the attractor states of a particular culture, such as racism, violence toward children–women, extreme polarities between the rich and poor, extreme religiosity, destruction of art and books, severe repressive forces in operation, and so forth. Note the viability of the nuclear and extended family structures of a given culture, for example, strong bonds, traditions, support, and so forth.

The ability on a smaller scale for the clinician to restructure components of the mesosystem can also be achieved. Although clinicians may have little effect on the larger components of the mesosystem, to conceptualize a case effectively, one must have knowledge of the contributory factors involved. Knowledge of the mesosystem and its multiple pathways of influence on the intrapsychic, dyadic, and triadic subsystems are critical to organizing an effective treatment strategy. As long as individuals, families, and societies have to contend with these destructive bionegative sociocultural forces, the individual personality system will converge and lead to dysfunction. Many of the problems in the mesosystem have significant impact on the development of psychopathological adaptations. As we have been informed by Maslow's theory of actualization, if lower level needs for security and safety are not met, higher level needs will often be neglected as survival becomes the predominate motivating life force.

Personality System Consultation and Mesosystem Restructuring

The mesosystem is the catalyst for personality development. When too many of the domains of the mesosystem are dysfunctional, toxic reactions to individual and family personality systems occur. Clinicians may offer their understanding of mesosystem processes by acting as consultants to community, national, and international problems. Mental health professionals and social scientists who are familiar with the principles of the personality-guided relational model can educate others about the effects of various dysfunctional subsystems on the development of the personality adaptations noted in previous chapters. The key is to be able to identify dysfunctional aspects of the mesosystem and the processes by which they are maintained and passed on from one generation to another. Clinicians who believe in a unified approach to psychotherapeutic change do not have to be confined to the traditional psychotherapeutic office but can leave their offices and become involved in community programs and innovations.

Empowerment Versus Demoralization

For individual clinicians on the front lines who work in hospitals, community mental health centers, and private practice, there is a tendency not to focus on problems in the mesosystem because these seem too chronic and daunting to tackle. As a result, clinicians can become immune or numb to them. Greater involvement with the mesosystem of clinicians and clinical and social scientists can counter the demoralization and lead to empowerment. This can be engendered in the system when the bionegative forces within these systems, such as poverty, crime, poor education, racism, and so forth, are addressed in a holistic way. In his compelling volume, *The Working Poor: Invisible in America,* Shipler (2004) proposed that poverty has multiple converging pathways and feedback loops that make it difficult to shift; small acts of kindness, however, can lift both the receiver and giver and ultimately affect the system from the bottom up.

An Example of Community-Based Mesosystem Restructuring

Tucker and Herman (2002) provided an example of mesosystem restructuring used to address the barriers to success experienced by many African American children:

> Abundant research indicates that African American children in general and socioeconomically disadvantaged African American children in particular are experiencing less academic and social success and more exposure to negative learning environments that cultivate behavior problems and violence than are their European American majority peers. (p. 763)

Tucker (1999) developed an innovative program that mobilizes various aspects of the mesosystem in a positive feedback loop where all participants gain self-empowerment. "There were yearly increases in students' adaptive skills and decreases in their frequency of engaging in maladaptive behaviors and school misconduct (Tucker & Herman, 2002, p. 769). The goal was to provide "culturally sensitive, multidimensional education through university –school–community" (Tucker & Herman, 2002). This multisystem intervention included parent and teacher training, tutoring by public school teachers, consulting, and mentorship by psychology graduate students. Elements of cognitive and affective restructuring as well as dyadic and triadic restructuring seem evident in their incorporation of various psychological strategies. Tucker and Herman (2002) noted that "it is important for psychologists to know how ecological factors such as racism, housing, economic status, and neighborhood affect the social behavior of African American children and families and how these social variables contribute to behavior problems (Comer & Hill, 1985)" (p. 770).

Intrapsychic, Dyadic, and Triadic Restructuring in the Mesosystem

Some of the mesosystem processes and systems identified in this chapter can be addressed using the restructuring methods presented in the previous chapters. One can imagine using intrapsychic, dyadic, or triadic restructuring to create an upward spiral and mesosystem restructuring creating a bidirectional flow, where healthy individuals, families, and groups demand more out of the institutions of the mesosystem while healthier institutions provide a better social milieu. Although this conceptual view is somewhat simplistic, small perturbations can have substantial impact, as in Victor Hugo's *Les Miserables*, where one act of kindness at the right time can have a transforming effect (Magnavita, 1997a). Restructuring of the mesosystem requires an understanding of the intrapsychic, dyadic, and triadic processes that are in operation. Clinicians need to have a through grounding in understanding mesosystem phenomena as they are expressed in their evolutionary processes. Social systems continue to evolve in never-ending adaptations. Restructuring of the mesosystem requires the ability to specify which component or process, structure, or function of a system is amenable to intervention and then find the fulcrum point, as discussed in the next chapter.

CHALLENGES FOR THE ECOLOGICALLY MINDED PSYCHOLOGIST

There are a number of arenas where the unified clinician can focus his or her energy and offer expertise to improve the functioning of institutions within the mesosystem. An exploration of these is far beyond the scope of this volume. The important point is that a unified approach, which considers whole–part relationships as part of the ecology and human development, will offer guidelines to reduce bionegativity at the mesosystem level of personality system adaptation and functioning. In the remainder of this chapter, one such problem of bionegativity that has substantial societal and personal impact is briefly explored.

Prison Systems

Using the unified model, we can see that prisons, as they exist and in the role that they serve, are an expression of extreme bionegativity of the mesosystem, with multiple converging domain–process components. It is unrealistic to believe that prisons as they are today will cease to exist anytime in the near future. There is, however, an increasing interest in addressing the dysfunctional aspects of the current model of incarceration without rehabilitation. For many inmates, prison tends to further antisocial personality systems; for the mentally ill, it represents a warehouse for those who would be better served in longer term treatment facilities. With as many as 2 million incarcerated members of society, this remains a major social, psychological, and political challenge.

Racism as an Expression of Extreme Generational Mesosystem Bionegativity

Racism is an expression of severe bionegativity in the mesosystem that has a multigenerational transmission pattern. Circular feedback loops are similar to those in operation with poverty. Racism requires an objectification of the "other" and subsequent dehumanization. Racism exists on many fronts and has assumed various forms over time. One problem that has drawn the attention of social scientists in recent years is the "persistent academic gap between white and black students" (Lee, 2002, p. B9). John Ogbu (2003) offered an interesting thesis in his book *Black American Students in an Affluent Suburb: A Study of Academic Disengagement*. Ogbu suggested that children of the middle-class Blacks, whom he compared with White youths and their families in an affluent Cleveland suburb with equal numbers of Whites and Blacks, differ in an important way. He proposed that they are using inappropriate role models, such as rap singers from the ghetto.

West (2001) described the problem of a consumer-driven culture and the special problems that this causes for Black youth:

> Since the end of the postwar economic boom, certain strategies have been intensified to stimulate consumption, especially strategies aimed at American youth that project sexual activity as instant fulfillment and violence as the locus of machismo identity. This market activity had contributed greatly to the disorientation and confusion of American youth, and those with less education and fewer opportunities bear the brunt of this cultural chaos. Ought we be surprised that black youths isolated from the labor market, marginalized by decrepit urban schools, devalued by alienating ideals of Euro-American beauty, and targeted by an unprecedented drug invasion exhibit high rates of crime and teenage pregnancy? (pp. 84–85)

SUMMARY AND CONCLUSION

This chapter presents mesosystem restructuring, the methods of which are less developed than are those for other systems, but the potential for change at this level is likely the most potent. The mesosystem has primarily been the domain of sociologists, political theorists, and others from related disciplines who are often interested in one component of the total ecological system. The future will be well served by interdisciplinary teams of scientists, ethicists, mental health professionals, anthropologists, environmentalists, and politicians who approach this final and largest nest of the personality system using a unified model that takes into consideration the interconnectedness of all the domains and seeks solutions that will work toward eliminating some of the root causes of personality system dysfunction.

IV

STRATEGIES AND
EMPIRICAL CHALLENGES

Chapter 11 is devoted to deepening understanding of various treatment strategies that are available to those who pursue a unified approach to treatment. With an understanding of the subsystems within the total ecological system and how they are related, it is easier to determine the fulcrum point for intervention that will provide the maximum momentum for restructuring and reorganization. Chapter 12 explores some of the empirical challenges that unification presents and the necessity for interdisciplinary collaboration to advance clinical science.

11

ENHANCING TREATMENT SYNERGY: FORMULATION AND DELIVERY OF TREATMENT PACKAGES

This chapter presents the daunting topic of navigating the total ecology of the personality system, from the microsystem to the mesosystem, to enhance treatment synergy by capitalizing on fulcrum points and using various modalities of treatment, either sequentially or combined. How does a clinician select from the four main methods of restructuring (intrapsychic, dyadic, triadic, mesosystem) and associated techniques from the array that is available? Furthermore, how does one select from the array of *treatment modalities* (individual, couples, family, group, etc.), *formats of treatment* (number of sessions, length of sessions), and *treatment frame* (short, intermittent, long) and organize intervention based on the component domains of personality? A major advance was made in the field of psychotherapy when Frances, Clarkin, and Perry (1984) offered the concept of "differential therapeutics." Their volume was based on the assumption that certain treatments are more likely to be effective with certain clinical syndromes and therefore should be selected in a logical manner. Prior to this development, most clinicians were adherents to one model of psychotherapy and generally unimodal in that they practiced individual, family, or group therapy according to a certain theoretical model and did not mix treatment modalities or visit alternative perspectives. When multiple modalities of treatment were offered, they were generally very structured, such as the child guidance model in which the child was seen for psychodynamic play therapy and the parent, generally the mother, was seen for supportive psychotherapy, by a different therapist from the one who worked with the child. The question of treatment specificity and treatment decision making has been a central concern in the field (Kiesler, 1966; Paul, 1967). The unified component system model in this volume takes significant next steps in advancing the concept of differential therapeutics by virtue of specifying, within the context of a conceptually coherent framework, the different levels (i.e., microsystem to mesosystem), methods of restructuring (intrapsychic, dyadic, triadic, mesosystem), and modalities that need to be considered when selecting these.

FLEXIBLE MOVEMENT FROM THE MICROSCOPIC
TO THE MACROSYSTEM

One of the most challenging aspects of conducting personality-guided relational therapy is the ability to conceptualize and move from subsystem to subsystem, both theoretically and in a given clinical situation, to understand which restructuring methods to apply and which treatment modalities to select. In the previous section of this volume, the various methods of restructuring systems are presented. Each offers the therapist strategies for intervention at various levels of abstraction from the microscopic to the macroscopic.

For example, a therapist must often be able to expand or contract the treatment frame and alternate or combine treatment modalities without unduly disrupting the therapeutic alliances that have been developed. An understanding of the ways in which systems function and subsystems interact is indispensable for the clinician looking for waypoints to assist in navigation, especially with more complex personality systems. Many therapists naturally shift among various perspectives, moving in close to understand how the individual's affective–cognitive matrix operates and regulates feelings with shifting defense. They may increase the angle of their lens for understanding the interpersonal workings in dyads and, further expanding the frame, take into account the triadic and ecosystem configurations and their interaction. This type of flexible movement from one component domain within these subsystems to another places increased demands on the clinician. It requires knowledge and expertise in multiple domains and skill using a range of methods and techniques. Although challenging, I believe this type of flexibility is superior to single domain or single modality therapies, especially when encountering more complex and dysfunctional systems.

THE BIOPSYCHOSOCIAL MODEL IN THE RELATIONAL MATRIX

The biopsychosocial model (Engle, 1980) offers a rich conceptual framework for conducting personality-guided relational therapy because it affords the clinician an opportunity to account for multiple factors at various levels of abstraction. Conceptualizing the interaction of these multiple factors is a central task that requires a broad knowledge base. Each level of abstraction in the system is only part of the whole personality system, but any level can become a target of intervention, which creates perturbations resonating throughout the entire system. Discovering the maximum change point can be used to increase the therapeutic leverage or "fulcrum" to effect change. The biopsychosocial model is a template, which all therapists should internalize, regardless of their theoretical orientation or loyalties to a particular school of thought.

MAXIMIZING TREATMENT DELIVERY

One of the goals of personality-guided relational therapy is to offer the most potent treatment from which the system can optimally benefit. There is always a fine line between too potent a treatment and one that may not be sufficient to mobilize the positive therapeutic forces and will of an individual or a family to embark on a journey of second-order change. Second-order, or systemic, change requires a tolerance for anxiety, because this is a by-product that can be disruptive. The system experiences a state of more intense disorder and destabilization before reconfiguring. Guidelines and accepted clinical procedures can help. Before I begin to discuss the topic of treatment modalities, it is worth exploring some of the fundamental principles for maximizing treatment applications.

Treatment Potency

We refer to *treatment potency* as the intensity of an individual modality or a combination of modalities to activate the change process in the shortest period of time. Treatment potency may be increased in a variety of ways, such as finding the fulcrum points, combining treatment modalities, increasing or decreasing the length of sessions, and strengthening the therapeutic alliance to prepare for the forces unleashed during the change process.

Principles for Determining the Maximum Treatment to Apply

- *Attend to the therapeutic alliance.* Most clinicians don't need this restated, yet it is a crucial function of conducting psychotherapy.

If the therapeutic alliance is not continually monitored for breaches, ruptures will occur that may lead to premature termination of psychotherapy.

- *Determine the level of motivation before proceeding.* The level of motivation that an individual or family possesses is a key to whether treatment can be safely intensified and potency maximized. If the level of motivation is low, generally speaking, the patient or family will not tolerate much treatment potency, at least initially, until motivational systems can be enhanced.
- *Determine the capacity of the system to tolerate higher levels of treatment potency.* Before offering a treatment or combination of treatments that may be potent, establish through careful assessment the capacity of the patient, couple, or family to handle the intervention offered. How have subsystems experienced and handled stress in the past? What is the highest level of functioning that an individual or subsystem reports? (See Magnavita, 1997a, for a complete description of how to assess these capacities in the intrapsychic–biological triangle and Magnavita, 2000a, for a comprehensive explanation on assessment of dyadic, triadic, and family systems.)
- *Try to maximize the forces of an already occurring transition stage.* It is often much easier to offer a maximum treatment intervention during a period of change, where the system is already destabilized. When a patient is going through a divorce, a family or couple is experiencing a developmental transition, or a substance abuser is in his or her first year of sobriety, more intensive treatment may be tolerated.

TREATMENT PACKAGING

Clinicians, after the main assessment phase of treatment, develop a strategy for intervention. This intervention, consisting of one or various treatment modalities, and the manner in which they are delivered are the way in which treatment is packaged. A collaborative agreement ensues accepting the treatment package or it is repackaged until acceptable. Most clinicians develop treatment packages in a rote fashion without fully considering how to maximize their intervention. It makes sense to fully explore the various aspects that, when combined, can maximize treatment potency and accelerate the process of redirecting the bionegative forces and restructuring the crucial subsystems engendering personality dysfunction.

Modalities, Combinations, Settings, Frames, and Formats

A *treatment package (TP)* includes the modalities of treatment, combinations or sequencing of modalities, treatment setting, framework of treatment, and the format in which it is delivered. These are important considerations that are generally discussed early in the treatment process and have major impact on outcome. TPs that do not have sufficient potency to affect the systems presenting for treatment will have little or no effect. Those that are overly ambitious can be too stressful and require too much in the way of resources, resulting in premature termination of treatment. The art of formulating an appropriate TP in a collaborative manner with the patient(s) is a challenge that occurs in the initial stage of treatment. In the following section, I discuss the major elements that comprise a TP and then formulate general principles to guide clinical practice. I begin with a review of treatment modalities.

Treatment Modalities

It is important to understand the indications and contraindications of various modalities of psychotherapy. Paolino and McCrady (1978) wrote about marital therapy, but their discussion is applicable to all forms of psychotherapy: "each therapist brings another viewpoint and style and . . . there is no infallible technique or answer to the multiple and complex problems of this work" (p. 113). Paolino and McCrady were addressing the issue of different theoretical orientations, but their comments have direct pertinence to the issue of treatment modalities as well. The art and science of treatment selection remains more a clinical art than an empirically based enterprise. Nevertheless, much clinical evidence and experience has accrued since clinicians, in their search for optimal treatment applications, began combining treatment modalities. Paolino and McCrady (1978) presented their view, one consistent with the perspective taken in this volume, as follows:

> Methods of diagnosis and classification, as well as treatment rationales, are based on the utilization of psychoanalytic, role, systems and learning theories. Since these theoretical positions are increasingly more often combined and tailored to the needs of each couple, the therapist should have an understanding of the principles of each orientation and its therapeutic application. Frequently, semantic systems and interactional models are deceptive. Therapeutic principles and procedures may not differ as much as their theoretical underpinnings would lead us to believe. (pp. 113–114)

Most therapists prefer and are more comfortable with a few treatment modalities; they rely on these, becoming expert as their experience and knowledge base increases. When confronted with a modality for which they have not been trained and have little experience, they tend to refer to other mental health professionals with suitable training. Early in the development of psychotherapy, most theoretical orientations or schools of therapy were aligned with a particular modality of treatment. For the first half of the 20th century, modern psychotherapy emphasized the modality of individual psychotherapy, emanating from the development of psychoanalysis. As new modalities of treatment, such as group, family, and marital, were developed, many therapists resisted combining modalities because of notions, again from the predominant psychoanalytic model, that the transference would be diluted or disturbed, especially if the same therapist provided more than one treatment. Contemporary writers such as Diana Fosha (1995) have challenged this taboo, among others, suggesting that many such psychotherapy taboos are related to its roots in psychoanalysis, which has always held that the unconscious is easily contaminated by therapeutic intervention. Against the backdrop of these considerations, the following is a brief review of the primary treatment modalities and some of their essential features.

Individual Psychotherapy

Individual psychotherapy has been the mainstay treatment modality, affording the patient an opportunity to engage in a relational experience with a trained psychotherapist who is able to bring patterns to awareness and develop strategies for change. Intrapsychic restructuring methods are primarily used (Magnavita, 1997c, 1998a). Most of the theoretical systems of psychotherapy have been developed using this modality. Individual therapy often has a narrow scope, focusing on processes in the intrapsychic–biological triangle; using a unified model allows the therapeutic process broader range, as suggested by Bowen and discussed in this volume.

Dyadic and triadic configurations as well as multigenerational transmission processes can be addressed in individual work. One suggestion that Bowen made is to encourage an individual to visit his or her family, even when it might be easier to untangle emotionally by avoiding them; he further suggested that the patient not allow himself or herself to be engaged and become reactive. This simple but challenging therapeutic restructuring can have broader impact on a dysfunctional system. One person changing can alter the dynamics in the entire system. Individual therapy is often the preferred modality when other members of an individual's personality system are not available or amenable to treatment. Individual psychotherapy also affords the opportunity to have a significant dose of intimacy and closeness that is difficult to attain in other modalities of treatment in which time with the therapist must be shared with family and group members.

Group Psychotherapy

This modality of treatment was developed after individual modalities became predominant. The understanding of group processes and the therapeutic harnessing of these forces were a significant advance in the development of psychotherapy. Group therapy affords a learning environment similar to individual therapy in which the patient can begin to identify component processes of the personality system and then use the group to develop more effective skills and relational patterns. Group therapy may not be a modality from which everyone can benefit. Some patients who have been severely traumatized require a phase of individual therapy before they are prepared to expose themselves to a larger and sometimes more threatening group process. Group therapy provides a relational matrix in which various methods of restructuring can be incorporated. Intrapsychic, dyadic, and triadic restructuring as well as mesosystem restructuring are all possible within this rich relational milieu.

Family Therapy

Family therapy emerged as a modality during the second half of the previous century. This modality was used cautiously at first because it challenged the dominant psychoanalytic model, which eschewed corrupting the therapeutic field. As noted earlier in this volume, family therapy was based on the development of a general system theory, which was a significant departure from the individual-oriented model in vogue at the time. Family therapy has developed into many branches that share a common view that dysfunction in an individual personality system cannot be understood without viewing the broader system. The other aspect of great relevance was in the explication of how functional and dysfunctional families communicate and are structured as well as how the processes are transmitted multigenerationally. As is the case with individual and group therapies, family therapy requires advanced training because the processes and methods differ from other modalities.

Couples and Marital Therapy

Another modality that was developed later in the evolution of psychotherapy was couples therapy (Synder, 1999). Couples therapy followed family therapy in the evolution of these modalities. It gained momentum during the human growth and potential movement that characterized the 1960s and grew out of the massive cultural shifts that occurred during the feminist movement in which woman were seeking equality in marriage and an increased focus on mutual sexual satisfaction emerged. Couples therapy is often the modality of choice for sexual dysfunction, but it is also a powerful modality for most forms of relational disturbance that are manifested by severely dysfunctional personality systems (Whisman & Synder, 1999).

Psychopharmacological Therapy

The use of psychotropic agents to treat emotional and psychiatric disorders has been an increasingly used treatment modality, even for those without severe psychiatric disorders. More often, medication is used as an adjunct to psychotherapy and in some cases as the primary treatment, although this may be a questionable trend. Clearly there is place for medications in a unified relational model. Understanding the dynamics of personality systems will enable more effective administration of pharamacotherapy. Medications are administered in a powerful relational matrix in which a variety of forces and counterforces may enable an individual to make use of medication or have trouble with it.

Couples Group Therapy

Another innovative modality is couples group therapy in which a number of couples come together to work on relational issues. It can be used when a psychoeducational focus is desired, as might occur when a number of couples have lost children to war, an accident, or a natural disaster. It is also beneficial for couples coping with certain medical or psychiatric disorders in the family, such as schizophrenia and other conditions that are chronic and place great stress on the couple. This modality of therapy has not been widely studied.

Multiple Family Therapy

Multiple family therapy entails bringing together nonrelated family systems to work conjointly on similar problems. This modality of therapy has a great capacity for healing. In general, multiple family therapy is a modality that has been used when members of families are hospitalized. The ability to learn and grow is substantial among families that are undergoing a particular challenge or experiencing dysfunction. Families that are in similar positions can model and share new ways of relating in a safe forum. This modality can mobilize powerful forces from multiple feedback sources, which can't be achieved as readily with other modalities. Family members can often assimilate feedback from other families more easily than that from their own family.

Treatment Settings

The setting in which treatment is delivered is also an important component of the treatment package, one usually related to the level of care and structure required during different phases of therapy. The setting becomes another aspect of the patient's ecosystem, which can periodically alter the current ecosystem, as when a patient leaves his or her family and is hospitalized or enters residential treatment. Treatment settings have powerful dynamics that can be constructive or destructive. In certain settings, there may be a parallel process between staff conflict and dynamics and patient dynamics. Anyone who has worked in an inpatient setting is aware of how staff conflict can be expressed through the patients in a parallel process. Knowledge of systems is of great benefit wherever multiple staff members are working together to treat and care for patients. Setting dynamics are also in operation in outpatient practices among professionals within a community who treat the same patients, as occurs among physicians and mental health clinicians. In these cases, diverse terminology and models that operate differently from one another may create obstacles to communication. Following are the three most common treatment settings.

Outpatient

The outpatient setting is the most frequently used to offer various treatment modalities. Outpatient therapy requires a certain level of autonomy and resources. If patients are unable to take responsibility for attending sessions as scheduled, they will likely not have the level of functioning necessary to make use of the modalities offered in this setting. Outpatient therapy can be delivered in a variety of venues from clinics (e.g., methadone maintenance programs) to private practice settings. The advantage is that the cost is considerably less than more intensive treatment settings, and the patient can maintain job and family responsibilities. The disadvantage is that only a certain degree of functional impairment can be tolerated before this setting becomes ineffective.

Inpatient

Treatment delivered on an inpatient basis is necessary in some circumstances. When the patient's functional capacities become too low or if the degree of self-destructiveness is unable to be managed effectively, inpatient care becomes necessary. It is unfortunate that, in this era of cost containment, few options are available for those who need extended care, unless patients or caregivers are able to pay expenses out of pocket. Inpatient hospitalization tends to focus primarily on patient stabilization and rapid discharge to less costly partial programs. The result is that many patients require multiple readmissions because they are discharged before they are ready to meet the demands of less restrictive types of care.

An advantage of an inpatient setting is that a treatment team is usually responsible for the patient, and therefore, in the case of extreme disturbances, a team shares the emotional demands of caring for a patient. Another clinical circumstance in which an inpatient setting is desirable is when a patient is undergoing a marked change in psychotropic medications or starting an entirely new regimen. The highly controlled environment of the inpatient setting allows clinicians and physicians to monitor the effects of medication or facilitate the adjustment to a new medication.

Partial Treatment

As the drive toward cost containment in mental health became the center of policymakers' attention, partial treatment became a much-used setting for the delivery of mental health services. The partial treatment setting is preferable to inpatient care in many instances because patients can stay in their home and community and there is less disruption in their lives. Partial programs are extremely flexible and can be used to deliver treatment during the day or evening and flexible enough to be delivered in the appropriate dosage from 1 day to 5 days a week.

Sequencing and Combinations of Treatment

The impact of treatment can be more or less potent based on how treatment modalities are selected, combined, and delivered. It makes sense that augmenting a treatment modality with another one will create greater potency in some cases. It is unfortunate that these relationships are complex, and little empirical evidence exists to guide these decisions. There are two major ways to conceptualize TPs: combining treatment modalities and offering them concurrently or delivering treatments sequentially. In complex cases, both multimodal and sequential treatment may be offered (Magnavita, 1998b, 1998c). Combining modalities and sequencing treatment is often done haphazardly. Clinicians who do not have training and experience with various modalities need to be familiar enough with them to understand their place in the treatment matrix so that they can make a referral to enhance treatment synergy.

Multimodal Combinations

Treatment modalities may be combined to offer a more potent treatment package (Lazarus, 1973, 1981). One might, for example, combine individual with couples therapy to maximize the treatment effect. Merely combining treatments or offering more modalities could have effects counter to what the clinician seeks, however. Only by understanding the systemic forces that are in operation will the clinician have what is needed to make an optimal decision. For example, based on the way in which a couple is managing its triadic anxiety, concurrent individual and couples work may reduce the anxiety available to the dyadic restructuring, which will defuse some of the couple's motivation to change. When a husband and wife are in therapy with separate therapists, the necessary emotional process needed to enhance the couple's growth may be diverted. Each case must be considered separately, and clinicians must avoid the urge to simplify treatment decisions by reducing them to a cookbook approach.

Sequential Combinations

Offering treatment modalities in a series is another manner in which to package treatment. In this case, one treatment is delivered and another follows. An individual might begin with individual therapy and at a certain point decide that group therapy would be a useful modality. Individual treatment can prepare the person for group treatment, which may be more threatening for some. Another common sequence occurs when a couple enters couples therapy and is unable to manage the anxiety that arises from it; they then choose to enter a phase of individual work to become more comfortable with couples work.

When examining the course of treatment for severely dysfunctional systems, a complex tapestry of treatment modalities and interventions often emerges over the course of time. As the clinician begins to understand and recognize the multiple overlapping triangular configurations that are in operation, often over generations, he or she can locate various fulcrum points where a course of focused treatment with an individual, dyad, or family can have enormous impact.

Treatment Frames

The treatment frame refers to the overall framework to which patient and therapist agree and that sets the parameters for treatment. The frame is an essential element of the treatment process. A long frame may indicate a more severe or refractory problem and lead to demoralization in some patients. For others, it may be an acceptable and comfortable offering. The treatment frame that the therapist offers or the patient(s) seeks will vary depending on many factors, including patient motivation, adaptive capacity, social support, and financial and logistical concerns. In addition, ideas and expectations about change will be influential in the decision about the frame. The frame may be predetermined by the nature of the institution where treatment is sought. For example, most university mental health centers limit their treatment to briefer frames and refer out when longer term treatment is required. A therapist's training and preference might also be a crucial element in setting the treatment frame. Some therapists prefer long-term therapy, and others avoid it; others do likewise with short-term therapy. The treatment frame is usually discussed during the first session after a review of systems has taken place and the patient's (or patients') expectations about the treatment process have been explored.

Short-Term Treatment Frame

Short-term treatment is the most common treatment frame used; all clinicians should be familiar with it and preferably be at least minimally trained in its application. A short-term treatment frame is established at the onset of treatment or shortly after assessment if it is deemed a suitable means by which to orient and deliver treatment. The essence of short-term treatment is the use of time as a way of mobilizing the forces of change and accelerating the therapeutic process. In some cases, it is advantageous to set a predetermined number of sessions; in others, it is preferable to allocate an approximate time frame, such as 3 months or 6 months, and then establish the format, which includes the frequency of sessions, spacing, length of session, and so forth. All modalities of treatment presented earlier can be delivered in a brief treatment format. Brief treatment generally places greater demands on the system and can be effective in mobilizing systemic changes. When formulating a TP, various treatment modalities may be offered within a brief treatment framework. It is often useful to offer various members and subsystems within a family the opportunity to have a brief focused intervention that is offered when the system seems most open to benefit from it.

When offering a short-term framework, the therapist needs to be prepared to shift to a different frame if necessary. Some systems that seem healthy at the onset of treatment can carry a greater load of dysfunction than was initially apparent. Conversely, systems that appear more dysfunctional can often have greater adaptive capacity and resources from which they draw, making briefer or intermittent treatment an ideal frame. A plethora of short-term models are available, some attempting rapid solutions in one or two sessions, others attempting personality reconstruction in a brief treatment frame. The models may be aimed at the individual, dyad, or family, but what they share is an attempt to maintain a focus on the issues that have been agreed on, a generally high activity level on the part of the therapist, the use of time limitations to counteract development of dependency, and the use of potent interventions that are strategic and often destabilizing to the system. Readers can refer to the array of volumes on this topic referenced in this volume and select a model or models that are most consistent with their work.

Long-Term Treatment Frame

Long-term psychotherapy is an important treatment frame in which many modalities of treatment and a variety of settings may be incorporated.

A long-term treatment frame generally has no predetermined number of sessions or expectations for a period of time with which to complete the therapeutic tasks. A long-term frame usually sets the conditions for the development of dependency on the therapist and therefore may be ideal when there is a need to address attachment disturbances in which the system has been hesitant or unable to establish trust in others. This is frequently required for dysfunctional systems in which there has been ongoing abuse, chronic neglect, and severe developmental insults. It is unfortunate that many parties, particularly insurance companies and health maintenance organizations, have discredited this frame. For many, long-term treatment allows for a substantial improvement in the quality of life; for some, it can preempt premature death.

Intermittent Treatment Frame

Intermittent therapy is another frame with which to deliver treatment in various modalities. The individual, couple, or family will usually seek out treatment when experiencing stressful periods, especially unexpected losses or trauma, or when navigating difficult developmental transitions. Although there are no available statistics on some fundamental aspects of practitioner patterns, this seems to be one of the mainstays of current clinical treatment. Individuals, couples, and families form long-term attachments with their therapists and often see them as a vital resource to be used when navigating the transitions and disruptions of life. This framework offers certain advantages. It allows a clinician to participate in the developmental progression and have a long-term historical perspective that can be essential to the change process. It also allows the clinician to understand the multiple influences of the four triangular configurations and the shifting influences of the multiple domains of the personality system over the course of time and development. This is essentially a family practice model that can ideally be offered by a group or in a clinic where there is long-term stability of clinical staff. It can also be valuable for prevention. The therapist can offer psychoeducation at critical developmental time points that can assist the patient(s) in preventing relapses or responding to increased stress in a dysfunctional manner. For example, a young couple that is planning to have children can be introduced to some of the issues they will face before they are in the trenches and can use this time to anticipate difficulties before they emerge.

Maintenance Treatment Frame

In some cases, the severity of dysfunction in a patient, dyad, or family requires that the frame be oriented toward maintaining the highest level of adaptive functioning. Maintenance therapy can be delivered in the most efficacious format once this has been established, usually by trial and error. The important point is to maintain a frame that is flexible enough to allow for increasing the intensity of contact when required. Many patients with chronic mental illness who require psychopharmacological treatment on an ongoing basis to prevent relapse are seen in a maintenance format. Again, it is important to remember that it may be beneficial to alter the format to respond to the needs of the system. In some cases, an intensification of therapy may suggest a shift to a brief treatment format to deal with an emerging issue, such as the development of a serious illness in a previous caretaking parental figure.

Treatment Format (Length and Spacing of Sessions)

The treatment format refers to the length and spacing of sessions. What has become standard for most forms of psychotherapy is weekly psychotherapy sessions of 45–50-minute duration or, in some cases, multiple sessions, usually two but sometimes three a week. Why has this format come to predominate the field of psychotherapy? Budman (1994) explained that the traditional model of once or twice a week 45–50-minute sessions is the result of "lock-in" and that these "closely held beliefs about the ways that psychotherapy should be delivered have more to do with accidents of history than with clearly defensible 'scientific' bases for treatment" (p. 2).

Brief Sessions (15–25 Minutes)

Brief sessions are often used for patients in a maintenance treatment framework. Frequent, briefer sessions may allow for more careful monitoring of high-risk patients and is often the most common protocol for those receiving pharmacological treatment after they have been stabilized.

Standard Session (45–50 Minutes)

The standard 45- to 50-minute session has been used extensively over the past century. It creates a unit of time that allows for ongoing work to be completed. There is little empirical evidence that either supports or challenges this format. Standard sessions can be offered to patients who are able to make a commitment to treatment and is often used in a long-term format. Brief sessions are not suitable for couple or family modalities because they do not afford enough time to establish a focus and complete a phase of restructuring.

Extended Sessions (90 or More Minutes)

Extended sessions have been in use since the beginning of modern psychotherapy. Freud made use of extended sessions, but the most important proponent of extending sessions was Ferenczi (Ferenczi & Rank, 1925). Many therapists have experimented with this format, and patients often report that it is superior to shorter sessions. Unfortunately, most insurance companies will not reimburse for extended sessions, thus making clinicians hesitant to use them. Extended sessions afford patients the opportunity to have an intensive treatment experience unlike any other format (Magnavita, 1997b). Extended sessions are not suitable for everyone, however. When a patient has problems maintaining energy or focus, they are contraindicated.

When sessions are extended, it may be beneficial to allow sufficient time between them to process the material and put new insights and patterns into practice. The ideal time between these sessions should be established with the unit of the system that is being treated. Based on a number of years of clinical practice in a variety of modalities, it seems that an extended session of 90 minutes is ideal for many. Others, however, respond to even longer sessions as long as sufficient breaks are scheduled to allow for refueling.

Consultation

Consultation can be another helpful format. A consultation is an opportunity to meet with a clinician or treatment team in an attempt to formulate a holonic map that will suggest various treatment options.

GENERAL GUIDELINES IN FORMULATING AND PRESENTING TPs

Conducting personality-guided relational therapy requires a through knowledge of the technologies of change so that TPs can be formulated with some degree of confidence. Once a holonic assessment is "complete" and the clinician has a multidimensional map of the of the personality system, a TP is offered to those seeking help. The general guidelines when formulating and delivering the TP to the patients include the following:

1. Start with a TP that is as parsimonious as possible. Greater complexity can be sought once engagement in treatment is solid.
2. Continually evaluate the potency of a TP by monitoring patients' responses carefully and making it clear that the format is flexible and based on what works best for them under the constraints that they are working with, such as finances, time, rapidity of change, effect on others in the system, and so forth.
3. Discuss the need to process the affects and changes that occur between sessions to find the most efficacious TP.

4. Attempt to offer the most potent treatment modality and frame that is acceptable to patients.

5. In severely dysfunctional personality systems, look for smaller changes and seek consultation when you feel demoralized by the resistance to change or are concerned that relapse will occur.

FINDING THE FULCRUM POINTS, USING THE FOUR TRIANGLES

The four triangles provide a useful point of reference in the context of treatment applications, incorporating the restructuring methodologies and various treatment modalities and processes that comprise a treatment package. A previous volume (Magnavita, 2000a) discussed the topic of finding fulcrum points within a system. A fulcrum point is where one can use a restructuring method or offer a treatment modality to derive the maximum treatment benefit. Each of the triangular configurations offers multiple fulcrum points to engender the change process. Finding fulcrum points requires the clinician to be attuned to the multiple levels of system dynamics. Clearly divergent therapeutic actions can have similar results, but the goal is to achieve the most efficacious and parsimonious action is selected to effect change by mobilizing the systemic forces.

Fulcrum Points Within the Intrapsychic–Biological Triangle

Within the *intrapsychic–biological triangle* are multiple fulcrum points that may appear during the course of treatment; when noticed, the clinician can respond to and address them using various modalities and treatment frames. Determining the fulcrum point in a system comes from understanding a unified model and being alert to important transition processes that may make a certain intervention timely. Each course of treatment offers multiple fulcrum points that may be selected at a particular time. It would be impossible to list all of these, but I offer some principles. In the context of the intrapsychic–biological triangle, consider a patient who is assessed to be fairly fluid in her affective system. There may have been a recent trauma or experience that has activated the core genetic code, and this intensifies the affective experience. In this case, one might readily consider that the most effective fulcrum point is to directly address the activated affective system. Among the restructuring methods that might be used are affective restructuring to metabolize the affect and cognitive–behavioral restructuring, such as eye movement desensitization reprocessing, used to process affect rapidly.

Fulcrum Points Within the Interpersonal–Dyadic Triangle

A variety of fulcrum points become available within the *interpersonal–dyadic triangle* during treatment. Fulcrum points can make themselves known when one member of dyad is suffering or when the dyad is experiencing destabilization due to external or internal shifts and stresses. A fulcrum point might occur when one member of a marital dyad expresses dissatisfaction with the relationship. This may arouse anxiety in the other and afford an opportunity to explore the dyadic configuration. For example, a married woman came into treatment feeling depressed and detailing long-standing marital dissatisfaction. When it was suggested that she might consider having her husband join her for marital therapy, she declared there was no way he would come for treatment and that he had been seen previously without any progress. The couple was clearly in a state of uncomfortable but familiar homeostasis. For one of the dyad to change, the dynamics of their relationship had to shift. They were both invested in maintaining the homeostasis but longed for something more fulfilling. The wife had been in individual treatment but was not satisfied with the progress in the marriage. The fulcrum point seemed to be in unbalancing the dyad so that they could break the stalemate. After discussion, the therapist suggested she refrain from talking about her therapy with her husband. This served the function of creating a therapeutic triangle in which the therapist became the third corner. This redistribution of anxiety, which was originally being absorbed by the couple's daughter, created leverage in the dyad as the husband became increasingly interested in his wife's therapy and her lack of reactivity to him. When he began to inquire about her experience, she timed her response well and invited him to join her, which he did. She had prepared herself by confronting their dissatisfaction and saying that she did not want to continue in their present state. They explored three options—continue as before, separate and divorce, or work on improving their relationship. Because she was able to say these things to him from a relatively nonreactive stance and discuss the options to which he agreed, the dyad was strengthened and a phase of intensive couple's therapy was initiated.

In another case, a patient was referred for treatment because he had a drinking problem. It became clear that there was a generational pattern of alcohol dependence. It became evident that the patient's alcohol use followed conflict with his wife. During exploration of the presenting issues, the patient began to react to the therapist in a manner suggesting that he expected the therapist to shame and humiliate him for his difficulties. Upon exploring his past relationship with his father, the patient made the link between the response he expected from the therapist and the relational schema from his father. Because of his emotional response, which included a wave of grief and anger, the fulcrum point was determined to be expected–

transactive restructuring. As a result of restructuring this schematic representation, the patient's drinking decreased and his relationship with his wife
showed some improvement, opening up another phase of therapy as he
began to explore how troubled his marriage had been because of these and
other factors. The therapist suggested he invite his wife in for a phase of
treatment to capitalize on this new dyadic fulcrum point that became available. Because the wife had seen improvement in his functioning and reduction in his alcohol consumption, she felt positive about entering treatment
with him.

Fulcrum Points of the Triadic Relational Configuration

Because of the ubiquity of overlapping triangular configurations in
dysfunctional systems, it is not difficult to find fulcrum points in the triadic–
relational configuration. Consider the case of a symptomatic child as the
impetus for entering treatment. At the outset of treatment, it is clear that
the child has an enmeshed relationship with his mother and a detached
and distant one with his father. There are many ways to capitalize on the
fulcrum points that this case offers. Depending on the unique configuration,
one could offer a variety of modalities that could strengthen the parental
dyad, enhance the quality of the father–son dyad, or increase the son's level
of differentiation. Determining how to proceed should be based on the
family's response to initial treatment moves. If the parents are completely
externalizing the difficulties to the son and joined around their view of him
being the problem, the initial move might be to see the son individually
or, if they tolerate it, using the modality of family therapy. If there is
some indication that the system might shift into a new configuration more
comfortably, seeing the father–son in dyadic work while finding a way to
engage the mother or get her to agree with the plan could be useful. The
point of the fulcrum is to move the child into a more autonomous position,
which will free up tension to emerge in the marital dyad and may be an
impetus for the couple seeking treatment.

Fulcrum Points of the Sociocultural–Familial Triangle

Finding the fulcrum points in the sociocultural triangle is complex but
offers multiple fulcrum points either within or outside of the traditional
therapeutic setting. On a broader scale, one might find a fulcrum point by
enhancing the quality of a school by developing a program that actively
encourages parents and school personnel to affirm ethnic differences. This
might be a valuable intervention in a community with newly arrived and
as yet unassimilated immigrants. A unified model helps clinicians think
outside the box of traditional domains. When we understand the fulcrum

points that may become available in the sociocultural–familial triangle, we must offer our knowledge to shape systems that are more functional.

Within the traditional therapeutic setting, finding the fulcrum points may take many forms. It may entail visiting a high-risk infant who has been referred by the community clinic and attempting to improve the parental function of the caregivers. It may mean inviting a culturally sensitive member from the patient's community to consult with the therapist about ways to proceed in a culturally sensitive manner or to incorporate healing practices relied on by the community. There are many culture-bound syndromes that are unique to certain ethnic groups. The therapeutic intervention should be tailored to each person's needs and culture.

SHATTERING SACRED ICONS ABOUT THE THERAPEUTIC FIELD

Psychotherapy continues to both benefit and suffer from some of Freud's conceptualizations. One of the most dearly held notions concerns the sanctity of the therapeutic relationship and the belief that allowing "outside" influences to intrude would corrupt it. Family system theorists, most notably Ackerman (1958), challenged this notion. The psychoanalytic stances of neutrality, anonymity, and confidentiality have been considered cornerstones of treatment and to some degree still influence practitioners today. Yet there is evidence to support the contention that Freud practiced very differently than he described in his clinical writing. Lynn and Vaillant (1998) examined 43 of his cases and determined the following:

> in all 43 cases Freud deviated from strict anonymity and expressed his own feelings, attitudes and experiences. Freud's expressions included his feelings toward the analysands, his worries about issues in his own life and family, and attitudes, tastes, and prejudices. Likewise, in 31 (72%) of the cases, Freud's participation in extra-analytic relations with analysands and/or his selection of analysands who already had important connections to himself or his family helped eliminate anonymity. These various expressions and relations obviated the anonymity and opacity prescribed in Freud's published work and gave each analysand a rich view of the real Freud. (p. 165)

Ferenczi's relational approach challenged these sacred icons in his relationally oriented approach to psychotherapy that gave the "real" therapist a more prominent position. The conceptual underpinnings of a contemporary relational analytic approach are presented by K. A. Frank (2002). Fosha (1995) wrote of the taboos of psychoanalytic treatment, including the ease with which the unconscious can be contaminated. She opined that if it is so easily contaminated, why can't we effect change more easily, if change is modifying the unconscious? Ackerman expressed a degree of "clinical artistry" (Guerin & Chabot, 1997, p. 206) that was similar to what has been described by those who knew Ferenczi's work more intimately. Ackerman, like many of the master therapists responsible for relational-oriented therapy, used himself in a way to engage the system emotionally. Guerin and Chabot (1997) described Ackerman's relational style as follows:

> He would provoke them into expressing their anger and would openly discuss their unconscious oedipal strivings. As a clinician in a family session he quickly took charge and made contact with each family member after playfully teasing the children, flirting with the women, and challenging the men in a fairly aggressive style. He was an activist, stirring up emotion by a process he called "tickling the defenses." He believed it was healthy to let emotions out, especially to express anger openly. (p. 206)

Just what stance should we assume?

Therapeutic Stance in Personality-Guided Relational Therapy

Much has been written about the stance a therapist should assume. *Stance* refers to the manner in which therapists conduct themselves and has many facets. The stance traditionally endorsed by psychoanalysis was neutral; the therapist was encouraged to present a "blank slate." Ferenczi's stance was much more relational and engaged with the patient. Whereas Freud sat behind the couch and was relatively passive, Ferenczi faced his patients directly and was active (although as noted earlier, there are more similarities than Freud's technical prescriptions suggest). Most orientations either explicitly prescribe a stance or covertly subscribe to one or another. Alexander (Alexander & French, 1946) was often accused of "manipulating" the stance by acting counter to the way the patient expected in the transference. Rogers (1951), on the other hand, felt that the best stance was a genuine one, accepting and nonjudgmental.

The topic of the "proper" stance is one of polemics. Which is the correct stance? This question is limiting, and as most therapists know it is not a useful one. Most of us say we do one thing and often do another. Videotapes of therapy sessions attest to this. The stance we choose and how we have come to this is influenced by our own personality systems, theoretical models, and training, as well as what we think a patient system requires. For some, we naturally assume a nondirective position; for others, we may be more authoritative. I suspect that unless a therapist practices in a very narrow scope, the therapeutic stance reflects to a degree the demands of the patient personality system. Of central importance is that the stance we choose be consistent with is who we are and that it meet the requirements of the system. The most effective therapists have used their own personality characteristics in a way that allows the therapeutic process to be intensified. Trying to adopt an artificial stance of a favorite therapist role model rarely, if ever, works. Finding one's own therapeutic and healing capacity is an essential part of the process of becoming a psychotherapist.

Practical Considerations and Controversies

Should a therapist see multiple members of a system or use multiple treatment modalities with the same family? This question is a controversial one that clinicians often face. Many therapists use multiple treatment modalities with the same family and its members but do not freely admit this to colleagues, as if there were something shameful or inappropriate about it. There are many permutations when combining treatment modalities and questions. Is it possible to conduct couples treatment, which includes individual sessions with each partner, and couples sessions as well? There is a lack of empirical research on how therapy is actually conducted, but informal surveys taken throughout the United States indicate that many therapists use multiple treatment modalities. Some therapists do so by necessity; others believe in the benefit of this approach with certain systems. Clearly, when a single clinician offers multiple modalities, he or she should discuss the advantages and disadvantages with the patient(s) and obtain informed consent. In some situations, this would be contraindicated, which should be determined on a case-by-case basis. An example is when one member of a couple's dyad reveals privately that he or she is having an affair. In this case, it is generally not useful to conduct couples therapy under false pretenses. If dyadic restructuring is going to create change, the extramarital relationship generally needs to end. Dyadic restructuring can, however, be useful for partners who want to end their relationship and come to a resolution, or if they have children, to restructure the dyad as a primary co-parenting one.

The Art of Modality Shifting

Effectively shifting from one treatment modality to another is more of an art than a science. Using a unified model can help us understand the core processes that are in operation and when these call for a shift. Consider shifting to another modality when optimal benefit has been reached with one modality or when the patient suggests it. For example, a couple came in for treatment during the initial session and asked whether it was possible for each of them to be seen individually. This is a good assessment strategy for some couples. After an initial session that allows observation of their process and the chance to gain understanding of the dyadic configuration, an individual session can demonstrate how the patient relates in the expected transaction with the therapist. Following the individual sessions, suggesting a treatment package to the couple is bound to be received with greater acceptance, because both parties feel they have been heard.

Multiple Clinicians

Things can become more complicated when there are multiple clinicians. The advantages of using multiple clinicians, especially for more refractory cases, outweighs the disadvantages, however. The most important concern is to have an open channel of communication. Sometimes patients may benefit from strategies such as seeing two therapists concurrently for individual work. These treatment interventions are beyond the realm of conventional approaches, but using a unified model allows greater therapeutic flexibility to respond to appropriate patient requests. When two or more therapists join together to further a patient or a system's growth, the results can be very positive.

Treatment Teams

A treatment team is a group of professionals who work together either by institutional demand or by choice. Such a team can be helpful when conducting therapy with complex and challenging systems. Treatment teams are compatible with a unified relational approach. Members of a treatment team with different perspectives can offer a highly synergistic treatment package. Psychologists, psychiatrists, medical practitioners, occupational therapists, and alternative healing specialists can augment the therapeutic matrix if coordinated by a team leader who has an overview of the case and coordinates all practitioners.

SUMMARY AND CONCLUSIONS

This chapter concludes the theoretical and clinical portion of this volume by addressing the issues of putting the personality-guided relational approach into practice. Treating personality systems is an extraordinarily complex endeavor, one that can be made clear through a unified theoretical model. This model incorporates interventions based on an optimal treatment package, blending components such as modality, setting, frame, and format and integrating these with a knowledge of the forces within each of the four triangular configurations and with a determination of the optimal fulcrum points for intervention. One of the fundamental elements of effective treatment is the patient's flexibility to respond to the unique needs of his or her total personality system. In many ways, this is a treatment delivered "outside the box" of any particular theoretical model or perspective, and it is fundamentally patient driven. This allows and encourages therapeutic creativity, with the ultimate stricture being "above all do no harm." Intensive treatment for severely dysfunctional personality systems must push the envelope of ritualistic, codified, and antiquated clinical methods and practice.

12

PARADIGM SHIFTS: EMPIRICAL CHALLENGES, CONVERGENCE, AND FUTURE DIRECTIONS

This chapter considers some of the empirical challenges and controversies as well as converging lines of evidence to support a unified model of personality-guided relational therapy. Of course, a unified model has not yet evolved to the point of sufficient "empirical" validation to support its use. Personality-guided relational therapy is, however, a theory-driven approach based on empirical and clinical findings from the personality-system domains presented in this volume. There is accruing evidence that the relational factors are the most potent ingredient of psychotherapy (Norcross, 2002). These multiple perspectives and cross-disciplinary findings provide converging evidence for a unified model and its continued development. As should be clear by this point, the theory is the wellspring from which sound clinical practice emanates and research interests evolve.

THE PLACE OF THEORY IN THE DEVELOPMENT OF SCIENCE

Theoretical models or paradigms are vital parts of science (Kuhn, 1970/1996). Scientific inquiry must be based on paradigms that attempt to unify our observations of the natural world and give direction to future research.

The paradigm presented in this volume attempts to join the domain systems of human functioning that have been identified during the first century of modern clinical science, psychology, and related disciplines. How these domain systems interrelate require continued elaboration, but the guiding assumption is that human functioning can only be understood when the entire ecology of the person is considered. It is hoped that the theory presented in this volume provides a framework for future exploration of the domains that have been identified as crucial to clinical science.

THEORY AND CLINICAL PRACTICE

The reality is that theory guides clinical work (Magnavita, 2004b). Empirical findings secondarily influence the practitioner's formulation, decision making, and intervention. A long-standing debate in the field of psychotherapy has been whether the results gleaned from psychotherapy research have relevance to the clinical practitioner. The simple answer is that they do, with limitations. Traditional psychotherapy research tends to focus on single domain treatments, which are applied to "discrete" clinical syndromes comparing the outcome. The "gold standard" for treatment research includes well-defined target symptoms, valid and reliable measures, specific treatment models, competent assessors, unbiased assignment to treatment conditions, and assessment and evaluation of adherence to a treatment manual (Foa & Meadows, 1997). The trend in psychotherapy research is on developing treatment manuals that are used by the clinicians delivering the treatment, to ensure that they are adherent to treatment and looking at outcome measures. For many clinical theorists and researchers, this research paradigm, which advances the science, is a model that should not be solely relied on. The results of these studies certainly build the empirical foundation of our clinical science but provide only one among many forms of verification. Such research does suggest which methods should be offered in certain clinical situations, such as the most efficacious restructuring methods for anxiety disorder and so on.

There has been an accumulation of literature suggesting that the most important aspect of any treatment is not the methods or techniques but the common factors that all "effective" therapies offer (Frank, 1973, 1991; Norcross & Goldfried, 1992; Striker & Gold, 1993) Thus, the relationship may indeed be more important than any method or technique. Much more research is required to address this controversy sufficiently. The current psychotherapy research paradigm based on the medical model of active treatments being compared with one another, or one model without the "active" agent of change, is a paradigmatic limitation to the advancement of a unified model. Research done in this manner reifies a paradigm that is based on the medical model of diagnosis and treatment. Again, although these research studies do advance the field, they do so within a paradigm that has limitations.

It is also of interest that in an examination of audiovisual recordings of various psychotherapy models, the actual clinical process is often more similar than different among various approaches. Many of the common processes of restructuring have been presented in this volume. All psychotherapies seem to share common core change processes (Mahoney, 1991). In fact, there has recently been more attention paid to transtheoretical models of change (Prochaska, DiClemente, & Norcross, 1992) and quantum change models (Miller & C'deBaca, 1994) that are essentially meta-models of how change processes occur. Without doubt, there are technical variations from school to school that can be considerable, but the fact remains that techniques are offered within the context of the relational matrix, and therefore capitalize either covertly or overtly on these relational–systemic forces.

SHATTERING ICONS—SCHOOLS OF THERAPY TOE-TO-TOE

Psychotherapy research by and large continues to focus its attention primarily on schools of psychotherapy that researchers, often the developers of these approaches, attempt to validate empirically. An example is a major report appearing in the *Journal of Consulting and Clinical Psychology* (2003) comparing the treatment of posttraumatic stress disorder using three treatments: exposure therapy, eye movement desensitization reprocessing, and relaxation training (Taylor et al., 2003). In terms of the unified model, these treatments are aimed at the restructuring the intrapsychic–biological triangle.

The trend to identify approaches that have been "empirically validated" has led to unnecessary contention in the field of psychotherapy, beginning with Eysenck's (1952) landmark research demonstrating the efficacy of behavior therapy over psychodynamic therapy. Psychotherapy researchers have followed the trends as various schools of psychotherapy have evolved, but most remain wedded primarily to the single domain school of thought, which attempts to prove the ascendancy of one approach over another. To do so, psychotherapy research by and large does not offer much of use to clinical practitioners; although there are some obvious times it has, as in the common factors research that examined the factors that cut across therapeutic schools and in providing support of certain methods for particular disorders. Yet if research is going to be useful, it needs to examine more closely what Rangell (1997) calls a "total composite theory" that is "unified and cumulative" (p. 1126). Again speaking from the vantage point of his perspective from psychoanalysis, Rangell urged a broader view:

> Every viable contribution made by alternative theories finds a home within this total composite theory. Accommodated under its embracing umbrella are drives and defenses, id, ego, and superego, self and object, intrapsychic and interpersonal, the internal and external worlds. This theory aims for both completeness and parsimony. Such a unitary theory is not monolithic, as some fear. Within it there are many principles of multiplicity. (p. 1126)

Millon et al. (1999) called his approach *psychosynergy*: Rangell (1997) described himself as a "id-ego-superego-internal-external-psychoanalysts-psychosynthesist" (p. 1117). *Synthesis, convergence,* and *total composite* are all terms that describe the move toward a unified model, one which has been backed by clinical evidence from the first century of modern psychotherapy and accruing empirical evidence from the neurosciences and other areas such as relational science, attachment theory, neuroscience, and affective science. Wilber (2000b) developed "integral psychology," which is yet another system of unified psychology. He wrote about the findings from various perspectives such as psychoanalysis, existentialism, transpersonal psychology, and cognitive science and their place within a unified model:

> What if, on the other hand, *all* of [these perspectives] were an important part of the story? What if they all possessed true, but partial, insights into the vast field of consciousness? At the very least, assembling their conclusions under one roof would vastly expand our ideas of what consciousness is and, more important, what it might become. The endeavor to honor and embrace every legitimate aspect of human consciousness is the goal of *integral psychology*. (p. 2)

THE CALL FOR A UNIFIED MODEL OF PERSONALITY SYSTEMIC RESEARCH

Another way to conceptualize psychotherapy research is to use a unified model of personality systemics that explores the interconnected domains of the personality system, which have been essential to development, psychopathology, and dysfunction. This echoes Sternberg and Grigorenko's (2001) call for a multidisciplinary team of researchers to examine these phenomena from multiple converging perspectives. This would entail a new approach to research that would look at processes within complex systems rather than cause–effect relationships. As Barabasi and Bonabeau noted, "Scientists have recently discovered that various complex systems have an underlying architecture governed by shared organizing principles" (2003, p. 60). These authors described the multiple network applications:

The brain is a network of nerve cells connected by axons, and cells themselves are networks of molecules connected by biochemical reactions. Societies, too, are networks of people linked by friendships, familial relationships and professional ties. On a larger scale, food webs and ecosystems can be represented as networks of species. And networks pervade technology: the Internet, power grids and transportation systems are but a few examples. Even the language we are using to convey these thoughts to you is a network, made up of words connected by syntactic relationships. (p. 62)

This complex system model would also require collaboration of scientists and clinicians from various orientations. Instead of being motivated to prove one form of therapy the winner over the rest of the field, this approach would encourage collaborative research among experts from the various domains of the personality system and encourage cross-disciplinary fertilization. We may have achieved the maximum possible benefit from trying to prove one domain-based model better than the others; in doing so, we can often miss the larger picture and artificially reduce the complexity of our subject. Researchers need to match more closely the processes that occur in real-life clinical practice, where much of what is practiced is gleaned from experience and trial and error, not from statistical findings about research, which never captures the complexity of the human beings we study. This surely would represent a paradigmatic shift, but one that would benefit all involved, especially the troubled patients in whom we try to alleviate suffering and reduce dysfunction. This is not to minimize the importance of basic research but to challenge the field of psychotherapy to shift to a more relevant model based on contemporary theories that emphasize convergence.

UNIFIED THEORY-BASED KNOWLEDGE AND SCIENCE

Clinical practice is driven by theoretical conceptualizations about the nature and the cause of human dysfunction, as well about, or beliefs about, modification and amelioration. The importance of theory in clinical science is a central tenet of this volume. L'Abate (1986) listed the following aspects of theory for reducing complexity: "(1) linkage between theory and practice, (2) diagnostic functions—classification, (3) therapeutic functions, (4) propedeutic (teachable constructs and methods), and (5) research functions" (p. 20). Stiles (2003) noted that

Theories are ideas stated in words (or numbers or diagrams or other signs), which communicate ideas between people—between author and reader in the case of research reports. To the extent that communication is successful, the reader experiences something similar to the author's understanding. Empirical truth—the goal toward which theoretical statements strive—can be understood as correspondence between theories and observed events. (p. 6)

These conceptual models draw substantially from other scientific models, which are often used as metaphors. The model might be mechanistic or based on fluid hydraulics, evolution, or another concept, yet to a large degree the model is limited by its explanatory metaphor. "Empirical truth is never general or permanent because different people experience the words and events differently, depending on their biological equipment, culture, life history, and current circumstances" (Stiles, 2003, p. 6). Wolfram (2002) wrote about his vision of a fundamental shift in science: "In the existing sciences much of the emphasis over the past century or so has been on breaking systems down to find their underlying parts, then trying to analyze these parts in as much detail as possible" (p. 3). This reductionistic approach was the predominant goal of behaviorism, for example, which was ascendant for many years in psychology. He adds: "But just how these components act together to produce even some of the most obvious features of the overall behavior we see has in the past remained almost a complete mystery" (p. 3). Behaviorism was at a loss to explain complex behavior such as language acquisition, which finally led to its downfall.

Wolfram (2002) summarized some of the important theoretical models that have broken ground in theoretical sciences, many of which are presented in this volume. Scientific advances are based on metaphors that approximate the subject of study. Freud based his model of psychodynamics on the theory of fluid dynamics. Since then, many other metaphors have been developed to explain natural phenomena. In the following list, I present those with the greatest relevance to our topic to familiarize readers with further possibilities.

- *Artificial intelligence* attempts to develop computer models capable of human thought processes.
- *Artificial life* imitates biological systems with computer simulation.
- *Catastrophe theory* demonstrates mathematically how discrete, nonlinear changes cause movements to and from different points of stability.
- *Chaos theory* demonstrates that even in simple systems, complex behavior can occur based on uncertainty.
- *Complexity theory* is the notion that complexity itself is a fundamental phenomenon that is independent of the systems we study.
- *Cybernetics* is the modeling of biological systems based on electrical machines.

- *Fractal geometry* is identification of the importance of nested shapes that seem arbitrary but replicate intricate patterns common in nature.
- *General systems theory* is the study of large networks of interrelated elements.
- *Nanotechnology* is the theory that simple structures can perform complex tasks.
- *Self-organization* is the observation that systems in nature may start out disordered and without features and then organize themselves into definitive structures. (Wolfram, 2002, pp. 12–16)

Wolfram (2002) wrote of the value of using a new kind of scientific theorizing based on his study of systems:

> From economics to psychology there has been a widespread if controversial assumption—no doubt from the success of the physical sciences—that solid theories must always be formulated in terms of numbers, equations and traditional mathematics. But I suspect that one will often have a much better chance of capturing fundamental mechanisms for phenomena in the social sciences by using instead the new kind of science. (p. 9)

Reductionistic attempts to capture the complexity of the therapeutic system or multiple domains of the personality system are likely to lead to dead ends. This type of research is costly and the findings often lack generalizability to clinical practice, where more complex disorders are typical.

THE MASTER THERAPIST AND THE POLITICALIZATION OF THE FIELD

Most of the dominant schools of psychotherapy originated from and gained prominence through the work and demonstrations of charismatic and gifted therapists. In many cases, these individuals are instinctive therapists who are able to read patient codes and processes in a highly accurate fashion and induce change in novel ways. Clinical experience often spawned theoretical systems, thus creating an integral relationship between clinical experience and the construction of theory, a dialectic evident in every clinical practitioner. If theoretical constructs do not prove to be utilitarian, they are jettisoned in favor for something that will be a better fit between clinical experience and theoretical constructs. This is particularly evident in Freud's development of psychoanalysis. Freud built and evolved his theory on his experience in the consultation room, which was his clinical laboratory. Many of these leading figures have attracted a cadre of devoted followers, an ongoing phenomenon beginning with Freud. In many cases, theoretical developments were rejected when the master fell out of favor. In other cases, the theoretical explanations describing how these figures conducted therapy was left for others to develop and codify.

The cult of the master therapist holds enormous sway. Theoretical systems do not develop solely from the scientific exploration of master therapists, but also through political agendas. The politics of science is well delineated and considered an important part of the evolution of new paradigms (Kuhn, 1996). Through political struggle, dominant models of psychotherapy often receive more funding for research. Theorists are often left with the task of empirically validating their own approach, which may lead to bias findings. Dominant schools of thought also draw more training therapists. Popularization of various formats also brings patients to those therapists who ascribe to the model. Psychotherapy becomes big business, which is not the best path for the field.

From another perspective, most therapists are said to believe that it is not the model of therapy that makes it effective, but the therapist. There continue to be practitioners whom others identify as "master therapists." A greater understanding of what characterizes effective psychotherapy might be gleaned from an in-depth examination of audiovisual recordings showing the manner in which master therapists work, searching for and isolating common processes. These therapists simply may harness common factors in such a fashion as to effectively promote change. These therapists simply may effectively use common factors that promote change. According to Messer and Wampold (2002), the substrate of the personality-guided relational model presented in this volume, is the centrality of the relationships in all domains of human functioning:

> common factors and therapist variability far outweigh specific ingredients in accounting for the benefits of psychotherapy. The proportion of the variance contributed by common factors such as placebo effects, working alliance, therapist allegiance, and therapist competence are much greater than the variance stemming from specific ingredients or effects. (p. 23)

CONVERGING LINES OF EVIDENCE

Accumulating research and clinical evidence over the last century supports the basic contention of this volume that it is our relationships that shape who we are and it is the therapeutic relational matrix that allows us to alter patterns. An examination of the accumulated literature from the critical domain areas within the personality system provide valuable support but are far beyond the scope of this volume. Readers may refer to the reference section for an in-depth examination of the findings from attachment theory, relational science, neuroscience, and the other domains of the unified system. There is, however, a growing force within the field to incorporate the findings and tools of neuroscience to verify many aspects of current theoretical constructs. This represents a major advance for the field if interdisciplinary cooperation can ensue.

Neurobiological Findings

Theories once considered clinical speculation now have support from neuroscience. It is beyond the scope of this volume to review the literature extensively, but I present here a few samples of these endeavors to give the reader who is unfamiliar with this groundswell an understanding of the kind of problems under investigation. Clinicians who treat individuals who have experienced early trauma are often struck by the capacity of the intrapsychic–biological triangle to maintain reactions to similar stimuli long past childhood. Evidence now suggests that early trauma can result in alterations in brain function and structure. This includes an actual decrease in hippocampal volume, possibly related to a decrease of cortisol, which is suppressed during trauma. There may also be activation of a series of complex neurobiological systems such as the hypothalamic–pituitary–adrenal (HPA) axis and the sympathetic nervous system, creating a "biological priming" for posttraumatic stress disorder (Heim, Meinlschmidt, & Nemeroff, 2003). Other studies support these findings. Preliminary evidence also suggests that early maltreatment may result in reduction in the size of the amygdala (Teicher, 2002). The limbic system plays a crucial role in emotional regulation and memory. As clinicians know, reversing the adverse effects of early maltreatment is arduous. Johnson (2003) wrote as follows:

> The trouble with emotional memories is they can be fiendishly difficult to eradicate. The brain seems to be wired to prevent the deliberate overriding of fear responses. Although there are extensive neural pathways from the amygdala to the neocortex, the paths running the reverse direction are sparse. Our brains seem to have been designed to allow the fear system to take control in threatening situations and prevent our conscious awareness from reigning. (pp. 38–39)

People who commit suicide also evidence structural changes in the orbital prefrontal cortex and a section of the brain stem (Ezzell, 2003). Early neglect and abuse may alter the brain and create a lifelong vulnerability to depression (Nemeroff, 1998). Again the HPA axis is implicated. Greenberg (2002) systematically articulated the interrelationship among the neurobiological and affect systems and the implications for psychopathology and psychotherapy.

Affective Processes From the Microsystem to the Macrosystem

The importance of affective processes is evident in just about every domain of the total ecological system. Affective processes can be conceptualized and studied at the nanosystem of brain function (as just described); at the intrapsychic, dyadic, and triadic systems; and at the larger socioeconomic and cultural systems. Affective dysfunction is implicated in all forms of psychopathology (Berenbaum, Raghavan, Le, Vernon, & Gomez, 2003) and is increasingly becoming the domain of neuroscientific investigation. Researchers using positron emission tomography scans can provide a view of emotional activation within neuronal networks, an advance that holds promise for documenting structural and functional changes in brain organization that result from psychopharmacological and psychotherapeutic intervention. Videotapes of psychotherapy using methods of emotional activation and regulation demonstrate the process and importance of giving affect a place in clinical treatment. Therapists of diverse persuasions are discussing the importance of following patient affect in the process of therapy. All of the therapeutic methods presented in this volume address anxiety regulation, emotion processing, and the assimilation of "hot" or emotionally laden cognitions.

Sociocultural and Familial Influence on the Development of Psychopathology—A Sample of Recent Converging Lines of Empirical Research

An accumulating body of empirical evidence provides support for the multiple domain research suggested by a unified model. The following brief sample of these provides a sense of the trend toward more complex investigation.

Research is beginning to tease apart the complex diathesis–stress that occurs in various forms of psychopathology. The effects of living in an urban environment on the development of dysfunction demonstrate the importance of a unified model. In a study examining the relationship between urban environment, family liability, and the occurrence of psychosis, researchers found support for a gene–environment interaction (van Os, Hanssen, Bak, Bijl, & Vollebergh, 2003). They summarized this interaction as follows:

> The risk-increasing effect of urbanicity on the occurrence of psychotic disorder was greater in those with higher familial liability for psychosis, independent of familial liability for other psychiatric morbidity. Between 60% and 70% of the psychosis outcome in probands exposed to both familial liability and urbanicity was attributable to the synergistic action of these two factors. (p. 480)

This type of research is critical to documenting the importance of a unified model that accounts for as many factors in the total ecological system as possible and suggests ways of prevention and intervention.

Familial factors are also being investigated as an important domain in the development of various disorders. Researchers have found a significant correlation between oppositional–defiant disorder and greater social and family dysfunction (Greene et al., 2002). The results of another study suggest that high levels of harsh and inconsistent parenting, lack of nurturing parenting, deviance-prone older siblings, and disadvantaged neighborhoods contribute to the development of conduct disorder in African American children (Brody et al., 2003).

The complexity of the interrelationships in the spectrum of domain systems is becoming evident in more sophisticated studies on psychopathology. A study on major depression in women described an "adversity pathway" that includes factors such as "disturbed family environment, childhood sexual abuse, and parental loss, flowing through low educational attainment, lifetime trauma, and low social support to ever divorced" (Kendler, Gardner, & Prescott, 2002, p. 1141).

In another study it was found that paternal substance abuse and antisocial personality were associated with children's affiliation with deviant peers (Moss, Lynch, Hardie, & Baron, 2002). The researchers concluded that their results "confirm that family functioning is comparatively worse in families in which there is parental substance dependence" (p. 612). These children tend to "drift" toward deviant peers. The authors described the mixture of domain systems: "A less functional family environment, a deviant peer environment, and paternal antisociality linearly interact to account for a greater degree of psychopathology in the child" (p. 613).

Recent research supports the importance of multiple domains in the development of and recovery from dysthymic disorder (low-grade chronic depression; Hayden & Klein, 2001). The researchers concluded: "The course and outcome of dysthymic disorder is best conceptualized within a multifactorial framework, with family history of psychopathology, early adversity, axis I and II comorbidity and chronic stress all making important contributions" (p. 1864). Another study using a family-focused approach for patients with bipolar disorder demonstrated that patients in family-focused treatment, compared with patients in individual therapy, had fewer mood disorder relapses and were less likely to be rehospitalized (Rea et al., 2003).

Childhood abuse constitutes an environmental risk for future suicide attempts and the development of impulsivity and aggression (Brodsky et al., 2001). They summarized their results as follows:

> Our main finding was that depressed adults who reported a history of
> either physical or sexual abuse in childhood were more likely to have

made a previous suicide attempt than those who did not report a history of abuse. They also had higher levels of trait impulsivity, higher levels of aggression, and a higher rate of comorbid borderline personality disorder. Thus, a childhood abuse history is associated with both suicidal behavior and impulsivity in depressed adults. (p. 1874)

In an extensive study of 8,000 participants, those who reported being victims of childhood physical or sexual abuse, those who had witnessed battering of the maternal figure, and those in an emotionally abusive family had decrements in mental health scores showing a dose–response relationship: The greater the incidence of abuse, the lower the mental health (Edwards, Holden, Felitti, & Anda, 2003).

Clear evidence suggests that the factors responsible for generating and maintaining disturbances at any level of the personality system are multifactorial and interrelated. Models of intervention that focus on a single domain are unlikely to be potent enough to undo these effects and address the multiple pathways that lead to dysfunction. In another study, Ehrensaft and colleagues (2003) found evidence for an intergenerational transmission of partner violence: "Our findings from this 20-year prospective study suggest that childhood behavior problems are among the most robust predictors of partner violence, and that conduct disorder (CD) appears to mediate the effect of child abuse, and that exposure to violence between partners and power assertive punishment during childhood significantly increased the risk for violent conflict resolution within intimate relationships" (p. 751). Portney (2003), in a review of the findings from children of the Holocaust, wrote: "Intergenerational transmission of trauma seems to have a particular significance in offspring of parents with a history of major trauma and subsequent PTSD" (p. 40). Using a unified model, either explicitly or implicitly, is the foundation of this type of empirical evidence and supports the search for a complex system process that will offer new ways to address the issue of how traumatic experience is encoded and passed to subsequent generations.

Relational Dysfunction and Psychopathology

The viability of a systemic approach to psychopathology is gaining momentum as can be seen from the research findings just reviewed. We need to learn more about the dynamic processes that occur in the various domains of the personality system. Relational dysfunction and psychopathology cannot be separated artificially. Patterson (2003) highlighted the pertinence of a dynamical systems perspective for understanding dysfunctional dyadic relationships, but his observations bear relevance for relational dysfunction beyond the dyad:

The recent upsurge in the use of dynamical systems is of particular interest to us because they can be used to provide "proof" of the existence of "relational disorders," and provide a means to explore the behavior of different types of dyadic systems over time. In particular, dynamical systems models can provide a solid foundation for arguing 1) that dyadic systems can have emergent properties, 2) that distinct subpopulations can diverge starkly despite similarity in initial starting points, 3) that some problematic relationship dynamics can become self-perpetuating, and 4) that dyadic systems can be "disordered" in the absence of disorder at the individual level. (pp. 15–16)

The conceptualization of relational dysfunction and psychopathology as emergent properties of complex human social and familial systems sounds basic, but if embraced by the field, it would represent a paradigmatic shift from the discrete-disorder medical model that has been the major paradigm for the study of psychopathological adaptations and syndromes.

Maximum Theoretical Utility

Theoretical systems evolve and are discarded as they become obsolete or fail to explain the phenomenon of their purview. In psychotherapy, theory is verified by basic research concerning the multiple domains of the personality system. For example, as shown earlier, substantial evidence indicates that trauma is implicated in most forms of dysfunction and that severe and ongoing sexual trauma in childhood results in forms of severe personality disturbance and complex posttraumatic stress disorder (Zanarini, 1997). This is useful for therapists confronted with severe disorders. Unified theory better guides our formulation and intervention than do single domain constructs, especially in complex cases. Psychoanalysis has been rightfully criticized over the past century for its lack of empirical support. Yet the theoretical systems spawned by the psychoanalytic movement continue to exert a strong influence on clinical practice because they help to organize clinicians' formulations in a way that has been useful enough not to retire it. "Good theories are useful. By accurately representing the process of psychotherapy, for example, a good theory can help practitioners understand their clients and how to be effective in helping them" (Stiles, 2003, p. 7). Theory needs to be verified by multiple perspectives. The fact that a theory is used in clinical practice does not guarantee its accuracy. In the long run, however, clinical science is self-correcting; theories that do not serve their purpose will be retired, and those that do will endure. How do most clinicians work when it comes to using theories in practice? Attempting to answer this question might provide useful data.

The Individual Clinical Theorist

All clinicians have a clinical theory that guides their work. Research has shown that theoretical models to which clinicians adhere strongly influence categorization of psychopathology (Benson, 2002). Each of us has an individualized and idiosyncratic clinical theory based on our training, experience, personality, and interests. All clinicians practice unified therapy, however implicitly or intuitively, in that they have a total composite understanding of how human functioning and the domains of the total ecosystem result in dysfunction. The individual clinical scientist whose consulting room is a scientific workbench considers the biopsychosocial matrix even if attention is being paid to a single domain or even multiple domains. We are also constrained by the paradigms in which we place our trust, especially if these models only map limited domains of the territory of human functioning. This is not to say that specialization is not an appropriate aspect of clinical science, but that an understanding of the unified system strengthens any formulation or intervention.

Case Studies

Much of what has been learned about psychology and psychotherapy over the last century was discovered in the consultation room or the hospital ward. The use of case studies continues to inform our science and should be elevated as a valuable method of clinical science. Case studies should no longer be reified, of course, but neither should they be denigrated as less substantial ways to understand clinical process and outcome. Stiles (2003) suggested that "case studies offer an alternative that can complement hypothesis-testing research. By simultaneously bringing many observations to bear on a theory, case studies offer both a way to test and an opportunity to improve theory" (p. 9).

SUMMARY AND CONCLUSIONS

This final chapter calls for a paradigmatic shift away from the comparative primary school model of psychotherapy research to one that emphasizes the processes and organization of the multiple networks encompassing the personality system. I suggest that a paradigmatic shift be made to a systemically based, multiple-domain model examining convergent lines of evidence and knowledge. This volume presents a basic framework to begin to conceptualize the multiple domain of the overall personality system. It is hoped that this perspective, evolving as new evidence is accrued, will provide a useful guide for clinical work and suggest new paths for unification of the component systems.

REFERENCES

Abbass, A. (2001). A case of OCD and schizophrenia treated with a modified STDP approach. *Quaderni di psychiatria practica, 17/18*, 143–145.

Ackerman, N. W. (1957). The emergence of family diagnosis and treatment: A personal view. *Psychotherapy: Theory, Research, and Practice, 4*, 125–129.

Ackerman, N. W. (1958). *The psychodynamics of family life: Diagnostic and treatment of family relationships*. New York: Basic Books.

Adams, H. E., Luscher, K. A., & Bernat, J. A. (2001). The classification of abnormal behavior: An overview. In H. E. Adams & P. B. Sutker (Eds.), *Comprehensive handbook of psychopathology* (3rd ed., pp. 3–28). New York: Kluwer Academic/Plenum.

Adams, H. E., & Sutker, P. B. (2001). *Comprehensive handbook of psychopathology* (3rd ed.). New York: Kluwer Academic/Plenum.

Ainsworth, M. D. S. (1979). Infant–mother attachment. *American Psychologist, 34*, 932–937.

Ajaya, S. (1983). *Psychotherapy East and West: A unifying paradigm*. Honesdale, PA: Himalayan.

Alexander, F. G., & French, T. M. (1946). *Psychoanalytic therapy: Principles and applications*. New York: Ronald Press.

Allport, G. W. (1961a). The open system in personality theory. *Journal of Abnormal and Social Psychology, 61*, 301–310.

Allport, G. W. (1961b). *Pattern and growth in personality*. New York: Holt, Rinehart & Winston.

Allport, G. W. (1968). *The person in psychology: Selected essays*. Boston: Beacon Press.

American Psychiatric Association. (1980). *Diagnostic and statistical manual of mental disorders* (3rd ed.). Washington, DC: Author.

American Psychiatric Association. (1994). *Diagnostic and statistical manual of mental disorders* (4th ed.). Washington, DC: Author.

Anchin, J. (2003). Cybernetic systems, existential phenomenology, and solution-focused narrative: Therapeutic transformation of negative affect states through integratively oriented brief therapy. *Journal of Psychotherapy Integration, 13*, 334–442.

Anchin, J. C., & Kiesler, D. J. (Eds.). (1982). *Handbook of interpersonal psychotherapy*. New York: Pergamon Press.

Anderson, J. L., Crawford, C. B., Nadeau, J., & Lindberg, T. (1992). Was the Duchess of Windsor right? A cross-cultural review of the socioecology of ideals of female body shape. *Ethology and Sociobiology, 13*, 197–227.

Angyal, A. (1941). *Foundations for a science of personality*. New York: Commonwealth Fund.

Angyal, A. (1982). *Neurosis and treatment: A holistic theory* (E. Hanfmann & R. M. Jones, Eds.). New York: Da Capo Press.

Arnett, J. J. (2002). The psychology of globalization. *American Psychologist, 57,* 774–783.

Aron, L. (1996). *A meeting of minds: Mutuality in psychoanalysis.* Hillsdale, NJ: Analytic Press.

Ashby, W. R. (1964). *An introduction to cybernetics.* London: Methuen

Bales, K. (2002). The social psychology of modern slavery. *Scientific American, 286,* 82–88.

Barabasi, A.-L., & Bonabeau, E. (2003). Scale-free networks. *Scientific American, 288,* 60–69.

Barber, N. (2002). *The science of romance: Secrets of the sexual brain.* Amherst, NY: Prometheus.

Barlow, D. H. (1988). Anxiety and its disorders: The nature and treatment of anxiety and panic. New York: Guilford Press.

Bartholemew, K., & Horowitz, L. M. (1991). Attachment styles among your adults: A test of a four category model. *Journal of Personality and Social Psychology, 61,* 226–244.

Bartholomew, K., Kwong, M. J., & Hart, S. D. (2001). Attachment. In W. J. Livesley (Ed.), *Handbook of personality disorders: Theory, research, and treatment* (pp. 196–230). New York: Guilford Press.

Bartlett, F. (1932). *Remembering.* Cambridge, MA: Cambridge University Press.

Bateson, G. (1958). *Naven* (2nd ed.). Stanford, CA: Stanford University Press.

Bateson, G. (1979). *Mind and nature: A necessary unity.* New York: Bantam Books.

Baumrind, D. (1967). Child care practices anteceding three patterns of preschool behavior. *Genetic Psychology of Monographs, 75,* 43–86.

Baumrind, D. (1971). Current patterns of parental authority. *Developmental Psychology Monograph, 41*(1), 101–103.

Beck, A. T. (1976). *Cognitive therapy and emotional disorders.* New York: International Universities Press.

Beck, A. T., Emery, G., & Greenberg, R. L. (1985). *Anxiety disorders and phobias: A cognitive perspective.* New York: Basic Books.

Beck, A. T., & Freeman, A. (1990). *Cognitive therapy of personality disorders.* New York: Guilford Press.

Beck, A. T., Rush, A. J., Shaw, B. F., & Emery, G. (1979). *Cognitive therapy of depression.* New York: Guilford Press.

Beitman, B. D., Goldfried, M. R., & Norcross, J. C. (1989). The movement toward integrating the psychotherapies: An overview. *American Journal of Psychiatry, 146,* 138–147.

Benedict, H. E., & Hastings, L. (2002). Object-relations play therapy. In F. Kaslow (Ser. Ed.) & J. J. Magnavita (Vol. Ed.), *Comprehensive handbook of psychotherapy. Vol. 1: Psychodynamic/object relations* (pp. 47–80). New York: Wiley.

Benjamin, L. S. (1993). *Interpersonal diagnosis and treatment of personality disorders.* New York: Guilford Press.

Benjamin, L. S. (1996). *Interpersonal diagnosis and treatment of personality disorders* (2nd ed.). New York: Guilford Press.

Benjamin, L. S. (2003). *Interpersonal reconstructive therapy: Promoting change in nonresponders.* New York: Guilford Press.

Benson, E. (2002). Thinking clinically: A new study shows how clinicians' theories could affect their diagnoses. *Monitor on Psychology, 33*(12), 30–31.

Berenbaum, H., Raghavan, C., Le, H.-N., Vernon, L. L., & Gomez, J. J. (2003). A taxonomy of emotional disturbance. *Clinical Psychology: Science and Practice, 10,* 206–226.

Berne, E., Steiner, C., & Dusay, J. (1973). Transactional analysis. In R. Jurjevich (Ed.), *Direct psychotherapy* (Vol. 1). Coral Gables, FL: University of Miami Press.

Berscheid, E. (1999). The greening of relational science. *American Psychologist, 54,* 260–266.

Binder, J. L., & Strupp, H. H. (1991). The Vanderbilt approach to time-limited dynamic psychotherapy. In P. Crits-Christoph & J. P. Barber (Eds.), *Handbook of short-term dynamic psychotherapy* (pp. 137–165). New York: Basic Books.

Bion, W. R. (1977). *Seven servants: Four works by Wilfred R. Bion.* New York: Aronson.

Bischof, L. J. (1970). Interpreting personality theories (2nd ed.). New York: Harper & Row.

Blanck, R., & Blanck, G. (1968). *Marriage and personal development.* New York: Columbia University Press.

Bleiberg, E. (2001). *Treating personality disorders in children and adolescents: A relational approach.* New York: Guilford Press.

Bleiberg, E. (2004). Treatment of dramatic personality disorders in children and adolescents. In J. J. Magnavita (Ed.), *Handbook of personality disorders: Theory and practice* (pp. 467–497). Hoboken, NJ: Wiley.

Blos, P. (1985). *Son and father: Before and beyond the Oedipus complex.* New York: Free Press.

Blum, D. (2002). *Love at Goon Park: Harry Harlow and the science of affection.* Cambridge, MA: Perseus.

Bowen, M. (1976). Theory and practice of family therapy. In P. J. Guerin Jr. (Ed.), *Family therapy: Theory and practice* (pp. 42–90). New York: Gardner Press.

Bowen, M. (1978). *Family therapy in clinical practice.* New York: Aronson.

Bowlby, J. (1969). *Attachment and loss. Volume 1, Attachment.* New York: Basic Books.

Bowlby, J. (1973). *Attachment and loss. Volume 2, Separation: Anxiety and anger.* New York: Basic Books.

Bowlby, J. (1977). The making and breaking of affectional bonds. I. Aetiology and psychopathology in light of attachment theory. *British Journal of Psychiatry, 130*, 201–210.

Bowlby, J. (1980). *Attachment and loss. Volume 3, Loss: Sadness and depression.* London: Hogarth Press.

Bradburn, N. M. (1963). The cultural context of personality theory. In J. M. Wepman & R. W. Heine (Eds.), *Concepts of personality* (pp. 333–360). Chicago: Aldine.

Bradt, J. O. (1980). The family with young children. In E. A. Carter & M. Mc-Goldrick (Eds.), *The family life cycle: A framework for family therapy* (pp. 121–146). New York: Gardner Press.

Brodsky, B. S., Oquendo, M., Ellis, S. P., Haas, G. L., Malone, K. M., & Mann, J. J. (2001). The relationship of childhood abuse to impulsivity and suicidal behavior in adults with major depression. *American Journal of Psychiatry, 158*, 1871–1877.

Brody, G. H., McBride Murry, V., Ge, X., Kim, S. Y., Simons, R. L., Gibbons, F. X., et al. (2003). Neighborhood disadvantage moderates associations of parenting and older sibling problem attitudes and behavior with conduct disorders in African American children. *Journal of Consulting and Clinical Psychology, 71*, 211–222.

Brody, S., & Siegel, M. G. (1992). *The evolution of character: Birth to 18 years: A longitudinal study.* Madison, CT: International University Press.

Bronfenbrenner, U. (1979). *The ecology of human development: Experiments by nature and design.* Cambridge, MA: Harvard University Press.

Bronfenbrenner, U., & Morris, P. A. (1998). The ecology of developmental processes. In W. Damon (Series Ed.) & R. M. Lerner (Vol. Ed.), *Handbook of child psychology* (5th ed., Vol. 1, pp. 993–1028). New York: Wiley.

Budman, S. H. (1994). *Treating time effectively: The first session in brief therapy* [videotape and manual]. New York: Guilford Press.

Buss, D. M. (1984). Evolutionary biology and personality psychology: Toward a conception of human nature and individual differences. *American Psychologist, 39*, 1135–1147.

Butz, M. R. (Ed.). (1997). *Chaos and complexity: Implications for psychological theory and practice.* New York: Taylor & Francis.

Byng-Hall, J. (1999). Family and couple therapy: Toward greater security. In J. Cassidy & P. R. Shaver (Eds.), *Handbook of attachment: Theory, research and clinical applications* (pp. 625–645). New York: Guilford Press.

Cairns, R. B. (1998). The making of developmental psychology. In W. Damon (Series Ed.) & R. B. Lerner (Vol. Ed.), *Handbook of child psychology* (5th ed., Vol. 1, pp. 25–105). New York: Wiley.

Cameron, N. (1963). *Personality development and psychopathology: A dynamic approach.* Boston: Houghton Mifflin.

Carson, R. C. (1982). Self-fulfilling prophecy, maladaptive behavior, and psycho-therapy. In J. G. Anchin & D. J. Kiesler (Eds.), *Handbook of interpersonal psychotherapy* (pp. 64–77). New York: Pergamon Press.

Carson, R. C. (1983). The social-interactional viewpoint. In M. Hersen, A. E. Kazdin, & A. S. Bellack (Eds.), *The clinical psychology handbook* (pp. 143–153). New York: Pergamon Press.

Carter, E. A., & McGoldrick, M. (Eds.). (1980). *The family life cycle: A framework for family therapy*. New York: Gardner Press.

Carter, R. (1998). *Mapping the mind*. Berkeley: University of California Press.

Cashdan, S. (1988). *Object relations therapy: Using the relationship*. New York: Norton.

Cassidy, J., & Shaver, P. R. (1999). *Handbook of attachment: Theory, research and clinical applications*. New York: Guilford Press.

Cattell, R. B. (1957). *Personality and motivation structure and measurement*. New York: World.

Chamberlain, L. L., & Butz, M. R. (Eds.). (1998). *Clinical chaos: A therapist's guide to non-linear dynamics and therapeutic change*. New York: Brunner/Mazel.

Charney, D. S. (2004). Psychobiological mechanisms of resilience and vulnerability: Implications for successful adaptation to extreme stress. *American Journal of Psychiatry, 161*, 195–216.

Cicchetti, D. (2000). Foreward. In E. M. Cummings, P. T. Davies, & S. B. Campbell (Eds.), *Developmental psychopathology and family process: Theory, research, and clinical implications* (pp. ix–xi). New York: Guilford Press.

Clarkin, J. F., & Lenzenweger, M. F. (1996). *Major theories of personality disorder*. New York: Guilford Press.

Colarusso, C. A., & Nemiroff, R. A. (1981). *Adult development: A new dimension in psychodynamic theory and practice*. New York: Plenum.

Comer, J. P., & Hill, H. (1985). Social policy and the mental health of black children. *Journal of the American Academy of Child Psychiatry, 24*, 175–181.

Costa, P. T., & McCrae, R. R. (1990). Personality disorders and the five-factor model of personality. *Journal of Personality Disorders, 4*, 362–371.

Costa, P. T., & Widiger, T. (Eds.). (1993). *Personality disorders and the five-factor model of personality*. Washington, DC: American Psychological Association.

Cramer, P. (1987). The development of defense mechanisms. *Journal of Personality, 55*, 599–614.

Cummings, E. M., Davies, P. T., & Campbell, S. B. (2000). *Developmental psychopathology and family process: Theory, research, and clinical implications*. New York: Guilford Press.

Damasio, A. (1999). *The feeling of what happens: Body and emotion in the making of consciousness*. New York: Harcourt Brace.

Darwin, C. R. (1859). *The origin of species by means of natural selection*. London: Murray.

Darwin, C. R. (1982). *The expression of emotions in man and animal*. London: John Murray. (Original work published 1872)

Dass, R. (1991). *The path of service: Here and now in the 90s, Part One*. Boulder, CO: Sounds True.

Davanloo, H. (Ed.). (1980). *Short-term dynamic psychotherapy*. New York: Jason Aronson.

Davidson, R. J. (2000). Affective style, psychopathology, and resilience: Brain mechanisms and plasticity. *American Psychologist, 55*, 1196–1214.

Davis, W. S. (1983). *A test of the predictability of collusion, ambivalence, and idealization in the mate selection process*. Unpublished doctoral dissertation, Florida State University, Tallahassee.

De Graaf, W., & Maier, R. (1994). *Sociogenesis reexamined*. New York: Springer-Verlag.

Dennett, D. C. (1991). *Consciousness explained*. Boston: Little, Brown.

Denton, W. H. (1996). Problems encountered in reconciling individual and relational diagnosis. In F. W. Kaslow (Ed.), *Handbook of relational diagnosis and dysfunctional family patterns* (pp. 35–45). New York: Wiley.

Diamond, G. M., Diamond, G. S., & Liddle, H. A. (2000). The therapist-parent alliance in family-based therapy adolescents. *Journal of Clinical Psychology/In Session: Psychotherapy in Practice, 56*, 1037–1050.

Doane, J. A., & Diamond, D. (1994). *Affect and attachment in the family: A family-based treatment of major psychiatric disorder*. New York: Basic Books.

Dollard, J., & Miller, N. E. (1950). *Personality and psychotherapy: An analysis in terms of learning, thinking, and culture*. New York: McGraw-Hill.

Donaldson-Pressman, S., & Pressman, R. M. (1994). *The narcissistic family: Diagnosis and treatment*. New York: Maxwell Macmillan International.

Donovan, J. M. (Ed.). (1999). *Short-term couple therapy*. New York: Guilford Press.

Dornelas, E. A., & Magnavita, J. J. (2001). High-impact therapy for smoking cessation. *Journal of Clinical Psychology/In Session: Psychotherapy in Practice, 57*, 1311–1322.

Edwards, V. J., Holden, G. W., Felitti, V. J., & Anda, R. F. (2003). Relationship between multiple forms of childhood maltreatment and adult mental health in community respondents: Results from the adverse childhood experiences study. *American Journal of Psychiatry, 160*, 1453–1460.

Ehrensaft, M. K., Cohen, P., Brown, J., Smailes, E., Chen, H., & Johnson, J. G. (2003). Intergenerational transmission of partner violence: A 20-year prospective study. *Journal of Consulting and Clinical Psychology, 71*, 741–753.

Ekman, P., & Davidson, R. J. (Eds.). (1994). *The nature of emotion: Fundamental questions*. New York: Oxford Press.

Elliot, C. (2000, December). A new way to be mad. *Atlantic Monthly*, 73–84.

Ellis, A., & Harper, R. A. (1961). *A new guide to rational living*. Englewood Cliffs, NJ: Prentice-Hall.

Emde, R. N. (1991). The wonder of our complex enterprise: Steps enabled by attachment and the effects of relationships on relationships. *Infant Mental Health Journal, 12,* 164–173.

Engle, G. L. (1980). The clinical application of the biopsychosocial model. *American Journal of Psychiatry, 137,* 535–544.

Erikson, E. H. (1950). *Children in society.* New York: Norton.

Erikson, E. H. (1968). *Identity: Youth and crisis.* New York: Norton.

Evoy, J. J. (1981). *The rejected: Psychological consequences of parental rejection.* University Park: Pennsylvania State University Press.

Eysenck, H. J. (1952). The effects of psychotherapy: An evaluation. *Journal of Consulting Psychology, 16,* 319–324.

Eysenck, H. J. (1982). *Personality, genetics, and behavior: Selected papers.* New York: Praeger.

Ezriel, H. (1952). Notes on psychoanalytic group therapy: Interpretation and research. *Psychiatry, 15,* 119–126.

Ezzell, C. (2003). The neuroscience of suicide. *Scientific American, 288,* 45–51.

Feigenbaum, M. (1980). Universal behavior in non-linear systems. *Los Alamos Science, 1,* 4–27.

Fenichel, O. (1945). *The psychoanalytic theory of neurosis.* New York: Norton.

Ferenczi, S. (1933). The confusion of tongues between adults and children: The language of tenderness and passion. In M. Balint (Ed.), *Final contributions to the problems and methods of psycho-analysis* (Vol. 3, pp. 156–167). New York: Brunner/Mazel.

Ferenczi, S., & Rank, O. (1925). *The development of psychoanalysis.* New York: Nervous and Mental Disease Publishing.

Festinger, L. (1957). *A theory of cognitive dissonance.* Stanford, CA: Stanford University Press.

Finger, S. (2000). *Minds behind the brain: A history of the pioneers and their discoveries.* New York: Oxford.

Firestone, R. W. (1997). *Combating destructive thought processes: Voice therapy and separation theory.* Thousand Oaks, CA: Sage.

Firestone, R. W. (2002). The death of psychoanalysis and depth therapy. *Psychotherapy, 39,* 223–232.

Florsheim, P., Henry, W. P., & Benjamin, L. S. (1996). Integrating individual and interpersonal approaches to diagnosis: The structural analysis of social behavior and attachment theory. In F. W. Kaslow (Ed.), *Handbook of relational diagnosis and dysfunctional patterns* (pp. 81–101). New York: Wiley.

Foa, E. B., & Meadows, E. A. (1997). Psychosocial treatments for post-traumatic stress disorder: A critical review. *Annual Review of Psychology, 48,* 449–480.

Fonagy, P., & Target, M. (2002). Psychodynamic approaches to child therapy. In F. W. Kaslow (Series Ed.) & J. J. Magnavita (Vol. Ed.), *Comprehensive handbook* of psychotherapy: Vol. 1: Psychodynamic/object relations (pp. 105–129). New York: Wiley.

Fosha, D. (1995). Technique and taboo in three short-term dynamic psychotherapies. Journal of Psychotherapy Practice and Research, 4, 297–318.

Fosha, D. (2000a). Meta-therapeutic processes and the affects of transformation: Affirmation and the healing affects. Journal of Psychotherapy Integration, 10, 71–97.

Fosha, D. (2000b). The transforming power of affect: A model for accelerated change. New York: Basic Books.

Fosha, D. (2001). The dyadic regulation of affect. Journal of Clinical Psychology/In session: Psychotherapy in Practice, 57(2), 227–242.

Fosha, D. (2002). The activation of affective change processes in accelerated experiential-dynamic therapy (AEDP). In F. W. Kaslow (Ser. Ed.) & J. J. Magnavita (Vol. Ed.), Comprehensive handbook of psychotherapy: Psychodynamic/object relations. (Vol. I, pp. 309–341). New York: Wiley.

Fowles, D. C. (2001). Biological variables in psychopathology: A psychobiological perspective. In H. A. Adams & P. B. Sutker (Eds.), Comprehensive handbook of psychopathology (3rd ed., pp. 85–104). New York: Kluwer Academic/Plenum.

Frances, A., Clarkin, J., & Perry, S. (1984). Differential therapeutics in psychiatry: The art and science of treatment selection. New York: Brunner/Mazel.

Frank, J. D. (1973). Persuasion and healing: A comparative study of psychotherapy. Baltimore, MD: Johns Hopkins University Press.

Frank, J. D., & Frank, J. B. (1991). Persuasion and healing: A comparative study of psychotherapy (3rd ed.). Baltimore, MD: Johns Hopkins University Press.

Frank, K. A. (1999). Psychoanalytic participation: Action, interaction, and integration. Hillsdale, NJ: Analytic Press.

Frank, K. A. (2002). The "ins and outs" of enactment: A relational bridge for psychotherapy integration. Journal of Psychotherapy Integration, 12, 267–286.

Freedheim, D. K. (Ed.). (1992). History of psychotherapy: A century of change. Washington, DC: American Psychological Association.

Freud, A. (1965). Normality and pathology in childhood. London: Penguin Press.

Freud, A. (1966). The ego and mechanisms of defense (rev. ed.). New York: International Universities Press.

Freud, S. (1939). Civilization and its discontents. London: Hogarth.

Freud, S. (1894). The neuro-psychoses of defence. In J. Strachey (Ed. & Trans.), The standard edition of the complete psychological works of Sigmund Freud (Vol. III, pp. 45–61). London: Hogarth Press.

Fromm, E. (1955). The sane society. New York: Holt, Rinehart and Winston.

Fromm, E. (1970). The crisis of psychoanalysis: Essays on Freud, Mark, and social psychology. New York: Holt, Rinehart & Winston.

Gabbard, G. O. (2001). Psychoanalysis and psychoanalytic psychotherapy. In W. J. Livesley (Ed.), Handbook of personality disorders: Theory, research, and treatment (pp. 359–376). New York: Guilford Press.

Gabbard, G. O. (2002). *The psychology of* The Sopranos: *Love, death, desire, and betrayal in America's favorite gangster family.* New York: Basic Books.

Gabbard, G. O., & Kay, J. (2001). The fate of integrated treatment: Whatever happened to the biopsychosocial psychiatrist? *American Journal of Psychiatry, 158,* 1956–1963.

Gardner, H. (1985). *The new mind's science: A history of the cognitive revolution.* New York: Basic Books.

Gerson, R. (1995). The family life cycle: Phases, stages, and crises. In R. H. Mikesell, D. Lusterman, & S. H. McDaniel (Eds.), *Integrating family therapy: Handbook of family psychology and systems theory* (pp. 91–111). Washington, DC: American Psychological Association.

Gleick, J. (1987). *Chaos: Making a new science.* New York: Viking/Penguin.

Glass, L., & Mackey, M. C. (1988). *From clocks to chaos.* Princeton, NJ: University Press.

Glick, I. D., & Loraas, E. L. (2001). Family treatment of borderline personality disorder. In M. M. MacFarlane (Ed.), *Family therapy and mental health: Innovations in theory and practice* (pp. 135–154). New York: Haworth Press.

Glickauf-Hughes, C., & Wells, M. (1995). *Treatment of the masochistic personality: An interactional–object relations approach to psychotherapy.* Northvale, NJ: Aronson.

Glickauf-Hughes, C., & Wells, M. (2002). Mastering developmental issues through interactional object-relations therapy. In F. W. Kaslow (Ser. Ed.) & J. J. Magnavita (Vol. Ed.), *Comprehensive handbook of psychotherapy: Psychodynamic/object relations* (Vol. I, pp. 283–307). New York: Wiley.

Goleman, D. (1995). *Emotional intelligence.* New York: Bantam Books.

Gordon, K. C., & Baucom, D. H. (1999). A multitheoretical intervention for promoting recovery from extramarital affairs. *Clinical Psychology: Science and Practice, 6,* 382–399.

Gould, S. J. (2002). *The structure of evolutionary theory.* Cambridge, MA: Belknap Press of Harvard University Press.

Greenberg, L. (2002). Integrating an emotion-focused approach to treatment into psychotherapy integration. *Journal of Psychotherapy Integration, 12,* 154–189.

Greenberg, J., & Mitchell, S. A. (1983). *Object relations in psychoanalytic theory.* Cambridge, MA: Harvard University Press.

Greenberg, L. S., & Paivio, S. C. (1997). *Working with emotions in psychotherapy.* New York: Guilford Press.

Greenberg, L. S., Rice, L. N., & Elliot, R. (1993). *Facilitating emotional change: The moment-by-moment process.* New York: Guilford Press.

Greenberg, L. S., & Safran, J. D. (1987). *Emotion in psychotherapy.* New York: Guilford Press.

Greene, R. W., Biederman, J., Zerwas, S., Monuteaux, M. C., Goring, J. C., & Faraone, S. V. (2002). Psychiatric comorbidity, family dysfunction, and social impairment in referred youth with oppositional defiant disorder. *American Journal of Psychiatry, 159,* 1214–1224.

Greenspan, S. I. (1997a). *Developmentally based psychotherapy*. New York: International Universities Press.

Greenspan, S. I. (1997b). *The growth of the mind and the endangered growth of intelligence*. Reading, MA: Perseus Books.

Greenspan, S. I. (2002). The developmental basis of the psychotherapeutic process. In F. K. Kaslow (Series Ed.) & J. J. Magnavita (Vol. Ed.), *Comprehensive handbook of psychotherapy: Vol. 1: Psychodynamic/object relations* (pp. 15–45). New York: Wiley.

Grigsby, J., & Stevens, D. (2000). *Neurodynamics of personality*. New York: Guilford Press.

Grossman, R. (2004). Psychopharmacotherapy of personality disorders. In J. J. Magnavita (Ed.), *Handbook of personality disorders* (pp. 331–335). Hoboken, NJ: Wiley.

Grotevant, H. D., & Carlson, C. I. (1989). *Family assessment: A guide to methods & measures*. New York: Guilford Press.

Groves, J. E. (1992). The short-term dynamic therapies: An overview. In J. S. Rutan (Ed.), *Psychotherapy for the 1990s* (pp. 35–59). New York: Guilford Press.

Guerin, P. J., & Chabot, D. R. (1997). Development of family systems theory. In D. K. Freedheim (Ed.), *History of psychotherapy: A century of change* (pp. 225–260). Washington, DC: American Psychological Association.

Guerin, P. J., Fogarty, T. F., Fay, L. F., & Kautto, J. G. (1996). *Working with relational triangles: The one-two-three of psychotherapy*. New York: Guilford Press.

Gurman, A. (1992). Integrative marital therapy: A time-sensitive model for working with couples. In S. Budman, M. F. Hoyt, & S. Friedman (Eds.), *The first session in brief therapy* (pp. 186–203). New York: Guilford Press.

Gurman, A. S., & Kniskern, D. P. (Eds.). (1981). *Handbook of family therapy*. New York: Brunner/Mazel.

Gurman, P. J., & Chabot, D. R. (1992). Development of family systems theory. In D. K. Freedheim (Ed.), *History of psychotherapy: A century of change*. Washington, DC: American Psychological Association.

Haley, J. (1963). *Strategies of psychotherapy*. New York: Grune & Stratton.

Haley, J. (1977). Toward a theory of pathological systems. In P. Watzlwick & J. H. Weakland (Eds.), *The interactional view* (pp. 31–55). New York: W. W. Norton.

Haley, J. (1987). *Problem-solving therapy* (2nd ed.). San Francisco: Jossey-Bass.

Hamberger, L. K., & Hastings, J. E. (1986). Personality correlates of men who abuse their partners: A cross validation study. *Journal of Family Violence, 1*, 323–340.

Hammer, W. (1990). *Reaching the affect: Style in psychodynamic therapies*. New Jersey: Aronson.

Harlow, H. F., & Harlow, M. K. (1962). Social deprivation in monkeys. *Scientific American, 203*, 136–146.

Harman, M. J., & Waldo, M. (2001). Family treatment of borderline personality disorder through relationship enhancement therapy. In M. M. MacFarlane

(Ed.), *Family therapy and mental health: Innovations in theory and practice* (pp. 135–154). New York: Haworth Press.

Hartmann, H. (1958). *Ego psychology and the problem of adaptation*. New York: International University Press.

Hartmann, H. (1964). *Essays on ego psychology: Selected problems in psychoanalytic theory*. New York: International Universities Press.

Havens, L. (2002). Foreword. In F. W. Kaslow (Editor-in-Chief) & J. J. Magnavita (Ed.), *Comprehensive handbook of psychotherapy: Vol. 1. Psychodynamic object relations* (pp. xi–xii). Hoboken, NJ: John Wiley & Sons.

Hayden, E. P., & Klein, D. N. (2001). Outcome of dysthymic disorder at 5-year follow-up: The effect of family psychopathology, early adversity, personality, comorbidity, and chronic stress. *American Journal of Psychiatry, 158*(16), 1864–1870.

Heider, F. (1958). *The psychology of interpersonal relations*. New York: Wiley.

Heim, C., Meinlschmidt, G., & Nemeroff, C. B. (2003). Neurobiology of early-life stress. *Psychiatric Annals, 33*, 18–26.

Herman, J. L. (1992). *Trauma and recovery*. New York: Basic Books.

Hetherington, E. M. (Ed.). (1998). Special issue: Applications of developmental science. *American Psychologist, 53*, 89–272.

Hinde, R. A. (1979). *Towards understanding relationships*. New York: Academic Press.

Hobson, J. A., & Leonard, J. A. (2001). *Out of its mind: Psychiatry in crisis*. Cambridge, MA: Perseus.

Hoffman, L. (1981). Foundations of family therapy: A conceptual framework for systems change. New York: Basic Books.

Horner, A. J. (Ed.). (1994). *Treating the neurotic patient in brief psychotherapy*. Northvale, NJ: Aronson.

Horner, A. J. (1995). *Psychoanalytic object relations therapy*. Northvale, NJ: Aronson.

Hunt, M. (1993). *The story of psychology*. New York: Doubleday.

Izard, C. (1994). Intersystem connections. In P. Ekman & R. J. Davidson (Eds.), *The nature of emotions: Fundamental questions* (pp. 356–361). New York: Oxford University Press.

Jackson, D. D. (1977). The study of the family. In P. Watzlawick & J. H. Weakland (Eds.), *The interactional view: Studies at the Mental Research Institute, Palo Alto, 1965–1974* (pp. 2–20). New York: Norton.

Jackson, S. W. (1999). *Care of the psyche: A history of psychological healing*. New Haven, CT: Yale University Press.

Jacobson, N. S., & Christensen, A. (1996). *Integrative couples therapy*. New York: Norton.

Jacobson, N. S., & Gurman, A. (Eds.). (2002). *Clinical handbook of couple therapy* (3rd ed.). New York: Guilford Press.

James, W. (1890). *The principles of psychology* (Vols. I & II). New York: Holt.

Jantsch, E., & Waddington, C. H. (1976). (Eds.). *Evolution and consciousness: Human systems in transition*. Reading, MA: Addison-Wesley.

Jensen, P. S., & Hoagwood, K. (1997). The book of names: *DSM–IV* in context. *Development and Psychopathology, 9,* 231–250.

Johnson, S. (2003). The brain and emotions. *Discover, 24,* 33–39.

Johnson, S. M., & Greenberg, L. S. (1995). The emotionally-focused approach to problems in adult attachment. In N. S. Jacobson & A. S. Gurman (Eds.), *Clinical handbook of couple therapy* (pp. 121–141). New York: Guilford Press.

Johnson, S. M. (1999). Emotional focused couple therapy: Straight to the heart. In J. M. Donovan (Ed.), *Short-term couple therapy* (pp. 13–42). New York: Guilford Press.

Johnson, S. M., & Whiffen, V. E. (1999). Made to measure: Adapting emotionally focused couple therapy to partners' attachment styles. *Clinical Psychology: Science and Practice, 6,* 366–381.

Joines, V., & Stewart, I. (2002). *Personality adaptations: A new guide to human understanding in psychotherapy and counseling*. Chapel Hill, NC: Lifespace.

Jones, C. W., & Lindblad-Goldberg, M. (2002). Ecosystemic structural family therapy. In F. W. Kaslow (Series Ed.), R. F. Massey, & S. D. Massey (Vol. Eds.), *Comprehensive handbook of psychotherapy: Interpersonal/humanistic/existential* (Vol. 3, pp. 3–33). New York: Wiley.

Jordan, J. V. (Ed.). (1997). *Women's growth in diversity*. New York: Guilford Press.

Jordan, J. V. (2004). Personality disorder or relational disconnection? In J. J. Magnavita (Ed.), *Handbook of personality disorders: Theory and practice* (pp. 120–134). Hoboken, NJ: Wiley.

Kahn, M. D. (1986). The self and the system: Integrating Kohut and Milan. In S. Sugarman (Ed.), *The interface of individual and family therapy* (pp. 50–64). Rockville, MD: Aspen

Kandel, E. R. (1998). A new intellectual framework for psychiatry. *American Journal of Psychiatry, 155,* 457–469.

Karasu, T. B. (1986). The specificity versus nonspecificity dilemma: Toward identifying therapeutic change agents. *American Journal of Psychiatry, 143,* 687–695.

Kaslow, F. W. (Ed.). (1996). *Handbook of relational diagnosis and dysfunctional family patterns*. New York: Wiley.

Kaslow, F. W. (Ed.). (2002). *Comprehensive handbook of psychotherapy* (Vols. 1–4). Hoboken, NJ: John Wiley & Sons.

Kelley, H. H., Berscheid, E., Christensen, A., Harvey, J. H., & Huston, T. L. (1983). *Close relationships*. New York: Freeman.

Kendell, R. E. (1988). Book review: American Psychiatric Association: Diagnostic and Statistical Manual of Mental Disorders, 3rd Edition, Revised (*DSM–III-R*). *American Journal of Psychiatry, 145,* 1301–1302.

Kendler, K. S., Gardner, C. O., & Prescott, C. A. (2002). Toward a comprehensive developmental model for depression in women. *American Journal of Psychiatry, 159,* 1133–1145.

Kernberg, O. (1974). Barriers to falling and remaining in love. *Journal of American Psychoanalytic Association, 22,* 486–511.

Kernberg, P. F., Weiner, A. S., & Bardenstein, K. K. (2000). *Personality disorders in children and adolescents.* New York: Basic Books.

Kerr, M. E. (1981). Family systems theory and therapy. In A. S. Gurman & D. P. Kniskern (Eds.), *Handbook of family therapy* (pp. 226–264). New York: Brunner/Mazel.

Kiesler, D. J. (1966). Some myths of psychotherapy research and the search for a paradigm. *Psychological Bulletin, 65,* 110–136.

Kiesler, D. J. (1982). Confronting the client–therapist relationship in psychotherapy. In J. C. Anchin & D. J. Kiesler (Eds.), *Handbook of interpersonal psychotherapy* (pp. 274–295). New York: Pergamon Press.

Kiesler, D. J. (1983). The 1982 interpersonal circle: A taxonomy for complementarity in human transactions. *Psychological Review, 90,* 185–214.

Kiesler, D. J. (1988). Therapeutic metacommunication: Therapist impact disclosure as feedback in psychotherapy. Palo Alto, CA: Consulting Psychologist Press.

Kiesler, D. J. (1996). *Contemporary interpersonal theory and research: Personality, psychopathology, and psychotherapy.* New York: Wiley.

King, B. J. (2002). *Biological anthropology: An evolutionary perspective, Parts I & II* (Lecture series). Chantilly, VA: Teaching Company.

Klein, D. F. (1967). The importance of psychiatric diagnosis in prediction of critical drug effects. *Archives of General Psychiatric, 16,* 118–126.

Klein, D. F. (1970). Psychotropic drugs and the regulation of behavior at activation in psychiatric illness. In W. L. Smith (Ed.), *Drugs and cerebral function.* Springfield, IL: Thomas.

Klein, M. (1964). *A contribution to the psychogenesis of manic–depressive states. Contributions to psychoanalysis, 1921–1925* (M. Klein, Ed.). New York: McGraw-Hill. (Original work published 1935)

Klerman, G. L., Weissman, M. M., Rounsaville, B. J., & Chevron, E. S. (1984). Interpersonal Psychotherapy of Depression. New York: Basic Books.

Kohut, H. (1971). *The analysis of the self.* New York: International Universities Press.

Kohut, H. (1977). *The restoration of the self.* New York: International Universities Press.

Kohut, H. (1984). *How does analysis cure?* Chicago: University of Chicago Press.

Kramer, P. D. (1993). *Listening to Prozac: A psychiatrist explores antidepressant drugs and the remaking of the self.* New York: Viking/Penguin Books

Krystal, H. (1988). *Integration and self-healing: Affect—trauma—alexithymia.* Hillsdale, NJ: Analytic Press.

Kuhn, T. S. (1996). *The structure of scientific revolutions* (2nd ed.). Chicago: University of Chicago Press. (Original work published 1970)

L'Abate, L. (1986). *Systemic family therapy.* New York: Brunner/Mazel.

Lachkar, J. (1992). *The narcissistic/borderline couple: A psychoanalytic perspective to marital conflict.* New York: Brunner/Mazel.

Lachkar, J. (1998). Narcissistic/borderline couples: A psychodynamic approach to conjoint treatment. In J. Carlson & L. Sperry (Eds.), *The disordered couple* (pp. 259–284). Bristol, PA: Brunner/Mazel.

Lachkar, J. (2004). *The narcissistic/borderline couple: New approaches to marital therapy* (2nd ed.). New York: Brunner-Routledge.

Lazarus, A. A. (1973). Multimodal behavior therapy; Treating the "BASIC ID." *Journal of Nervous and Mental Disease, 140,* 80–86.

Lazarus, A. A. (1981). *The practice of multimodal therapy: Systematic, comprehensive, and effective psychotherapy.* New York: McGraw-Hill.

Lazarus, R. S. (1991). *Emotion and adaptation.* New York: Oxford University Press.

Leary, T. (1957). *Interpersonal diagnosis of personality: A functional theory and methodology for personality evaluation.* New York: Ronald Press.

LeDoux, J. E. (1995). Emotion: Clues from the brain. *Annual Review of Psychology, 46,* 209–227.

Lee, F. R. (2002, November 30). Why are black students lagging? A new theory in a thorny debate points to the minorities themselves. *New York Times,* p. B9.

Lerner, R. M. (1998). Theories of human development: Contemporary perspectives. In W. Damon (Series Ed.) & R. M. Lerner (Vol. Ed.), *Handbook of child psychology* (5th ed., Vol. 1, pp. 1–24). New York: Wiley.

Levant, R. E. (1997). Nonrelational sexuality in men. In R. F. Levant & G. R. Brooks (Eds.), *Men and sex: New psychological perspectives* (pp. 9–27). New York: Guilford Press.

Levenson, H. (1995). *Time-limited dynamic psychotherapy: A guide to clinical practice.* New York: Basic Books.

Levenson, H. (2003). Time-limited dynamic therapy. An integrationist's perspective. *Journal of Psychotherapy Integration, 13,* 300–333.

Levenson, H. (2004). Time-limited dynamic therapy. In J. J. Magnavita (Ed.), *Handbook of personality disorders: Theory and practice* (pp. 254–279). Hoboken, NJ: Wiley.

Levinson, D. J., Darrow, C. N., Klein, E. B., Levinson, M. H., & McKee, B. (1978). *The seasons of a man's life.* New York: Knopf.

Levine, M. P., Piran, N., & Irving, L. M. (2001). Disordered eating behavior in adolescents. In T. Gullotta & M. Bloom (Eds.), *The encyclopedia of primary prevention and health promotion.* New York: Kluwer Academic/Plenum Publishers.

Lewin, K. (1935). *A dynamic theory of personality.* New York: McGraw-Hill.

Linehan, M. M. (1993). *Cognitive–behavioral treatment of borderline personality disorder.* New York: Guilford Press.

Luhrmann, T. M. (2000). *Of two minds: The growing disorder in American psychiatry.* New York: Knopf.

Lusterman, D. (1995). Treating marital infidelity. In R. H. Mikesell, D. Lusterman, & S. H. McDaniel (Eds.), *Integrating family therapy: Handbook of family psychology and systems theory* (pp. 259–269). Washington, DC: American Psychological Association.

Lynn, D. J., & Vaillant, G. E. (1998). Anonymity, neutrality, and confidentiality in the actual methods of Sigmund Freud: A review of 43 cases, 1907–1939. *American Journal of Psychiatry, 155*(2), 163–171.

Lyons-Ruth, K., & Zeanah, C. H. (1993). The family context of infant mental health: I. Affective development in the primary caregiver relationship. In C. H. Zeanah, Jr. (Ed.), *Handbook of infant mental health* (pp. 14–37). New York: Guilford Press.

Maccoby, E., & Martin, J. (1983). Socialization in context of the family: Parent–child interaction. In E. M. Hetherington (Ed.), *Handbook of child psychology: Vol. 4. Socialization, personality, and social development* (4th ed., pp. 1–101). New York: John Wiley & Sons.

Maddi, S. R. (1963). Humanistic psychology: Allport and Murray. In J. W. Wepman & R. W. Heine (Eds.), *Concepts of personality* (pp. 162–205). Chicago: Aldine.

Magnavita, J. J. (1993a). The evolution of short-term dynamic psychotherapy: Treatment of the future? *Professional Psychology: Research and Practice, 24,* 360–365.

Magnavita, J. J. (1993b). The treatment of passive-aggressive personality disorder. Part I. *International Journal of Short-Term Psychotherapy, 8,* 29–41.

Magnavita, J. J. (1997a). *Restructuring personality disorders: A short-term dynamic approach.* New York: Guilford Press.

Magnavita, J. J. (1997b). Accelerated methods for treating personality disorders: Upgrading your clinical toolbox. *Psychotherapy in Private Practice, 16,* 17–34.

Magnavita, J. J. (1997c). Treating personality disorders: Psychotherapy's frontier. *Psychotherapy Bulletin, 32,* 23–28.

Magnavita, J. J. (1998a). Challenges in the treatment of personality disorders: When the disorder demands comprehensive treatment. *In Session: Psychotherapy in Practice, 4,* 5–17.

Magnavita, J. J. (1998b). Introduction: Advancements in the treatment of personality disorder: Special edition. *In Session: Psychotherapy in Practice, 4*(4), 1–4.

Magnavita, J. J. (1998c). Methods of restructuring personality disorders with comorbid syndromes. *In Session: Psychotherapy in Practice, 4*(4), 73-89.

Magnavita, J. J. (2000a). *Relational therapy for personality disorders.* New York: Wiley.

Magnavita, J. J. (2000b). Introduction: The growth of relational therapy. *Journal of Clinical Psychology/In Session: Psychotherapy in Practice, 56,* 999–1004.

Magnavita, J. J. (2000c). Integrative relational therapy of complex clinical syndromes: Ending the multigenerational transmission process. *Journal of Clinical Psychology/In Session: Psychotherapy in Practice, 56,* 1051–1064.

Magnavita, J. J. (2001a). Affirmation and active defense restructuring: Accelerating access to the unconscious. *Quaderni di Psichiatria, 6*(17/18), 77–79.

Magnavita, J. J. (2001b). Restructuring personality disorders to metabolize affect associated with trauma. *Quaderni di Psichiatria*, 6(17/18), 149–156.

Magnavita, J. J. (2002a). *Theories of personality: Contemporary approaches to the science of personality*. New York: John Wiley & Sons.

Magnavita, J. J. (2002b). Psychodynamic approaches to psychotherapy: A century of innovations. In F. W. Kaslow (Series Ed.) & J. J. Magnavita (Vol. Ed.), *Comprehensive handbook of psychotherapy: Volume 1: Psychodynamic/object relations* (pp. 1–12). New York: Wiley.

Magnavita, J. J. (2002c). Relational psychodynamics for complex clinical syndromes. In F. W. Kaslow (Ser. Ed.) & J. J. Magnavita (Vol. Ed.), *Comprehensive handbook of psychotherapy: Volume 1: Psychodynamic/object relations* (pp. 435–453). New York: Wiley.

Magnavita, J. J. (2002d). Contemporary psychodynamics: Major issues, challenges, and future trends. In F. W. Kaslow (Ser. Ed.) & J. J. Magnavita (Vol. Ed.), *Comprehensive handbook of psychotherapy: Volume 1: Psychodynamic/object relations* (pp. 587–604). New York: Wiley.

Magnavita, J. J. (2002e). *Comprehensive handbook of psychotherapy: Psychodynamic/object relations* (Vol. 1). Hoboken, NJ: John Wiley & Sons.

Magnavita, J. J. (2004a). Classification, prevalence, and etiology of personality disorders: Related issues and controversies. In J. J. Magnavita (Ed.), *Handbook of personality disorders: Theory and practice* (pp. 3–23). Hoboken, NJ: Wiley.

Magnavita, J. J. (2004b). The relevance of theory in treating personality disorders. In J. J. Magnavita (Ed.), *Handbook of personality disorders: Theory and practice* (pp. 56–75). Hoboken, NJ: Wiley.

Magnavita, J. J. (2004c). Toward a unified model of treating personality dysfunction. In J. J. Magnavita (Ed.), *Handbook of personality disorders: Theory and practice* (pp. 528–553). Hoboken, NJ: Wiley.

Magnavita, J. J. (2004d). *Handbook of personality disorders: Theories and practice*. Hoboken, NJ: John Wiley & Sons.

Magnavita, J. J., & MacFarlane, M. (2004e). Family treatment of personality disorders: Historical overview and current perspectives (pp. 3–39). In M. MacFarlane (Ed.), *Family treatment of personality disorders: Advances in clinical practice*. Binghamton, NY: Haworth Press

Magnavita, J. J. (in press-a). Systems theory foundation of personality disorders: Components of a unification paradigm. In S. Strack (Ed.), *Handbook of personology and psychopathology*. Hoboken, NJ: Wiley.

Magnavita, J. J. (in press-b). The Millon Multiaxial Inventory in clinical practice: Enhancing clinical efficacy. In R. J. Craig (Ed.), *New directions in interpreting the Millon Clinical Multiaxial Inventory (MCMI): Essays on current issues*. Hoboken, NJ: John Wiley & Sons.

Mahler, M. S. (1968). *On human symbiosis and the vicissitudes of individuation*. New York: International Universities Press.

Mahler, M. S., Pine, F., & Bergman, A. (1975). *The psychological birth of the human infant: Symbiosis and individuation*. New York: Basic Books.

Mahoney, M. J. (1991). *Human change processes: The scientific foundations of psychotherapy*. New York: Basic Books.

Main, M., & Cassidy, J. (1988). Categories of response to reunion with the parent at age 6: Predictable from infant attachment classifications and stable over a 1-month period. *Developmental Psychology, 24*, 415–426.

Main, M., & Goldwyn, R. (1985). *An adult attachment classification system*. Unpublished manuscript, University of California Department of Psychology, Berkeley.

Main, M., & Morgan, H. (1996). Disorganization and disorientation in infant Strange Situation behavior: Phenotypic resemblance to dissociative states. In L. K. Michelson & W. J. Ray (Eds.), *Handbook of dissociation: Theoretical, empirical, and clinical perspectives* (pp. 107–138). New York: Plenum Press.

Malan, D. H. (1979). Individual psychotherapy and the science of psychodynamics. London: Butterworth.

Maruyama, M. (1963). The second cybernetics: Deviation-amplifying mutual causal processes, *American Scientist, 51*, 164–179.

Mashek, D. J., & Aron, A. (Eds.). (2004). *Handbook of closeness and intimacy*. New York: Lawrence Erlbaum Associates.

Maslow, A. H. (1962). *Toward a psychology of being*. New York: Van Nostrad.

Masterson, J. F. (1988). *The search for the real self: Unmasking the personality disorders of our age*. New York: Free Press.

May, R. (1953). *Man's search for himself*. New York: Signet.

Mayne, T. J., & Bonanno, G. A. (Eds.). (2001). *Emotions: Current issues and future directions*. New York: Wiley.

Mayne, T. J., & Ramsey, J. (2001). The structure of emotion: A nonlinear dynamic systems approach. In T. J. Mayne, & G. A. Bonanno (Eds.), *Emotions: Current issues and future perspectives* (pp. 1–37). New York: Guilford Press.

McCullough, L. (1998). Short-term psychodynamic therapy as a form of desensitization: Treating affect phobias. *In Session: Psychotherapy in Practice, 4*, 35–53.

McCullough Vaillant, L. (1997). *Changing character: Short-term anxiety regulating psychotherapy for restructuring of defenses, affects, and attachments*. New York: Basic Books.

McDermott, J. J. (Ed.). (1981). *The philosophy of John Dewey* (Vols. I and II). Chicago: University of Chicago Press.

McGoldrick, M., & Gerson, R. (1985). *Genograms in family assessment*. New York: Norton.

McWilliams, N. (1994). *Psychoanalytic diagnosis: Understanding personality structure in clinical practice*. New York: Guilford Press.

Meissner, W. W. (1978). The conceptualization of marriage and family dynamics from a psychoanalytic perspective. In T. J. Paolino & B. S. McCrady (Eds.), *Marriage and marital therapy: Psychoanalytic, behavioral and systems theory perspectives* (pp. 25–88). New York: Brunner/Mazel.

Meissner, W. W. (1981). Meissner's glossary of defenses. In H. I. Kaplan & B. J. Sadock (Eds.), *Modern synopsis of comprehensive textbook of psychiatry* (3rd ed., pp. 137–138). Baltimore: Williams & Williams.

Menninger, K. (1958). *Theory of psychoanalytic technique.* New York: Basic Books.

Menninger, K., Mayman, M., & Pruyser, P. (1963). *The vital balance.* New York: Viking Press.

Messer, S. B. (1988). Philosophical obstacles to unification of psychology. *International Newsletter of Uninomic Psychology, 5,* 22–24.

Messer, S. B., & Wampold, B. E. (2002). Let's face facts: Common factors are more potent than specific therapy ingredients. *Clinical Psychology: Science and Practice, 9,* 21–25

Metzinger, T. (Ed.). (2000). *Neural correlates of consciousness.* Cambridge, MA: MIT Press.

Mikesell, R. H., Lusterman, D. D., & McDaniel, S. H. (Eds.). (1995). *Integrating family therapy: Handbook of family psychology and systems theory.* Washington, DC: American Psychological Association.

Miller, W. R., & C'deBaca, J. (1994). Quantum change: Toward a psychology of transformation. In T. F. Heatherton & J. L. Weinberger (Eds.), *Can personality change?* (pp. 253–280). Washington, DC: American Psychological Association.

Millon, T. (1981). *Disorders of personality: DSM–III: Axis II.* New York: Wiley.

Millon, T. (1985). *Modern psychopathology.* Prospect Heights, IL: Waveland Press. (Original work published 1969)

Millon, T. (1990). *Toward a new personology: An evolutionary model.* New York: Wiley-Interscience.

Millon, T. (2004). *Masters of the mind: Exploring the story of mental illness from ancient times to the new millennium.* Hoboken, NJ: John Wiley & Sons.

Millon, T., Blaney, P. H., & Davis, R. D. (1999). *Oxford textbook of psychopathology.* New York: Oxford University Press.

Millon, T., & Davis, R. (1996). *Disorders of personality: DSM–IV and beyond.* New York: Wiley.

Millon, T., & Davis, R. D. (1999). Developmental pathogenesis. In T. Millon, P. H. Blaney, & R. D. Davis (Eds.), *Oxford textbook of psychopathology* (pp. 29–48). New York: Oxford University Press.

Millon, T., Davis, R., Millon, C., Escovar, L., & Meagher, S. (2000). *Personality disorders in modern life.* New York: Wiley.

Millon, T., Grossman, S., Meagher, S., Millon, C., & Everly, G. (1999). *Personality-guided therapy.* New York: Wiley.

Minuchin, S. (1974). *Families and family therapy.* Cambridge, MA: Harvard University Press.

Mischel, W., & Shoda, Y. (1995). A cognitive-affective system theory of personality: Reconceptualizing situations, dispositions, dynamics, and invariance in personality structure. *Psychological Review, 102,* 246–268.

Mitchell, S. A. (1988). *Relational concepts in psychoanalysis: An integration.* Cambridge, MA: Harvard University Press.

Mitchell, S. A. (1993). *Hope and dread in psychoanalysis.* New York: Basic Books.

Monroe, S. M., & Simons, A. D. (1991). Diathesis–stress theories in the context of life stress research. *Psychological Bulletin, 110,* 406–425.

Moss, H. B., Lynch, K. G., Hardie, T. L., & Baron, D. A. (2002). Family functioning and peer affiliation in children of fathers with antisocial personality disorder and substance dependence: Associations with problem behaviors. *American Journal of Psychiatry, 159,* 607–614.

Muran, J. C., & Safran, J. D. (2002). A relational approach to psychotherapy. In F. W. Kaslow (Series Ed.) & J. J. Magnavita (Vol. Ed.), *Comprehensive handbook of psychotherapy: Psychodynamic/object relations* (Vol. I, pp. 253–281). New York: Wiley.

Murphy, G. (1947). *Personality: A biosocial approach to the origins and structure.* New York: Harper & Brothers.

Murray, H. A. (1938). Explorations in personality. New York: Oxford University Press.

Murray, H. A. (1959). Preparations for the scaffold of a comprehensive system. In S. Koch (Ed.), *Psychology: A study of a science* (Vol. 3). New York: McGraw-Hill.

Narrow, W. E., Regier, D. A., Rae, D. S., Manderscheid, R. W., & Locker, B. Z. (1993). Use of services by persons with mental and addictive disorders: Findings from the National Institute of Mental Health Epidemiologic Catchment Area Program. *Archives of General Psychiatry, 50,* 95–107.

Neborsky, R. J., & Solomon, M. F. (2001). Attachment bonds and intimacy: Can the primary imprint of love change? In M. F. Solomon, R. J. Neborsky, L. McCullough, M. Alpert, F. Shapiro, & D. Malan (Eds.), *Short-term therapy for long-term change* (pp. 155–185). New York: Norton.

Nemeroff, C. B. (1998). The neurobiology of depression. *Scientific American, 278,* 42–49.

Nemiroff, R. A., & Colarusso, C. A. (Eds.). (1990). *New dimensions in adult development.* New York: Basic Books.

Nichols, W. C. (1988). *Marital therapy: An integrative approach.* New York: Guilford Press.

Norcross, J. C. (Ed.). (2002). *Psychotherapy relationships that work.* New York: Oxford University Press.

Norcross, J. C., & Goldfried, M. R. (Eds.). (1992). *Handbook of psychotherapy integration.* New York: Basic Books.

Ogbu, J. U. (2003). *Black students in an affluent suburb: A study of academic disengagement.* New York: Lawrence Erlbaum Associates.

O'Leary, K. D. (1999). Developmental and affective issues in assessing and treating partner aggression. *Clinical Psychology: Science and Practice, 6,* 400–414.

Olson, D. H. (1996). Clinical assessment of treatment interventions using the family circumplex model. In F. W. Kaslow (Ed.), *Handbook of relational diagnosis and dysfunctional family patterns* (pp. 59–101). New York: Wiley.

Omer, H., Winch, G., & Dar, R. (1998). Therapeutic impact in treatments for smoking and test taking. *Psychotherapy Research, 8,* 439–454.

Paolino, T. J., & McCrady, B. S. (1978). *Marriage and marital therapy: Psychoanalytic, behavioral and systems theory perspectives.* New York: Brunner/Mazel.

Paris, J. (1999). A diathesis–stress model of personality disorders. *Psychiatric Annals, 29,* 692–697.

Patterson, T. (Ed.). (2003). *Comprehensive handbook of psychotherapy: Cognitive-behavioral approaches* (Vol. 2). Hoboken, NJ: Wiley.

Paul, G. (1967). Strategy of outcome research in psychotherapy. *Journal of Consulting Psychology, 31,* 109–118.

Pawl, J. H., & St. John, M. (2002). Infant mental health. In F. Kaslow (Series Ed.) & J. J. Magnavita (Vol. Ed.), *Comprehensive handbook of psychotherapy. Vol. 1: Psychodynamic/object relations* (pp. 81–104). New York: Wiley.

Perlmutter, R. A. (1996). *A family approach to psychiatric disorders.* Washington, DC: American Psychiatric Press.

Perls, F. S. (1969). *Gestalt therapy verbatim.* Lafayette, CA: Real People Press.

Perry, H. S. (1982). *Psychiatrist of America: The life of Harry Stack Sullivan.* Cambridge, MA: Belknap Press of Harvard University Press.

Perry, J. C., & Cooper, S. H. (1989). An empirical study of defense mechanisms. *Archives of General Psychiatry, 46,* 444–452.

Pilkonis, P. (1988). Personality prototypes among depressives: Themes of dependency and autonomy. *Journal of Personality Disorders, 2,* 144–152.

Pine, F. (1985). *Developmental theory and clinical progress.* New Haven, CT: Yale University Press.

Pinsof, W. M. (1995). *Integrative problem-centered therapy: A synthesis of family, individual, and biological therapies.* New York: Basic Books.

Pipher, M. (2002). *The middle of everywhere: The world's refugees come to our town.* New York: Harcourt.

Plutchik, R. (1980). *Emotion: A psychoevolutionary synthesis.* New York: Harper & Row.

Plutchik, R. (2000). *Emotions in the practice of psychotherapy: Clinical implications of affect theories.* Washington, DC: American Psychological Association.

Portney, C. (2003). Intergenerational transmission of trauma: An introduction for the clinician. *Psychiatric Times, XX*(4), 38–40.

Prochaska, J. O., DiClemente, C. C., & Norcross, J. C. (1992). In search of how people change: Applications to addictive behaviors. *American Psychologist, 47,* 1102–1114.

Rachman, A. W. (1997). *Sandor Ferenczi: The psychotherapist of tenderness and passion.* Northvale, NJ: Aronson.

Rangell, L. (2002). The theory of psychoanalysis: Vicissitudes of its evolution. *Journal of the American Psychoanalytic Association, 50,* 1109–1137.

Rangell, L. (1997). Into the second psychoanalytic century: One psychoanalysis or many? The unitary theory of Leo Rangell, MD. *Journal of Clinical Psychoanalysis, 6,* 451–612.

Rayner, E. (1991). *The independent mind in British psychoanalysis.* Northvale, NJ: Jason Aronson.

Rea, M. M., Tompson, M. C., Miklowitz, D. J., Goldstein, M. J., Hwang, S., & Minz, J. (2003). Family-focused treatment versus individual treatment for bipolar disorder: Results of a randomized clinical trial. *Journal of Consulting and Clinical Psychology, 71,* 482–492.

Reich, W. (1933). *Character analysis.* Leipzig: Verlag.

Rennie, J. (Ed.). (2004). The brain: A look inside [Special issue]. *Scientific American, 14*(1).

Rogers, C. (1951). *Client-centered therapy.* Boston: Houghton Mifflin.

Rogers, C., Perls, F., & Ellis, A. (1965). *Three approaches to psychotherapy: A therapeutic interview with Gloria* [Video]. Corona Del Mar, CA: Psychological & Educational Films.

Roth, G., & Wullimann, M. F. (2000). *Brain evolution and cognition.* Hoboken, NJ: Wiley.

Rottenberg, J., & Gross, J. J. (2003). When emotion goes wrong: Realizing the promise of affective science. *Clinical Psychology: Science and Practice, 10,* 227–232.

Rotter, J. B. (1954). *Social learning and clinical psychology.* Englewood Cliffs, NJ: Prentice-Hall.

Rotter, J. B., Chance, J. E., & Phares, E. J. (1972). *Applications of a social learning theory of personality.* New York: Holt, Rinehart and Winston, Inc.

Royce, J. R. (1987). A strategy for developing unifying theory in psychology. In A. W. Staats & L. P. Mos (Eds.), *Annals of theoretical psychology* (Vol. 5, pp. 11–54). Plenum.

Rychlak, J. F. (1973). *Introduction to personality and psychotherapy: A theory-construction approach.* Boston: Houghton Mifflin.

Safran, J. D., & Muran, J. C. (2000). *Negotiating the therapeutic alliance: A relational treatment guide.* New York: Guilford Press.

Sameroff, A. J. (1993). Models of development and developmental risk. In C. H. Zeanah, Jr. (Ed.), *Handbook of infant mental health* (pp. 3–37). New York: Guilford Press.

Sameroff, A. J., & Chandler, M. J. (1975). Reproductive risk and the continuum of caretaking casualty. In F. D. Horowitz, E. M. Hetherington, S. Scarr-Salapatek, & G. Siegel (Eds.), *Review of child development research* (Vol. 4, pp. 187–244). Chicago: University of Chicago.

Sapir, E. (1963). *Selected writings of Edward Sapir in language, culture, and personality* (D. G. Mandelbaum, Ed.). Berkeley: University of California Press.

Satir, V. (1967). *Conjoint family therapy*. Palo Alto, CA: Science and Behavior Books.

Satir, V. (1972). *Peoplemaking*. Palo Alto, CA: Science and Behavior Books.

Scharff, D. E., & Scharff, J. S. (1991). *Object relations family therapy*. Northvale, NJ: Aronson.

Schlosser, E. (2001). *Fast food nation: The darkside of the all-American meal*. New York: Houghton Mifflin.

Schnarch, D. M. (1991). *Constructing the sexual crucible: An integration of sexual and marital therapy*. New York: Norton.

Schuldberg, D., & Gottlieb, J. (2002). Dynamics and correlates of microscopic changes in affect. *Nonlinear Dynamics, Psychology, and Life Sciences, 6*, 231–257.

Seligman, M. E. P. (1975). *Helplessness: On depression, development, and death*. San Francisco: Freeman.

Shapiro, F. (1995). *Eye movement desensitization and reprocessing (EMDR): Basic principles, protocols and procedures*. New York: Guilford Press.

Shapiro, F. (2001). Trauma and adaptive information-processing: EMDR's dynamic and behavioral interface. In M. F. Solomon, R. J. Neborsky, L. McCullough, M. Alpert, F. Shapiro, & D. Malan (Eds.), *Short-term therapy for long-term change* (pp. 12–129). New York: Norton.

Shea, M. T., Benjamin, L. S., Clarkin, J. F., & Magnavita, J. J. (1999). Personality disorders: A discussion of current status and future directions for research, practice, and policy. *Journal of Clinical Psychology/ In Session: Psychotherapy in Practice, 55*, 1371–1384.

Shedler, J., & Westen, D. (2004). Refining personality disorder diagnosis: Integrating science and practice. *The American Journal of Psychiatry, 161*(8), 1350–1365.

Shipler, D. K. (2004). *The working poor: Invisible in America*. New York: Knopf.

Shore, A. N. (2003a). *Affect dysregulation and disorders of the self*. New York: Norton.

Shore, A. N. (2003b). *Affect regulation and the repair of the self*. New York: Norton.

Shore, B. (1996). *Culture in mind: Cognition, culture, and the problem of meaning*. New York: Oxford University Press.

Shotter, J. (1994). The sociogenesis of processes of sociogenesis, and the sociogenesis of their study. In W. De Graaf & R. Maier (Eds.), *Sociogenesis reexamined* (pp. 73–91). New York: Springer-Verlag.

Siegel, D. J. (1999). *The developing mind: Toward a neurobiology of interpersonal experience*. New York: Guilford Press.

Silverman, W. (2001). Editorial: Clinicians and researchers: A bridge to nowhere? *Psychotherapy, 38*, 249–251.

Skinner, B. F. (1953). *Science and human behavior*. New York: Free Press.

Skolnick, N. J., & Warshaw, S. C. (Eds.). (1992). *Relational perspectives in psychoanalysis*. Hillsdale, NJ: Analytic Press.

Skynner, A. C. R. (1976). *Systems of family and marital psychotherapy*. New York: Brunner/Mazel.

Sluzki, C. E., & Beavin, J. (1977). Symmetry and complementarity: An operational definition and typology of dyads. In P. Watzlawick & J. H. Weakland (Eds.), *The interactional view: Studies at the Mental Research Institute, Palo Alto, 1965–1974* (pp. 71–87). New York: Norton.

Smelser, N. J., & Smelser, W. T. (1963). *Personality and social systems*. New York: John Wiley & Sons.

Solomon, M. F. (1989). *Narcissism and intimacy: Love and marriage in an age of confusion*. New York: Norton.

Solomon, M. F. (1998). Treating narcissistic and borderline couples. In J. Carlson & L. Sperry (Eds.), *The disordered couple* (pp. 239–258). Bristol, PA: Brunner/Mazel.

Solomon, M. F., & Lynn, R. E. (2002). Object-relations couples therapy. In J. J. Magnavita (Vol. Ed.), *Comprehensive handbook of psychotherapy: Psychodynamic/object relations* (Vol. I, pp. 387–433). Hoboken, NJ: Wiley.

Spitzer, R. L. (1999). Harmful dysfunction and the *DSM* definition of mental disorder. *Journal of Abnormal Psychology, 108*, 430–432.

Staats, A. W. (1983). *Psychology's crisis of disunity: Philosophy and method for a unified science*. New York: Praeger.

Staats, A. W. (1987). Unified positivism: Philosophy for the revolution to unity. In A. W. Staats & L. P. Mos (Eds.), *Annals of theoretical psychology* (Vol. 5, pp. 11–54). New York: Plenum.

Staats, A. W. (1991). Unified positivism and unification psychology: Fad or new field? *American Psychologist, 46*, 899–912.

Stampfl, T. G. (1966). Implosive therapy: The theory, the subhuman analogue, the strategy, and the technique. In S. G. Armitage (Ed.), *Behavior modification techniques in the treatment of emotional disorders* (pp. 12–21). Battle Creek, MI: Veterans Administration.

Stampfl, T., & Lewis, D. (1973). *Implosive therapy: Theory and technique*. Morristown, NJ: General Learning Press.

Stanton, M. (1991). *Sandor Ferenczi: Reconsidering active intervention*. Northvale, NJ: Aronson.

Stasch, M., Cierpka, M., Hillenbrand, E., & Schmal, H. (2002). Assessing reenactment in inpatient psychodynamic therapy. *Psychotherapy Research, 12*, 355–368.

Steinglass, P. (1978). The conceptualization of marriage from a systems theory perspective. In T. J. Paolino & B S. McCrady (Eds.), *Marriage and marital therapy: Psychoanalytic, behavioral and systems theory perspectives* (pp. 298–365). New York: Brunner/Mazel.

Stern, D. N. (1985). *The interpersonal world of the infant: A view from psychoanalysis and developmental psychology*. New York: Basic Books.

Sternberg, R. J., & Grigorenko, E. L. (2001). Unified psychology. *American Psychologist, 56,* 1069–1079.

Stewart, I., & Joines, V. (1987). *TA today: A new introduction to transactional analysis.* Chapel Hill, NC: Lifespace.

Stiles, W. B. (2003). Research corner: When is a case study scientific research? *Psychotherapy Bulletin, 38,* 6–11.

Striker, J., & Gold, J. (Eds.). (1993). Comprehensive handbook of psychotherapy integration. New York: Plenum Press.

Stone, M. H. (1993). *Abnormalities of personality: Within and beyond the realm of treatment.* New York: Norton.

Stone, M. H. (1997). *Healing the mind: A history of psychiatry from antiquity to the present.* New York: Norton.

Strupp, H. H., & Binder, J. L. (1984). *Psychotherapy in a new key.* New York: Basic Books.

Sugarman, S. (1986). The interface of individual and family therapy. In S. Sugarman (Ed.), *Individual and family therapy: An overview of the interface* (pp. 1–16). Rockville, MD: Aspen.

Sullivan, H. S. (1953). *The interpersonal theory of psychiatry.* New York: Norton.

Swenson, C. (1973). *Introduction to interpersonal relations.* Glenview, IL: Scott, Foresman.

Synder, D. K. (1999). Affective reconstruction in the context of a pluralistic approach to couple therapy. *Clinical Psychology: Science and Practice, 6,* 348–365.

Taylor, S., Thordarson, D. S., Fedoroff, I. C., Maxfield, L., Lovell, K., & Ogrodniczuk, J. (2003). Comparative efficacy, speed, and adverse effects of three PTSD treatments: Exposure therapy, EMDR, and relaxation training. *Journal of Consulting and Clincial Psychology, 71,* 330–338.

Teicher, M. H. (2000). Wounds that time won't heal: The neurobiology of child abuse. *Cerebrum, 2,* 50–75.

Teicher, M. H. (2002). Scars that won't heal: The neurobiology of child abuse. *Scientific American, 286,* 68–75.

Terkelsen, K. G. (1980). Toward a theory of the family life cycle. In E. A. Carter & M. McGoldrick (Eds.), *The family life cycle: A framework for family therapy* (pp. 21–52). New York: Gardner Press.

Thomas, A., & Chess, S. (1977). *Temperament and development.* New York: Brunner/Mazel.

Tomkins, S. S. (1962). *Affect imagery consciousness. Volume I: The positive affects.* New York: Springer.

Trujillo, M. (2002). Short-term dynamic psychotherapy of narcissistic disorders. In F. W. Kaslow (Series Ed.) & J. J. Magnavita (Vol. Ed.), *Comprehensive handbook of psychotherapy: Psychodynamic/object relations* (Vol. I, pp. 345–364). New York: Wiley.

Tucker, C. M. (1999). *African American children: A self-empowerment approach to modifying behavior problems and preventing academic failure*. Needham Heights, MA: Allyn & Bacon.

Tucker, C. M., & Herman, K. C. (2002). Using culturally sensitive theories and research to meet the academic needs of low-income African American children. *American Psychologist, 57*, 762–773.

Tucker, G. J. (1998). Putting *DSM–III* in perspective [Editorial]. *The American Journal of Psychiatry, 155*, 159–161.

Turner, S. M., & Hersen, M. (1997). *Adult psychopathology and diagnosis* (3rd ed.). New York: John Wiley & Sons.

Tyrer, P., Gunderson, J., Lyons, M., & Tohen, M. (1997). Extent of comorbidity between mental states and personality disorders. *Journal of Personality Disorders, 11*(3), 242–259.

Vaillant, G. E. (1971). Theoretical hierarchy of adaptive ego mechanisms. *Archives of General Psychiatry, 24*, 107–118.

Vaillant, G. E. (1977). *Adaptation to life*. Boston: Little, Brown.

Vaillant, G. E. (Ed.). (1992). *Ego mechanisms of defense: A guide for clinicians and researchers*. Washington, DC: American Psychiatric Press.

van Os, J., Hanssen, M., Bak, M., Bijl, R. V., & Vollebergh, W. (2003). Do urbanicity and familial liability coparticipate in causing psychosis? *American Journal of Psychiatry, 160*, 477–482.

von Bertalanffy, L. (1968). *General systems theory: Foundations, development and applications*. New York: Braziller.

Wachtel, P. L. (1993). *Therapeutic communication: Principles and practice*. New York: Guilford Press.

Wakefield, J. (1997). When is development disordered? Developmental psychopathology and the harmful dysfunction analysis of mental disorders. *Development and Psychopathology, 9*, 269–290.

Wakefield, J. C. (1999). Evolutionary versus prototype analyses of the concept of disorder. *Journal of Abnormal Psychology, 108*, 374–399.

Wallerstein, J. S. (1994). The early psychological tasks of marriage: Part 1. *American Journal of Orthopsychiatry, 64*, 640–650.

Wallerstein, J. S. (1996). The psychological tasks of marriage: Part 2. *American Journal of Orthopsychiatry, 66*, 217–227.

Watson, W. H., & McDaniel, S. H. (2000). Relational therapy in medical settings: Working with somatizing patients and their families. *Journal of Clinical Psychology/In Session: Psychotherapy in Practice, 56*, 1065–1082.

Watzlawick, P., & Beavin, J. (1977). Some formal aspects of communication. In P. Watzlawick & J. H. Weakland (Eds.), *The interactional view: Studies at the Mental Research Institute, Palo Alto, 1965–1974* (pp. 56–68). New York: Norton.

Watzlawick, P., Weakland, J., & Fisch, R. (1974). *Change: Problem formation and problem resolution*. New York: Norton.

Weiner, N. (1961). *Cybernetics: Or control and communication in animal and machine.* New York: MIT Press.

Weinfield, N. S., Sroufe, L. A., Egeland, B., & Carlson, E. A. (1999). The nature of individual differences in infant–caregiver attachment. In J. Cassidy & P. R. Shaver (Eds.), *The handbook of attachment: Theory, research, and clinical applications* (pp. 68–88). New York: Guilford Press.

Weissman, M. M., Markowitz, J. C., & Klerman, G. L. (2000). *Comprehensive guide to interpersonal psychotherapy.* New York: Basic Books.

Werner, H. (1948). *Comparative psychology of mental development.* New York: International Universities Press.

Werner, H. (1957). The concept of development from a comparative and organismic point of view. In D. B. Harris (Ed.), *The concept of development* (pp. 125–148). Minneapolis: University of Minnesota Press.

West, C. (2001). *Race matters* (2nd ed.). New York: Vintage Books.

West, M., & Sheldon, A. (1988). Classification of pathological attachment patterns in adults. *Journal of Personality Disorders, 2,* 153–159.

Whisman, M. A., & Synder, D. K. (1999). Affective and development considerations in couple therapy: Introduction to the special series. *Clinical Psychology: Science and Practice, 6,* 345–347.

Whitaker, C. A. (1986). Becoming a psychotherapist. In S. Sugarman (Ed.), *The interface of individual and family therapy* (pp. 113–116). Rockville, MD: Aspen.

Whitaker, C. A., & Keith, D. V. (1981). Symbolic-experiential family therapy. In A. S. Gurman & D. P. Kniskern (Eds.), *Handbook of family therapy* (pp. 187–225). New York: Brunner/Mazel.

Wiener, N. (1961). *Cybernetics: Or control and communication in the animal and machine.* New York: MIT Press.

Wiggins, J. S., & Trobst, K. K. (1999). The fields of interpersonal behavior. In L. A. Pervin & O. P. John (Eds.), *Handbook of personality: Theory and research* (pp. 653–770). New York: Guilford Press.

Wilber, K. (2000a). *A theory of everything: An integral vision for business, politics, and spirituality.* Boston: Shambhala.

Wilber, K. (2000b). Integral psychology: *Consciousness, spirit, psychology, therapy.* Boston, MA: Shambhala.

Wilmot, W. W. (1987) *Dyadic communication* (3rd ed.). New York: McGraw-Hill.

Wilson, E. O. (1975). *Sociobiology: The new synthesis.* Cambridge, MA: Harvard University Press.

Wilson, E. O. (1998). *Consilience: The unity of knowledge.* New York: Knopf.

Wilson, R. A., & Keil, F. C. (Eds.). (1999). *The MIT encyclopedia of the cognitive sciences.* Cambridge, MA: MIT Press.

Winnicott, C., Shepherd, R., & Davis, M. (Eds.). (1989). *Psychoanalytic explorations: D. W. Winnicott.* Cambridge, MA: Harvard University Press.

Wolfram, S. (2002). *A new kind of science.* Champaign, IL: Wolfram Media.

Wolpe, J. (1958). *Psychotherapy by reciprocal inhibition.* Stanford, CA: Stanford University Press.

Wolpe, J. (1973). *The practice of behavior therapy* (2nd ed.). Elmsford, NY: Pergamon Press.

Woodward, W. R., & Devonis, D. (1993). Towards a new understanding of scientific change: Applying interfield theory to the history of psychology. In H. V. Rappard, P. J. van Strien, L. P. Mos, & W. J. Baker (Eds.), *Annals of theoretical psychology Vol. 9* (pp. 87–123). New York: Plenum.

Wynne, L. C. (1984). The epigenesis of relational systems: A model for understanding family development. *Family Process, 23,* 297–318.

Yalom, I. (1985). *The theory and practice of group psychotherapy.* New York: Basic Books.

Yancher, S. C., & Slife, B. D. (1997). Pursuing unity in a fragmented psychology: Problems and prospects. *Review of General Psychology, 1,* 235–255.

Zanarini, M. (1997). Evolving perspectives on the etiology of borderline personality disorder. In M. Zanarini (Ed.), *Role of sexual abuse in the etiology of borderline personality disorder. Progress in Psychiatry, No. 49* (pp. 1–14). Washington, DC: American Psychiatric Press.

AUTHOR INDEX

SUBJECT INDEX

Anxiety, *continued*
    sources, 156–157
    striated muscle pathway,
      142–143
    symptoms, 141
    systemic, 142
    triadic, 106, 145–146
    types of, 141–142
    vertical/horizontal, 106
Anxiety-siphoning defenses, 98
Apotemnophilia, 263–264
Assessment. *See also* Diagnostic
    classification
    affective functioning, 154
    anxiety, 140–141, 143, 144–145,
      146, 147
    attachment patterns/style, 84–86,
      149–152
    clinical approach, 137, 169
    cognitive functioning, 154–155
    conceptual basis, 139–140
    couple personality system, 133
    defensive system, 92–93, 155,
      177–178
    for dyadic restructuring, 210, 212–
      213, 225–226
    family systems, 165–166
    genetic code, 134, 168
    goals, 137, 138
    holonic, 74–76, 80–81, 167–168
    instrument selection, 168
    interpersonal–dyadic matrix, 159–
      160, 200–201
    of interpersonal style, 225–226
    intimacy and closeness, 158
    intrapsychic–biological matrix,
      81–91
    for intrapsychic restructuring,
      196–197
    marital dyad, 219
    of multigenerational conflict,
      247–248
    neurobiological, 82–83, 149
    personality, 135
    personality system, 79–80
    relational system, 138–139
    to set intensity of treatment,
      277–278
    sociocultural matrix, 166–167
    temperament, 83–84
    triangular configurations, 81

Attachment. *See also* Infant–caretaker
    relationship
    affective functioning and, 89
    angry–withdrawn, 152
    anxious avoidant, 150
    anxious resistant, 150
    assessment, 84–86, 149–152
    biopsychosoical model, 37–38
    in component systems model, 34
    compulsive care-seeking, 152
    compulsive self-reliant, 152
    as determinant of relational develop-
      ment, 102–103, 104–105, 107
    developmental significance, 34,
      150–151
    dismissive, 151
    disorganized/disoriented, 150
    dyadic–interpersonal anxiety and,
      145
    fearful–avoidant, 151–152
    interpersonal insensitive, 152
    neurobiology, 82–83, 85
    object relations theory, 8
    obsessive–compulsive, 152
    origins of psychopathology in, 57,
      59–60, 123
    patterns/styles, 84–86, 149–150,
      151–152
    preoccupied, 151
    profiling, in dyadic restructuring,
      212
    relational model, 82
    secure, 86–87, 150
    separation and individuation pro-
      cesses, 117–119
    stability over time, 84–85
    therapeutic relationship and, 151
Attractor state(s)
    affective restructuring, 188–189
    genetic code and, 134
    mesosystem relationships, 266–267
    trauma as, 56–58
Avoidance behavior, 96

Behavior therapy
    conceptual development, 9
Bionegativity, 55, 56–58, 64
Biopositivity, 55
Biopsychosocial model, 14, 37–39
    therapeutic framework, 277

Diagnostic and Statistical Manual of Mental Disorders, 52, 65–66, 69, 74
Diagnostic classification, 13, 52, 65–69
 current inadequacies, 15–16, 19
 systems theory and, 18–19
 vs. holonic assessment, 74–75
Dialectic behavior therapy, 194
Diathesis–stress, 14–15, 61–63
 anxiety assessment, 141
 process, 167
 in relational–triadic matrix, 232–233
 symptom expression, 167–168
Displacement, 95–96
Dissociation, 94
Divorce and separation, 128
Dyadic restructuring, 21
 assessment for, 210, 212–213, 225–226
 conceptual basis, 201–203, 226
 containing affect in, 213–214
 emotional differentiation in, 220–221
 enhancing communication in, 222–223
 expected–transactive, 203–205
 goals, 200
 indications, 199–200
 of marital dyad, 218–219
 mechanism of change, 200
 relational–dyadic, 209–210
 self-differentiation in, 221–222
 self–other restructuring, 205–209
 technique and process, 219–223, 225
 theoretical and technical origins, 200
 therapeutic focus, 210–213
 therapeutic holding environment, 220
 types of, 203
Dysthymia, 309

Eating disorders, 110, 264
Ecological model of psychology, 30–33, 37–39, 254, 255, 300
 development in, 130
 personality system, 111
 psychopathology conceptualization, 63–65
Economic systems, 110–111, 269
Ecosystem relationships, 39

Ego psychology, 8
Ego-syntonic/ego-dystonic defenses, 98
Einstein, A., 3, 7
Emotional differentiation, 129, 200
 in dyadic restructuring, 220–221
Emotional intelligence, 188
Empathy, 90
Engrams, 116
Evolutionary theory, 30, 49
 affective functioning, 87–88
 attachment theory, 86–87
 punctuated equilibrium, 47
Existential anxiety, 141, 156–157
Existential–humanistic movement, 10
Expected–transactive restructuring, 203–205
Externalization, 94
Eye movement desensitization reprocessing, 194

Family system. See also Infant–caretaker relationship; Marital dyad; Relational–triadic matrix
 adolescent development, 125–126, 127–128
 assessment, 165–166, 247–248
 constricted–flexible, 124–125
 as developmental container, 115–117
 development of child personality system, 120–125
 in development of psychopathology, 122–123, 160–161
 diathesis–stress in, 232–233
 dysfunctional personologic systems, 161–165, 233, 234, 237–238, 251
 emotional cutoff in, 108
 influence of, 133
 in-law triangles, 231
 life cycle development, 127–128
 multigenerational transmission of relational patterns, 108–109, 160–161, 236–237
 nuclear family emotional system, 107
 organized–disorganized, 124
 parenting styles, 128–129, 233–235
 personality theory, 72
 projection in, 107–108
 relational system, 107

personality systems in, 72–73
repetitive maladaptive patterns, 212
self-differentiation and, 129–130,
221–222
symmetry in, 42–43
symptomatic expression, 211–212
triangular configurations, 40–42
Interpersonal psychiatry, 8–9
Intimacy, 157–158
Intrapsychic–biological matrix, 3, 21, 42.
See also Intrapsychic restructuring
affective/cognitive–anxiety–defensive
matrix, 152–157
affective components and processes,
87–89
anxiety in, 90, 142–143
assessment, 81–91
attachment and, 82–87, 149–152
defensive operations in, 91–92
development, 90–91, 173–174
dysregulation, 81–82
fulcrum points, 290
neurobiological substrate, 148–149
personality system assessment,
147–158
Intrapsychic restructuring, 21
assessment for, 196–197
goals, 173, 174
mechanism of change, 174–175
methods, 174. *See also specific method*
Introjection, 94, 105, 202
Isolation, 96

Learned helplessness, 9
Learning theory, 9
experience of novelty in, 47–48
Limbic system, 88

Macrosystem relationships, 32
in unified model, 38–39
Marital dyad
assessment, 219
clinical significance, 214
divorce and separation effects within
family, 128
downward spiraling, 216
extramarital affairs, 216–217, 230,
246
fusion fantasy, 215

myths of marriage, 214
parent–child problems, 217
as personality system, 214–215
symptoms of dysfunction in,
216–218
therapy, 218–219
triadic configurations, 229–232
Mesosystem relationships, 32
clinical significance, 266
domains and elements, 39, 257–266
function and purpose in, 265–266
patterns, 265
process, 265
restructuring. *See* Mesosystem restructuring
societal, 258–259
sociocultural–familial, 44–45
structure, 264–265
in unified model, 39
Mesosystem restructuring, 22, 172,
270–271
applications, 269–270
clinician knowledge for, 266–267,
269
community-based, 268–269
conceptual basis, 254–257
goals, 267–268
indications, 253
personality system consultation and,
267–268
Metabolization, 36
of affect, 192–193
Microsystem relationships, 32
in unified model, 38
Millon Clinical Multiaxial Inventory,
168

Nanotechnology, 305
Narcissism
dysfunctional personologic systems,
162–164
self psychology theory, 8
Narratives, 74
Neurobiology
affective system, 88
assessment, 82–83
of attachment, 83, 85
in component systems approach, 29,
33–34
current understanding, 33, 307

Neurobiology, *continued*
of intrapsychic–biological matrix,
148–149
neurotransmitter mapping, 148–149
in psychotherapy, 33–34, 42
restructuring, 21, 59, 61, 196
trauma effects, 59, 61, 83, 307

Object relations, 8, 158
cognitive restructuring, 183
Obsessive–compulsive personality disorder, 100
Oedipal complex, 41, 44
Organized–disorganized family systems, 124
Orthogenetic principle, 53, 129
Outpatient therapy, 283

Paranoid dysfunctional personologic systems, 164–165
Passive–aggressive behavior, 94, 176
Personality
adolescent personality system, 125–131
adult personality system, 131–132
assessment, 135, 139–140
assumptions of unified theory, 11–12, 13, 51–52
child personality system, 120–125
clinical significance, 13
components systems model, 20–21
core genetic code in, 133–134
couple personality system, 132–133
developmental personology, 114–115
developmental progression, 115–120, 134–135
differentiation processes, 129
disorders. *See* Personality disorders
ecological model, 111
family personality system, 72
feedback system, 46–47
individual differences in infants, 119–120
individual personality system, 71–72
interpersonal personality system, 72
intrapsychic–biological components assessment, 147–158
levels of organization, 71
mesosystem relationships, 254–257

models of psychopathology and, 12, 13, 52–55, 63–64
relational personality system, 72, 139
requirements of unified theory, 11–12, 13, 51–52
societal–cultural personality system, 73
systemics. *See* Personality systemics
systems model, 17–19, 36–37, 62–63, 69–73
temperamental variation, 83–84
trauma theory, 56–63
Personality disorders
assessment, 79–81
in children, 120–121
concept of complex syndromes, 16–17
severely disturbed couples, 218–219
systems model, 18, 69
Personality-guided therapy, 296–297
biopsychosocial perspective in, 276–277
conceptual basis, 20–21, 51, 139–140, 299–300
empirical research, 299
historical conceptual development, 6
movement among component domains in, 276
as system theory, 17–19
therapeutic relationship in, 294–295
treatment potency, 277–278
Personality systemics, 114
infant–caretaker, 117
purpose, 137
research role, 302–303
Personologic systems, dysfunctional, 161–165, 233, 234, 237–238, 251
Pharmacotherapy, 282
neurotransmitter mapping, 148–149
Pleasure–pain polarity, 173
Political systems, 110–111
anxiety pathways, 147
personality development and, 259
scientific development and, 306
Prison work, 269–270
Projection, 93, 202
family process, 107–108
multigenerational transmission of relational patterns, 108–109, 236–237
in therapy, 203
transference patterns, 211

Projective identification, 95
Psychoanalysis–psychodynamic therapy,
    3–4, 7, 8–9, 44
    conceptual and technical evolution,
        175–176
Psychopathology
    attachment disruptions in, 84–86
    biopsychosoical model, 14
    chaos theory, 48–49
    characterological conceptualization,
        67
    classification, 13, 15–16, 52, 65–69
    concept of complex syndromes,
        16–17
    conceptual development, 13
    cultural context, 263–264
    cybernetic account, 41–42
    developmental, 114–115, 122–123
    development in relational–triadic
        matrix, 106
    diathesis–stress model, 14–15,
        61–63
    dimensional conceptualization,
        66–67
    dyadic model, 42–43
    dysfunctional personologic systems,
        161–165
    ecological model, 63–65
    family systems in development of,
        122, 123, 309–310
    as harmful dysfunction, 64–65
    holonic assessment, 74–76
    holonic conceptualization, 68–69
    intrapsychic dysregulation, 81–82
    multifactorial conceptualization,
        308–310
    neurobiology, 42
    personality theory and models of, 12,
        13, 52–55
    prototypical conceptualization, 67
    relational model, 19–20, 67–68,
        310–311
    requirements of unified theory,
        11–12
    sociocultural factors, 308–309
    systems model, 18, 52–53,
        54–55
    trauma theory, 56–63
    triadic relationships in, 43–44
Psychotic dysfunctional personologic sys-
    tems, 164

Racism, 270
Rationalization, 96
Reaction formation, 96
Reenactment, 210–211
Regression, 94, 99
Reich, W., 97
Relational–dyadic restructuring, 21,
    209–210
    formation of relational–triadic
        matrix, 229, 235–238
Relational matrix
    assessment goals, 80–81
    component systems model, 35
    developmental significance, 115
    functional domains, 3
    model of psychopathology in, 19–20,
        67–68, 310–311
    primary triangular configurations, 3,
        20–21, 42–45
    restructuring, 21–22
    theoretical and clinical significance,
        3, 19–20, 306–312
Relational psychoanalysis, 9
Relational–triadic matrix, 3, 21, 43–44.
    See also Family systems
    affect, 232
    components and processes, 106–108
    developmental context, 106–107,
        160–161
    diathesis–stress model, 232–233
    family processes in, 107, 160–161
    formation of, 229, 235–238
    fulcrum points, 292
    marital configurations, 229–232
    restructuring, 21–22, 172. See also
        Triadic restructuring
    sources of dysfunction, 229–238,
        251–252
Relaxation training, 194
Religion and spirituality, personality de-
    velopment and, 259–260
Repression, 95
Role relations, 104–105

Schemas, 100–101
    cognitive restructuring, 183
Schizoid fantasy, 94
Scientific development, 260, 263
    to advance unified theory of psychol-
        ogy, 303–305

common features among theoretical approaches, 301
defensive restructuring, 177–183
dyadic restructuring, 203–214, 219–223
family therapy, 138–139
fulcrum points, 290–293
requirements of unified theory, 12, 51–52
restructuring relational matrices, 21–22
role of theory development, 300
triadic restructuring, 240–244
unified component system approach, 39–40
Therapeutic relationship
attachment and, 151
conceptual evolution, 293–294
in defensive restructuring, 178–179, 180–181
dyadic relationship, 159
in dyadic restructuring, 213
as mechanism of change, 306
movement among component domains and, 276
in personality-guided therapy, 294–295
relational model, 20
restructuring, 21
in self–other restructuring, 205–209
treatment intensity and, 277–278
Transactive restructuring, 184, 186–187
Transference, 203, 211
relational model, 20
Trauma experience
classification, 60
developmental context, 60–61
diathesis–stress model, 61–63
family system in, 58
intergenerational transmission, 310
intrapsychic restructuring goals, 174–175
neurobiological change and, 83, 307
psychopathogenesis in, 56–57, 59, 174, 309–310, 311
theoretical conceptualization, 56
trauma as attractor state, 56–58
Treatment. *See also* Personality-guided therapy; Therapeutic process and technique
challenges in, 276

couples therapy, 281–282
differential therapeutics, 275–276
family therapy, 281
frames, 285–288
group therapy, 281, 282
individual psychotherapy, 280
inpatient, 283–284
intermittent, 287
length and spacing, 288–289
long-term, 286–287
maintenance therapy, 287–288
measures of effectiveness, 300–302
methods of restructuring, 171–172. *See also specific method*
movement among component domains, 276
multiple clinicians, 296
outpatient, 283
packaging, 278–279, 289–290
partial, 284
pharmacotherapy, 282
selecting modalities, 279–280, 295–296
sequencing and combinations, 284–285
settings, 282–283
short-term, 286
team treatment, 296
Triadic–relational anxiety, 145–146
Triadic restructuring, 21–22
conceptual basis, 227–228
containing emotional reactions in, 250
core affective exchange in, 250
detriangulating a child, 246–247
extramarital triad, 246
with extremely dysfunctional family, 251
family education intervention, 249
focus, 239–240
goals, 232, 238, 244–246
individual therapy, 238
modeling tolerance in, 250
primary conflict intervention, 251
realigning family hierarchy, 248–249
redistributing family power, 249
regulating anxiety in, 250–251
relational, 238, 240–243
reorganizing dysfunctional triads, 248

ABOUT THE AUTHOR

Jeffrey J. Magnavita, PhD, ABPP, FAPA, is a licensed psychologist and marriage and family therapist in active clinical practice. A diplomate of the American Board of Professional Psychology and fellow of the American Psychological Association, Dr. Magnavita has received awards for his work in the practice and theory of psychotherapy and personality disorders, on which he speaks at a national level. He is the founder of Glastonbury Psychological Associates, PC, and the Connecticut Center for Short-Term Dynamic Psychotherapy and is an affiliate professor of clinical psychology at the University of Hartford and lecturer at Smith College of Social Work. He authored *Restructuring Personality Disorders: A Short-Term Dynamic Approach*, *Relational Therapy for Personality Disorders*, and a textbook, *Theories of Personality: Contemporary Approaches to the Science of Personality*, and was the volume editor of the *Comprehensive Handbook of Psychotherapy: Psychodynamic/Object Relations: Volume 1* and the *Handbook of Personality Disorders: Theory and Practice*. He is on the editorial board of the *Journal of Clinical Psychology/In Session: Psychotherapy in Practice*. He is a member of the affiliate medical staff at a number of Hartford, Connecticut area hospitals, where he consults and conducts training. He is an active member of the International Society for the Study of Personality Disorders, Society for Psychotherapy Research, New York Academy of Science, and Society for the Exploration of Psychotherapy Integration and is a founder of the International Association for Experiential Dynamic Therapy.